AF361612

Breakaway Americas

Published in Cooperation with the

William P. Clements Center for Southwest Studies

Southern Methodist University

BREAKAWAY AMERICAS

The Unmanifest Future of the Jacksonian United States

Thomas Richards, Jr.

Johns Hopkins University Press

Baltimore

Johns Hopkins University Press
2715 North Charles Street
Baltimore, Maryland 21218-4363
www.press.jhu.edu

Library of Congress Cataloging-in-Publication Data
Names: Richards, Thomas, Jr., 1993– author.
Title: Breakaway Americas : the unmanifest future of the Jacksonian
United States / Thomas Richards, Jr.
Description: Baltimore : Johns Hopkins University Press, 2020. |
Includes bibliographical references and index.
Identifiers: LCCN 2019023256 | ISBN 9781421437132 (hardcover) |
ISBN 9781421437149 (ebook)
Subjects: LCSH: Separatist movements—History—19th century. | United
States—History—Autonomy and independence movements. | United States—
History—19th century. | United States—Politics and government—19th century.
Classification: LCC E337.5 .R53 2020 | DDC 973.5—dc23
LC record available at https://lccn.loc.gov/2019023256

A catalog record for this book is available from the British Library.

This material is neither made, provided, approved, nor endorsed by
Intellectual Reserve, Inc., or the Church of Jesus Christ of Latter-day Saints.
Any content or opinions expressed, implied, or included in or with the
material are solely those of the owner and not those of Intellectual Reserve,
Inc., or the Church of Jesus Christ of Latter-day Saints.

*Special discounts are available for bulk purchases of this book. For
more information, please contact Special Sales at specialsales@press.jhu.edu.*

Johns Hopkins University Press uses environmentally friendly book materials,
including recycled text paper that is composed of at least 30 percent
post-consumer waste, whenever possible.

For Jill

CONTENTS

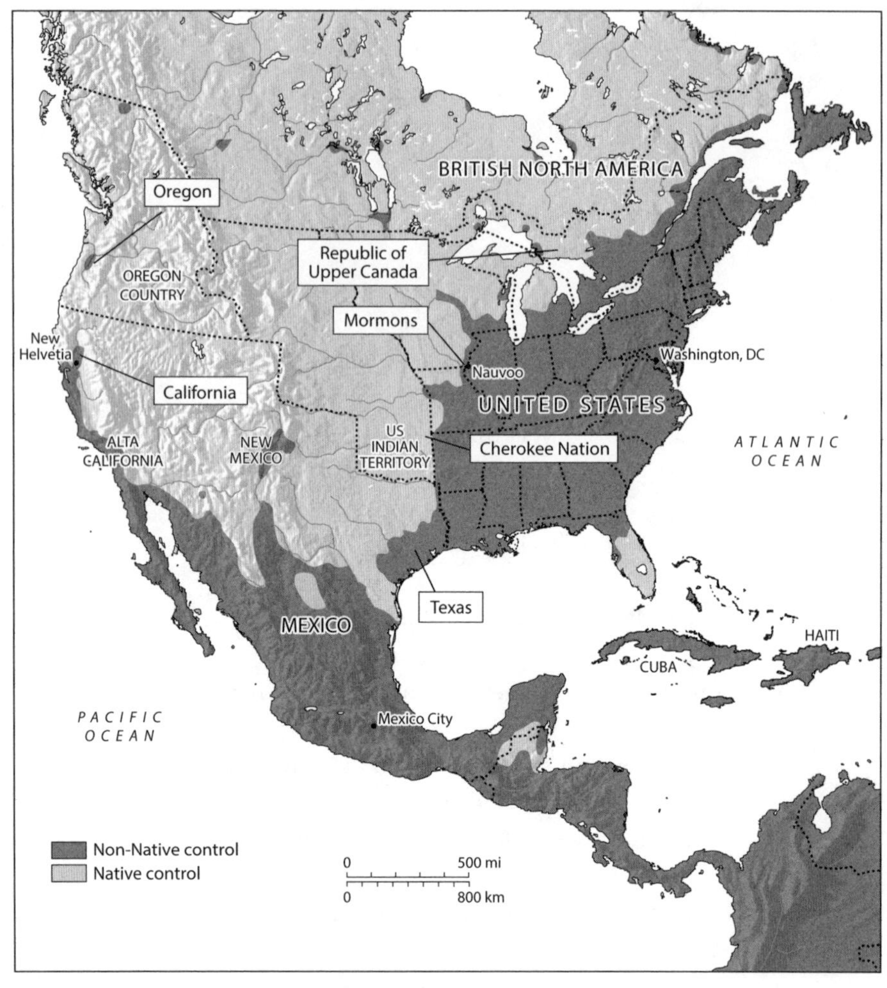

Breakaway Americas, 1835–1848. Map by Bill Nelson.

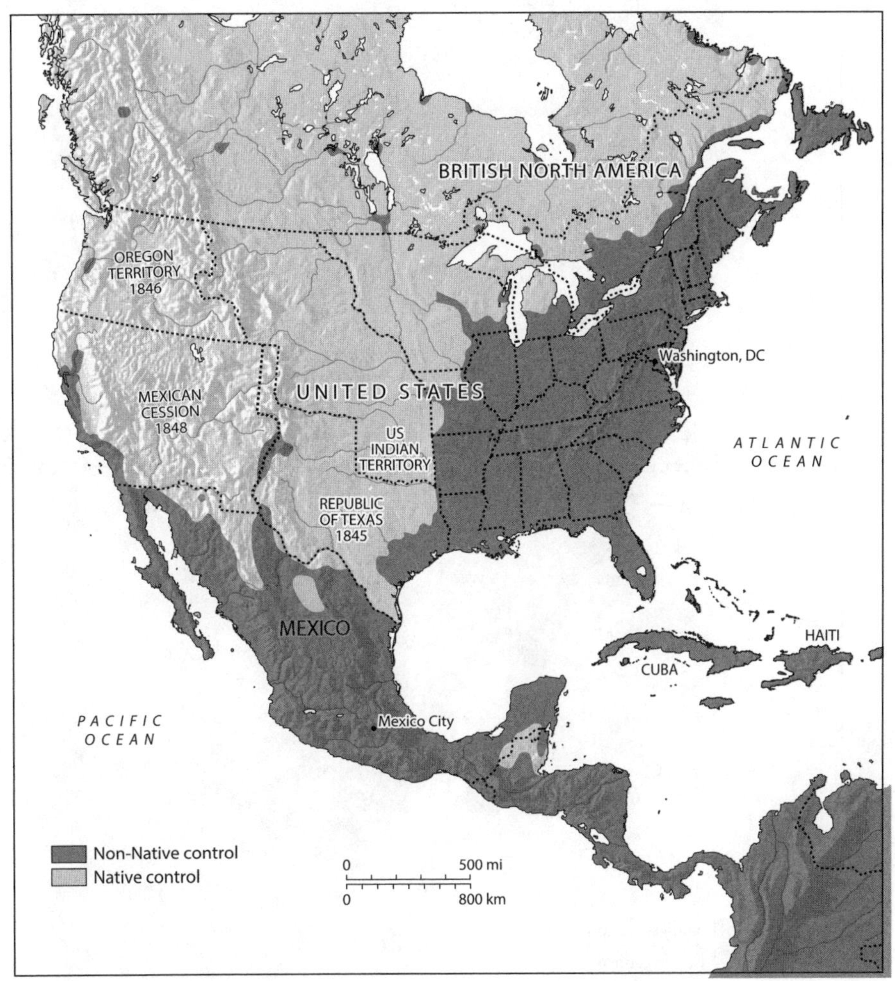

Territorial gains by the United States, 1845–1848. Map by Bill Nelson.

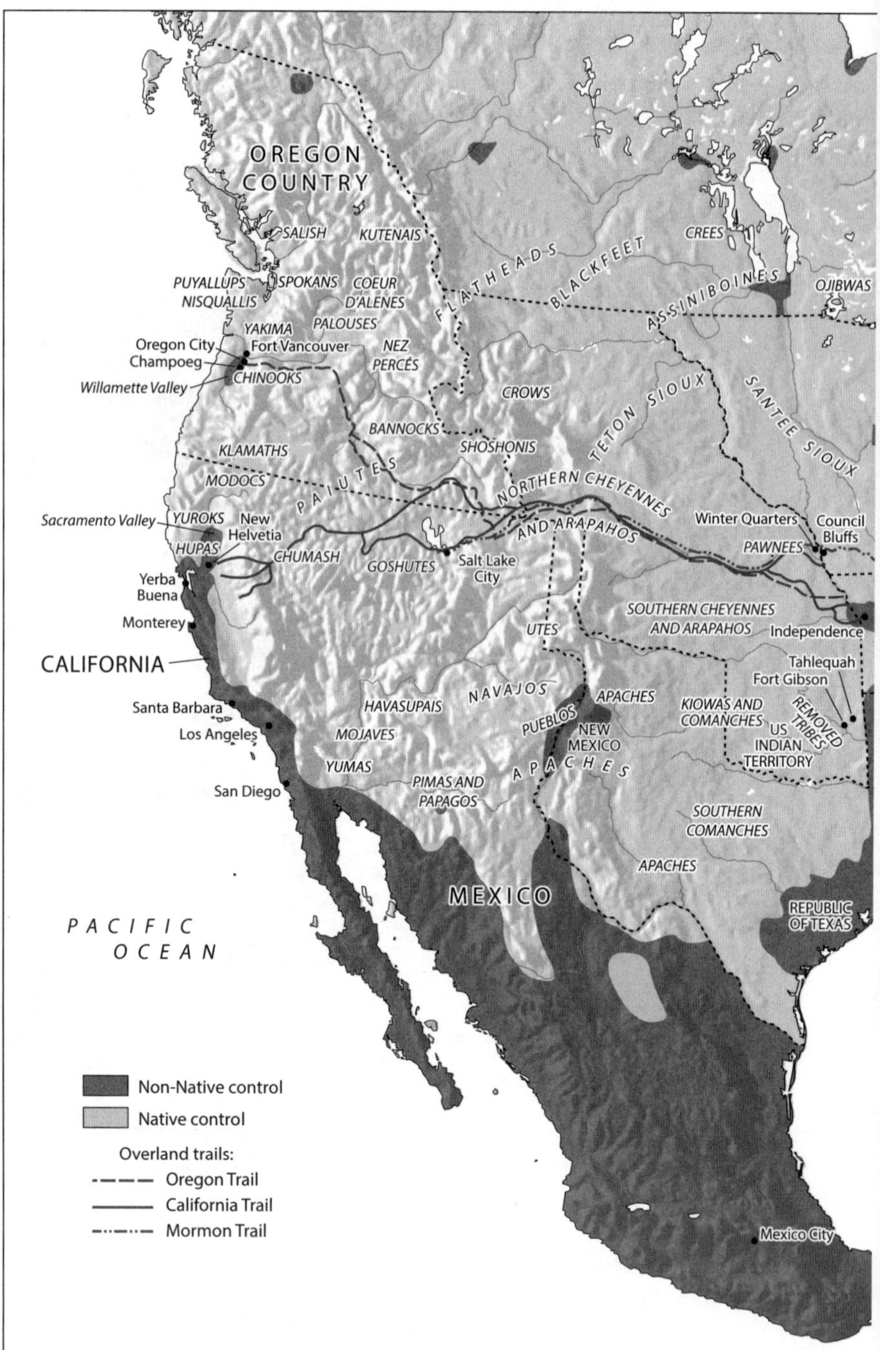

North America, circa 1840, with some select later locations and overland trails. Areas under Native and non-Native control are approximations since these borders were constantly fluctuating. Map by Bill Nelson.

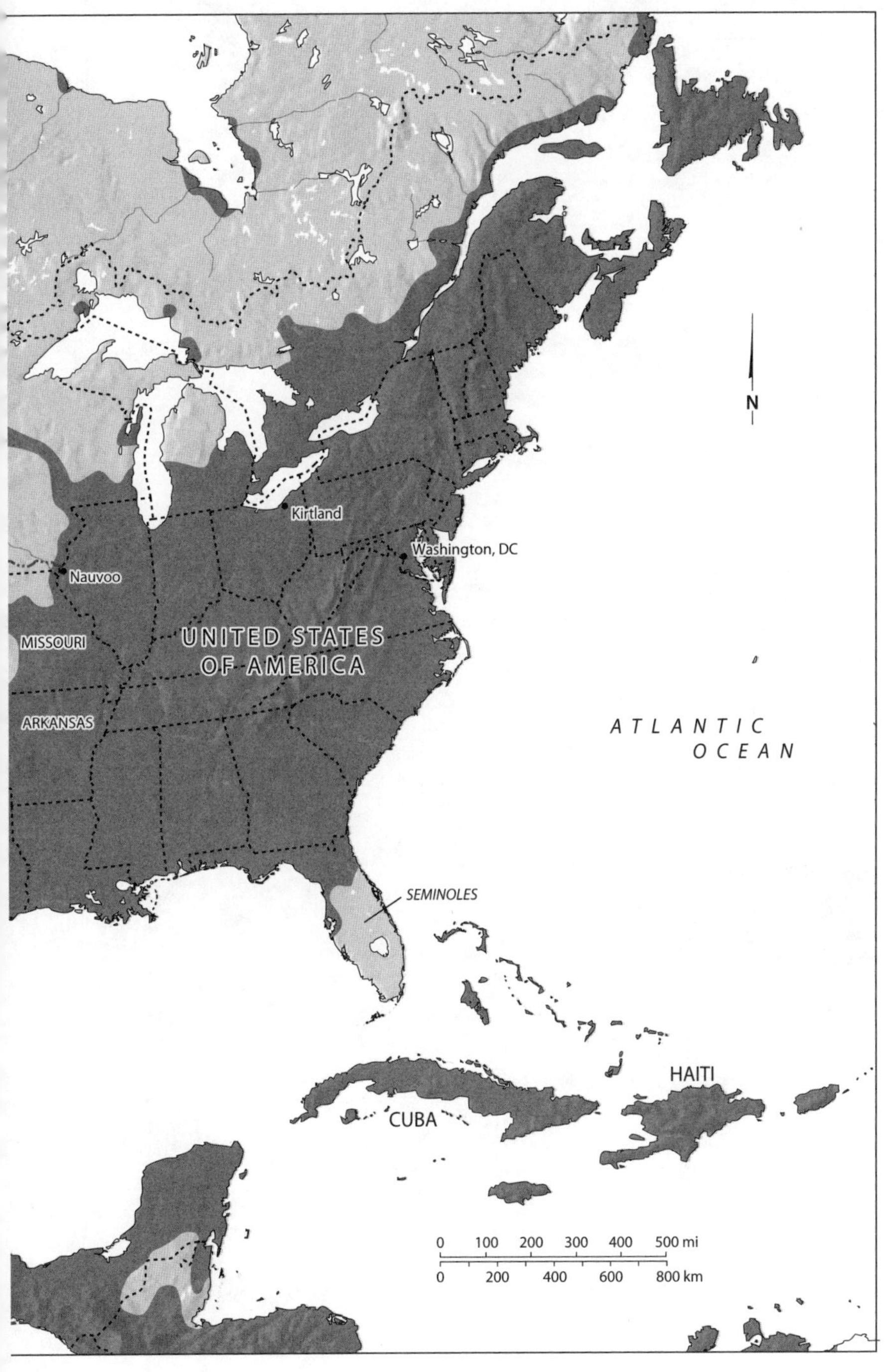

N
Kirtland
Washington, DC
Nauvoo
MISSOURI
UNITED STATES
OF AMERICA
ARKANSAS
ATLANTIC
OCEAN
SEMINOLES
CUBA
HAITI
0   100   200   300   400   500 mi
0   200   400   600   800 km

ACKNOWLEDGMENTS

This book could not have been written without the immeasurable support and generosity of countless people. It began as a dissertation at Temple University under the tutelage of my adviser Drew Isenberg. Drew first cultivated my interest in the American West, and—perhaps more important—in the spring of 2012, Drew decided that he would consider Upper Canada part of the West and allow me to write a research paper on the Patriot invaders of Canada for his American West seminar. This book began with that paper. More generally, Drew's valuable advice and guidance have shaped this project at every turn, and this book could not have been written without him. While Drew is not always right (e.g., he does not believe Philadelphia is the greatest city in the world), he was pretty much always right in his suggestions for this project. Thank you for everything, Drew.

It also could not have been written without the unfailing support of David Waldstreicher, my first adviser at Temple, who remained an unofficial adviser throughout the project. I first went to Temple to write about the politics of the American Revolution with David. When I told him I was thinking about writing instead about the Jacksonian West, he never questioned my drastic shift in focus but rather continued to provide unshakable encouragement. He was constantly open to new ideas, and he too was pretty much right about everything when it came to this project. I continue to relish our marathon breakfasts at the deli, and I continue to appreciate his enthusiasm for all facets of early American history (although not his enthusiasm for the Mets). Thank you for everything, David.

Many others at Temple shaped this project at various stages. In particular, Travis Glasson read multiple drafts and gave impeccable feedback, and he always provided a sense of calm in the chaos that often is the life of a grad student. Jessica Roney's pointed critiques were invaluable, as have been our continued conversations in recent years in the hallways of various conferences and in the McNeil Center reception area. I workshopped two chapters at her Temple Early American seminar, and both became much better because of it. At these seminars many scholars, especially Alexandre Caillot and Monica Hahn, provided valuable feedback. I wrote what became the second chapter for this book in Jon Wells's research seminar; his advice on writing and research techniques was refreshingly practical and continues to be useful. I also worked through many of my ideas in the classes of Harvey Neptune, Gregory Urwin, and Petra Goedde, and they all shaped this project in beneficial ways. Vangie Campbell and the late Pat Williams alleviated administrative headaches and provided a breath of proverbial fresh air in the cement confines of Gladfelter Hall. My grad cohort at Temple, in particular Jess Bird, Tom Reinstein, Grant Scribner, Seth Tannenbaum, and John Worsencroft, made it enjoyable to come to campus on a daily basis. Although they studied "current events" (the twentieth century) and not what they called "ancient history" (the nineteenth century), they were always there, offering advice and support. Steve Hausmann and I had terrific conversations about the American West. In retrospect, our twelve hours at the Minneapolis airport was time well spent. Catherine Murray was always able to pick me up with words of encouragement. Brenna Holland remains a close friend who is wise beyond her years; she really should appear in multiple sections of these acknowledgments. Finally, David Thomas was essentially my fellow muse at Temple. We had similar research interests, we liked similar books, and we were annoyed with similar historiographic trends. Some of the best advice I got on this project came from David in our car rides from East Falls to North Philadelphia, and while David hails from Ohio by way of Tennessee by way of Seattle, I consider him a fellow Philadelphian at heart (which, to him, is a compliment).

I wrote much of this book while on a yearlong fellowship at the McNeil Center for Early American Studies at the University of Pennsylvania. There, my scholarship truly progressed. I offer thanks to the incomparable Dan Richter, whose deep and wide historical knowledge, valuable advice, generosity, gregariousness, ties, and puns made the year a remarkable one. Amy Baxter-Bellamy and Barbara Natello made things come together on a daily basis. Much appreciation to the many attendees of my McNeil seminar at the Historical Society of Pennsylvania. Thanks also to my fellow fellows who read parts of this work and often pushed me out of my comfort zone in helpful and meaningful ways: Dee Andrews, Jessica Blake, Dan Couch, Lori Daggar, Elizabeth Eager, Liz Ellis, Rachel Engl, Alexandra Finley, Nicholas Gliserman, Sarah Gronningsater, Andrew Inchiosa, Christopher Jones, Lauren Kimball, Alex Manevitz, Don James McLaughlin, Alexandra Montgomery, Tony Perry, Gabriel Rocha, and Laura Soderberg. Three individuals deserve particular mention: Kevin Waite and I always had terrific discussions about western history. Maxime Dagenais was (and is) my go-to connection for all things Canada—Canadian history, Canadian historians, Canadian historiography, poutine, Montreal bagels, hockey, and bad weather. Rachel Walker was the best officemate—and fellow cynic—I could have had, and our daily conversations made this book so much better and my days at work so much more entertaining.

Much of the work of turning my dissertation into this book took place at the Clements Center for Southwest Studies at Southern Methodist University, where I spent a year as a postdoctoral fellow. Thanks to those who attended my manuscript workshop, in particular the Steves—Stephen Aron and Steven Hahn—who both provided incalculable written and oral feedback. So too did workshop attendees Brian Franklin, Eric Schlereth, Whitney Stewart, Patrick Troester, and Ben Wright. The genial Ed Countryman, with his expansive historical knowledge, was a treasure trove of all things American history and improved this work in numerous immeasurable ways. Jimmy Bryan's support and guidance have been valuable and much appreciated. My other fellows, Sarah Pearsall, Sarah Rodríguez, and Aimee Villareal, never tired of friendly discussions over Texas barbecue, and Sarah Rodríguez in particular deserves to appear multiple times throughout these acknowledgments. Andy Graybill and Neil Foley both offered ceaseless encouragement about the project and life more generally (Andy's positivity and Neil's love of sport especially stand out). Finally, my year at the Clements Center ran so smoothly because of the tireless work of Ruth Ann Elmore, who defines the center in many ways. When she retires in a few decades, SMU won't be the same. The Clements Center was truly a home away from home (it was even better because I was able to celebrate an Eagles Super Bowl win in Dallas), and it was all because of the support and, above all, friendship of Sarah P., Sarah R., Aimee, Andy, Neil, and Ruth Ann.

Over the years, I have been lucky to have many other scholars read my work and offer their thoughts at conferences and workshops. First and foremost, Rachel St. John was unquestionably the right choice to be the outside reader of my dissertation, and she has continued to shape this project both via comments on my work and by sharing her own. At the western history dissertator's workshop in Taos, I was privileged to get helpful feedback from Bill Deverell, John Faragher, Katrina Jagodinsky, and Louis Warren. Maurice Crandall provided vital commentary on chapter 4. Other scholars who have offered suggestions include Juliana Barr, Andrew Bonthius, Brian DeLay, Ruth Dunley, Amy Greenberg, Nick Guyatt, Patty Limerick, Julien Mauduit, Jason Opal, Benjamin Park, Andrés Reséndez, Robert Richard, Nora Slonimsky, and Stephen Smith.

Much of this book is based on archival materials found in libraries throughout the United States and Canada, all of which possessed knowledgeable and generous staff who made this work possible (and much less stressful than it could have been). Thanks to the archivists at the American Philosophical Society Library, the Archives of Ontario, the Bancroft Library, the Buffalo and Erie County Historical Society, the DeGolyer Library at SMU, the Detroit Free Library, the Historical Society of Pennsylvania, the Huntington Library, the LDS Church History Library, the Library of Congress, the National Archives and Records Administration, the Newberry Library, the Oregon Historical Society, St. Lawrence University, the University of Michigan's Bentley and Clements Libraries, the University of Puget Sound, and the Western History Collections at the University of Oklahoma Library. Thanks also to the staff at Temple University's Paley Library, the University of Pennsylvania's Van Pelt Library, and Southern Methodist University's Fondren Library for allowing me to check out hundreds of books at a time and putting up with my almost daily interlibrary loan requests.

Generous financial support was provided by the Bancroft Library, the Charles Redd Center for Western Studies, the Huntington Library, and Temple University. Several individuals deserve special mention. At the LDS Church History Library, Gerrit Dirkmaat, Matthew Grow, and Brent Rogers provided me with a warm welcome, and Brent especially has continued to offer encouragement and advice. At the Huntington, Peter Blodgett was a wealth of archival information, and Juan Gomez provided terrific hospitality and Pasadena ice cream.

I have long heard rumors that the final stages of turning a manuscript into an actual published book are often the most tedious. Thankfully, this has not proven to be the case for me—far from it. The kind, talented, helpful, and responsive staff at Johns Hopkins University Press have made everything remarkably easy. Thanks especially to Laura Davulis for taking a chance on this project and for all her hard work and knowledge, which have made it into the best book possible. Thanks too to Esther Rodríguez for her diligence and for making all the difficult logistics seem easy. Merryl A. Sloane was a profoundly skilled copyeditor who had a remarkable ability to fix my countless mistakes while still letting my own voice remain throughout the book's pages. Thanks too to Kyle Kretzer, Juliana McCarthy, Hilary Jacqmin, and Kathryn Marguy, all of whom have helped bring this book to fruition.

It is rare that an argument can be seen in visual form, but thanks to Bill Nelson, the maps in this book do just that. Thanks, Bill, for dealing with my many complicated requests and for putting the vision that I had in my head onto paper better than I could have ever expected.

I finished this book while teaching at Springside Chestnut Hill Academy in Philadelphia, which has truly been a privilege. SCH's inquisitive students, tireless administrators, and dedicated and selfless teachers have continued to inspire this project and—more important—have made it rewarding to come to work each morning. The members of the History and English Departments deserve special mention, particularly Danielle Gross, Kevin Harris, Josh Mattingly, and Sarah McDowell, all of whom have discussed this project with me. Most notably, following our very interesting first conversation, David Salmanson has offered ceaseless encouragement and advice (and many more interesting conversations). Thanks to all!

The genesis for the ideas for this book has a long, unknowable history, as I likely began formulating some of its contents long before I ever considered I would write a book. Thanks goes to a series of wonderful academic institutions I attended before Temple that nurtured my love of history: the Shipley School, the College of Arts and Sciences at the University of Pennsylvania, and the General School of Education at the University of Pennsylvania. Thanks in particular to my history teachers at Shipley, Tom Nammack, George Wrangham, and Jim White, and to Penn professors Ann Greene and Karen Clark, who both saw my potential as a scholar.

Finally, this book could not have been written without my friends and family. While I do not think any friends helped with the actual content of this book (as they themselves would certainly admit), they bring fun, joy, laughter, and needed stupidity to my life on a regular basis: Fuller, Tanner, Sam S., Tim, Tucker and Alex, Rob, Mike M., Mike M., Kyle, Andrew and Kate, Conor, Ryan, Tripper, Blondon, Andre, Chris, Sam M., Dan L., Maria and Anthony, Teddy, Doug P., J. Embiid, and many, many others not named (from Shipley, Troop Rugby, Penn, and life). Over the past decade I have been lucky to become a part of an amazing second family, the sprawling, gregarious, and endlessly fun Gosselin and Lawless clans. Particular appreciation goes to Deanne,

Mary Ann, the late Pop Pop Dan, Johnnie, Beth, and Chris, all of whom have welcomed me to the family despite my very few, ever-so-slight foibles. Here's to many more college graduation parties!

Thank you to my extended family—the Fifers, the Stricklers, and the Safnauers—for their senses of humor, their generosity, their inspiration, and their willingness to put up with me. Thanks especially to Uncle Mark, whose love of history movies and Westerns inspired this book in countless unknowable (and probably good) ways, and also to Aunt Gay, who has always offered unflinching support through the many perils of higher education. My grandparents are not alive to see this book come to fruition, but my memories of them and their love for me hover all around its pages. Thank you, Bup and Goggy, and Nannie and Dada.

My dog, Struan, gets his own separate, much-deserved paragraph. I arrived at many of my ideas while taking him on quiet and/or bark-filled walks through East Falls and Skunk Hollow. This project is almost as old as he is, and he's been there with me, quite literally, every step of the way.

My brothers, Will and Corey, have always been there to support me (even when they have not quite understood me). They both know intuitively that sometimes the best solution to writer's block is to have a thirty-minute conversation using only *Seinfeld* quotations. I am lucky to have both of them in my life, ruined birthdays notwithstanding. My parents, Sandi and Tom, have always believed in me and have offered me love, reassurance, and comfort in both good times and bad. I could not have written this book without them. When I was three years old, my mom outfitted me with a belt to wear around my sweatpants so I could hold the various toy swords, toy pistols, and sticks that constituted my childhood arsenal, and then my dad drove me for three hours to visit the Gettysburg battlefield. Although my Civil War reenacting ended at some point in elementary school, it was at that early age that my love of history began, and it was all thanks to my parents. I still cherish these memories. Thanks, Mom and Dad, for everything.

Fran and Caleb, my amazing kids, are both too young to read and thus won't be too excited when this book first appears in print. Hopefully one day, they will pull an old dust-covered copy off the storage shelf of some library, read these acknowledgments, and smile. Fran and Caleb, I love you both so, so much. You bring hilarity, craziness, wonder, and joy to my life every single day.

And, finally, a paragraph for my wife, Jill, although in truth she deserves a chapter or even a book of thank yous. A few months before we married, I told Jill I was going to quit my job and go back to school so I could eventually write a history book that would be published almost a decade in the future. By any sane metric, this was a questionable decision. Amazingly, Jill still said yes both to marriage and to my return to grad school, and she has continued to offer unconditional love, support, laughter, and excellence in Microsoft Excel every day. She is a special person, and I cannot thank her enough for everything she has done for me, for us, and for our family. I owe you so much, Jill, but only have a little to give: this book is dedicated to you.

An earlier version of chapter 2 appeared in my essay "The Lure of a Canadian Republic: Americans, the Patriot War, and Upper Canada as Political, Social, and Economic Alternative, 1837–1840," in *Revolutions across Borders: Jacksonian America and the Canadian Rebellion*, ed. Maxime Dagenais and Julien Mauduit (Montreal, QC: McGill-Queen's University Press, 2019), and earlier versions of parts of chapters 5, 6, and 7 appeared in my article "Farewell to America: The Expatriation Politics of Overland Migration, 1841–1846," *Pacific Historical Review* 86, no. 1 (2017): 114–152.

Breakaway Americas

Introduction

On June 19, 1839, in the New York town of Lewiston, "thousands of American people" welcomed Gilbert Belnap as he crossed the US-Canadian border. They greeted him with "loud hurrahs" and bursts of cannon fire and then escorted him through two long lines of men and women, "young and old," to the aptly named American Hotel, where he was feted with food and drink for hours into the night. Belnap was overjoyed with the reception, writing years later, "To this day, my pen, when grasped between my fingers, is too weak an instrument to convey the most distant emotions of my soul for my deliverance from British tyranny." Months before, Belnap had joined the Patriot army, a combined force of American and Canadian volunteers who sought to liberate Canada in the aftermath of the failed Canadian rebellions. He had been captured by British and Loyalist Canadian forces and then held prisoner in Toronto for several months, until the British agreed to escort him and three other Patriots across the border out of "politeness," at least according to Belnap. More likely, Belnap was part of a prisoner exchange. Whatever the reason, when Belnap arrived in Lewiston he was a free man once again.[1]

Belnap remembered the welcoming throng of Americans as his fellow countrymen; even though Belnap was Canadian, the discrepancy rarely mattered along the northern border. Like many Upper Canadians, he had deep roots in the United States. Before emigrating to Canada, his parents had lived in New York, and his paternal grandfather had even fought against the British in the American Revolution. Orphaned at the age of ten, Belnap became indentured to a wheelwright in Canada, but his master fled to the United States to escape his debts, bringing Belnap along. For several years in New York, Belnap suffered harsh discipline at his master's hands. Eventually, however, he learned that his contract was not enforceable on US soil, so he promptly fled his master to search for his siblings in Canada. It was at that point that the Canadian rebellions erupted, and Belnap volunteered for the Patriot army.

After being lauded in Lewiston, Belnap traveled west, taking odd jobs here and there as he tried to survive in the midst of a devastating economic depression that had begun in 1837 and continued through the mid-1840s. Eventually he found work chopping wood in Kirtland, Ohio, a center of the early Church of Jesus Christ of Latter-day Saints, whose followers were commonly referred to as Mormons. Belnap soon became enthralled with the fledgling faith. In 1842, he was baptized into the church, and within two years he traveled west again, to the Mormon city of Nauvoo in the state of Illinois. There, in the spring of 1844, he met Joseph Smith, the founder of the Mormon faith and the political leader of Nauvoo, which had become an independent city-state in all but name. Belnap became captivated with Smith's power and presence, recalling that, even during their first meeting, "[Smith] seemed to read the very recesses of my heart."

Perhaps because of his prior service in the Patriot army, Belnap was quickly made one of Smith's armed protectors, at a time that was the most perilous in Smith's life and in the history of early Mormonism. To the non-Mormons who lived around Nauvoo, Smith possessed a dangerous amount of political power; he was no longer seen as the founder of a small branch of Christianity but as the autocrat of a growing Mormon theocracy. In late June 1844, five years after a mob of Americans had welcomed Belnap across the border with open arms, another mob of Americans forced Belnap and several other Mormons to flee the town of Carthage, Illinois, where Joseph Smith was locked in jail. Belnap was one of the last Mormons to see Smith alive. The next day, a group of anti-Mormons murdered Smith in his jail cell. In Belnap's eyes, the "boasted land of liberty and equal rights" had become a farce. Within two years, he and thousands of other Mormons started the journey west from the US borders to the Salt Lake Valley, then part of Mexican territory, as they abandoned the now-fallen United States for good.

At some point in 1845, Gilbert Belnap almost certainly met Lewis Dana, for Dana was also a Mormon convert who had achieved a position of prominence in the church. Even in the unlikely case that they never met face-to-face, Belnap assuredly knew of Dana, for Dana was unique among the Mormons: he was Native, an Oneida chief originally from the tribe's homeland in northern New York. In the 1820s Dana and many other Oneidas had been forced by the US government to move west, to Wisconsin Territory, and in 1840 one segment of the Oneidas sent him on a mission to investigate possible settlement even farther west, beyond the Mississippi. On his journey downriver, Dana stopped in Nauvoo, where he immediately became taken with Mormonism—and Mormon leaders became taken with him, with good reason. His ethnicity meant that he was what Mormon theology deemed a "Lamanite," a descendant of the sinful inhabitants of North America who would one day be redeemed through Mormon outreach. Dana was baptized into the faith, and over the next several years he traveled between Nauvoo, Wisconsin Territory, Michigan Territory, and US Indian Territory, where he acted both as the Oneidas' agent to the US government in their quest to migrate farther west and as the Mormons' agent among the Oneidas, preaching the Mormon faith.[2]

In 1845, however, Dana's unique dual identity as both Native and Mormon made him truly important for the Mormons' plans. After Smith died, Brigham Young assumed leadership of the Mormon majority. He, along with countless other Mormon leaders, desired revenge against the United States for its culpability in Smith's murder and its continued apathy toward anti-Mormon violence. The Mormon leaders' plan was simple: seek out the Lamanites, especially those Natives already "removed" to US Indian Territory. Surely, Mormon leaders thought, they too wanted revenge, and they would join with the Mormons in an anti-US alliance at the same time as they converted to the Mormon faith. Lewis Dana was sent to US Indian Territory to bring this ambitious plan to fruition.[3]

Countless Native peoples inhabited US Indian Territory, but the Cherokees in particular received Dana's attention for reasons both geopolitical and cultural. The Cherokees numbered almost 20,000; their leaders had famously acculturated themselves to US cultural and legal norms in the 1820s; and thanks to their alliance with New England missionaries, they had held out the longest against President Andrew Jackson's racist, obdurate removal policies. If the Cherokees decided to ally with the Mormons, presumably other less populous and less "civilized" tribes would follow suit—or so Mormon leaders hoped.

Yet, when Dana actually contacted a Cherokee chief, his Mormon identity dropped out, and his Native identity took over. In fact, he never mentioned Mormonism at all. Instead, he claimed that the Oneida people planned to investigate land in the West on which they could settle permanently. He wanted the Cherokees to join him and "unit[e] with us to explore the western continent for the purpose of finding some resting place for our people."[4] He continued, "This invitation is not confined to you alone, but may be intended through you" for other removed Native peoples. In his response, Chief John Brown maintained that he had "not the least doubt" that the Cherokees would "do something" and shared his desire for a Native alliance, writing that he hoped the "Great Spirit the ruler of all things will forward your views and bring about a change that will be the means of uniting all the Red People together."[5] What Dana did not seem to know was that this idea of an alliance among removed Natives had already been discussed in 1843 at the Cherokee Nation's capital of Tahlequah. And, alas for Dana, he had contacted the wrong person, for Chief John Brown opposed the Cherokee leaders who had sought to bring this alliance to fruition. Whatever his claims in his letter to Dana, Brown was in no position to facilitate a mass Cherokee migration. Ultimately, the Mormon-Native alliance came to nothing. Within a year, Dana was on the trail west with the Mormons, acting as an emissary to the Omahas and other Native peoples whose lands the Mormons wanted to pass through.

While Lewis Dana and Gilbert Belnap probably knew one another, neither likely ever met Lansford Warren Hastings, which was to the benefit of all parties. Hastings began his own journey west beyond the US border around the same time as Dana and Belnap, but the Americans who traveled with him had no desire to encounter Mormons, for they were Missourians, and it was Missourians who had forced the Mormons to flee from their state to Illinois in the late 1830s. While on the Overland Trail, therefore, most Missourians feared Mormon reprisals and sought to avoid all contact. Hastings, a self-identified expert in the overland route to Oregon and California, was the trail leader for roughly a dozen migrants. They put faith in him largely because he had written *The Emigrants' Guide to Oregon and California*, which had become the go-to travel guide for anyone interested in traversing the Overland Trail.[6]

As his authorship evinced, Hastings had journeyed west before. In 1842, the twenty-one-year old Ohio lawyer had left his state for Oregon Country, which at that point was jointly shared by the United States and Great Britain by treaty although still largely controlled by Natives on the ground. In Oregon, the Hudson's Bay Company's chief factor, John McLoughlin, hired Hastings as his lawyer, hoping to protect his land claims from encroaching Americans. Hastings was present to witness the birth of Oregon politics at the village of Champoeg, where immigrants organized the Oregon provisional

The only extant image of Lansford Warren Hastings. This photograph appeared in later editions of *The Emigrants' Guide to Oregon and California* (originally published 1845). Courtesy of Wikimedia Commons.

government. Within months, however, Hastings tired of Oregon and left for the Mexican territory of Alta California. There he met John Sutter, whose fort presided over the Sacramento Valley, and then Hastings traveled south along the Pacific Coast, where small numbers of Californios presided over vast ranchos worked by Native laborers. As he traveled, he became captivated with California's economic potential, and he resolved to awaken Americans to its promise of prosperity. The result was his best-selling *Emigrants' Guide*.[7]

At some point on this journey, Hastings started dreaming bigger. Hidden beneath his desire to increase American migration to California was a remarkably ambitious political goal: to overthrow Mexican sovereignty and establish an independent American republic on the Pacific Coast. Why Hastings believed that California and not Oregon—at that point a much more popular destination for American migrants—was the place to realize this goal remains unprovable, but he saw firsthand the genesis of Oregon politics, which were decidedly conservative in their ambitions. The Oregon provisional government's modesty was apparent in the name itself: it was designed as a placeholder until US annexation arrived (which, it turned out, did not come any time soon). California had no such baggage. On the contrary, John Sutter's de facto independence testified that ambitious, risk-taking men could achieve political power quite easily in the distant Mexican territory. Now Hastings just needed to find those types of men in the United States—men who not only were willing to hazard a dangerous transcontinental journey, but who sought power and glory, which they thus far had failed to realize within US borders.

A republic of Upper Canada. The Mormon city-state of Nauvoo. A united Indian Territory. A Mormon empire in the Salt Lake Valley. Autonomous Alta California. A shared Oregon Country. A California or Pacific republic. Belnap, Dana, and Hastings traveled through, attempted to create, and participated in a dizzying number of political formulations between the years 1838 and 1846. Of course, none of these formulations lasted for very long, and none ever achieved international recognition of its self-sovereignty. Despite the precarious and brief existence of these creations, however, thousands of people—mostly Americans—dedicated themselves to their construction. At various points, Americans traveled hundreds of miles, wrote political documents, created political bodies, cleared farmland, started businesses, joined armies, and even fought and died for polities that, at least in retrospect, had little hope of surviving.

At the time, however, many participants in and many more observers of these quasi-independent polities thought they would continue for quite a long time and thought their economic and political potential quite good. There was a good reason for this belief. A sovereign nation had just been created south of the US border: the Republic of Texas. In 1836, a majority of the Anglo and Tejano inhabitants of Texas had rebelled against the newly established centralist Mexican government and established their own independent republic. In the aftermath of their closely won (and still quite temporary) victory, most Texans hoped to annex their new country to the United States, but for many political and economic reasons, the US government could not comply. Texas would remain independent, and to most observers it would do so for quite some time. Thus, when other Americans throughout the continent thought of establishing their own independent polities, they thought of Texas, spoke of Texas, wrote of Texas, and, in some cases, imagined themselves as would-be Texans. Texas became a language through which to understand the future geopolitics of the continent. Its independent existence augured an era when not just Texas but other independent polities would arise on the continent. In this book I term this the "Texas Moment." During the Texas Moment, Americans living both within and outside US borders imagined a future in which the United States did not bestride the continent, but instead existed alongside separate American "sister" republics.[8]

This is not how this era is often treated—quite the contrary. Instead of Americans imagining a future of multiple republics in North America, historians portray Americans imagining a future of an expansionist, "spread-eagle" United States encompassing Texas, Mexican California, Oregon, and, in some cases, Canada, Cuba, and all of Mexico.[9] A preponderance of Americans, so it is argued, believed that this was the United States' Manifest Destiny, a term coined by John L. O'Sullivan (or more likely, by ghostwriter Jane McManus Storm Cazneau) in an 1845 article in the *United States Magazine and Democratic Review*.[10] Not only did Americans imagine this future, but they acted to fulfill it—electing James Polk as president on an expansionist platform, volunteering in droves for the US-Mexican War, supporting Polk's bellicosity with Great Britain over the fate of Oregon Country, and—crucially—migrating to places beyond the US borders that Americans believed would soon be part of the United States. By seizing Texas from Mexico, migrating to Oregon by the thousands, and rebelling against Mexican rule in California, these Americans paved the way for US expansion.

Yet this portrayal is only possible in retrospect, for it fails to take into account the in-the-moment precariousness of the expansionist project, which required a series of unlikely or unforeseen events to unfold, including Polk's election, a successful war with Mexico, and successful diplomacy with Great Britain. From the perspective of the late 1830s, when the United States entered the most severe depression in its short history, or even the mid-1840s, when Polk remained a long-shot, dark-horse candidate, nothing about US expansion looked destined. Americans who remained within US borders had this outlook, but so too did Americans who left those borders to create their own polities. They did not leave to fulfill the United States' Manifest Destiny to conquer the continent; instead, they possessed political, social, economic, and ideological goals of their own, which rarely aligned with the wishes of US expansionists. Their destinies were fundamentally personal and thoroughly pragmatic, not national and romantic, and the polities they created were rarely intended as extensions of the United States.

In many ways, these independent polities echoed the distant American past, when English people founded colonies in North America in the seventeenth century that both mimicked and diverged from their native country. Puritan New England, Quaker Pennsylvania, slaveholding South Carolina, and cosmopolitan New York, among others, all resembled England and rejected it at the same time—some, like the Puritans, consciously so, and others more by happenstance. Yet, even the Puritans of New England acknowledged that their claim to rule over North America and its Native peoples remained rooted in the fact that they were claiming the land *for* England and *by leave* of the English government. The connection between England and its seventeenth-century colonies was loose and often tenuous, but it was a connection nevertheless.[11] Nineteenth-century Americans shared their ancestors' conception of a colony, but unlike them, they rejected the term. They were not colonists, and they were not founding colonies. They did not intend their polities to be extensions of the mother country, for they believed they had essentially severed themselves from US sovereignty when they embarked on their political experiments.[12] They were founding colonies *of Americans*, but they were not founding *American* colonies, if "American" equates to being connected to the United States.

Indeed, the distinction between "American" and the "United States" reflects one of the crucial arguments of this study. But first, a note on terminology: in this book, I use "American" to describe a person whose culture and heritage was rooted in the United States: English-speaking, most likely Protestant, a celebrator of the American Revolution, an adherent to laws and customs rooted in early US history and the pre-revolution British colonies. I am fully aware that this terminology is problematic, for it aggrandizes the people of the United States over those from every other country in the Americas, all of whom have just as much claim to being "American" as do people from the United States. For this reason, the architect Frank Lloyd Wright once tried to popularize "Usonian" as a term to refer to someone or something rooted in US culture and history.[13] Yet, while Usonian is a more appropriate and more accurate term in many ways, for this book Usonian—or other such terms— not only detracts from my argument, but in fact is exactly the opposite of what I am contending: the Americans I discuss in this book had little interest in the future of the United States. They may have been rooted in US history and culture, but they distinguished their American identity from their connection to the United States as a state.

The people I am discussing, who cared about independent polities, were in effect "breakaway Americans," and they were seeking to create "breakaway Americas." To be clear: this is my term, not theirs, and one that I impose historically to describe these people's common actions and ideologies. At the time, some breakaway Americans consciously identified themselves as American, even when they had left US borders and were creating their own polities. Others, however, would have questioned or even rejected this term. Some Anglo-Texans referred to themselves as Americans, but others saw themselves as Texians—a term that also connoted a connection to an Anglo-American culture and history. The Mormons, by contrast, would certainly have seen themselves as Americans until 1844, when the murder of Joseph Smith caused them to consciously reject this identity. Nevertheless, the polity they founded in the Salt Lake Valley remained thoroughly American, and their religion arguably is *the* American religion. Most problematically for my usage, no matter the time period, the Cherokees would have rejected the label outright. They saw themselves as members of the Cherokee Nation; they were Native, not American. Yet their leaders were thoroughly American*ized*, and the polity they created was perhaps more similar to a US society—in their case, the slaveholding society of the US Southeast—than any other breakaway America found in this book. By defining groups as diverse as the Cherokees, Mormons, and Texians as breakaway Americans, I do not seek to ignore their self-identities nor collapse the vast differences between them, but rather this terminology is intended to highlight their similar geopolitical goals and shared cultural values.

Each breakaway America both mimicked and rejected aspects of US society and culture. Viewing the panorama of breakaway Americas is like viewing the Jacksonian United States through a prism or, perhaps more appropriately, a funhouse mirror. Each one exaggerated certain aspects of US society and eliminated others. Most often, these aspects revolved around four areas: land, gender, race, and the history of the United States. This should come as no surprise. After all, these were arguably the four key areas over which not just breakaway Americans, but all Americans debated.

Breakaway Americans interpreted these issues differently depending on the polity they created. Wherever they traveled, they sought landownership, which had eluded them in the United States, but some sought to become yeomen farmers, others slaveowning patriarchs, and others something else entirely. While breakaway Americans were both men and women, in the male-dominated Jacksonian world—a world in which married women were legally "merged" with their husbands under the doctrine of coverture—it was men who made the decision to leave US borders.[14] Beyond US borders, these men sought to assert their masculinity. Some did so through landownership, while others did so through the more aggressive methods of military service and violent conquest. And, beyond US borders, breakaway Americans hoped to solve the racial issues that seemed to be imperiling the United States' future. Most breakaway Americans were white, and like most white Americans, they considered African Americans to be inferior and degraded. They were uncomfortable with the position that black people occupied in the ambiguously half-slave, half-free United States, and thus they created two unambiguous types of polities: ones that unequivocally embraced slavery and mandated that all black people should be enslaved, and ones that unequivocally rejected slavery but mandated that free black people could not live in the polity at all.

In the racial hierarchy of the Jacksonian United States, Native people occupied a loftier and vaguer position than African Americans. Few white Americans considered them equals, but some believed they could be equal, under the right tutelage; other white Americans, Andrew Jackson most famously, believed they would forever remain "savage," no matter how much they acculturated themselves to US society. Thus, in contrast to the binary place of African Americans, the roles of Native people in breakaway Americas could be placed on an extended continuum. On one extreme end were the Anglo-Texans, who believed that the United States had been far too tolerant of Native peoples and subsequently embarked on a genocidal policy of expulsion and suppression. On the other end were the polities of Native peoples themselves, above all the Cherokees, who sought to create a sovereign republic of their own. Between these two extremes were many other Anglo-American visions of white-Native relations, from converting Natives to Protestantism, to forcing them to labor as virtual slaves, to allying with them against the United States.

For all breakaway Americans, issues of land, masculinity, and race were bound up with various understandings of the United States' brief but all-important history. To breakaway Americans, the recent past was an idealized past, in which American men had been able to acquire land, display martial prowess, provide for their families, and perhaps participate in government and lead other men. Some breakaway Americans looked back to the American Revolution and others to the height of Andrew Jackson's influence in the early and mid-1830s, but by the late 1830s, all thought that the United States had fallen away from its revolutionary and Jacksonian promises—although which era they emphasized depended on their worldview. Thus, in a seemingly counterintuitive phenomenon, breakaway Americans believed they could be more American by leaving US borders, for beyond the borders they could perfect their own ideal of Americanness.

This belief separated the breakaway Americans I discuss here from the various filibusters and breakaway movements of previous generations. Since the American Revolution, Americans had created breakaway polities, such as Vermont, Franklin, and the Republic of West Florida. They also had joined ones that already existed, such as the Late Loyalist migration to British Canada, the American settlements in Spanish Louisiana, or, most famously, the migration to Mexican Tejas led by Stephen Austin in the 1820s.[15] Yet these earlier migrants did not bring their Americanness with them wholesale when they left US borders. In some cases, they were willing to give loyalty to non-republican polities. Or, if they were forming their own republics, it was because they saw the American Revolution through a cosmopolitan lens, as something to be copied over and over again, not revered as a single founding moment.[16] The breakaway Americans of the late 1830s and early 1840s, by contrast, believed in *the* revolution, and they were not willing to give ultimate loyalty to polities that were not governed by Americans. They would not convert to Catholicism in exchange for land nor learn another language to facilitate commerce. Fifty years of an idealized US history had made Americans a distinct ethnic and cultural group that refused to assimilate.

In this sense, breakaway Americans were adamant *American* nationalists, which seems counterintuitive considering their willingness to depart from US borders and found their own polities. But American nationalism during this time period was eminently flexible and its relationship to the US state ambiguous and ever-changing, always dependent on the Americans' differing backgrounds and worldviews.[17] For Whigs like Daniel Webster, John Quincy Adams, and Henry Clay, nation and state were tied closely together; an allegiance to and investment in one equated to an allegiance to and investment in the other. Democrats like Andrew Jackson, meanwhile, saw nationhood as more a matter of culture, background, and, fundamentally, American blood (by which they meant *white* American blood).[18] Democrats nevertheless participated in US institutions, including local, state, and national governments and, for men like Jackson, the US Army. Jackson may have supported states' rights and a small national government, but he fought for the United States for decades as an army officer and then sought to maintain the Union as president, most notably during the nullification crisis. Breakaway Americans, by contrast, fully separated nation from state. Their allegiance to the US state was wholly conditional, and it was dependent on how well the United States displayed the breakaway Americans' conception of American ideology—an amorphous combination of local democracy, individual liberty, social equality, and the ownership of private property. According to this mindset, the United States could in fact become un-American, and if it did, it was up to breakaway Americans, individually and collectively, to reassert American values beyond US borders.

Once beyond US borders, the desire to display their Americanness separated breakaway Americans from other assertions of sovereignty that occurred during the same years throughout the North American continent. During these years New Mexico, Yucatán, and other Mexican states rebelled against Mexico's centralist government, and Native peoples, most notably the Comanches, aggressively expanded their power across the Great Plains.[19] From simply the perspective of power, examining breakaway Americas is focusing on a distinctly secondary story, as these small polities were often islands in a sea of Native sovereignty. The Comanches, the Lakotas, and countless other Native groups were wielding sovereignty based on a long history of Native political, social, and economic practices. Breakaway Americans, by contrast, were doing so based on practices and traditions embedded in early US and European colonial histories. It is this distinction that makes the Cherokee Nation, along with smaller Native polities in US Indian Territory, a breakaway America. Although the Cherokees would have rejected calling themselves "Americans," they nevertheless argued, both before and after removal, that the Cherokee Nation mirrored other American-style polities in its political and social organization.

That both white and Native breakaway Americans believed that independent polities were possible in North America seems, in retrospect, to be stunningly naïve, even delusional. After all, this was the era of Manifest Destiny, when the United States doubled in size in only a few years. Yet scholars, by and large, have given too much credit to that ideology, reifying it historically in an attempt to understand its implications. The sheer number of (often excellent) works with titles invoking "manifest," "destiny," or both is a testament to the paradigm's overarching influence.[20] Certainly, historians no longer ascribe to Manifest Destiny as it was intended by its original adherents: as a moral and righteous nonviolent expansion. Instead, they have revealed the racist and violent notions that undergirded the expansionist ideology. And in defense of historians: many Americans *did* ascribe to an expansionist mentality. But as I demonstrate below, they believed that expansion could be undertaken by Americans as a people or by the United States as a state, and these were not the same. Nevertheless, for this era, scholars have lost the sense that history could have turned out differently. They have lost the notion that contingencies directed the geopolitics of the period just as much as broad social forces, complicated ideologies, mass movements of people, and the day-to-day minutiae of US national politics.

The failure to take into account alternative futures is unique for this particular era of early American history. For example, historians have little trouble imagining a history in which the American Revolution did not happen as it did, or one in which the United States failed to survive its first several decades of independence intact.[21] The entire revolutionary era is usually narrated with a sense that the project that became the United States was always shaky and constantly subject to disruption. That the Patriots won and the United States survived was "almost a miracle" and reflected that there had been an "angel in the whirlwind"—to make use of the titles of two books on the subject, both of which paraphrase Patriot leaders.[22] The road to the Civil War and the eventual Union victory reflects a similar sense of contingency. Historians understand that the decade-long countdown to the war, from the Compromise of 1850 to Fort Sumter, was not ordained; secession could have happened differently, or perhaps not at all.[23] During the war, the Confederacy could have won if not for crucial military and political turning points.[24] With these alternative futures in mind, we study the seemingly failed political movements of the moment: from Loyalist ideology, to the Articles of Confederation and the Hartford Convention, to the South Carolina Nullifiers and the Know-Nothings, and ultimately to the Confederate States of America. Although historians have brought back a sense of contingency to the US-Mexican War and have revealed that the United States' victory was much more closely run than assumed in the popular imagination (then and now), US expansion more generally continues to be a certitude.[25] In the historical imagination, it remains both manifest and destined.

However, Americans living at the time, both the thousands leaving US borders and the millions who remained in the United States, believed no such thing. On the contrary, a majority of Americans in the late 1830s, particularly in the aftermath of the Panic of 1837, did not foresee US expansion in the immediate future. Nothing about the current political, social, or economic milieus indicated as such. It appeared to most Americans, even—or especially—those who longed for US expansion, that if expansion happened, it would come in the medium-to-distant future. That it did not happen this way, that expansion occurred within less than a decade, a stunningly short time, may mean this was an inaccurate prediction, but it was not illogical. The path from the late 1830s to the mid-1840s, from US weakness to seeming US strength, from no conquest to immense conquest, was marked by a vast number of unforeseeable contingencies. Those contingencies, above all, erased the brief but fascinating history of breakaway Americas in the early 1830s and 1840s, collapsing their existence into the grand narrative of Manifest Destiny.

CHAPTER ONE

The Texas Moment

In December 1843, Henry Clay wrote a letter to his fellow Kentucky Whig senator John Crittenden, in which Clay responded to recent hints from President John Tyler that Texas would be more successful joining the United States than remaining independent. Clay offered Crittenden three reasons that Tyler's position was untenable: first, the United States already possessed enough territory; second, since annexation required the approval of two-thirds of the Senate and only half of all senators supported it, it was utterly impracticable—and thus hardly worth discussion; and third, if Texas entered the union as a slave territory, then non-slaveholding expansionists would push for the annexation of Canada in order to maintain the sectional balance, leading the United States into a precarious international position. Clay then laid out his own vision for Texas's future: "Texas is destined to be settled by our race, who will carry there, undoubtedly, our laws, our language, and our institutions, and that view of her destiny reconciles me much more to her independence than, if it were peopled by another and an unfriendly race. We may live as good neighbors, cultivating peace commerce and friendship."[1] To Clay, Texas and the United States would march into the future as allied—but separate—republics.

Clay's vision would prove to be spectacularly wrong. Within a year of Clay's letter, Democrats were pushing for Texas annexation; within two, they had succeeded. Yet from the perspective of 1843, Clay's reasons for believing Texas's independence would prove permanent were quite rational. Most Whig politicians, from both the North and South, shared Clay's disdain for adding any more territory to the union, and they commanded a Senate majority. Texas's annexation could not muster a majority, let alone the two-thirds support needed to approve a treaty, making the prospects for annexation dim indeed. Moreover, Whigs could count on support from many northern and western Democrats who believed adding slave territory would prove destabilizing—not, as Clay thought, because northern expansionists would then target Canada, but because they feared a sectional rift in their party over slavery's expansion. One of these Democrats was Martin Van Buren, the party's likely 1844 presidential nominee, and another was the preeminent western Democrat Thomas Hart Benton, each of whom commanded an important faction of the party.

Considering the many barriers arrayed against Texas annexation, Clay's prediction was not only logical, but *likely*. Of course, this assertion is ultimately unprovable, for what may have been likely never came to pass. Instead of Clay's prediction of a permanently independent Texas existing side by side with its northern sister republic, the history of the United States in the mid-1840s is defined by James Polk, Texas annexation, the Oregon Treaty, the US-Mexican War, Manifest Destiny, and the Wilmot Proviso—and, with the Wilmot Proviso, the inexorable countdown to the Civil War. Yet to understand the many other—very real—possibilities of the era, we must forget these events entirely and not deem any of them foreseeable, let alone inevitable. From the perspective of 1843—or even 1846—Manifest Destiny was neither manifest, nor destiny. Instead, we must consider US politics and the union more generally as its citizens did in the late 1830s and early 1840s. During these years, James Polk was a twice-defeated candidate for the Tennessee governorship who was contemplating the end of his political career; the Republic of Texas elected a president who longed to expand the new republic's borders and decisively opposed annexation to the United States; Oregon was firmly in the hands of the Hudson's Bay Company and its Native allies; and Americans living in western states believed they had been forgotten by the US government and were confronting a multitribal Native alliance without federal support.

Also during these years the Panic of 1837 initiated an economic depression that devastated many parts of the union. In its wake, multiple states declared bankruptcy, hundreds of local banks folded, thousands of Americans fled to Texas to escape their debts, and tens of thousands experienced some level of destitution. Meanwhile, violence and lawlessness reigned across the country. Anti-abolitionist and nativist mob violence erupted in countless towns and cities. Americans illegally invaded Canada in 1838, preyed on the Cherokees as they were forced west in 1839, and attacked Mormon settlements in Missouri in the late 1830s and in Illinois in the early 1840s. In Florida, the US

Army floundered at defeating a few hundred Seminoles, which cost the federal government millions of dollars—money that it could ill afford to spend amid the depression. As to the federal government itself, little seemed to be going right. Two presidents, Martin Van Buren and John Tyler, were despised by wide swaths of the population, including significant factions within their own parties; a third, William Henry Harrison, whose campaign in 1840 had energized much of the electorate, died within a month of taking office.

Given the union's malaise, it is no wonder that many white Americans, in countless local newspapers and hundreds of letters to their friends and family members, envisioned a very different future for the continent—and, perhaps, for themselves on that continent. Many still adhered to a belief that existed even before the American Revolution, which held that Americans—by which they meant *white* Americans like themselves—would one day conquer the continent through a combination of demographics and military prowess. At times these people were wedded to a polity: the British Empire before the American Revolution or the United States after. Yet this did not need to be the case: Americans might also conquer the continent without the guidance or support of the United States. Indeed, if the United States maintained its current level of dysfunction, then Americans could and should create republics beyond US borders. They were doing so in Texas; perhaps California and Oregon, or even British Canada, would next become neighboring American sister republics. Perhaps some time in the future, these American republics would voluntarily join the United States, but whether this would happen in five years, in fifty years, in a hundred years, or never was anyone's guess. The future was uncertain, and anything could happen.

1836–1837: The Texas Moment Begins

On April 21, 1836, in only eighteen minutes, the fate of North America turned. On that day, in that brief period of time, Sam Houston's outnumbered Army of the Republic of Texas decimated Mexican president Antonio López de Santa Anna's unprepared force. The Texans killed 630 Mexican soldiers and took 730 prisoners at the cost of 9 casualties. The following day brought the coup de grace: the Texans captured Santa Anna, who had been hiding in a nearby marsh. Although 4,000 Mexican troops remained in Texas under the command of General Vicente Filisola, the overwhelming nature of the Mexican defeat, coupled with Santa Anna's capture, persuaded Filisola to retreat south. Texas's independence was secured—at least for the immediate future.[2]

The Battle of San Jacinto was a stunningly unambiguous ending to a Texas history that had been littered with ambiguities. In the early 1820s, Stephen Austin and thousands of other white American migrants had traveled to the Mexican territory of Tejas precisely because they believed Mexico offered better prospects than the United States did. At the time, Mexico claimed more territory than the United States and had a much longer history of European settlement. Following its successful war of independence against Spain, which ended in 1821, Mexico's future looked bright. Even more important for men like Austin, Mexico offered the prospects for locally autonomous rule in a remarkably decentralized federal republic. More tangibly—and probably more important for most migrants—it also offered enormous tracts of land at minimal cost. In Texas, a head of a family could obtain a square league of land (4,428 acres) for a low fee (four cents per acre) that was payable in installments, none of which were due until the fourth year after arrival.[3] To be sure, a majority of American migrants still arrived as illegal squatters, but unlike in the United States, they did not feel the pressures from speculators and governmental officials to obtain legal title. At the same time, empresarios like Austin had every incentive to make the squatters legal landholders, for empresarios received additional land for each family they settled in Texas. With such inducements, American migration to Texas skyrocketed in the 1820s, reaching 20,000 by 1830.

Meanwhile, the United States in the early 1820s was suffering. The US economy had collapsed during the Panic of 1819, and many Americans blamed the depression on the centralized banking policies of Washington. Moreover, land in the United States was expensive, and much of it had already been purchased by wealthy landowners or speculators. While prices differed among different states and localities, US land policies were on the whole decidedly conservative. Landowners themselves were not necessarily secure from hardship, and countless people lost their land during the depression. Thus, the United States pushed while Texas pulled. Once in Texas, expatriated Americans argued that their once-great nation had betrayed the ideal of the yeoman farmer that Thomas Jefferson had exalted decades before.[4] Whether Mexico would offer an improvement remained to be seen.

The first Anglo-Texans represented one strand of a portion of the US population that rejected the 1787 constitutional settlement from a populist standpoint. Including the frontier anti-Federalists of the late 1780s, the Whiskey Rebels of 1791, and the proponents of relief in the aftermath of the Panic of 1819, this populace was heterogeneous and ever fluctuating, but generally shared four core beliefs. First, the path to economic prosperity and social power lay in landownership, and thus it was the duty of the federal and state governments to support widespread land acquisition for as many Americans as possible. Second, unlike landownership, land *speculation* was immoral and corrupt, and thus governments should prioritize the interest of squatters at the expense of speculators. Third, landownership bequeathed political power at the local level, and while the federal and state governments ought to facilitate land acquisition, they should largely stay out of local affairs, a principle the historian Saul Cornell labeled "plebeian populism." Finally, these three tenets all buttressed a fourth: the glorification of the white male who, by owning land and asserting local sovereignty, also wielded power over his dependents: his wife, his children, and in some cases, enslaved people.[5]

While plebeian populists were a crucial voting bloc in the Jeffersonian and, later, Jacksonian coalitions, their support was neither consistent nor automatic. Neither Thomas Jefferson nor Andrew Jackson nor many of their more established supporters embraced true plebeian populism. On the contrary, both men embraced speculation as a means of personal enrichment, and both asserted a fundamental right to private property and the inviolability of contracts. Egalitarianism among all white American males was a worthy goal in theory, but to prominent Jeffersonians and Jacksonians, it should never be accomplished by redistributing property or devaluing specie. Jackson in particular may have paid homage to the common white man, but his rhetoric rarely translated into actual policies that helped common white men in the real world, particularly during economic downturns.[6] While conservative financial policies were troublesome for yeomen during boom times, they were disastrous for them in hard times, especially because federal and state courts, with the approval of wealthy landholders like Andrew Jackson, overruled any state legislation that provided Americans with some relief from foreclosure and indebtedness. Indeed, at the same time as the first American migrants left for Texas in the early 1820s, Jackson was busy in Tennessee countering the pro-relief government that threatened his property interests.[7]

In their opposition to the United States' conservative financial policies, dissenters consistently argued for their quintessential Americanness. They believed that they, not those currently in charge of the federal and state governments, embodied the true principles of the American Revolution. Anglo-Texans in particular did not see their commitment to Mexican Texas as representing a rejection of either their Anglo-American ethnicity or their heritage. In their political loyalties, they were fundamentally flexible and pragmatic. They could orient themselves outward toward the United States to the north or Mexico to the south or, as would be the case after 1836, inward toward their own fledgling institutions—as they believed best benefited their interests. This pragmatism was not something Mexican authorities had in mind when they devised the terms of settlement. In return for land titles, Anglo-Texans were supposed to assimilate to Mexican culture and customs, and to a certain extent, they did. They learned Spanish, converted to Catholicism, and generally got along with their Tejano neighbors. Anglo-Texans also celebrated Mexican federalism wholesale, and with good reason: Mexico left them alone while still providing them with abundant access to cheap and fertile land.[8]

Yet Anglo-Texans' commitment to Mexico was always partial. They were hardly committed Catholics, but converted because it simply was part of the terms of landownership.[9] Many continued to honor their American heritage through celebrations of the Fourth of July, and they continued to pay homage to the revolutionary generation.[10] Most important, despite Mexico's prohibition of slavery, Anglo-Texans maintained the practice, sometimes working around the law by declaring that the black men and women who labored in their fields were not actually slaves, but debt peons in the process of paying off the "debts" that they had supposedly accrued on the journey from the United States to Texas. Moreover, and most concerning in the eyes of Mexican authorities, the Texan economy remained firmly oriented north, much more a part of the United States' economic orbit than Mexico's. Yet during the 1820s, this concern never assumed priority among Mexican officials, both because Texas was distant and only marginally populated by non-Natives and because Mexican federalism—to which many Mexican officials were deeply committed—mandated that Texas, like all Mexican states and territories, should be free to manage its own affairs.[11]

The amity between Anglo-Texans and Mexican officials did not last. By 1835 Texas was in open rebellion against Mexico due to two factors that had combined to exacerbate the breach. First, like the inhabitants of many Mexican states and territories, most Texans, both Anglo and Tejano, were dedicated to the principle of Mexican federalism. Second, however, unlike other Mexican states and territories, Texas was populated overwhelmingly by Anglos who refused to abandon American economic and cultural norms. Texas was thus both federalist and foreign. Mexican officials, in particular General Manuel de Mier y Terán, who had been sent to the territory to assess the situation, emphasized the latter, arguing that Anglos' failure to assimilate presaged inevitable rebellion. Therefore, in 1830 the Mexican government had issued the Law of April 6, which prohibited both future American immigration and chattel slavery.[12]

But it was Texas federalism, not its foreignness, that ultimately precipitated outright rebellion. Relations between Texas and Mexico continued to deteriorate for several more years, and they were fully sundered in 1835, when centralists in Mexico City overthrew the beleaguered federalist government. Led by General Santa Anna, who had once been a federalist, the centralists revoked the 1824 constitution, replacing it with a new constitution that stripped Mexican states of much of their autonomy. Federalists not just in Texas but in other Mexican states, such as Zacatecas, Yucatán, New Mexico, and Alta California, rose in rebellion.[13] Yet, while the beginnings of the Texas Revolution may have mirrored the federalist-centralist struggles in other parts of Mexico, Texas's foreignness—its majority Anglo population, its proximity to the United States, and the previous years of tension—led events in Texas to take a profoundly different path than the rebellions elsewhere. In 1835, Texans seized San Antonio de Béxar, the capital of the territory, one of several state and territorial capitals across northern Mexico to fall to federalist forces. In no other rebellion, however, did Anglo-American migrants constitute even a significant number of the rebels, let alone a majority as they did in Texas. Because these migrants could be deemed American and not Mexican, Santa Anna could play to incipient Mexican nationalism by concentrating on Texas as a hotbed of federalist secession at the expense of other rebellious states and territories.[14] At the head of an army of 6,000 men, Santa Anna initiated a military campaign whose events are quite familiar to students of Texas, US, and Mexican history: Mexican victories (or, in Texans' eyes, heroic defeats) at the Alamo and Goliad; the Texas Declaration of Independence at Washington-on-the-Brazos; the Runaway Scrape and seeming collapse of Texan forces; and ultimately, Texans' stunning victory at San Jacinto and the capture of Santa Anna.

And yet, for all of the legends told about the Texas Revolution (among other things, the problematic term "revolution" presumes a world-changing event), the Republic of Texas was really never meant to be. For most Tejanos and for the majority of older Anglo-Texan migrants known as the Peace Party, rebellion was always conditional. Once the constitution of 1824 was reinstated, these rebels maintained that Texas would reenter the Mexican republic as a loyal territory. However, Santa Anna's massive invasion—and in particular his willingness to execute captured Texas rebels, whom he deemed traitors—caused all support for moderation to collapse and laid the groundwork for the rapid ascendancy of the War Party. This group argued from the beginning that reconciliation with Mexico was both impossible and undesirable.

Most members of the War Party were young American men who had only recently arrived in Texas. They represented a crucial transition in the history of North America when the pragmatism of earlier American migrants leaving US borders gave way to the strident and increasingly racialized American nationalism of later migrants.[15] Members of the War Party were, in essence, the first breakaway Americans. Unlike the earlier Anglo-Texans, who were halfway sincere in their commitment to Mexico and dedicated to pragmatic self-interest above a dedication to any specific nation, these new migrants came as Americans—and Americans they would remain, no matter what steps Mexico took to incorporate them. They reinvigorated and radicalized the struggle, taking it over from the demoralized group of older settlers. It was these arrivals who pushed for the Texas Declaration of Independence in March 1836. Behind this declaration stood a larger goal: Texas's annexation to the United States.[16]

The War Party's pro-annexation stance stemmed from reasons both emotional and practical. As predominantly single young men hailing from southwestern states like Mississippi, Alabama, Louisiana, and Arkansas, they were ardently proslavery and stridently racist toward non-Anglos, including toward the countless Tejanos who had also supported rebellion. Yet there were also practical reasons to connect Texas to the United States, and these concerns led many members of the Peace Party to also support US annexation following Santa Anna's invasion, uniting the two factions. Both groups of rebels understood Texas's severe limitations as an independent republic, particularly in regard to Texan military strength vis-à-vis Mexico. While the Battle of San Jacinto had rescued Texans from the brink of total defeat, the result did not solve the larger geopolitical problem. In the battle's aftermath, Mexicans of all political affiliations refused to recognize Texas's independence. Anglo-Texans realized all too well that if Mexico could get its act together politically, it could then launch another devastating invasion of Texas that the Texans would be unlikely to defeat on their own. Annexation provided an immediate solution to Texas's weakness: either Mexico would choose not to invade a US Texas for fear of US strength, or Texas would have US protection if Mexico chose to still hazard war.

Yet pro-annexationists had a problem: the US government would not accede to annexation, even though many Americans in the United States were willing partners, especially southern Democrats and the proslavery bloc led by John C. Calhoun, who sought to expand slave territory, and an emerging contingent of more general expansionists throughout the union who desired all territory, both slave and free. In his final year in office, President Andrew Jackson agreed with them on a personal level, but he feared that adding slave-holding Texas would split the Democratic coalition along sectional lines. His vice president and successor, Martin Van Buren, agreed. Further, Van Buren, more so than Jackson, pursued peace and moderation in his foreign policy, and Texas annexation would potentially initiate a war with Mexico, thereby breaking an 1832 US-Mexico peace treaty.[17] When the Panic of 1837 erupted only a month into Van Buren's presidency, it proved the final nail in the coffin for annexation, as even pro-annexationists throughout the union turned their attention to more pressing matters.

Texans now understood that the chances for immediate annexation were abysmal. Writing from Washington, DC, in late 1837, the Texas secretary of state, R. A. Irion, noted that most Americans "would vote against" annexation and then lamented, "I do not believe that any future administration will attempt such a negotiation."[18] Texas was on its own. Thus was born the "accidental republic," an eminently fitting nickname. The Peace Party had wanted Texas to rejoin Mexico on federalist terms, while the War Party had desired Texas annexation to the United States. Very few, it seems, really wanted permanent Texas independence, but it happened anyway. The Texas republic's accidental nature has led its ten years of independence to be glossed over as if it hardly happened. In this treatment, Texas existed in a holding pattern until it could safely land in its rightful place in the United States.[19] On its surface, this stance seems logical. After all, Texas's population of 50,000 in 1836 was tiny compared with that of the United States (17 million) or Mexico (7 million); its economy was for the most part in shambles; its military was ineffectual; and Mexico refused to recognize its independence.[20] For Texas historians (and many Texans more generally), the republic's existence as an anomalous, separate Anglo-American polity on the continent made (and makes?) Texas exceptional, but this exceptionalism does not necessitate taking permanent Texas independence seriously.[21]

Yet this stance ignores historical contingencies and parallels. Begin with the fact that the Texas republic's "accidental" status was hardly anomalous in the Western Hemisphere. For most Latin American republics (including Mexico), independence only became an option when France conquered Spain in the early 1800s, meaning that the centrally governed Spanish Empire no longer had a center.[22] In response, countless ayuntamientos sprang up across Latin America, claiming sovereignty in the name of the Spanish king, now that Spain itself was under French domination. In the years following independence, however, Latin American republicans ignored this complicated history, replacing it with nationalist narratives that described their inevitable birth—a phenomenon that was at work in the Republic of Texas as well.[23] Moreover, weakness and instability do not mandate that a sovereign state will necessarily fail to survive, let alone prosper. Texas in the late 1830s was no more unstable or ineffectual than the United States was during the confederation period. Nor should the Republic of Texas be skipped over simply for its brevity. Texas lasted longer as an independent country than the Confederate States of America did, and it lasted longer than the United States did as it was first governed under the Articles of Confederation, both polities that have received intense historical attention. Even the lack of enthusiasm among Anglo-Texans for permanent Texas independence is no reason to be dismissive of Texas's independent existence. After all, many of the soon-to-be founding fathers of the United States were ardent *British* patriots in the 1760s, deeming Britain "home" despite never having set foot there. By the early to mid-1770s, however, these patriots summoned and manufactured enthusiasm for independence—as the Texans would do also.

Of course, no historical analogy is perfect. Texas *was* small, underpopulated, and weak, and its inhabitants were decidedly unsure about going it alone on the international stage. Yet, flawed grand historical parallels aside, there is reason to take Texas independence seriously. From 1837 through as late as 1844, it looked more probable to both Texans and Americans that the Republic of Texas would remain permanently independent from the United States. Indeed, events of the late 1830s and early 1840s made Texas annexation to the United States seem quite unlikely. If an impartial observer during those years had to place a bet on what would happen to Texas, the safest wager would have been on Texas independence for the foreseeable future. And if Texas independence seemed to be permanent, perhaps other American republics would also arise on the continent. The Texas Moment had begun.

A Tale of Two Republics

In December 1838, newly elected Texas president Mirabeau Lamar offered a grandiose vision of the future of the infant republic in a stirring inauguration speech. Following what he and many Anglo-Texans perceived as the vacillating presidency of Sam Houston, Lamar offered an unambiguously glorious future. He described Texas's "vast extent of territory, stretching from the Sabine to the Pacific" and explained how "mountains of minerals" and "immense and exhaustless wealth" would provide for the "peace, plenty, and protection" of every Texan. He looked to a future of free trade and "improvements . . . in government" and noted that all of these benefits would stem from Texas's "present independent position as the sun courses the heavens."[24]

One month later, US lieutenant general Winfield Scott outlined a very different future for the United States in a letter to Secretary of War Joel Poinsett. Scott was writing from the northern border, where he was attempting to quell American "Patriots" bent on invading Canada in the aftermath of the Canadian rebellions. To Scott, the Patriots represented US society at its worst for their unwillingness to obey US neutrality laws, but the Patriots were only part of a larger problem. To Scott, the union's ills were many: "Canadian excitement among our peoples[,] . . . peace societies, antimasonry, nullification, Mormon difficulties, and abolitionism." All of these, Scott noted, were "cankers of a long peace and a calm world." He then prescribed a drastic solution, writing that a "good but foreign war only could save the union, and our free institutions, by effectually curing our people of those moral distempers."[25]

Both Lamar and Scott were decidedly wrong in their predictions—and, in Lamar's case, even in his assessment of Texas's geopolitical clout. The Republic of Texas's official territory did not in fact stretch to the Pacific, and the republic's power remained minimal in many of the western regions it did claim. It was Native people, particularly the Comanches, Kiowas, and Apaches, who wielded effective sovereignty over western Texas. Texas's economy was in disarray, and its military power was weak. Only Mexico's political instability, not fear of Texas's might, kept Mexican forces from trying to reconquer the territory. And in regard to Scott's vision of the United States, actual civil war remained far off—and, when a "good . . . foreign war" did finally arrive, against Mexico in 1846, it quickly exacerbated rather than alleviated the United States' political instability.

Although both Lamar's and Scott's predictions were wrong, their outlooks on the state of their respective countries exemplified the dominant popular moods in the United States and Texas. Let me begin with Scott's United States. In the mid-1830s, the United States' economy was booming. Politically, President Andrew Jackson and his coalition stood at the height of their popularity, while also engendering an intense opposition by reformers and evangelists. This heated political divide, however, did not negate the United

States' positive geopolitical position on the continent and in the wider world: it seemed to be an up-and-coming power. Jackson certainly believed so, as he offered to purchase two valuable regions from Mexico: Texas in 1829 and then California in 1835. It was this forward-looking United States that Alexis de Tocqueville toured in the early 1830s, when he predicted that the United States and Russia would one day be the preeminent great powers in the world.[26]

All changed in 1837. That spring, only five weeks after the inauguration of Martin Van Buren, the United States entered the most severe depression in the nation's short history. Fueled by a combination of rampant speculation, transatlantic miscommunication with British financiers, and Jackson's ad hoc banking policies, the Panic of 1837 devastated Americans of all social classes and backgrounds.[27] Although the economy rebounded briefly in 1838, it cratered again in 1839, this time for several years, only rebounding in 1846. During this time nine states defaulted on their debts. Prices collapsed across the union, and one historian estimated that 30,000 businesses failed, with the amount of specie available reduced by half.[28] The human cost of these developments was incalculable. With minimal federal or state aid for the millions affected, debt and bankruptcy invariably led to destitution, malnutrition, and starvation.[29]

Nationwide depression and individual hardship led Americans to begin to wonder if the United States' future was no longer bright, particularly when they added other ills into the equation. In this sense, the depression was just as much a psychological phenomenon as a fiscal one, fostering what one historian termed an "ideology of failure."[30] Failure, in turn, led to disorder. New York's Anti-Rent Wars, for example, began when landlords asked their tenants to settle their accounts during the depths of the depression, causing tenants to respond with violence.[31] In Philadelphia, the panic caused the city's trade union to collapse and threw many out of work, which became a driving factor behind the nativist Kensington riots of 1844.[32] In this vein, various local, regional, and sectional crises like abolitionism, nullification, urban riots, the Mormon War in Missouri, and other—in Winfield Scott's words—"moral distempers" combined to create a feeling of malaise about the future of the country. The union seemed a bubbling cauldron of small and medium crises, and soon the cauldron overflowed, to which Americans from all regions of the country attested. From Missouri, one writer described a "want of all confidence in the United States."[33] An Ohioan believed that the United States would "soon be broke down by civil wars and contentions, etc."[34] In Buffalo,

Thomas Love, a former member of the House of Representatives, bewailed that the country was "laboring from a spirit of disunion—of revolution both social and sectional, of anarchy and violence."[35] From Philadelphia, printer James Ronaldson wrote that an "evil state now afflicts the country," lamenting that the "business of the whole people is ill done or entirely neglected."[36] By 1840, some believed the economy was improving. The *New York Mercury* observed, "We have had so much growling about hard times, ruin, bankruptcy, distress, mystery, and the utter prostration of business, that we thought it would be a source of happiness to our readers, to hear of a thorough revival of all business, not only in this city but throughout the Union."[37] Yet the paper's hopes were misplaced, and hard times continued. In 1843, one father lamented to his son that there was still a "real scarcity of money now in U.S. states."[38] When and how the United States would finally overcome the depression was anyone's guess.

For many individuals, particularly male heads-of-households or would-be heads-of-households, whether the United States would withstand the depression was beside the point. What truly mattered was making ends meet on a day-to-day basis. Even before the depression, this had become increasingly difficult, as the full emergence of capitalism in the 1820s eroded many of the traditional familial and societal structures of the post-revolution period in both the North and South. By the 1830s, wage labor dominated northern cities while wealthy southerners sought to exponentially increase the output from enslaved people while simultaneously profiting through intensified speculation in southwestern lands.[39] As capitalism ruptured US society in countless ways, Americans responded with countless solutions: some advocated "moral reform" to ease social ills, others the building of internal improvements to facilitate economic connections across the country. To one crucial set of Americans, however, the solution could be found in reverting to what they assumed was the bedrock of the union: landownership. Like the Americans who migrated to Texas in the 1820s, this amorphous population romanticized the yeoman farmer and longed to return to this Jeffersonian ideal, which seemed to be going extinct.[40] Thus, agrarian families in both the North and South moved and moved again in search of cheap land. The desire for land even emerged in cities in the guise of the National Reform Association, which sought to move urban inhabitants to rural areas by guaranteeing them a free homestead.

Unfortunately, the seemingly abundant land in the western United States was less abundant than supposed. Wealthy speculators bought much of the prime real estate, and squatters were often uprooted from their small farms.[41] While these conditions were present before the Panic of 1837, the depression exacerbated and widened the hardship. In 1836, in an effort to curb rampant speculation, the Jackson administration's Specie Circular mandated that public lands could only be purchased with gold or silver. Yet the Specie Circular failed to prevent the panic, and when the depression arrived it only made things worse, for the plethora of bank failures across the country ensured that there was no specie available except to the most wealthy and well connected.[42] Moreover, while land prices dropped precipitously and ostensibly made land more affordable, this also only benefited speculators. In 1841, Congress finally tried to alleviate squattership when it passed the Preemption Act, which guaranteed a squatter the right to the land that he farmed. However, the act limited claims to 160 acres, not enough for a would-be patriarch to divide among many sons, and payment was required upon purchase, which most squatters did not have.[43] Most land still remained under the control of speculators, and squatters continued to be reduced to tenancy or were forced to take out loans at usurious rates in a Sisyphean effort to eventually purchase the land they worked.

The depression was felt not just economically, but socially, particularly among men who were already experiencing the Jacksonian era as a crisis of masculinity. Landownership was the essential precondition of manliness in the American republic. It made men "independent" of the market and allowed them to provide for their families in the present, to bequeath to their sons land in the future, and to gain access to political power. However, the growth of capitalism and its various progenies—wage labor, land speculation, factories, and proto-factories—eroded this independence for countless American men.[44]

Moreover, as the revolutionary generation passed away, Americans were increasingly concerned that the second generation was not living up to the founders' legacy. Young men in particular searched for new outlets to display their martial prowess.[45] In the 1830s, however, opportunities were few and far between. The US Army in 1837 numbered a paltry 12,500 men, which Congress further reduced in the aftermath of the panic.[46] This force was not enough to defeat Seminole fighters in Florida (where the army was mired in a brutal seven-year campaign), let alone wage a national war against a European adversary like Great Britain. Militia service, long an area in which men could exhibit soldierly aptitude and leadership skills, was also on the wane, for in most regions east of the Mississippi there was no enemy left to fight besides potential rebels among enslaved people and urban rioters—hardly opponents that created manly reputations.[47]

Other divisions also afflicted the country. Slavery increasingly split northerners from southerners, and although northern abolitionists and southern fire-eaters remained small minorities in their respective sections, the debate over the gag rule in the House of Representatives showed that the politics of slavery would continue to plague the union. Partisanship had reached new heights, as the United States officially entered what is now termed the "second party system." Although thousands of Americans embraced this partisanship and dedicated themselves to their favored party, others found it distasteful and espoused an ideology that one historian labeled "anti-partyism."[48] Moreover, partisanship, along with nativism and racism, bred social discontent, which spawned countless riots that engulfed eastern cities.[49] Farther west, Mormons and anti-Mormons fought pitched battles in Missouri and later in Illinois. Americans who were lucky to live in areas relatively free of conflict were nevertheless informed of all types of disturbing news via the penny press or their newly arrived neighbors, as the United States experienced a stunning rate of geographic mobility.[50] The penny press in particular may have aggravated feelings of disorder and disunion by bringing unwelcome information into homes and businesses.[51] Amid what the historian Steven Mintz defined as the "specter of social breakdown," it is no wonder that Winfield Scott believed only a national war would deliver a shock to the malaise afflicting the land and once again unite all Americans around a common cause.[52]

To be sure, the United States still possessed many advantages. A nadir was not a collapse. No matter the extent of the depression, the United States remained on a vastly better financial footing than Mexico, which was bankrupt and confronting actual—rather than anticipated—rebellions throughout its northern and southern borderlands.[53] As numerous scholars have shown, in certain areas the US federal government possessed the attributes of a strong state, notably an effective court system, a sprawling postal service, an efficient customs house, and direct power over its territories.[54] Moreover, while the depression caused many Americans to move in search of better opportunities, a majority did not, and most of those that did moved within US borders rather than beyond them.

But Americans were not analyzing their prospects in the United States according to how they compared to the experience of Mexican citizens, nor were they giving credit to the United States for simply maintaining institu-

Edward Williams Clay, "The Times" (1837). This pro-Whig political cartoon shows Americans in various states of distress in the aftermath of the Panic of 1837. It blames the depression on the policies of Andrew Jackson, whose hat, eyeglasses, and pipe appear in the sky beside the mocking word "Glory." The US flag displays "July 4th 1837," sarcastically celebrating Independence Day. Courtesy of the Library of Congress, Prints and Photographs Division, Washington, DC.

tions that had been created in the past. It was a matter of perception: to many Americans, the United States was once a vibrant nation that had ensured opportunity for all its (white and male) inhabitants, but now was beset with divisions, anxieties, and failed expectations. Indeed, the various strengths of the US state were, as the historian Brian Balogh argued, largely invisible to everyday Americans, and it is unsurprising that Americans failed to give the United States credit for its continued successes.[55] The Panic of 1837, therefore, was just as much a moment of clarification and crystallization as a moment of real financial hardship. Many believed that eventual redemption was still possible for the United States, but at present the situation was precarious.

Contrast the economic depression and social divisions pervading the United States with the virtues of and opportunities in the Republic of Texas, which Mirabeau Lamar outlined in his inaugural speech. Whereas the United

States offered partisanship, Lamar sought "union amongst the people [of Texas]" and deplored the emergence of "factious dissensions."[56] While the United States suffered from depression, Lamar described the Texans as a "powerful and prosperous people."[57] In Texas, "the ploughshare of the husbandman is driven in peace and safety," Lamar said, painting a verbal portrait of a land of small farms and hardworking yeomen farmers. The fact that most of the recently arrived Anglo-Texans aspired to become not yeomen but plantation patriarchs did not diminish the image's comforting appeal. As the example of Thomas Jefferson had long evidenced, Americans had no problem paying homage to a yeoman society while seeking much greater profits in their personal lives (and, in the case of slaveholders like Jefferson, never doing any actual physical work).

To these broad platitudes Lamar added more specific benefits of Texas. Once an opponent of US tariff policy, Lamar celebrated Texas's "example of free trade," which would eventually cause all nations to cast off the "thralldom of tariff restrictions."[58] He maintained that in Texas the written law would be revered, and it would prove a bulwark against a "popular chief who shall discard its authority under the hollow pretext that he is acting for the good of the people."[59] Even though he did not name names, Lamar was clearly referencing Andrew Jackson, whom he disdained for Jackson's stance against South Carolina during the nullification crisis. To Lamar, Jackson's populism had exposed a flaw in the US Constitution, and while Lamar noted that this document was undoubtedly "the highest effort of political wisdom," he maintained that "a fair trial of fifty years ha[d] detected in that chart many se[r]ious and alarming errors."[60] The Texas constitution, explained Lamar, had corrected these.

Discussing more sensitive topics, Lamar was less direct. Slavery was crucial to his vision of Texan prosperity, and he believed the republic's explicit protection of the enslaved property of owners would lead to a massive slaveholder migration from the United States. In Texas their property (enslaved people) was safe from abolitionist "fanaticism."[61] In an earlier draft of his address, Lamar even described how the United States' failure to protect slavery would eventually destroy the union.[62] He decided to leave this part out of his inaugural speech, most likely because he was all too aware that Texas's future prosperity required international recognition from antislavery Great Britain. Nevertheless, he still decried the dangers of abolitionists, describing them as "communities [in the United States] who are known to be opposed to her peculiar and essential interests." Abolitionism's influence in the United

States, Lamar maintained, should give Texans who desired US annexation pause.[63] To slaveholders versed in the language that described their "peculiar institution," Lamar's careful phrasing would have been easy to understand.

Just as he was an unapologetic slaveholder, Lamar was also a virulent hater of the continent's Native people. As a former Georgia resident, he was a staunch supporter of Indian removal in the United States, and once in Texas he was disgusted with Sam Houston's relatively peaceful policies toward Texas Natives.[64] In his speech, however, Lamar hardly referenced this topic, only promising to "protect the frontiers" and arguing that Texas should avoid annexation so as to retain the "right of controlling the Indian tribes within her borders."[65] When this view was coupled with his vision of an expanding Texas empire, there could be little doubt that the Republic of Texas could only be built through the expulsion and destruction of Native peoples. One migrant who had been in Texas for no more than a few months clearly understood Lamar's intention, informing his friend in the United States, "The Indians it is true are troublesome uppon [*sic*] the frontier but I think the course the President is taking will soon quell them."[66]

But Lamar's grandiose vision came nowhere close to reality, for the Texas government barely functioned, and the Texas army hardly existed. Moreover, Lamar's dream of an independent, expansionist Texas was not shared by all Texans. Quite the contrary: in the aftermath of San Jacinto, a striking majority of Texans had voted for annexation to the United States: 3,277 votes for annexation, 91 against.[67] By Lamar's presidency, however, hopes for US annexation had been dashed, perhaps permanently. Whether they wanted to or not, Texans had to turn away from the United States. Now Mirabeau Lamar voiced their only acceptable alternative: an independent, expansive, and prosperous Anglo-American Republic of Texas.

Thus, as the United States rejected Texas, Lamar and his constituents rejected the United States. Lamar's inaugural speech defined Texas as a second, *improved* Anglo-American republic in North America. The United States allowed northern abolitionists to threaten the institution of slavery, but Texas would explicitly protect the rights of slaveholders. The United States would hem and haw as it negotiated with Natives for removal, but the Texas government would expel them at any cost, no matter how brutal. Land was prohibitively expensive in the United States, but it was cheap and abundant in Texas. The new republic would avoid the rank partisanship in the United States, and it would reject the United States' hated tariff. The recently created myths of the Texas Revolution—Lamar already deemed its heroes the "sons of the Revolution" in his address—even offered a new generation of founding fathers.[68] Incoming migrants could join this illustrious group themselves.

Lamar's rejection of the United States was not a rejection of his Anglo-American cultural background and heritage. Texas would ascribe to the principles of the US Bill of Rights, and Lamar explicitly celebrated freedom of the press and freedom of religion in his address. The new republic would embrace Anglo-American culture, American history, and most of the United States' economic practices, particularly the South's booming cotton market. As Lamar noted, the US Constitution was "nearly" perfect. Texas, however, would be fully perfect, serving as the fulfillment of the promise of the United States, preserving its many virtues while casting off its few vices.

This vision may have been idealistic, but it was hardly unrealistic from the perspective of the late 1830s. Despite all of their severe fiscal and military issues, Anglo-Texans had ample reason for hope. In the aftermath of the Texas Revolution, migration from the United States boomed, reaching 20,000 migrants per year (including enslaved people) into the early 1840s.[69] By 1845, a remarkable 125,000 non-Natives lived in Texas, compared to 40,000 in 1836. In the first two years of independence, migrants were pulled by cheap land, military glory, and a chance of adventure. Indeed, all of these were wed together, as the Texas government granted all men who served in the Texas army free land for their service. After 1837, however, migrants had an additional push: the Panic of 1837. As one American republic's economy collapsed, a second American republic offered hope with its affordable and abundant land. While the panic was a transatlantic fiscal crisis and devastated the Texan economy alongside that of the United States, the new republic nevertheless offered greater financial flexibility than the much more heavily populated and regulated United States. It also offered legal relief, for creditors and US law could not pursue debtors beyond US borders.[70] As one US newspaper reported, "In the Southwest [of the United States], emigration to Texas is the order of the day" because in those US states "money-matters are as bad as they can be."[71] When they left for Texas, indebted emigrants carved "G.T.T." or "G.T." on their doors to inform their creditors that they had "Gone to Texas," a tactic borrowed from previous debtors during the Panic of 1819 who had made up the first, smaller American migration to Texas. The initials and phrase soon became a common idiom throughout the United States.[72]

This migration kept the republic afloat. Texas may have been, in historian Andrew Torget's words, a "barnyard republic," because its government hardly functioned and its military hardly existed. Yet thousands of yearly immigrants helped mitigate these problems, particularly in regard to Texas's external and internal enemies. While few migrants wanted to join the Texas army, many were more than willing to act as militiamen and join the Texas Rangers. During Lamar's presidency, Texan forces waged a genocidal war against the Comanches, pushing the boundaries of white settlement farther north and west.[73] At the same time they expelled the Texas Cherokees, whom Sam Houston had previously promised could remain in Texas. The influx of Anglo settlers also meant that the once influential Tejano minority would be helpless to prevent the increasing Americanization of the land they once claimed as solely their own.[74] In essence, Anglo-American migration to Texas ensured that the new republic could be expansionist and aggressive in spite of its many failings. As Lamar exemplified in his speech, to Anglo-Americans and Anglo-Texans, the future of Texas seemed bright. On the other hand, while the United States was larger and vastly more functional than its new sister republic, its future appeared hazy. No wonder tens of thousands of Americans departed their republic of birth for a new republic of opportunity.

In some ways, this phenomenon was nothing new. I have already mentioned that an earlier generation of Anglo-Americans chose to travel to Mexican Texas in the 1820s. At various points over the first decades of the early US republic, Americans also chose to leave the United States for Canada, for Spanish Florida, for Spanish-French Louisiana, and for western regions whose borders lay within the United States but whose political destiny remained tenuous (e.g., the state of Franklin). Many of these Americans were responding to the same factors of push (lack of economic opportunities) and pull (availability of land, promise of adventure) that drove Americans to Texas in the mid-1830s. Yet, while general emigration from the United States was nothing new, the migration to Texas represented a different phase in this process due to a combination of two factors. First, earlier migrants were generally traveling to lands controlled by a foreign, non-Native power—Great Britain, France, Spain, and eventually Mexico. In order to gain economic prosperity, they needed to accommodate themselves to that power, at least to a certain extent. The Late Loyalists in Canada became dependable British subjects, while the early Anglo-Texans were willing if not always enthusiastic participants in the project of Mexican federalism. Accommodation, however, was not necessary in the Anglo-dominated Republic of Texas. On the contrary, for proslavery, southern, and indebted American men, Texas was even more welcoming than the United States. Second, while the Republic of

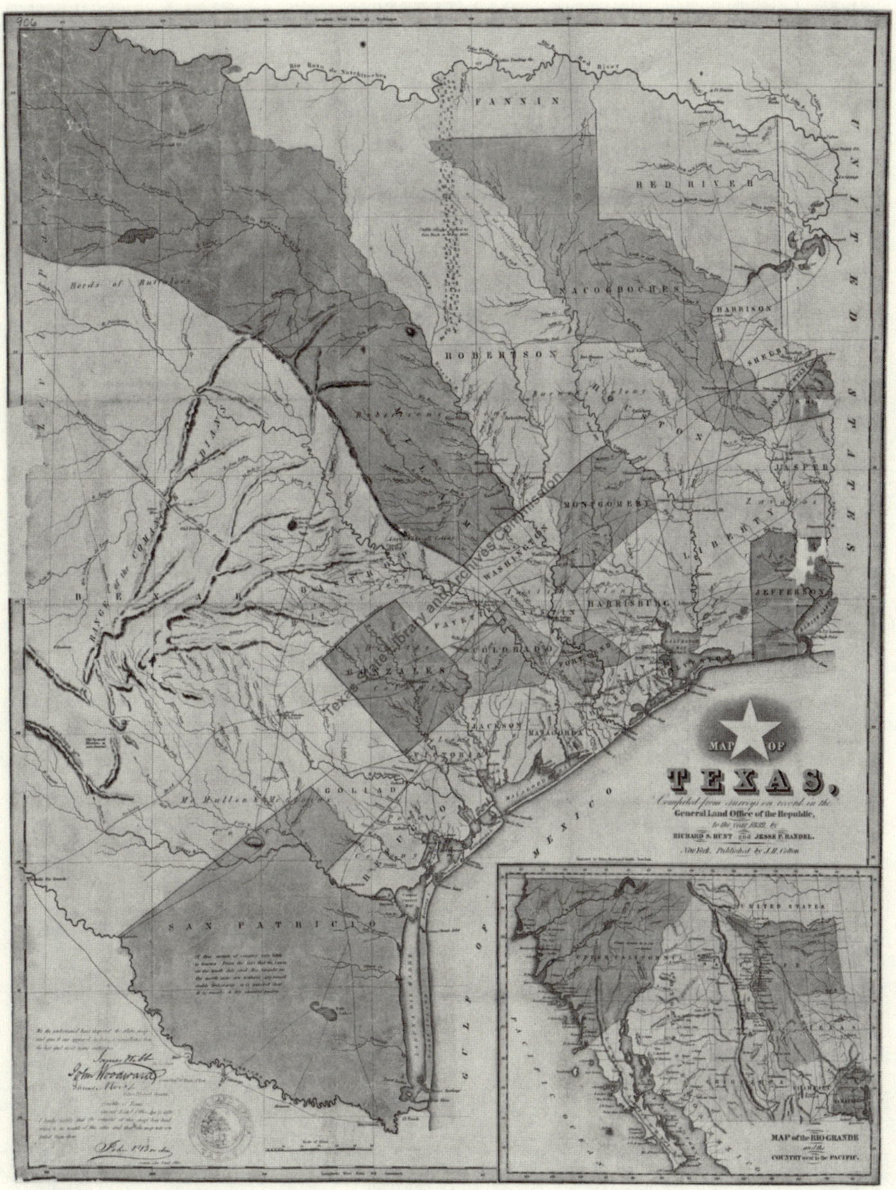

"Map of Texas" (1839). This map was one of many reproduced from an original first published by Stephen Austin in 1830. This updated iteration shows the Texas border stretching as far south as the Rio Grande, and the insert shows the lands west of Texas as far as the Pacific Ocean, thereby implicitly arguing for Texas's expansion. The definitive boundary lines suggest an orderly settlement that did not match reality, while the "Range of the Comanche Indians" to the west shows that not just mountains but the Comanches and other Natives stood in the way of western conquest. Map 00906, courtesy of the Texas State Library and Archives Commission.

Texas was not the first Anglo-American republic that was created beyond US borders, the others were almost always some combination of small, brief, and geopolitically precarious. Franklin and Vermont, arguably the two most geopolitically significant non-US Anglo-American republics, were not recognized on the international stage and did not possess dreams of a Pacific empire. Texas did.

Not all of the sufferers of the 1837 depression fled to Texas, of course. Many more remained in their homes and fought their creditors, clogging the dockets of state courts throughout the country.[75] Others, particularly debtors in the North, moved to cities or to rural areas, finding work in mills and factories.[76] Finally—and most important for this book—thousands of others who wanted to own land and were willing to leave US borders to attain it were unwilling to move to slaveholding Texas. A slave society may have attracted many white southerners, but it repelled most white northerners as well as some non-slaveholding yeomen farmers from the South.[77] Instead, these men and their families most often moved to places within US borders, most likely to a state or territory farther west than their current home. This was nothing new. Even before the depression, thousands of families had moved west time and again in order to obtain cheap land, which one anonymous East Coast resident lamented as the "withering curse" of western migration.[78] Yet in many cases, western migration was only a temporary solution, particularly for the squatter majority. At some point, US and state laws and the intervention of wealthy speculators would catch up with them. The ultimate goal—legal title to a modest amount of free land in a non-slaveholding territory—remained elusive. Neither Texas nor the United States offered a permanent solution.

There were other reasons that deterred certain groups from migrating to Texas. For the Whiggish reformers, Texas represented a step back from the moral progress that the United States had made. It was widely noted that the new republic was a haven not just for debtors, but for other criminals with more nefarious purposes. Moreover, although the Texas government sought to recruit migrants with families, most were single men, further adding to the republic's stigma of immorality.[79] To reformers seeking a refuge for the truly virtuous, Texas was not the answer. Beverly Waugh, the first Methodist bishop of Texas, believed that only married missionaries would be able to withstand the moral assault that would come upon arrival, writing that Texas was not "the place, at present, to send young, untried, and unmarried men."[80]

A New England migrant agreed, reporting to his family, "I have no great opinion of the people [in Texas] anyhow[.] I would advise no one to bring their family here at present altho a wife is a valuable article in this place."[81] Whatever its economic potential, in some people's eyes Texas remained an immoral republic.

Last, Texas was clearly not a destination for two other groups of US inhabitants who may have welcomed an alternative to the United States: African Americans and removed Natives. Texas's staunch proslavery stance, which included a measure that allowed for the enslavement of free black people if they did not leave the republic within two years, meant that neither free black people nor those who had escaped slavery would look to Texas for emancipation and opportunity (although enslaved people in Texas looked to the Mexican border).[82] During the Texas Moment, black people in the United States continued to migrate to the places where they had gone for decades: northern cities in the United States, British North America, and, for a few thousand, the African American colony of Liberia across the Atlantic Ocean.

For eastern Natives, Texas had once beckoned. In the 1820s, roughly a thousand Cherokees, along with a conglomerate of other migrating Native peoples, like the Shawnees, had found a home in the region. Later, in the mid-1830s, when the much larger group of Cherokees living in the state of Georgia became increasingly desperate in the face of the removal threat, several leaders contemplated moving to a "Country out of the United States which we may live in" and even tried to contact the Mexican government to settle in northern Mexico.[83] Texas's proslavery stance would not have deterred them: the Cherokee elite, along with many Creeks, Choctaws, and Chickasaws, were just as committed slaveholders as the Anglo-Texans. Sam Houston was sympathetic to Native settlement, but his policies were disliked by a majority of Anglo-Texans, as Native leaders knew all too well.[84] And if there were any doubts as to Texas's stance toward Native people, they were answered by Mirabeau Lamar's genocidal policies, which he directed just as much against "civilized" Natives like the Cherokees as he did against the Comanches.

Thus, the Republic of Texas was not just an alternative American republic to the United States, but a specific type of alternative: slaveholding, localist, Indian-hating, aggressively expansionist, and willing to sell land at vastly cheaper sums than the United States was. This alternative attracted tens of thousands of white Americans in the late 1830s and early 1840s, but it did not attract everyone. Texas was just a small portion of the vast North American continent that lay beyond US borders. Perhaps other American republics could be realized somewhere else, too.

Many Manifest Destinies

In November 1839, during the depths of the post-panic depression, John L. O'Sullivan (or, more likely, ghostwriter Jane McManus Storm Cazneau) penned his second-most-famous essay, which anticipated the more famous 1845 "Annexation," in which he would proclaim the United States' "Manifest Destiny."[85] Like its later iteration, this earlier version was an assertion of confidence in all things American—the United States' republican governance, its literature, and its schools. These things, O'Sullivan claimed, were what made the United States great in the present, and they would make it even greater in the future. In contrast, adhering to European practices would only bring the nation misery, and it was this tendency, particularly in regard to debt and speculation, he argued, that had led the United States into its current depression. However, even misguided Americans clinging to European practices would be unable to prevent the United States from becoming the preeminent nation of the world. As O'Sullivan famously wrote, "We may confidently assume that our country is destined to be *the great nation* of futurity."[86]

How could the *United States Magazine and Democratic Review* make such claims at a time when the US Army numbered fewer than 10,000 men, when nine states had defaulted on their loans, when many Americans believed that the United States was on the verge of disunion in some form or another? At the time the article was published, the immediate future of the United States looked bleak. On its face, "The Great Nation of Futurity" was either stunningly blind to the severity of the times or remarkably (perhaps luckily) prescient in its prediction of unprecedented US expansion a decade later, for in 1848 the United States did indeed appear to be the "great nation of futurity."

Looking deeper, however, it is clear that O'Sullivan's confidence in the future went hand in hand with his ambiguity about *when* the United States would fulfill its promise as a great nation. To O'Sullivan, this moment lay somewhere in the "far-reaching" and "boundless" future. He wrote, "The expansive future is our arena, and for our history."[87] Whether the depression would last a year or a decade, it was a small blip in O'Sullivan's timeline of infinity. In his sense of the future's boundlessness, O'Sullivan was not alone, even during the depression years.[88] Many other Americans had confidence in the future of the United States, particularly in its territorial expansion, although they differed from O'Sullivan in terms of not only when this expansion would occur, but which actors would perform the expansion. The future lay not with the United States as a polity, but with Anglo-Americans as a people.

A vast majority of white Americans agreed that they would eventually overrun the continent through sheer demographics. This belief was rooted in both fact and fantasy. It is a fact that the demographic growth of the Anglo-American population at this point was extraordinary. In the mid-nineteenth century, the United States really was outbreeding most other nations in the world. This demographic exceptionalism (along with some immigration) allowed the United States' population to surge ahead of Mexico's by the 1830s, when it had been only slightly more populous in the early 1820s.[89] But white Americans also believed in a fantasy, holding that their superior racial, ethnic, and cultural stock would make the tide of expansion all but irresistible in the long run; the historian Reginald Horsman labeled this "Anglo-Saxonism." Only Americans of Anglo-Saxon heritage, it was held, had the unique racial composition to make the land productive and expand "civilization." The "Anglo" aspect was somewhat flexible, as not just those of English background but all Northern European Protestants and their descendants could essentially assimilate to Americanism. The fantasy was also flexible in terms of the polity behind the expansion: Mirabeau Lamar, a proponent of Texas expansion, could use words quite similar to those of John L. O'Sullivan, a supporter of US expansion, for both were celebrating Americans' demographic dominance. However, Anglo-Saxonism was inflexible when it came to Natives, black people, and Mexicans, all of whom would neither be able to resist the Anglo-American tide nor assimilate into it.[90]

Hardly a unique development of the 1830s, Anglo-Saxonism existed in modified form even before the American Revolution, when patriotic Britons on the continent (many of whom became patriotic Americans) assumed Great Britain's inevitable dominance. By the Jacksonian era, Anglo-Saxonism was the consensus among white Americans, despite the deepening divisions in US society. Even Whigs, who almost unanimously opposed the US annexation of Texas, celebrated Anglo-American demographic expansion. Henry Clay, for example, wrote, "I have ever been desirous to see our race, and our institutions, more and more diffused over this Continent."[91] Daniel Webster noted that although he opposed the US annexation of Texas, he was quite pleased with the Texans' success.[92] Indeed, Whigs recognized that American demographic expansion was such an unstoppable force that they hoped to harness it as a means to develop the already-settled states of the East. Rather than the Democratic policy of preemption, which sought to settle the West as fast as possible, Whigs supported "distribution," whereby the United States would sell western lands at fixed prices, and this money would then be distributed to the states to use for internal improvements. As Whigs themselves admitted, distribution was also an attempt to slow down western settlement and make it more orderly, but the preemption-distribution debate revolved around *how* Americans should settle in the west, not *whether* it would be settled. Both parties agreed on the latter point.

If white Americans believed in destiny in the Jacksonian era, it was in the expansion of themselves as a people, which to some made the immediate future practically irrelevant. As Ralph Waldo Emerson observed, "The question of the annexation of Texas is one of those which look very differently to the centuries and to the years. It is very certain that the strong British race which have now overrun so much of this Continent, must also overrun that tract & Mexico & Oregon also, and it will in the course of ages be of small import by what particular occasions & methods it was done."[93] Emerson opposed the immediate conquest of the continent as immoral, but future Anglo-American racial conquest was nevertheless inevitable and undeniable. Only a small cadre of northern abolitionists was explicitly opposed to American demographic expansion, arguing that the racism of white Americans and the United States' protection of slaveholding made expansion not only immoral, but perilous to black people and other nonwhites who would be subsumed in the process.[94]

While most white Americans believed in demographic expansion, they differed on how the United States should be involved. Should the United States seek to incorporate future far-flung American settlements into the union? And if so, how quickly should it do so? On this question, there were more defined lines of disagreement.[95] To some, the answer was clear: US expansion should be prevented at all costs, for it would prevent the union from strengthening itself internally. As Webster wrote, "There must be some boundary, or some limits, to a Republic which is to have a common centre."[96] In his view, as Americans spread across the continent, they would create new republics—as they had just done in Texas and as he believed they would do in Oregon.[97] Opinions like Webster's were a vestige of a viewpoint that had once been much more prominent. It was Thomas Jefferson, after all, who had famously articulated an "independent empire" of Americans in the West, "unconnected with us but by the ties of blood and interest."[98] By the 1830s, however, this attitude was largely confined to New England Whigs. At the other extreme were mostly southern and western Democrats. This group believed in the immediate US annexation of Texas, a more aggressive stance toward settling and annexing Oregon Country (a territory then shared with the British), and more generally a fast-paced process of expansion—which, among southern Democrats in the case of Texas, was also tied into support for slavery's expansion. Yet this aggressively expansionist mindset faded in the aftermath of the Panic of 1837, when it became clear that, first, the United States did not have the means to assert continental superiority, and second, the Republic of Texas had turned its back on annexation.

Between these neatly delineated extremes was a much murkier middle, whose answer as to whether the United States should incorporate new American settlements was an ambiguous "eventually." These "conditional annexationists" (my term) included southern and western Whigs like Henry Clay, northern and some western Democrats, and the nominally Democratic adherents of John C. Calhoun. Calhoun best defined this strategy of expansion when he advocated that the United States practice "masterly inactivity" when it came to Oregon Country, for "time is acting for us."[99] In his mind, the United States was weaker than Great Britain from a military standpoint so acting aggressively in the near term would prove counterproductive. However, he and many others believed that Americans would eventually dominate Oregon from a demographic standpoint, so simply waiting for a few years would make US annexation assured. Conditional annexationists differed from one another not so much in final vision, but in immediate strategy, as Democrats were willing to sanction more aggressive measures, particularly when it came to Native relations. In contrast, Whigs desired slow and orderly expansion, with each step of the way backed by legal treaties and carefully engineered diplomacy with Native peoples and European powers. Moreover, Democrats and Whigs differed over the ideology of expansion: for Democrats, expansion *should* occur in order to improve the United States, while Whigs believed expansion *could* occur after the United States had been improved. Yet when it came to the practical implications of expansion more generally, the two sides largely agreed. The United States would eventually expand, but there was no immediate hurry to facilitate the process.

A third question about expansion, the *how*, was answered similarly by almost all white Americans. The process, whether undertaken by Americans as a people or the United States as a nation, would occur peacefully. Neither people nor polity would wage wars of aggression; neither would, in essence, act like the hated Great Britain or other European states. Few white Americans, of course, gave much thought to the fact that the supposedly peaceful expansion of the United States up until the 1830s had been anything but, as Americans had fought ruthless wars against various Native peoples in the Trans-Appalachian West through the end of the War of 1812, with scattered moments of violence, like the Black Hawk War, still erupting in later decades. Most whites did not give much thought either to the fact that Native peoples beyond the Mississippi not only continued to resist conquest, but often were expanding their own geopolitical power. Sovereignty in the Trans-Mississippi West may have been officially divided among the United States, Great Britain, and Mexico, but in most places, it was actually wielded by Native peoples. Americans, some consciously and some not, adhered to the centuries-old "doctrine of discovery," which held that people of European descent gained possession of indigenous land by simply showing up.[100] Armed with this belief, most white Americans ignored the inconvenient fact of Native power and land claims and deemed eventual US expansion "destiny"—but when, how, and where this would be accomplished remained ambiguous.

Thus, the most definitive statement that describes Jacksonian Americans' geopolitical vision is this: *there was no definitive vision.* The only viewpoint that truly came close to unanimous was a negative one: white Americans believed that Natives would eventually succumb to demographic and/or military pressure and lose their political independence. Beyond this, white Americans imagined a plethora of geopolitical possibilities, from a United States that spanned the entire continent, to a continent composed of three or four transcontinental republics (the United States, Texas, Mexico, and—eventually—a republican Canada), to the emergence of a Pacific republic on the West Coast. The wide range of opinion was reflected in the US press. When printing stories from the majority of the continent that lay beyond US borders, editors frequently made predictions about what exactly this news portended for the future geopolitical shape of North America.

Because Texas was already an independent republic, it received the most newspaper attention and therefore generated the most commentary. Moreover, because the new republic was settled and founded by Anglo-Americans (at least in the eyes of Americans in the United States, who ignored the important albeit diminishing influence of Tejanos), newspapers could easily portray Texas's growth as a logical example of Anglo-American demographic expansion. In this vein, the *New Orleans Bulletin* offered a stirring—and decidedly racist—prediction of Texas's future: "Peopled with an intelligent, adventurous, bold, and fearless race . . . the career of this young republic will, it is probable, be fraught with future greatness and glory. . . . Like the aboriginal inhabitants of America, the emasculate[d] and unworthy Mexicans are doomed to recede before the certain and steady encroachments [of the Texans]. . . . Ere long, neither the Neces [*sic*] nor the Rio Grande will prove a sufficient boundary to the daring march of our sister Republic."[101] Mirabeau Lamar could not have said it better.

The *New Orleans Bulletin* failed to mention what the United States' role on the continent would be if Texas remained independent, but other newspapers did. In the *National Intelligencer*, "A Traveller" celebrated, "To the two Anglo-Saxon masses of North and Centre, we may add another, Texas to the South; and therefore, as the middle of this century approaches, we behold three immense colonies of this commanding family of nations fixed on Eastern North America, and all with very different physical force, and much difference of moral[ity], increasing in mass, and spreading westward with a steadiness and force nothing can resist, and yet with almost the silence and omnipotence of time."[102] Here, then, was US expansion without Texas; Mexican California and Oregon would presumably join the United States, but Texas would not.

Or perhaps the United States would remain confined east of the Rocky Mountains, and California and Oregon would go their own way. At least, that was how many Whigs viewed the West. Daniel Webster thought this about Oregon, which he envisioned as a "great *Pacific Republic*, a nation where our children may go for a residence, separating themselves from this government, and forming an integral part of a new government."[103] Because this republic would mostly be settled by Americans and "some settlers . . . from England," it would undoubtedly flourish. The Whig-leaning *New Orleans Bulletin* believed that Webster's vision also described the fate of California. In California, Americans would soon plant a "colony" akin to the one they had established in Texas twenty years prior, and eventually they would seize the region from the impotent Mexican government. Predicted the *Bulletin*, "To a harder and more civilized raced will belong the glory of founding an empire of Federal Republican States along the Pacific Coast."[104]

To many, the emergence of a Pacific republic would be in the best interests of the United States. Whigs in particular were pessimistic about the value of the West and believed it was best to leave the region to itself. The *Louisville Journal*, for example, argued that "Russia has her Siberia, England has her Botany Bay, and if the United States should ever need a country to which to banish its rogues and scoundrels, the utility of . . . Oregon will be demonstrated."[105] Until that time, the paper had urged the United States to leave Oregon to Indians, trappers, and nature. Others failed to predict the triumph of the railroad and telegraph and believed that the Pacific Coast was simply too far from the United States to ever be governed effectively. As the *St. Louis New Era* described, residents in Oregon and California "will soon find that their peculiar and local interests will be neglected by a distant General Government and that they have many interests separate from and conflicting with those of the Atlantic States." The paper suggested that Oregon and California join together to form a "great independent Republic on the Pacific."[106]

Democrats argued vociferously against such visions, but they nevertheless believed that a North America composed of many republics was still an unfortunate possibility. For example, in a response to Webster's support for a Pacific republic, the *Southern Patriot* of Charleston countered, "The day that declares [Oregon] a republic by itself, will find our continent a nest of little republics, spitting and snarling and spattering at each other from morning until night."[107] By 1845 John O'Sullivan (or Jane Cazneau) agreed, at least in the long term, as he noted in "Annexation." While he believed that California would be independent for a period of time—perhaps a hundred years— eventually the railroad would knit together the East and the West, and the United States would bestride the continent. To O'Sullivan, anything but a continental United States was unthinkable and would lead to economic stagnation that would mirror the situation with the Latin American republics: "Away, then, with all the idle French talk of *balances of power* on the American Continent. There is no growth in South America!"[108] Only US continental conquest would foster continuous economic growth.

Americans contemplated that Canada, alongside Texas, Oregon, and California, would soon become a sister republic. During the Canadian rebellions in 1837, many presumed this republic to be imminent, and thousands of American "Patriots" flocked to the cause of the rebels, as I detail in chapter 2. Canadian Loyalists and the British army soon crushed the Patriots, yet many Americans continued to believe that a Canadian republic was on the near or at least distant horizon.[109] Henry Clay was an ardent opponent of Patriot activity in 1838, but only six years later he believed that soon Canada would become independent from Britain, which would create a harmonious geopolitical situation for the United States: "With the Canadian Republic on one side, that of Texas on the other, the United States, the friend of both, between them, each could advance its own happiness. . . . They would be natural allies, ready, by cooperation, to repel an European or foreign attack upon either. Each would afford a secure refuge to the persecuted and oppressed driven into exile by either of the others."[110] At one point, in an interesting reversal of arguments, Clay opposed the (theoretical) US annexation of Canada because it would spur the clamor for Texas annexation.[111] Like Clay, many other Americans tied Texas to Canada in their geopolitical visions. For example, the *Albany Evening Journal* agreed with Clay, claiming, "We neither want Texas nor Canada. But we do want sister Republics, and it should be our aim to encourage their establishment."[112] These were decidedly Whig visions, and Democrats disagreed, many predicting in the manner of the *Daily Madisonian* that Canada would be an "inevitable acquisition, sooner or later."[113] Nevertheless, Americans of all political persuasions recognized that geopolitics remained fluid throughout the continent.

This fluidity reached new heights when we take into account the people who remained within US borders. The federal government had removed thousands of Natives from the Southeast and Old Northwest to the US western border in the 1830s, and until 1848 US politicians contemplated a "permanent Indian barrier" that would stand between the United States and the Great Plains, which white Americans termed the "Great Western Desert."[114] While white Americans agreed that Natives throughout the continent would lose their political independence, not all envisioned that Native autonomy would cease entirely. Some Americans imagined an Indian state in the West, either as one of the many states of the American union or as a sort of quasi-autonomous polity that was loosely connected to the United States.[115] This belief was shared by whites living next to Indian Territory, many of whom feared Native attacks and often became frantic over the federal government's failure to control the region. However, the US government largely left its western border and removed Natives alone. Natives were left to carve out a precarious sovereignty that they hoped would continue indefinitely.

Americans also predicted that the Mormons, whether they were living in Missouri in the late 1830s or Illinois in the early 1840s, possessed geopolitical goals beyond US borders. According to the *Richmond Enquirer*, for example, "That the Mormons are determined to form the new empire in California, there is not the least doubt."[116] Revealingly, a few papers even argued that the United States should leave the Mormons to create their polity, whether it was in California or somewhere else. For example, the *New York Sun* maintained that the Mormons "never will annex themselves to any government on earth; nor is it desirable they should, as they are determined to be governed by their own laws."[117] Therefore, the United States should acquiesce to Mormon independence.

More often than they predicted the future of the continent, US newspapers simply reported continental news, which was also revealing, particularly when it pertained to Texas. For all of the fervor among southerners and westerners to annex Texas in 1836–1837 and again in 1844–1845, in the intervening years the Republic of Texas's existence became entirely unremarkable. Papers printed accounts from the fledgling republic on almost a daily basis and about almost any subject—politics, war, economics, migration, and so on. Often this news came without comment underneath headings such as "From Texas" or "The Affairs of Texas," demonstrating the normality of Texas's existence. News from Texas was treated like news from Europe or South America, although at times a paper would conclude with a glowing assessment of Texas's prospects. For example, in 1840, after reporting on a host of Texas subjects—the policies of President Lamar, a new bill in the Texas Congress, Texas's war against the Comanches—the pro-annexation *Baltimore Sun* concluded, "Every thing appears to be going on as well as the most sanguine of the well wishers of the Republic could desire."[118] In this manner, Democratic papers could implicitly support annexation by demonstrating that Texas's success meant that annexation would not require a substantial US commitment—namely, waging war against Mexico. Interestingly, Whig papers also celebrated Texas's success but for precisely the opposite reason: success meant that there was no need for US intervention, for Texas would "constitute a peaceable and good neighbor to the United States and Mexico."[119] In the South, Whig papers added an additional reason to celebrate Texas's independence: because it was an explicitly proslavery republic, Texas would be a permanent haven from abolitionists and therefore act as an international ally of southern slaveholders in the United States.[120] In a great majority of cases, however, whether the paper was Whig or Democratic, Texas articles ended without editorial comment. Reports from Texas were simply part of the broader category of international news that needed no editorializing. The ubiquity of these articles furthered the normalization of the permanent existence of the Republic of Texas and at the same time offered proof that Texas independence was already normal to a broad swath of the US public. Just as important, the constant printing of Texas's success in its early years of independence fed continued migration, which in turn supported Texas's success, a mutually reinforcing loop.

And yet, for newspapers that advocated the expansion of US borders alongside the demographic expansion of the American people, there was a looming peril: Great Britain. Expansionists worried that the British would eventually seize Oregon and California and intervene in Mexico and the Caribbean. With Canada already under British sovereignty, Great Britain would soon encircle the United States with what Andrew Jackson termed an "iron hoop."[121] It was crucial, therefore, for the US federal government to act decisively to counter such a disastrous future. Invariably, the significantly more anglophobic Democrats were far more concerned with British interference. Indeed, their vast range of predictions about the locations and methods of British meddling matched the array of potential geopolitical settlements they envisioned to such an extent that it is hard to find a place where expansionists did *not* think the British would soon interfere. Whether it was in Texas, Oregon, California, Indian Territory, or East Coast ports and cities or an invasion from Canada, the British specter was everywhere. In some cases, observers put all of these possibilities together. Writing from London in 1838, US ambassador Richard Rush warned that the 45,000 newly removed Natives would ally with Britain, putting the United States in "a state of blockade by the English navy on one side and *the Canadas, Mexico, and the Indians* on the other."[122] Rush was taking a continental view from his perspective in London, but on the ground in the western United States the threat was perceived just as acutely. The *St. Louis Republican*, for example, printed news that a few British officers were traveling through Missouri to hunt bison in the West, and then it connected this seemingly innocuous information with other developments—Indian depredations, controversy over the northeastern boundary, and the expanding influence of the Hudson's Bay Company— to suggest that something more sinister was afoot. The *Republican* wished that these British men "had chosen the other side of the line for their excursion, or some other time in making it."[123] The actual connection between all of these events was left by the paper to the reader's imagination.

In a few cases, the geopolitical influence of British abolitionism also became a danger, although not to the point it became by the mid-1840s, when the Republic of Texas looked to Britain to secure its increasingly precarious independence in case US annexation failed. But in its early years, Texas's staunch proslavery stance made the southwestern flank of the United States safe from slave revolts and abolitionist ventures, and thus it was the least concerning region for US slaveholders.[124] Instead, the primary threat of abolitionism came from the Atlantic Ocean and possible British landings on US soil and from Canada to the north. John C. Calhoun listed the United States' "maritime frontier" as the most vulnerable to British might, perhaps recalling how a British alliance with enslaved people in coastal Virginia and Maryland wreaked havoc during the War of 1812.[125] To Calhoun, any money the United States received from western land sales should immediately go toward strengthening Atlantic coastal fortifications.[126] Other observers took more expansive views of the abolitionist threat. For one newspaper, danger came from the Far West, where the British "scheme to colonize the Californias with negroes and mulattos," thereby permanently barring the United States from expanding west of the Rocky Mountains.[127] Although unsubstantiated and outlandish, this type of speculation reflected a larger truth: many white Americans perceived themselves to be at the mercy of British meddling.

The problem was, in the late 1830s and early 1840s, that there was little the United States could do in response. Joel Poinsett, the secretary of war under Martin Van Buren, understood this all too well from his incoming correspondence. Whether it came from the North, East, South, or West, every letter told the same story: there were not enough troops to handle any threat, real or imagined. From the front lines of the Seminole War in Florida, Poinsett received word that "we cannot defend from the frontier."[128] From the Arkansas border with Indian Territory, he was instructed that a "cordon of posts which should have been commenced *two years ago* is still neglected."[129] This carelessness meant that the United States could be "overwhelmed by a combined attack of Mexicans and Indians."[130] From the Great Lakes region, where thousands of American Patriots were hoping to restart the failed Upper Canadian rebellion of 1837, Poinsett received regular word that there were not enough federal troops to quell any Patriot invasion of Canada.[131] Farther east on the northern border, Maine threatened war against Britain over its disputed boundary with New Brunswick in the Aroostook War, and there the US Army presence was also negligible. The concern was that if either Patriots or the Maine militia invaded Canada, this could prompt Great Britain to declare war on the United States. To prepare, Poinsett urged the Massachusetts governor, Edward Everett, to raise funds to upgrade the Boston fortifications, but Everett could not get the Massachusetts Senate to agree. This left Boston, in Everett's words, "defenseless."[132] The United States' inability to defend itself had created, as Philadelphia printer James Ronaldson described to Poinsett, the "present listless confidence in our security."[133] For those concerned about US power and stability, the future seemed precarious.

For many other Americans, meanwhile, US weakness was not a concern. On the contrary, it provided a geopolitical opening. If the United States could not wield power effectively, then beyond or on the margins of US borders new polities could be created—ones that, unlike the United States, offered opportunity, hope, and prosperity.

CHAPTER TWO

Perfecting America in Canada

In the era of the Texas Moment, never was there such a gap between a break-away polity's rhetoric and its reality as in the 1837 Republic of Upper Canada. In theory, this proclaimed state had all the trappings of legitimacy, possessing a provisional government, a declaration of rights, and a national bank. It even possessed an impressive army—more than 500 men from both Canada and the United States, equipped with arms largely stolen from US arsenals. Yet the extent of the Republic of Upper Canada's jurisdiction was miniscule. Its flag flew over 300-acre Navy Island, situated on the Niagara River, which separated the United States from Upper Canada, and while the island was officially a part of the latter, the republic's writ ended at the water's edge. Across the river in Canada proper, thousands of British soldiers and Loyalist Canadian militiamen awaited an expected attack, while on the US side Winfield Scott cajoled US officials to remain neutral. After a month, realizing the obstacles they faced, the republicans revised their strategy and abandoned the island to fight another day. Today, the Republic of Upper Canada is so little remembered that only private boats can access Navy Island, and only a small plaque commemorates the republic's existence. Few Canadians, Americans, or historians of either country take it seriously.[1]

Yet the hundreds of Americans who volunteered to fight for Canadian freedom during what has been termed the Patriot War were deadly serious. They not only volunteered at Navy Island in late 1837, but also fought in several pitched battles against British forces in Canada in 1838, all in an effort to revive the failed Canadian rebellions of 1837. That year, French Canadian Patriotes in Lower Canada, followed by Anglo-Canadians in Upper Canada, rebelled against British rule. Quickly defeated, the failed rebel leaders fled across the US-Canadian border to carry on the struggle. Although these Canadians provided the impetus, Americans soon dominated the Patriot ranks. While the reasons they joined and eventually assumed leadership of the Patriot War were myriad, they all revolved around one central factor: an Upper Canadian republic represented a political, economic, and social alternative to the United States, where Americans imagined they could achieve political power and financial gain, which seemed no longer possible in the post-panic United States. The Patriot War was, in essence, a northern counterpart to the Texas Revolution, and the Canadian republic was the northern counterpart to the breakaway America of Texas.

American Patriots made this comparison themselves, often as a way to criticize US interference in their struggle, which they contrasted to the federal government's laissez-faire attitude toward the Texas Revolution. Yet their self-serving rhetoric contained a great degree of historical truth. In both cases, Americans invaded neighboring countries in order to aid people whom they perceived as fellow Americans. In both cases, volunteers sought the distinction of military glory and potential political power. In both cases, participants believed that free land awaited them after military victory. In both cases, the hundreds who invaded Texas and Canada were augmented by the thousands of Americans who donated money and arms to the struggle but never crossed the border themselves. Even the number of American participants—roughly 4,000—was remarkably similar. Ultimately, the crucial distinction between the Patriot War and the Texas Revolution was not internal difference, but the nature of the enemy and the geographic landscape of the extended battlefield. Texans defeated a divided and untrained Mexican army, using the vast expanse of the Texas prairie to their advantage when they confronted military setbacks; the Patriots had little hope against the British forces arrayed along the thickly settled northern border, especially when the United States also cracked down on Patriot activity. Confronting such odds, the Patriot movement was bound for inevitable failure.

Yet it is the movement's persistence and popularity that matter for this chapter. The Patriot War proves that the Texas Moment was truly a continent-wide phenomenon. When an opportunity to create a breakaway America arose, Americans responded in a similar fashion, in similar numbers, for similar reasons—whether they lived in the South, West, or North. If the Patriot War stands as the northern anomaly of this book, it is because the geopolitical situation in North America made it so—not because the quest for a northern breakaway polity was more marginal or less dynamic. Moreover, the federal government's crackdown on the Patriots provides a crucial window on the

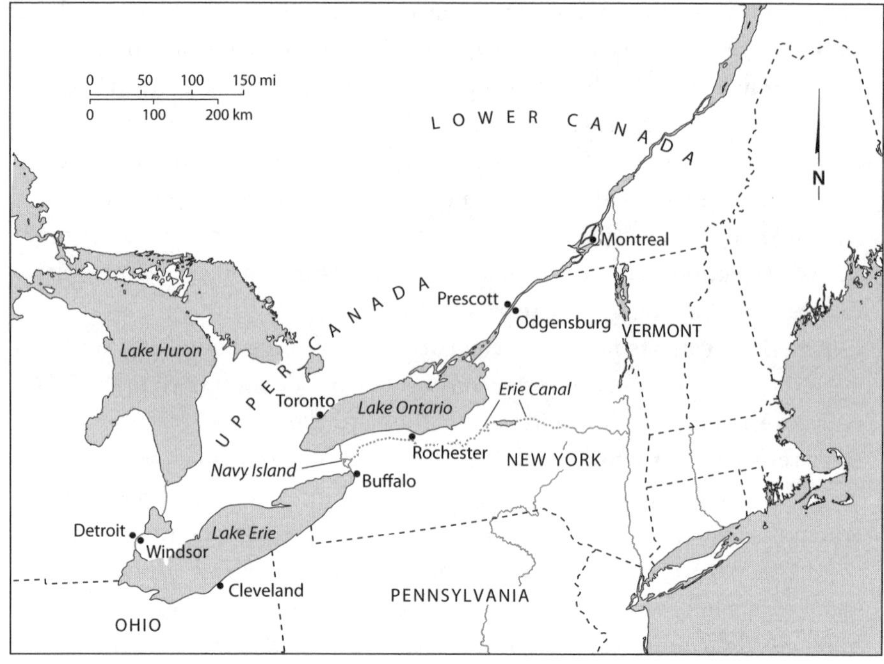

The Patriot War theater, 1837–1842. Map by Bill Nelson.

ideology of breakaway Americans, which is largely unavailable for the other case studies of this book. When Americans left US borders to travel to Texas, California, or Oregon, they almost never needed to explain their decisions publicly, for the United States had no desire to prevent their emigration. In the case of the Patriot War, however, the Patriots were forced to battle US officials with rhetoric as they simultaneously battled the British with arms—and this rhetoric demonstrated that they sought an improved American republic across the northern border.

The Persistent Northern Borderland

According to most historians, the War of 1812 separated Anglo-Americans and Anglo-Canadians into two distinct peoples, as the border war augmented nationalism on both sides. After the war, the Great Lakes region went from borderland to "bordered land," destroying Native autonomy in the process.[2] In the years that followed, older borderland notions of accommodation and hybridity gave way to uncontested sovereignty and imperial rivalry. Yet, while the structures of power along the border were no longer fluid, the economic and social connections between Americans and Canadians remained so. The border, while real, remained leaky, and its permeability had ramifications in 1837.

Before 1837, this porosity was hardly a secret, especially along the Upper Canada–US border. At the far western end of the St. Lawrence River, Upper Canada was the most isolated of Britain's North American colonies. Encircled on three sides by an economically booming United States, the colony was much more in the US economic orbit than in the British. Most goods to Upper Canada traveled through New York via the Erie Canal, and US towns along the Canadian border acted as transport hubs for people and goods moving to and from the colony.[3] Social ties augmented these economic ones. While British authorities largely prohibited American migration to Upper Canada after 1810, even in 1837 a majority of Upper Canadians were either Anglo-American migrants or their descendants.[4] These people received their news from easily obtained US newspapers, followed US politics, traded with Americans, and married Americans.[5] Across the border, Americans reciprocated in kind.[6]

In contrast to Upper Canada, Lower Canada, with its French-speaking majority, its traditional Catholic culture, and its proximity to the Atlantic, was much more isolated both socially and economically from the United States. Vermont's and Maine's small cities were far from the border, and their economies hardly matched those of New York or Ohio. While some Lower Canadian trade traveled south along the Richelieu River–Lake Champlain corridor between New York and Vermont, most went north via the St. Lawrence. In a few regions, particularly in the Lower Canadian Eastern Townships, where New Yorkers had settled in the 1810s, substantial connections remained, but not to the same colony-wide extent as Upper Canada.[7]

In 1837, both Lower and Upper Canadians rebelled against British rule. In Lower Canada, thousands of radical Patriotes, largely of French Canadian background but including some Anglo-Canadians, had peacefully struggled to overturn the colony's oligarchic government for almost a decade. After continued British intransigence, the Patriotes took up arms and created the paramilitary group Société des Fils de la Liberté (Society of the Sons of Liberty).

In Upper Canada, the Patriot cause was less popular and driven more by personality, propelled primarily by the Scottish immigrant and newspaper publisher William Mackenzie. Despite their fewer numbers, Mackenzie and his allies, like their Lower Canadian counterparts, were also frustrated with their inability to implement democratic reforms in the colony. Tellingly, a majority of these radicals were either descendants of Anglo-Americans or American migrants themselves.[8]

Violence first began in the more volatile Lower Canada, as the Patriotes finally rebelled. They gained an initial victory, only to be crushed by British forces in two subsequent battles. William Mackenzie feared the British would use the Lower Canadian conflict to justify a political crackdown in Upper Canada, and he preemptively launched his own rebellion in Toronto. In western Upper Canada, another group of radicals followed his lead. Both groups of Upper Canadian rebels were defeated even more thoroughly than their Lower Canadian counterparts. In the days after their defeat, large numbers of rebels from both colonies crossed the US border. While many rebel leaders hoped to escape capture, they also believed that they could carry on the struggle from inside US territory, using the United States as a staging point to restart the abortive rebellions. The Patriot War had begun.

When the failed rebels crossed the border, the underlying American-Canadian social and economic connections immediately resurfaced. In US border cities and towns, thousands of Anglo-Americans welcomed Mackenzie and other rebels with open arms, pledging to support their cause by any means necessary. Buffalo, Rochester, Cleveland, Detroit, and other border towns became frenzied hubs for Patriot activity, with hundreds and perhaps thousands joining pro-Patriot rallies.[9] As one Detroit resident wrote, "Canada—Canada, is in the mouth of every one, even the women have caught the torch of liberty and are passing it on from the other with as much enthusiasm as the most devoted Canadian revolutionist. . . . Why? Because many of the citizens of this city and the adjoining country are Canadians, or have been, they have many friends there, and to a man they are opposed to the General Government."[10] The final ambiguous "they" in this statement (Americans? Canadians? both?) reveals just how much Americans identified with the Canadian cause. Buttressed by their new allies, the rebels now planned for a second time to free Upper Canada.

Meanwhile, when the Patriotes crossed the Lower Canada–Vermont border, they too were heartily welcomed with rhetorical support. American newspapers praised both rebellions as struggles for liberty against the tyrannical British, and Americans provided safe havens for both sets of Canadian rebels. Yet only across from Upper Canada did Americans actually join the Patriot ranks in any significant numbers. The Patriote armies that congregated along the Vermont border during the following year were predominantly composed of French Canadian refugees. Very few Americans enlisted in these forces, and those who did deserted before fighting began.[11]

The Anglo-American propensity to join the Upper Canadian rebels and not their Lower Canadian counterparts was not based on any rational military assessment. On the contrary, the Patriotes were better organized than the Upper Canadian rebels, had achieved a battlefield victory, and were more threatening to British sovereignty in Canada. If Anglo-Americans wanted to volunteer for a cause that had more chance of success, they should have joined the Patriotes. That they did the exact opposite reveals that their commitment to the two conflicts was related to their social and cultural connections to each; they would fight with and for Anglo Upper Canadians and cheer on the French-dominated Lower Canadians from the sidelines. To border Americans, Lower Canada remained a foreign land, whether the British ruled or not. Upper Canada, by contrast, would become the third Anglo-American republic on the continent, alongside the United States and Texas.

Fighting for a Breakaway America

In the weeks after their arrival in the United States, Canadian Patriots in Buffalo, Detroit, and Vermont organized their mushrooming forces. While Detroit and Vermont were important sites of Patriot activity in the following months, it was outside Buffalo, on Navy Island, where the largest number of Patriots assembled. As a place to proclaim the provisional government of the Canadian republic, Navy Island offered several advantages. Situated in the middle of the Niagara River, the island was officially British territory, thus giving the Patriots an aura of political legitimacy. Moreover, the island was closer to the US shore than to the Canadian shore, facilitating easy transport from the United States but making any attack by the British extremely difficult.[12] In late December 1837, Americans from the surrounding counties and Canadian refugees gathered on the island to enlist in the newly created Patriot army. Soon the army grew to hundreds or even a thousand men, and Mackenzie and other Patriot leaders in Buffalo named Rensselaer Van Rensselaer to be commander in chief.[13] Van Rensselaer was a scion of New York's renowned Dutch family, members of whom had fought in the American Revolution and the War of 1812. He was also the editor of the Albany *Daily Advertiser*, a paper that had predicted a rebellion in Canada as early as 1831. When rumors of the rebellion reached Albany, he set off for Buffalo, enthusiastic to help.[14] However, his enthusiasm and family name seem to be the only reasons for his appointment; Van Rensselaer had no military experience. He spent the next month on Navy Island drunk, unhinged, or both.

Despite his incompetence, Van Rensselaer's role as an American leading a multinational force offers a starting point to examine exactly who joined the Patriots and why they did so. Some Patriots were, of course, Canadian. Having failed to overthrow the British in Canada itself, rebels like Mackenzie carried on the struggle in US territory. From the outset, however, Americans like Van Rensselaer made up perhaps two-thirds of the Patriot forces.[15] As one observer noted, it was not Canadians but "Americans citizens" who were "creating warfare."[16] And the Americans' dominance of the movement only increased. By November 1838 a Patriot convention held in Cleveland consisted mostly of Americans, and Americans outnumbered Canadians by six to one in a major Patriot battle a few weeks later.[17]

According to American Patriots, they fought, above all, to liberate Canada. As one soldier from Rochester wrote to Van Rensselaer, "I am for liberty. My whole soul is in it and if I am called to defend it I am willing to shed the last drop of blood in my veins rather than surrender this glorious boon."[18] Americans at a Patriot meeting longed "to plant and sustain the tree of liberty."[19] Van Rensselaer later wrote that he agreed to lead the Patriots because of his "hatred of tyranny," which brought him to join a cause "so desirable to all the republican world."[20] That the Patriots were fighting the British only added to the motivation. Many American Patriots imagined themselves as heirs to the revolutionary generation, none more than the aptly named Thomas Jefferson Sutherland. Like Van Rensselaer, Sutherland was a newspaper printer who quickly assumed a leadership position among the Patriots, and also like Van Rensselaer, he quickly disappointed, as his actions rarely matched his rhetoric. Sutherland frequently compared himself and other Patriots to "Lafayette, DeKalb, Steuben, Pulaski, Kosciusko, and other illustrious foreigners" who had aided Americans during the revolution.[21] He believed his mission was twofold: first, to spread democracy throughout North America, and second, to "oppose British influence" wherever it appeared.[22] Other volunteers noted that their fathers and grandfathers—or, in a few cases, they themselves—had fought the British in the past, and now they would do so again.[23]

Yet spreading liberty and opposing the British were not the sole explanations for why Anglo-Americans joined the Patriots. If they were, then Anglo-Americans throughout the country should have also volunteered, for they too hoped to spread liberty, and they too disdained the British.[24] These feelings became even more acute after the night of December 29, 1837, when British soldiers, fearing that a steamship named the *Caroline* would be used by the Patriots to cross into Canada, attacked and burned it in US waters. In the melee, the British killed one US sailor, and some presses printed that casualties reached a dozen or more.[25] Along the border, the burning of the *Caroline* was immediately appropriated as a symbol that represented the perfidy of the British—and by extension, the righteousness of the Patriot cause. Cries of "Remember the *Caroline*" echoed throughout the region.[26] Yet despite their public outcry, American Patriots privately wrote little on the *Caroline* in the weeks immediately following the incident.[27] In reality, the Patriots invoked the *Caroline* for propaganda purposes, as they hoped to induce Americans outside the Great Lakes region to also join the cause; this, alas, proved ineffective. While the *Caroline* affair outraged Americans outside the Great Lakes region, notably few clamored for war, and fewer still acted by enlisting in the Patriot cause.

If the *Caroline* affair did little to induce Anglo-Americans on the border to join the Patriots, the desire for US annexation of Canada was even more insignificant, at least in the heat of the struggle. At the time, no Patriot expressed an interest in an imminent US seizure of Canada. Many believed a "convergence" between the United States and Canada was possible down the road, but as with Texas's connection to the United States, when and how—and whether—this would occur was anyone's guess.[28] Just like the Texas revolutionaries, the Patriots put aside thorny questions about diplomacy and geopolitics for the immediate goal of military victory. Eventually, Mackenzie broached the idea of a US-Canada union in an effort to reassert his leadership, but he was greeted with silence and disdain. One American sympathetic to the Patriots admonished Mackenzie that no union was necessary, for two separate republics could easily exist side by side.[29]

While the Patriot cause was never about revenge or expansion, it was more complicated—and self-interested—than simply a fight for Canadian liberty. Interests augmented ideology: the Patriots desired a free Canadian republic, but they also saw opportunities for themselves in that republic—glory, fame, wealth, and personal independence. Many Americans who volunteered, particularly those with military backgrounds, did so with the caveat that they would assume a certain rank in the Patriot army.[30] Generally these requests were embedded in support for the cause, subsuming their personal interest within statements praising freedom. An Ohio brigade major, George Russell, succinctly tied the two together when he wrote, "[The commanding officer] and his staff are at your command, providing you can give them the same rank in your army, that they now hold in the militia of Ohio. Our reasons for tendering you our services are, that we are willing to aid in the cause of LIBERTY."[31] Whether Russell would fight for "LIBERTY" if he did not receive a proper rank, he did not say. Others who did not seek an appointment themselves at least sought, as good republicans, to vote for their own officers, a common practice among state militias for much of the early republic.[32]

Due to the rebellion's eventual failure, determining the end goal for individual American Patriots remains elusive. Some likely envisioned that after defeating the British, they would return to the United States as American Lafayettes and achieve national fame and universal acclaim for their heroism in a foreign cause. Others may have planned to remain as heroes in the newly established Canadian republic among friendly Anglo-Canadians, a place and people already familiar to border-state Americans. The most ambitious may have hoped that fame would translate into higher military rank or a prominent political position in either the United States or Canada. As Andrew Jackson had evinced, political power could be achieved through military glory. Indeed, Jackson was an apt role model for American Patriots, for he too had crossed US borders illegally—in Florida in 1817—and had quickly ridden his notoriety to even greater heights of popularity.

However, for Americans yearning for martial glory, much had changed in the two decades since Jackson's infamous actions. Within US borders, at least, there seemed to be no more wars to fight, but the Patriot War provided a new opportunity. Such was the case for Rensselaer Van Rensselaer. As a Van Rensselaer, he had little financial incentive to join the Patriots. Instead, he looked for glory, claiming he joined because he hoped to emulate "the chivalrous example of the South in the Case of Texas." Van Rensselaer's citation of Texas was an attempt to portray the Patriot cause as a similar fight for liberty and republicanism, yet his comparison was also unintentionally revealing. For some soldiers in Texas, most famously Sam Houston and David Crockett, the conflict had offered an opportunity to rebuild failed lives in the United States. Canada could work the same wonders for Van Rensselaer, a drunken and insecure man (doubly) weighed down by a famous name.[33]

Unlike Van Rensselaer and his type, many American Patriots sought more immediately tangible incentives: land and money. From the outset, Patriot leaders promised volunteers 300 acres in Canada and $100 in silver, all to be paid after the Patriot victory.[34] Eventually the Patriots formed the Bank of

Upper Canada, with a proposed capital of $7.5 million, from which some funds could be used to pay Patriot soldiers their promised salary of $10 per month, about the same pay as a day laborer in the region.[35] Unsurprisingly, the volunteers left out these baser requests from their letters to Mackenzie and Van Rensselaer, although at times Patriot recruiters gave hints that more men would come with "a little assistance."[36] The Americans hostile to the Patriots were less oblique, denouncing them as "riotous loafers" who wanted to "plunder neighboring Canada or ourselves."[37] This rhetoric was inflated: the Patriots did not want to plunder, but they did want to get paid.

While freedom, fame, and fortune were all factors that pulled Anglo-Americans into the Patriot ranks, there was also one crucial push factor: the Panic of 1837, which hit the Great Lakes region particularly hard.[38] In the midst of the depression, Americans joined the Patriots in the hopes of escaping financial distress. Unlike the Van Rensselaer types, for these men it was not the war itself, but what happened after that truly mattered. They hoped Patriot service would eventually provide a financial restart, representing a northern counterpart to the concurrent "Gone to Texas" phenomenon in the South. A Michigan Patriot officer, W. W. Dodge, illustrates the point. Dodge likely entered Patriot service to pay his debts, and over the next two years he was captured by the British, made a spectacular escape from Quebec, returned to Michigan, and then fled the state to avoid his debtors. He traveled to New York, where he was eventually arrested again for not paying his debts.[39] One can imagine that if Canada had provided opportunities for cheap land and debt evasion before the Patriot War, then Dodge and many other American Patriots would have already "Gone to Canada" to rebuild their lives. Thousands of Americans had done exactly that in the aftermath of the American Revolution, when the British had welcomed them as Late Loyalists. However, unlike Canada in the 1790s or Texas in 1837, Canada in 1837 did not welcome Americans—*unless* the Patriot War was won and a Canadian republic was consummated. Patriot leaders understood this crucial dynamic, and unsurprisingly they believed that continued economic hardship would lead to more recruits.[40]

Whether rich or poor, selfless or self-interested, both Anglo-American and Anglo-Canadian Patriots felt extremely optimistic about their cause in early January 1838, when Patriot forces on Navy Island reached their high point. Their outlook was quite rational, based on their own assessment of the geopolitical situation in the Great Lakes borderland. On the Canadian side of the river were thousands of silent sympathizers (or so the Patriots thought).

The bungled nature of the rebellion in Toronto meant that this group had never had a chance to join the rebels, but with a successful landing in Canada they would rally to the cause. Moreover, the Patriots faced only Canadian militia of dubious loyalty (or so the rumors went), for the British army was quelling insurrection in Lower Canada. In the United States, meanwhile, thousands of supporters were eager to join the Patriot army, or at least provide financial and rhetorical support.

The cause had united a cross-border region whose inhabitants were intimately familiar with one another. The momentum seemed to be with the Patriots. Revolution would not be stopped. Then, on January 10, 1838, US Army officers arrived in Buffalo, drastically changing the Patriots' outlook.

An Americanized Canada and an Un-American United States

President Martin Van Buren had learned of the *Caroline* affair and the Patriot buildup at Navy Island in early January, and he rightfully feared war with the British—a war for which the United States, with a standing army of only 8,000 men ineffectively fighting Seminoles in Florida and guarding the western frontier, was by no means prepared.[41] While Van Buren played on Americans' anglophobia by denouncing Britain's violation of US waters, he also issued a proclamation to US citizens that directed them to avoid involvement. He then sent Major General Winfield Scott, the United States' foremost military leader, to the border to enforce neutrality.[42] Scott's arrival marked a transition in the Patriot War, changing the dual British-Patriot struggle to a more complicated tripartite US-British-Patriot conflict. Over the next few years Scott and other army officers would use all manner of influence to prevent Patriot activity. At first their means were severely limited, for they only possessed a handful of new recruits and no professional soldiers.[43] Yet they had the power of persuasion and access to US funds, which one Patriot described as a strategy of "bullying and buying."[44] These measures would prove consequential.

Scott was soon able to cut off all supplies to Navy Island. Without replenishment and with substantial numbers of British militia dug in across the water, Van Rensselaer and Mackenzie had little hope of even maintaining their force on the island, let alone achieving victory. Scott met with Van Rensselaer to persuade him to give up the cause.[45] By January 14 Van Rensselaer agreed, and the Patriots dispersed from Navy Island, many going west to continue the struggle along the Michigan frontier.[46] The failure of the Navy Island campaign, along with defeats at the Michigan and Vermont borders, marked an end to the first phase of the Patriot War. Now the US government would attempt to hinder Patriot activity wherever it arose.

Remarkably, many American Patriots continued their armed struggle, and many more Americans continued contributing rhetorical and financial help. Some did abandon their support when they realized the United States now opposed the Patriot movement, but a majority of Patriots remained Patriots despite the US stance. Most Patriots simply went underground, forming a secret society throughout the border region known as the Hunters Lodges. The name and idea were drawn from a Lower Canadian secret society, the Frères Chasseurs (Hunter Brothers), but in contrast to the French-dominated movement, which remained centered in Lower Canada, the American-dominated Hunters Lodges took root almost solely in the United States.[47]

Estimates of the number of Hunters Lodge members ranged from 15,000 to 200,000, although the higher figure was almost certainly an exaggeration.[48] However, while membership may have not reached 200,000, the number of sympathizers may have been significantly higher. Any number remains suspect, for the Hunters destroyed all of their documents after their final defeat, which served the dual purpose of erasing both their illegal activity and their involvement in what had become an embarrassing cause.[49] They likely numbered in the tens of thousands, most of whom hailed from the border region, although a few came from as far as Philadelphia and Washington, DC.[50] Of these members possibly 4,000 bore arms, and half of these actually fought in battle.[51] Crucially, most Hunters held allegiance to each other and their planned Canadian republic—and decidedly not to the United States.

To gauge how the Hunters thought of themselves within the United States, one can view the border region's inhabitants on a continuum. On one end were those who, from the outset, desired to uphold national honor and international treaties and were disgusted by the lawlessness they perceived in the Patriot cause.[52] Although anti-Patriot Americans proved decisive as the struggle continued, at first they were decidedly in the minority.[53] Next on the continuum were those who supported the Patriots during the first month of the conflict but changed their tune when they perceived both the hostility of the US government to the Patriots and the huge obstacles preventing Patriot victory. This group included politicians like New York governor William Marcy and Michigan governor Stevens Mason, both of whom sought to maintain their popularity among the pro-Patriot border population until outright US opposition made this stance, in effect, treasonous for prominent elected officials.[54]

Yet Americans seeking to suppress the Patriots could only do so much. With few US soldiers on the border, those charged with enforcing order required local citizens—juries in local courts, state and local officials, and local militia—to support them. All were undependable. Either state officials refused to enforce the newly updated Neutrality Act or juries refused to convict—developments widely known to the Patriots.[55] As one Patriot commented, juries would not convict because "young and old, and all classes . . . are advocates of Canadian freedom."[56] Patriot arms came almost exclusively from US arsenals, where state officials conveniently left weapons "just where they might be stolen" by the Patriots. If this did not work, Patriots forged letters from US officials ordering the weapons to be released.[57] State militias were entirely unreliable, and Winfield Scott requested militias from nonborder states that were "uninfected" with Patriot sympathizers.[58] A US officer, William Worth, even wrote to Secretary of War Joel Poinsett that some militiamen would not only refuse to obey orders, but would "openly ally themselves with the insurgent cause."[59]

A Patriot sympathizer, however, did not make a Patriot. While willing to look the other way when the Patriots broke national laws, sympathizers did not actively counter the United States. Allegiance to their country was strained, but it did not break. In contrast, stalwart Patriots, on the other end of the continuum, volunteered for a cause that directly contradicted the laws of the United States and the wishes of a majority of Americans outside the northern border region. The Hunters Lodges, in essence, represented a breakdown of nationality, where dedication to Canadian republicanism outweighed obedience to US law. Many observers noted these skewed allegiances. As the anti-Patriot *Daily Intelligencer* stated, the Patriots "hovered between the two countries, not deserving the name of United States citizens, or subjects of Great Britain."[60] Daniel Webster observed, "If war breaks out [between the United States and Britain], [American Patriots] do not propose to join the forces of the United States, but to unite themselves with the disaffected in Canada, declare the province free, and set up another government."[61]

Anglo-American Patriots, on the other hand, never doubted that their actions were both legal and moral, and their dedication to Canadian republicanism remained resolute. Despite several defeats by British forces and the opposition of the United States, their work continued unabated for almost a year. They clandestinely planned a three-front invasion of Canada, formed a provisional government for the Republic of Canada in Cleveland, opened pro-Patriot presses throughout the border region, and frustrated US officials who hoped to stop their actions. Like Anglo-Americans in Texas who first supported Mexico and then the Republic of Texas, Anglo-American Patriots put their faith in the future Republic of Canada. Although they had not yet physically expatriated themselves as the Anglo-Texans had done, their membership in the Hunters Lodges represented a preliminary ideological expatriation. Indeed, in one telling newspaper ad, a gunsmith named L. W. Babbitt stated he would devote one day per week to repairing arms for free for all Patriot "emigrants," implying that American Patriots were planning to live in Canada for good.[62] An Upper Canadian republic, like both Mexican and independent Texas, represented a political and economic alternative to the United States, but unlike in Texas, victory had not yet been realized.

Here, then, was the power of breakaway Americanism at work. Canada remained a breakaway America in name only, for British power stood in the way. Yet to the thousands of Hunters Lodge members, the very idea of a Canadian republic propelled the Patriot movement to continue despite repeated military defeats by British forces and persistent opposition by the US federal government. Indeed, in regard to the US-Patriot conflict, the Patriots effectively won—at least for a time. For more than a year, they wrested the entire border region from US control. By October 1838, it was clear to federal authorities that army officers alone could not suppress Patriot activity, forcing Van Buren to send 2,000 troops to the border.[63] Yet even these troops were not enough. During high points, such as the November 1838 gathering of Patriot soldiers in the New York town of Ogdensburg prior to another invasion of Canada, the Patriots, not the United States, controlled the town.

The power of the Patriot movement rested not just with American Patriots' desire to further the cause of liberty and help out neighbors oppressed by the hated British. A potential Canadian republic also attracted Americans because it promised opportunity, whereas the United States no longer did. A Canadian republic would solve many of the issues that the United States increasingly looked unable or unwilling to address, becoming the ideal republic that the United States no longer was. This idea did not emerge in the first weeks of the conflict, as Americans were too busy picking up guns and flocking to Patriot armies to offer cogent explanations of their long-term goals. However, once it became clear that the Patriots would have to defeat both Loyalist forces in Canada and the federal government in the United States, they began to outline how exactly the United States had gone wrong—and how, presumably, Canada would go right.

Criticism of the United States began with its anti-Patriot stance. To American Patriots, the US federal government was betraying the principles of the union, and now it was the Patriots, not the United States, who held true to American values. Central to this argument were the twin Jacksonian defenses of democratic majority rule and the sanctity of individual liberty. With a majority of Americans along the border either sympathizing or joining with the Patriots, the imposition of federal power looked decidedly anti-democratic and authoritarian, especially when it came at the hands of 2,000 federal troops. Although the number of US regulars did not compare to the 10,000 British soldiers across the border, it was a remarkable force by US standards. By comparison, 700 troops were placed in South Carolina during the nullification crisis, and only during the Whiskey Rebellion had more professional soldiers been deployed against US citizens.[64]

The Patriots attacked this display of federal power. As the editor of the pro-Patriot *Detroit Morning Post* maintained, federal troops had no right to arrest any Patriots, for the Patriots commanded majority support in the city, and "the people are sovereign."[65] At the least, federal authorities had no right to supersede state power. As one Patriot wrote, "We shall not let the U.S. authorities wrest the few rights which as a sovereign state we possess."[66] Moreover, federal interference represented "shameful conduct of a free government."[67] At a Hunters Lodge meeting in Detroit, one Patriot proclaimed that while he understood that the federal government did not want war with Britain, there were "constitutional privileges" that could not be violated for any reason. The Hunters at that meeting issued a series of resolutions that condemned US actions on the border; reiterated the importance of state sovereignty, free speech, and the right to bear arms; and warned of the dangers of "consolidation." These resolutions argued that allegiance to the United States was conditional on US actions: "We are for sovereignty of the states, and for the union of the states; but we will not submit to martial law in a time of peace."[68] To American Patriots, their movement, and not a newly autocratic United States, truly represented the American people.

In this regard, Anglo-American insurgents' embrace of the name "Patriot" is revealing. French Canadian political leaders in Lower Canada originally coined "Patriote" for their political party in the 1820s as an assertion of French Canadian democratic nationalism, which they saw as in opposition to the aristocratic "English" party that continued to hold power. The term was then co-opted by Mackenzie and his allies in Upper Canada during their rebellion, and they continued to employ it upon their arrival in the United States. For both Lower and Upper Canadian radicals and rebels, the term made sense in both a current national sense—the Patriots represented the "true" Canadian nation—and a historical sense, as these Canadian Patriots saw themselves as heirs of the Patriots of the American and French Revolutions.[69] But how could *American* invaders of *British* Canada be termed "patriots" when the United States was bent on neutrality? To Edmund Kirby, the paymaster of the US Army and therefore someone whose profession relied on the preservation of the United States, the terminology made no sense, for "most of [the Patriots] are citizens of the United States and have nothing to do with Canada."[70] To Kirby, a true Patriot was someone who upheld the laws of their own country instead of illegally invading another.

Yet Anglo-American Patriots had no problem appropriating the term for themselves for several reasons. First, they perceived Anglo-Canadians as fellow Americans culturally, racially, and temperamentally. The US border may have stopped at Canada, but the *American* nation and the *American* people went beyond it. Patriotism was defined by common blood, not borders, and thus they were just as much Patriots as any Canadian rebel.[71] Second, because most Americans who lived near the Canadian border supported the Patriot cause, Patriots understood their struggle as both patriotic and nationalist, even from within the confines of the United States. When a mass of Detroit residents prevented federal authorities from arresting a band of Patriots, one Patriot commented, "The rebuke of the people had terrified and subdued the authorities. They saw only their legitimate sovereigns would be masters; and that they must be content to submit to their will."[72] American blood and the exercise of local sovereignty—these were the essence of the American nation, not the undemocratic mandate of a distant federal government.

Much of this rhetoric echoed the language of the radical Locofoco wing of the Democratic Party, and a majority of American Patriots were indeed Democrats. They were drawn to Mackenzie's radical agrarian ideology and espousal of egalitarian principles, particularly in the midst of the depression. If radical Democrats could not create the republic they desired in the United States, perhaps they could create it in Canada. The Patriots' appropriation of Democratic ideology proved a problem for Democratic newspapers that condemned the Patriot War, for they had difficulty countering the Patriots' conception of an American nation united by blood and a states-dominant union—unlike Whig papers, which consistently maintained the supremacy of federal law. Not wanting to admit they feared war with Britain and unable to debate the Patriots ideologically, Democratic papers effectively ceded to American Patriots their constitutional arguments and changed tactics. Instead of attacking the American Patriots for their illegal actions vis-à-vis US laws, they attacked them for their alliance with the Canadian rebels, contending that the rebels' weakness mandated staying out of the conflict. If the Canadians were really meant to have freedom, so the argument went, then they would have taken it for themselves. Instead, the Canadian rebels had shown themselves to be "subservient," "leaderless," and undeserving of freedom—and therefore undeserving of American help. Judging by the continued popularity of the Patriots in the fall and winter of 1838, these arguments were unpersuasive.[73]

Even though Democratic ideology predominated, American Patriots deliberately portrayed their movement as nonpartisan. As the Patriot newspaper the *Canadian* proclaimed at the head of its first (and seemingly only) issue: "The *Canadian* is edited by a refugee—published by a Democrat—printed by a Whig, and read by the whole world."[74] One Detroit official even wrote to Secretary of War Poinsett that the Patriots comprised a political party of their own.[75] Proclaiming their explicit nonpartisanship was in some ways a Patriot propaganda ploy to argue for their cause's widespread appeal, yet these protestations also rested on a key truth: although outnumbered by Democrats, there were also many Whig Patriots. Although these men may not have identified as much with Patriot politics, other factors enticed them. For a prominent Whig like Rensselaer Van Rensselaer, for example, this was military glory and potential political power. For many other Whigs, it was the relations along the Great Lakes borderland: American political stances became irrelevant when Canadian friends' and business partners' very liberty was at stake.

Patriots on both sides of the political spectrum valued this cross-party nature of the struggle, and they became enraged when Mackenzie abandoned his own nonpartisanship and began openly engaging in US party politics. By the summer of 1838 Mackenzie stepped down from his leadership position, believing that his talents would best be utilized by starting a nonpartisan, pro-Patriot press to rally more supporters. Yet he could not help his political nature and soon began lambasting Whig policies in his paper, equating the US Whigs with British Tories.[76] The blowback was immediate, as outraged Whig Patriots canceled their subscriptions, while frustrated Democratic Patriots admonished him for getting involved in US politics. Even Mackenzie's son James, living in the New York town of Lockport, pointed out to his father that while the Whigs in the federal government in Washington were unsympathetic, the Whigs in New York were "our best friends."[77] One Patriot from

Watertown put it more succinctly: "The die is cast, and you are cursed by all good patriots, both Jackson and Whig."[78] The writer was correct: subscriptions to *Mackenzie's Gazette* dropped dramatically, and the nonpartisan Patriot movement left the Democrat Mackenzie by the wayside.

The Patriots' vehement assertion of their nonpartisanship was unsurprising from the perspective of 1838. Between the dreadful depression and the combined efforts of both national Democrats and Whigs to crush their cause, partisanship offered the Patriots little. As James Mackenzie described, "Neither of the political parties of the day will assist or countenance equal rights and privileges" because monopoly had become "so deeply rooted."[79] Moreover, Democratic Patriots could argue for their Democratic ideology, but they could not link themselves to the Democratic *Party* when it was Martin Van Buren, the Democratic president, who was primarily responsible for the United States' anti-Patriot stance.

The geography of the Patriot War gives further hints of this disillusionment with partisanship. Throughout the Jacksonian era, counties along the northern border, especially those in New York and Ohio, were especially prone to populist third party candidates who offered answers to problems that neither major party could. In these counties, the Anti-Masonic Party in the late 1820s and especially the Free Soil Party in the 1840s drew support. In 1838, the third party movement was represented by the Patriots, who would create in Upper Canada the ideal—nonpartisan—republic.[80]

And like the Free Soil Party ten years later, Patriots maintained that the new Canadian republic would not countenance slavery. William Mackenzie had always been a vehement opponent of the "peculiar institution," and he included a clause in his proposed constitution for Upper Canada acknowledging that the colony had been a haven in the past for people escaping slavery.[81] This attitude clearly resonated with many American Patriots. Of the few who became famous in the decades after the Patriot War, most became known for their antislavery principles. Patriot general Lucius Verus Bierce was a friend of John Brown, and he supplied Brown with weapons for his actions in Bleeding Kansas.[82] A. D. Smith, elected as the "president of Canada" in an Ohio Hunters Lodge meeting, became a Wisconsin judge and decreed the Fugitive Slave Law unconstitutional in 1854 in the case *Ableman v. Booth*, although the Supreme Court would overturn his ruling five years later. During the Civil War, he would fight for freedmen's right to landownership in the South Carolina Sea Islands.[83] Preston King, a Patriot supporter although not an active Patriot army volunteer, became a Free Soil congressman and one of the crafters of the Wilmot Proviso. Other, less famous Patriots also expressed antislavery principles, some at the time, others in later decades.[84]

However, like the later Free Soilers—and in contrast to the more radical abolitionist movement that was also gaining steam in the late 1830s—the Patriots did not harbor sentiments of racial equality. Upper Canada would be a free soil, *white* republic. At first this assertion seems to contradict several of Mackenzie's statements of racial egalitarianism, in which he blamed perceived "uncivilized" qualities in the black population of North America on the effects of slavery.[85] Yet the Loyalism of Canadian black people grated on him. Less than a year before the rebellion, he wrote: "[Black people] are so extravagantly loyal to the Executive, that to the utmost of their power they uphold all the abuses of government, and support those who profit by them."[86] In the days before the rebellion, Mackenzie played on white Canadians' fears of Loyalist black people, claiming that British authorities would unleash them—as well as Natives—on a defenseless white populace if Anglo-Canadians did not swiftly revolt. While Mackenzie primarily disliked black people for their Loyalism, his racial rhetoric also played well with racist American Patriots who disliked black people simply because they were black. The Patriot movement was, in essence, united by whiteness—*antislavery* whiteness, but whiteness nonetheless.[87]

The Patriots never explicitly expressed this white racial unity, but considering that the population of the Great Lakes region on both sides of the border was overwhelmingly white, this is unsurprising. When racial "others" entered the discourse, it was evident that race played a role. Like Mackenzie, Patriots often directed racism toward British-allied black people, which, in a certain respect, was logical, for Canadian black men joined the Loyalist militia in proportions far exceeding other Canadians—for good reason. They were ready and willing to fight for an empire that protected their freedom from the slaveholding republic to the south.[88] Further, the Anglo-American Patriots did not just condemn black men from Canada; those who lived in the United States were also held in suspicion. They represented a potential British fifth column on American soil, who would stop at nothing to destroy the Patriot cause. In the first weeks at Navy Island, rumors spread among the Patriots that black cooks planned to poison them, leading Thomas Jefferson Sutherland to warn Van Rensselaer, "For God's sake look out for the negroes."[89] In Detroit, reports circulated that the "negroes are destroying things" across the river in Canada and would soon unleash their destruction on Detroit itself.[90] Some Patriots uttered frustration with abolitionists who were so concerned with enslaved black people, but cared nothing for the "white slaves" in Canada.[91]

The Patriots also demonized Native people. Rumors of a British-incited Native American invasion surfaced on a regular basis. Like the animosity toward black people, these rumors also had some rationale: Canadian Natives, like Canadian black people, proved overwhelmingly loyal to the British during the rebellion.[92] One letter writer even feared the British would unleash both black and Native people in a multipronged attack on the Patriots, arming enslaved people in the South and inviting them north and simultaneously rousing Natives in the West to attack east.[93] Of course, these reports were outlandish. While Canadian black and Native people were indeed overwhelmingly loyal to the British, at no point did their small numbers merit the panic of Patriots' imagination. This rhetoric helped unite Anglo-American and Anglo-Canadian Patriots around their shared whiteness, while also providing an excuse for their continued failures: it was black and Native "others" who were preventing Patriot victory, not the loyalty (or, at least, passivity) of the bulk of the Anglo-Canadian population or the sheer power of British arms.

The racial dynamic of the Patriot War in the Great Lakes region becomes even clearer when placed alongside the Patriot War on the Lower Canada–Vermont border. In Upper Canada, Anglo-American and Anglo-Canadian Patriots fought the British, black people, and Natives—the three bête noires of the early republic. In Lower Canada, by contrast, Americans perceived the conflict as an ethnic one, in which French Canadians possessed a "considerable spice of national prejudice and hatred" toward the British.[94] This perception, at least at first, was incorrect, for some Anglo-Canadians in Lower Canada also supported the Patriotes. Yet in the eyes of Americans, the Lower Canadian conflict was fundamentally a foreign war. As a result, only a few dozen Americans joined the French Patriotes when they crossed the border. The dearth of American volunteers did not mean Americans along the Lower Canadian border were anti-French—quite the opposite, for many wished the Patriotes victory. Yet Americans believed that French Canadians were fundamentally different from themselves, for they were not a revolutionary people—a sentiment that became more prevalent as a rebel victory became increasingly doubtful. As one letter writer put it, "The 'habitants,' generally, are an illiterate and peaceably disposed body of men, rather inclined to be penurious, and caring more for their 'peculiar habits of life' than for the kind of government under which they live."[95] That Patriote leader Robert Nelson's proposed Lower Canadian Declaration of Independence called for the equality of all Canadian Natives could only have further alienated Americans from the struggle.[96] While it had been several generations since joint French-Native invasions had terrorized northern New England, these raids remained in both public memory and popular culture, notably in James Fenimore Cooper's recently published *Leatherstocking Tales* and other works.[97] No wonder, then, that Americans could envision a future for themselves in the (supposedly) similar Anglo Upper Canada but not in the (supposedly) very different French Lower Canada.

The whiteness of an Upper Canada republic would be buttressed by its masculinity. From the outset, issues of manhood permeated the Patriot movement, most obviously in the Hunters Lodges, whose membership was reserved for men only. Modeling themselves on Masonic lodges—at first, one region of lodges was known as the "Patriot Masons"—the Hunters established elaborate initiation rituals, secret signs and passwords, and a complicated hierarchy of rank ranging from Snowshoe (the lowest) to Patriot Hunter (the highest).[98] It is uncertain how many Hunters were also Freemasons, but during a time when the Masons were under attack, the Hunters provided an alternative, more legitimate form of organization.[99] Lodge meetings also offered large feasts and copious alcohol to their members, providing what the historian Mary Ann Clawson labeled a "culture of fraternalism."[100]

Beyond fostering male camaraderie, the Patriot War also validated the manhood of its Anglo-American volunteers. These volunteers believed that their belligerence demonstrated masculinity, which mirrored the masculinity of their fathers and grandfathers who had fought in the American Revolution. Even dead Patriots were deemed "manly corpses."[101] In contrast, the federal government's pro-British measures represented a fundamental shift away from a masculine United States; in this, too, the United States had lost its way. As one Anglo-American Patriot wrote, "We think more of the establishment of Banks, the price of stocks . . . prosperity of our foreign trade, the preservation of our . . . bales and silks, than the preservation of that ennobling and glorious spirit of manly independence, that guided and directed the conduct of our fathers in the 'age of revolution.'"[102] Van Buren received particular opprobrium. To one observer, unlike his predecessor Andrew Jackson, Van Buren had "not acted with manly forwardness."[103] That Van Buren was deferring to Queen Victoria of all people was especially galling. She was, in one writer's eyes, a "two legid strumpet" to whom no "states men or soldier" should "bow."[104]

The Patriots' assertion of masculinity was aimed not just at US policy in the moment, but at broader trends in US society. In the increasingly market-oriented North, many men's personal independence was rapidly eroding, but the Patriots gave this ideal renewed life. Patriot volunteers could prove their martial prowess at a time when both state militias and the US Army offered diminishing prospects for glory and personal advancement.[105] Moreover, Patriot volunteers could acquire a significant amount of free land in a Canadian republic that still possessed ample undeveloped regions, which would allow them to maintain the custom of bestowing on all of their sons significant landholdings. To preserve this traditional economic custom, thousands of American families would move west in the early 1840s, but in 1838 this option seemed possible in much closer Canada.[106] Or, for those Americans who had already moved west from New York to Ohio or Michigan in pursuit of cheap land, Canada was the next stop. This was the case for the aforementioned "president of Canada," A. D. Smith. Smith originally hailed from a small New York town fifty miles from the Canadian border, but in the mid-1830s he moved to Ohio and soon found himself caught up in the Patriot fervor.[107] One British official even believed that many Americans who failed in the West now "looked to the Canadas" for similar remedies.[108] In this way, the Patriot struggle affirmed the ideal of the yeoman farmer. Whether this ideal had ever matched the yeoman reality remains contested among historians, but countless Jacksonian era Americans thought it had once been reality. The economic plans of Mackenzie and his radical Democratic allies clearly pointed to this archetype and, more generally, to an economic system in which a man would be less beholden to the market and more in charge of his own—and his family's—future. In this fashion, the Patriot cause provided a means to reassert the republican ideal of manhood in a world of increasingly unsettled gender categories.[109]

Anglo-American Patriots presumably put their visions for a Canadian republic on paper in the fall of 1838, when they and a diminishing number of Anglo-Canadian Patriots organized a provisional government in Cleveland. Alas, their plans have not survived. Judging by the political beliefs of the attendees of the convention, their constitution probably combined various Locofoco, workingman's, and relief policies—thereby wedding urban and rural "plebeian populist" interests—that put preeminence on local control and republicanism, with a particular stress on the economic equality of all (white) men.[110] Indeed, on this latter point, there is a surviving document: Canadian rebel Charles Duncombe's outline of his "people's bank," which would be run along democratic lines and in which all citizens would reap the bank's profits equally and would have a voice in its policies.[111] According to this vision, Canada would become a republic that promised economic opportunity for all, in contrast to a United States that seemed to be run along increasingly aristocratic lines.

The number of deep-seated reasons for joining the Patriot struggle explains its remarkable persistence in the face of US opposition. In the nine months after the Navy Island campaign, Patriot military plans continued unabated. Over the spring and summer of 1838, Patriot leaders sent small raiding parties across the border in order to conceal their larger end game: a full-scale, three-pronged invasion in the winter after the rivers froze, which would facilitate large-scale border crossings. A predominantly French Canadian army would revolt in Lower Canada, while American-dominated Patriot armies would invade from northern New York and Detroit. These successful invasions would be followed—it was hoped—by the mass uprisings of Upper and Lower Canadians in Canada, and the Canadian Revolution would begin anew. Anticipating victory, Anglo-American Patriots organized the aforementioned provisional government for Upper Canada in Cleveland, while the French Canadian–dominated Patriote exiles in Vermont did the same for Lower Canada. Yet US officers and state officials who remained loyal to the federal government, backed by 2,000 troops Van Buren had sent to the border and wielding the powers of the Neutrality Act, increasingly hindered the Patriots. While they seemed to be able to hold meetings without interference, the Patriots were unable to organize along the border itself. And, of course, the British had been preparing for months for these invasions.

With the obstacles of British arms in Canada and hostile laws in the United States, the result was never in doubt. The Patriot armies were defeated piecemeal—first in Lower Canada, then on the New York border, and finally at Windsor, across the river from Detroit. At each battle, the Patriots were defeated primarily by British arms, not US interference. Yet at each battle, US actions solidified Patriot misfortunes, as US officials patrolled their side of the border, preventing Patriot reinforcements from reaching Canada and preventing the Patriot armies from retreating into the United States to fight another day. The Battle of the Windmill, fought near the modern Ontario town of Prescott, illustrates this.[112] The Patriot army planned to embark from Ogdensburg, New York, across the St. Lawrence River, and occupy the Upper Canadian town of Prescott, but fearing US authorities, this force departed hurriedly without waiting for reinforcements. Although numbering fewer

Site of the Battle of the Windmill, Prescott (artist unknown). This contemporary print shows the setting of the Battle of the Windmill from the British and Loyalist Canadian perspective. Patriot defenders made their final stand for a Canadian republic from the confines of the windmill. The New York town of Ogdensburg, from which Americans cheered on the Patriots from the rooftops, lies across the St. Lawrence River at the right of the image. Courtesy of the Library and Archives Canada / Henry Francis Ainslie Collection / c000527k.

than 300 men, the Patriots still attacked Prescott, but they were easily repulsed by Canadian militiamen, who had been warned by British spies in the United States. Their next stop was a stone windmill downriver, which acted as both defensive protection and a place to await reinforcements: Canadians in the surrounding region and American Patriots across the river. The Canadian rebels never materialized, but some Americans did gather in Ogdensburg to aid the Patriots—at least until US colonel William Worth arrived.

For a day Ogdensburg had been under the complete control of the Patriots. When Worth reached the town, he immediately issued warrants to arrest the Patriot commanders for violating the Neutrality Act. These leaders had already crossed the Canadian border, but the purpose of the warrants was just as much about warning potential Patriots from involvement as it was about arresting those already fighting. Then, with the aid of a few loyal local officials, Worth seized several schooners that had been supplying the Patriots across the river. Now the Patriots in the windmill were alone. There was no longer any possibility of reinforcement or resupply. A few American sympathizers did undertake a rescue mission, possibly with the tacit approval of Worth, but it ended in failure.

For several days the Patriot army held out in the windmill as more and more British troops surrounded their position. Across the river, hundreds of people in Ogdensburg cheered on their endeavors, but this only added insult to injury. As one Patriot remembered bitterly, the hundreds of spectators never had the "moral courage" to aid the Patriots, although it seems unlikely any could have reached the Patriots with Worth patrolling the river.[113] Once the British heavy guns arrived and started pummeling the windmill, the Patriots had no choice but to raise the white flag. In the end, 161 Patriots surrendered to the British; in the weeks that followed 60 were exiled to Van Diemen's Land, and 11 were executed.

The Meaning and Legacy of the Patriot War

The November 1838 invasions of Canada marked the apogee of the Patriot movement. After three crushing defeats, most Anglo-American Patriots—meaning, by now, most of the Patriots—gave up the struggle. Some Patriots changed their strategy, and through border raids hoped to provoke a US-British war. These diehards were desperate and deluded (anti-Patriot rhetoric finally matched the reality), and former leader Mackenzie perceived as much.[114] For several years Patriot activity persisted on a low level, ebbing and flowing depending on US-British relations. Briefly the Hunters Lodges saw a marked resurgence during the trial of Alexander McLeod. McLeod was a Canadian sheriff involved in the *Caroline* affair, and in New York in 1840 he was arrested for the murder of the one US sailor who had been killed. Patriots hoped a guilty verdict for McLeod, followed by his execution, would lead to war between Britain and the United States, but effective and discreet management by the federal government led to an acquittal, further dampening Patriots' hopes. In 1839 Lord Durham issued his famous report recommending responsible government for Canada, and in 1842 the United States and Britain signed the Webster-Ashburton Treaty, settling the *Caroline* affair and all other border controversies. These measures killed the Patriot movement for good.[115]

Thus, the Patriots stand as an anomaly in this book. Unlike the other breakaway Americas I discuss, the Patriots were not incorporated by the unprecedented US expansion of the mid-1840s. Instead, they were countered directly by the US state in the late 1830s—and defeated directly. The federal government's seemingly uniquely activist position in this case, which is in contrast to its laissez-faire approach to most other measures on the continent at this point, had nothing to do with the ideology of American expansion. Rather, it was a simple calculation of realpolitik: no matter how much US officials loathed the British, they all realized the United States could ill afford a war with such a powerful enemy. Between the tiny size of the US Army, the devastating depression, the massive British troop buildup in Canada, and the overwhelming dominance of the British navy, the United States' prospects in this war were terrible. No wonder the Van Buren administration cooperated with the British in crushing Patriot activity. The direct US countermeasures and the subsequent Patriot defeat provide a contemporary historical lens on the imagined breakaway republic of Canada, which is unavailable with the other polities discussed in this study. In this case, Americans were forced to contemplate the meaning of the Patriot movement—and breakaway Americanism more generally—in ways they did not have to in 1846, when US expansion subsumed all in its path.

As the Patriot movement disappeared, most former members tried to forget their involvement. Some ex-Patriots sought anonymity or erasure. The cause of a Canadian republic had been an embarrassing failure, and involvement in the Hunters Lodges was proof of illegal activity, and it seems most American participants simply returned to their lives, destroying evidence of their connection to the Hunters in the process. However, famous Patriot leaders and those exiled to Van Diemen's Land could not hide their participation, and some wrote memoirs justifying their actions. One strategy in their justifications was internationalizing the scope of the Patriot War by comparing the struggle to the 1836 Texas Revolution. This comparison achieved two important goals. First, it provided legitimacy for what had become an illegitimate movement. Van Rensselaer demonstrated this when he explained his actions as a northerner in Canada "emulating the chivalrous example of the South in the case of Texas."[116] Using this reasoning, Van Rensselaer could argue that he was not a discredited vagabond (as many had begun to portray him) but a northern Sam Houston, and therefore he deserved praise for his noble actions. In this case, the Texas link attempted to restore honor to the Patriot cause.

Second, the Texas comparison shifted the blame for Patriot defeat away from the Patriots themselves and to the US government, thereby avoiding the bitter pill of giving credit to the strength of British Loyalism or the potency of the British military. Daniel Heustis, one of the exiles to Van Diemen's Land, lamented that in the case of Upper Canada, "Troops were sent to the frontier, not to punish our insatiable foe, but to assist her in crushing the republican spirit which threatened to uproot British power in Canada." Yet during the Texas Revolution, troops came and went "without molestation" by the US government.[117] Other Patriots took this narrative one step further, claiming that the differing US policies toward the northern and southern borders reflected the dominance of slaveholder interests in the government.[118] These statements were both self-serving and inaccurate: the different US actions in Texas and Canada had little to do with slavery and everything to do with the vastly different military capabilities of Mexico and Great Britain. Nevertheless, they tapped into a larger debate in the United States that also compared Texas and Canada and spoke to the relationship between the United States as a state and Americans as a people.

Despite the drastically different outcomes, it was logical for Americans to compare the Texas Revolution and the Patriot War, for they did mirror one another in important ways. In both, due to a combination of personal interests and republican ideology, Americans left the United States to fight for what was technically a foreign cause, but one that American volunteers perceived as their own. In both conflicts, several thousand Americans actually fought, but they were buttressed by tens of thousands who donated money and arms.[119] Most important, in both cases, volunteers envisioned futures for themselves in these new republics. But there was a crucial difference between the two when it came to national opinion: the results of San Jacinto guaranteed that Americans did not have to confront the ideological ramifications of their fellow Americans expatriating themselves and fighting for a foreign country. In contrast, the Patriots' endurance in spite of initial defeats, coupled with the implications of British power and US interference, compelled such consideration.

The exploration of the relationship between the state and its people began from the moment the Patriots occupied Navy Island, when the pro-Whig *Buffalo Daily Commercial Advertiser* outlined the stakes of the conflict in a perceptive editorial, worth quoting at length:

> We are naturally a warlike people, we love a fight, and have so much of John
> Bull [a fictional personification of England] in our composition, that a broil
> cannot occur near our borders, without us feeling an earnest desire to ex-

change a few blows with one or the other side. Each man feels a right to cock his beaver [i.e., aim his gun] as independently as a king, and when we hear of people who are fighting for liberty, we are almost irresistibly impelled to join, without stopping very nicely to examine whether they have the right or not. This feeling induced thousands to engage in the Texas contest. They cared nothing for the laws of nations, neither did they take the trouble to inquire with what justice Texas raised the standard of independence. A field for wild adventure and distinction was opened—this, together with a rude love of liberty in the abstract, and perhaps an eye to main chance—for Yankees, whether at the south or north, rarely forget that—induced them to espouse heart and soul the cause of Texas. The Canada contest presents the same motives for action, and we see that it daily produces similar effects. The whole country is alive with a feeling in favor of the Canadians, and bands of from five to ten, fifty, and one hundred persons, from the interior towns and villages, are [in a] very little while marching towards the frontier, all fully armed and burning for active service.

Despite this relatively sympathetic description of American participation, the paper made two pleas. First, while individuals may want to fight in Canada, national self-interest necessitated peace, especially in the wake of the Panic of 1837. In essence, the needs of the US state superseded the desires of individual Americans. Second, if war did come, it should come as a national war between the United States and Britain, proclaimed "openly and above board," with the United States espousing the Patriot cause as its own. This, rather than "sneaking aid to the insurgents," was a "more manly course" (notice the assertion of masculinity to counter the Patriots' own gendered language).[120] To this editor, the people must follow the flag, and the nation must either be completely neutral or totally committed to war. Americans should not be at war while the United States was at peace.

Other observers also defined the Patriot War in similar terms. John Brooks, a Detroit merchant, was unsure how he felt about Americans fighting without US approval. On the one hand, the Patriots were a "damn pack of rascals," but on the other hand, the "General Government" was leaving American citizens to be "kicked, cuff'd, kill'd, and kidnapped" by the British. Ultimately he decided that if the state would not protect the people, he was "glad to see that the people are trying to take redress without regards to the General Government."[121] Henry Clay took a different stance, writing to Buffalo politician Peter Porter, "It is a monstrous spectacle to behold our government at peace and our people at war."[122] A firsthand observer of the Battle of the Windmill echoed Clay: the Patriot War was "a war of people without government."[123] The Patriots would have retorted that it was nothing of the sort, for a provisional government had been planned in detail (twice!). Outside the border region, however, few were sympathetic to their arguments, especially in the halls of Congress.

In January 1838, in response to events on Navy Island and along the northern frontier, Congress began debating an updated Neutrality Act. This law would strengthen the original Neutrality Act of 1818 by giving officials more leeway to prevent armed men and supplies from crossing US borders. The law expanded the definition of what could be seized, and it allowed officials to act temporarily without a warrant if they suspected a violation of US neutrality.[124] Pennsylvania senator James Buchanan first proposed the law, leading one paper to deem it "Buchanan's neutrality bill."[125] In his proposal, Buchanan maintained that it was against all "reason and justice" that Americans should be allowed to cross US borders and engage in war. He went on, "If this be tolerated, then it is in the power of the people along the borders of our country to force the whole nation into war."[126] Therefore, US borders needed to be controlled. Seemingly lost on Buchanan was the irony that US borders had been porous for more than half a century, with Americans easily traveling into Florida, Louisiana, and Texas. Along the northern border, where the British stood ready, this long-ignored border-crossing pattern was now unacceptable. The Senate never acknowledged this hypocrisy and speedily passed the bill.

In the House of Representatives, the Neutrality Act was debated for much longer after several congressmen added words that would strengthen the bill's measures. During these discussions, past events and possible future events in Texas constantly entered the discussion. Multiple congressmen questioned just what, exactly, Americans had a right to do on the border. Did Americans have a right to leave the United States with arms? If so, what if these arms were going to be used to fight the country they entered? And if they were, should this alter US policy? After a few days of debate, Tennessee representative John Wesley Crockett, son of Alamo martyr David Crockett, had had enough of the Texas talk, and he rose to defend the actions of Americans in Texas. Key to his defense was the goal of Americans who had left for Texas. Because these men planned to become citizens of Texas, Crockett argued, they were only exercising their "unquestionable rights" in leaving the United States as armed, private citizens. James Garland, a Democrat from Virginia, countered Crockett, "It would be . . . an anomaly in the history of nations, that your citizens could be at war, while your Government was neutral. [I do] not believe in this doctrine, that your citizens can fit out expeditions against other Governments on the plea that they were going to expatriate themselves."[127] Of course this "anomaly" was just what the Patriots argued for, hoping the federal government would simply leave them alone to plan their Canadian invasions. One week later, however, more congressmen sided with Garland than with Crockett (and the Patriots), passing the Neutrality Act.

Although the Neutrality Act increased the power of US agents on the border, it remained limited in both scope and duration: officials could only arrest violators after they returned to US soil, and the act expired after two years. However, as part of the bill the federal government placed 2,000 troops on the border (out of a total of 8,000 in the entire US Army) and appropriated $625,000 for border security, measures that added some teeth to the bill's limitations.[128] Judging by the statements of the Patriots, many of whom were arrested under the statute, its effects were very real.[129] A few years later, after the McLeod case caused a resurgence of Patriot activity, Winfield Scott bemoaned its expiration for restricting his powers, demonstrating that it had proven crucial to squelching cross-border activity, its limitations notwithstanding.[130]

Beyond the immediate goal of curbing the Patriots, the Neutrality Act held a larger importance that went unnoticed at the time. The nonpartisan Patriot movement was met by a bipartisan and multisectional response from the US government: Whigs and Democrats, northerners, southerners, and westerners—most supported the bill. For Whigs, the traditional proponents of a strong state, this support was to be expected. Jacksonian Democrats, however, had traditionally defended the rights of states and the actions of individuals vis-à-vis the federal government. By 1837, however, a majority of Democrats in Congress, pushed by the Democratic Van Buren administration, voted to enforce US borders and prevent individual Americans from waging war as they saw fit. Democrat James Buchanan shepherded the Neutrality Act through the Senate, while fellow Democrat James Polk, as speaker of the House, oversaw its passage through the House. Eight years later, President Polk, with the support of Secretary of State Buchanan, would provoke a border war himself, sending the US Army across the disputed US-Mexican border.

In contrast to 1846, US officials in 1837 were much less sure of themselves. The congressional debate on the Neutrality Act revolved around themes of rampant movement, violence, and lawlessness—topics that other Americans also stressed when they contemplated the Patriot War and its relevance to the larger United States. Thomas Love, a former congressman from northern New York, wrote a long diatribe against the Patriots, predicting that their lawlessness would lead to war with Britain, which invariably "would be followed by intestine convulsions."[131] Other observers of the Patriot War also predicted some sort of national calamity.[132] When added to the border crossing of the Texas Revolution, the Patriot conflict provided even more evidence that the United States simply could not control its own citizens.[133] Indeed, to Kentucky representative Richard Menifee, one begat the other, for allowing Americans to enter Texas at will had led to a "lawless" feeling among American citizens along the northern border.[134] The editor of the *Detroit Free Press*, observing the Patriots firsthand, believed that Americans had "degenerated to the spirit of mobocracy."[135] To many, the Patriot War was but one part of a larger disorder afflicting a United States mired in depression and unrest. Of course, American Patriots knew this malaise well, for it was why they had volunteered.

In the end, the Patriot efforts were all for naught. Britain's potent military routed the Patriots at every engagement, and US involvement augmented the impossibility of Patriot success. In its opposition, the United States ensured that no Patriot invasion of Canada would be able to call on reinforcements from across the US border. In this lies the final and perhaps most important meaning of the Patriot War for the Americans involved. Despite a plethora of anti–United States rhetoric, American Patriots never fought the United States. Some expressed a desire to, and US and British officials worried they would, but no Patriot-US battle—or any type of violence—ever occurred.[136] In spite of widespread disaffection, the United States survived the crisis intact because American Patriots were unwilling to attack fellow Americans. In a legal sense, certainly, they committed treason against the United States, yet this never translated to violence against other Americans. In the few instances where the Patriots confronted a sizable number of US troops, their peaceful submission to US authority can be explained as self-preservation. More often, the Patriot numbers dwarfed the few federal officials and US soldiers present, but nonetheless the Patriots disbanded when ordered. Such was the case when Colonel Worth arrived in Ogdensburg during the Battle of the Windmill. His presence single-handedly changed the situation, as Patriots who planned to aid their comrades across the river acceded to Worth's demands. Ultimately, despite widespread dissatisfaction with US actions and the extensive economic hardship caused by the panic, the continued identity of American Patriots as Americans prevented civil war.

Perhaps it was this lack of internal violence that ensured that most contemporary Americans quickly forgot about the Patriot War. For those on the border, however, the conflict remained a vivid memory, despite what seems to have been an unofficial policy of silence in the decades that followed.[137] For more than a year, a fervor to free Canada had reigned on the border. Thousands of Americans had volunteered, and ultimately more than a hundred Americans died in the struggle. Many, such as postmaster Preston King, simply could not forget. King was a prominent Ogdensburg citizen with many family connections to Canada, and in the aftermath of the Canadian rebellions he became a staunch promoter of the Patriot cause.[138] However, initial Patriot failures caused King to abandon active assistance for the struggle. Over the next year he remained a passive supporter, judging by his continued subscription and support for *Mackenzie's Gazette*.[139] During the Battle of the Windmill, King made an effort to rescue the besieged Patriots, but when he arrived on the Canadian shore one of his companions lied to the Patriots that 500 reinforcements were on their way. Hearing this news, the Patriots refused to leave the windmill. Soon the British fired on King's boat from the shore, forcing him to return to Ogdensburg empty-handed.

Despite his efforts on behalf of the Patriots, King was subjected to a smear campaign by the Patriot press in the weeks that followed. This vindictiveness, coupled with executions of the Patriots whom King had hoped to rescue, caused him to descend into depression. Eventually he checked himself into a Hartford asylum, emerging three months later a seemingly cured man. King went on to be an influential Democratic congressman in the 1840s. His free soil principles then caused him to leave the Democrats and join the Republicans, and he served as a Republican senator from 1857 to 1863. In 1865 President Abraham Lincoln appointed King to be the collector of the New York City Port, a post King did not seek nor want. He was soon overwhelmed by the duties of the job, and he fell into a "morbid state," according to a friend.[140] On November 12, 1865, King rowed into the middle of the East River, weighed himself down with rocks, and jumped overboard. His suicide prompted New York papers to equate his recent state of depression with his behavior after the Battle of the Windmill almost three decades prior.[141] The *Albany Argus* turned this comparison into an attack, claiming that he had once again suffered from a "cause deserted and companions betrayed."[142] The

New York press had clearly not forgotten the Patriot War, and it seems Preston King had not forgotten either. Although no paper noticed at the time, the date of King's suicide was the anniversary of the first day of the Battle of the Windmill.

CHAPTER THREE

Mormon Zion and the Quest for an American Theocracy

In the spring of 1844, another group of North American dissidents convened in the Illinois city of Nauvoo to discuss something far more ambitious and radical than anything discussed at Hunters Lodge meetings several years prior. The Hunters had sought to revolutionize Canada, but the leaders of the Church of Jesus Christ of Latter-day Saints sought to create a government that would first inspire and eventually revolutionize the whole world. They assembled in the store of Joseph Smith, the church's prophet and founder, in the first meeting of what was soon called the Council of Fifty. The council's immediate purpose was twofold: first, to act as the political arm of the Mormon Church; and second, to explore options for settlement somewhere on the continent, as it was becoming increasingly apparent to Smith that anti-Mormon sentiment would soon force the Mormons from Illinois. Texas, coastal California, Oregon Country, Mexico, and British Canada were all on the table, as was the Salt Lake Valley, which was officially part of Mexican California. In one of these places, as the chairman of the council, Sidney Rigdon, described, the Mormons would "form a Theocracy according to the will of Heaven, planted without any intention to interfere with any government of the world. We wish to have nothing to do with them. . . . We will hunt a spot somewhere on the earth where no other government has jurisdiction and cannot interfere with us and there plant our standard."[1]

Rigdon's words, the archived minutes of the Council of Fifty, and the general political plans of Mormon leaders during these years seem to support the continued treatment of the Mormons as an exceptional group in both US history and the history of the American West.[2] Yet from the perspective of the Texas Moment, neither the Mormons' disaffection with the United States nor their plans to create an improved society beyond US borders were exceptional. Already I have shown that thousands of Americans felt similarly about Texas and Canada, and thousands more looked to California and Oregon for similar reasons (see chapters 5 and 6).

What *was* exceptional was the Mormons' theological basis for migration and their stunning ambitions, both geopolitical and theological. Unlike the secular goals of most breakaway Americans, the Mormons sought migration both as a result of and in order to fulfill their unique religious beliefs. Unlike other breakaway Americans, almost all of whom were also breakaway *republicans*, the Mormons were breakaway *theocrats*, although their religious goals remained hidden from public view. And unlike other breakaway Americans, the Mormons were not ambiguous about their short- and long-term political goals: they disdained any further connection to the United States and instead sought an independent "empire" in the West that would act as "Zion," the founding of which would eventually lead to the Second Coming of Christ. Until then, the Mormon empire would be a powerful geopolitical player. As one Council of Fifty member put it, "We are the hammer of the whole earth and we will break it in peices [*sic*]."[3]

The Latter-day Saint theology was crucial to this outlook. The Mormons believed they were doing the work of God, and thus God would engender their success. Yet their millennialist outlook went hand in hand with their fundamental pragmatism, and their geopolitical goals were rooted in this pragmatism.[4] Acute readers of continental news and western travelogues, the Mormons believed that they could achieve their geopolitical ambitions because the political fate of the North American West was uncertain. With more than 20,000 converts in the United States and a trained militia of several thousand men known as the Nauvoo Legion, Mormon leaders understood that they could wield significant power in geopolitically fluid places like Texas, Oregon, or California. They also understood that the United States was in no position to take advantage of this fluidity. As one Mormon leader stated when pondering whether the Mormons should go to Oregon, "It is well known the course the United States is taking to grasp Oregon but there is not stability enough among them to do any thing."[5] The Mormons would seek to take advantage of this.

More than the history of any other group of breakaway Americans, the story of the Mormons' pursuit of a theocratic empire in the West demonstrates both the alternative geopolitical visions Americans possessed during the Texas Moment and the many continental futures that were actually possible. This is because, more than any other group of breakaway Americans (and perhaps more than most Americans generally), the Mormons possessed an all-encompassing vision of continental geopolitics that took into account events in the United States, Texas, California, Oregon, and British North America at the same time. Moreover, the story of the Mormon empire demonstrates the importance of contingency to the history of the Texas Moment. Time and again, the best-laid plans of Mormon leaders went awry due to circumstances that were unforeseen and impossible for the Mormons to control. Beginning in 1844 they sought to leave US borders and create an independent empire, and they hoped to do so with the aid of some continental ally. By 1848 they found themselves once again within US borders and once again without allies. In the end, the Mormons' unity of purpose, knowledge of the West, military strength, and dedication to their cause crashed against a series of unpredictable and unlikely contingencies.

The Apotheosis of Joseph Smith's Political Dreams

In the spring of 1844, Joseph Smith could boast of remarkable achievements for the Church of Jesus Christ of Latter-day Saints, which he had founded in western New York in the late 1820s. This faith was based on the Bible and on Smith's revelatory Book of Mormon, which soon gave the name "Mormons" to his adherents. The Book of Mormon relates the history of several migrations from ancient Israel to North America, most prominently that of Lehi and his son Nephi, who fled Israel in advance of Jerusalem's destruction by the Babylonians in 586 BCE. Later, the Book of Mormon recounts how, following his resurrection, Jesus Christ came to North America and preached to the descendants of these prophets, inaugurating a golden age that eventually collapsed into civil war. The book concludes with the narratives of Mormon and his son Moroni, who recorded these events on golden plates in order that a later prophet could find them. Thus, as countless scholars have noted, Mormonism is fundamentally rooted in a vision of the deep American past, and the scriptures routinely refer to North America as a promised land: at one point, Jesus himself declares America a "land of liberty."[6] Thus, even when a majority of Americans feared and disdained Mormonism as anti-American, Mormon leaders could argue that they practiced the most thoroughly American religion: American exceptionalism was rooted in the faith itself.

In an increasingly insecure Jacksonian America, Mormonism offered inspiration, reassurance, and security—religiously, psychologically, economically, and politically.[7] Thus, despite rising opposition from fellow Americans, Mormonism thrived, and the number of its adherents grew exponentially. In its early years, when it was based in Kirtland, Ohio, Smith urged his followers to settle in Missouri, which he believed would be the Mormon Zion. However, Missourians quickly turned against the Mormons, despising them as northern abolitionists (which they were not, although they did hold antislavery beliefs) and pro-Indian for their proselytizing among Missouri Natives. Violence quickly increased in the mid-1830s, culminating with the 1838 Mormon War and the deaths of two dozen Mormons and several non-Mormons. During the war, Missouri governor Lilburn Boggs issued an "extermination order," which directed all Missourians to kill Mormons or drive them from the state.[8] Without any other options, the refugee Mormons migrated to Illinois and founded the town of Nauvoo.

Nauvoo flourished, rapidly becoming the second-largest city in the state. As Nauvoo grew, so did Mormon power. The Mormons voted as a bloc, and when the population of Illinois numbered half a million, several thousand Mormon votes could—and did—prove decisive.[9] Moreover, in the early days of Nauvoo, when the Mormon settlement appeared harmless and even desirable to Illinoisans, the state legislature granted the Mormons a town charter that granted two extraordinary provisions. First, the charter allowed the Nauvoo municipal court the right to grant habeas corpus, ensuring that Smith or any other Mormon could not be dragged from Nauvoo for trial elsewhere.[10] Second, it granted Nauvoo a militia that would be virtually independent from any state oversight, making it an anomaly not just in Illinois but in the entire United States.[11] Joseph Smith was commissioned the lieutenant general of the legion, and by 1844 he commanded more than 3,000 men, with rumors estimating twice that number. To compare, the US Army at the time numbered 8,500.[12] Nauvoo had become for all intents and purposes a prosperous, powerful, self-governing city-state.

At the time, Nauvoo's city-state status meant it enjoyed a unique political position in the United States, yet this status also reflected the ambiguities and uncertainties of where, exactly, sovereignty ultimately resided in the republic during the Jacksonian era. While the US Constitution mandated a delicate balancing act between federal and state sovereignty, many Americans believed that local sovereignty—in which towns and cities controlled their own laws and borders—was just as fundamental. The founding of Nauvoo demonstrated this, but so too did the Patriot movement, which flourished at the same time. Indeed, the Patriot arguments that federal and state inter-

Temple on the Hill (1846). This photograph, taken just before the Mormons' final departure from Nauvoo, is reportedly the only one that remains of the city from the time when the Mormons called it home. The Nauvoo Temple towers over the city, revealing Mormons' ambitions. The surrounding desolation and emptiness, meanwhile, reveal tragedy. Courtesy of the Church History Library, Church of Jesus Christ of Latter-day Saints, Salt Lake City, UT.

ference in local matters was unconstitutional revealed a political worldview similar to that of the Mormons in Nauvoo. The call for states' rights meant little when it was the state itself—Missouri in the Mormon case, the Great Lakes states in the Patriot case—that was the oppressor.

Of course, the importance of local sovereignty was in the eye of the beholder. To the Mormons, the founding and formulation of Nauvoo was a legitimate safeguard that protected them from the persecution they had experienced in Missouri. To an increasing number of non-Mormons in Illinois, however, these developments combined religion and politics in a disturbing fashion. Certainly, politics and religion often went hand in hand in the US republic, and Mormonism was only one of a plethora of religious movements of the era that sought political change. Some of these movements were predicated on reforming the existing US religious landscape. Evangelicalism swept through Baptist and Methodist congregations, and dynamic ministers like Lyman Beecher and Charles Grandison Finney offered a cross-denominational appeal to its call. While Mormonism was rooted in some of the same issues in what has been termed the Second Great Awakening, it also offered a radical break with evangelicalism, particularly in its adherence to the Book of Mormon and its predication on continuing revelation.[13]

Meanwhile, other religious movements, such as the Perfectionists, Owenites, Shakers, and Rappites, sought to remove themselves from society entirely and offered Americans futures of communitarianism and utopianism.[14] Like these communities, Mormons broke decisively with currently accepted Christian doctrine, but unlike these communities Mormons refused to withdraw from American society and, crucially, refused to abandon participation in US politics. In the Mormons' millennialist outlook, their community would not be a refuge *from* the world, but a participant *of* the world. As early as 1831 Smith had prophesied a millennial vision in which he would lead the kingdom of God—on earth, in the United States. For a time this polity would coexist with other world governments, and Nauvoo would function as Zion, a place of "gathering," where all followers would converge.[15] The city would then become the "center stake" of an ever-expanding tent, as Mormon missionaries planted more stakes beyond its borders.[16] While divinely inspired, Smith's goals could only be temporally and politically realized.[17]

It was Mormons' unique melding of religion and politics that made them particularly threatening to their non-Mormon neighbors around Nauvoo. From a strictly religious perspective, Mormonism seemed bizarre to most Americans, yet religious prejudice by itself does not explain the rampant hostility toward the Latter-day Saints, for no other millennialist Christian sect engendered such persistent persecution for such an extended period of time. The problem was not polygamy—not yet. While much would be made of what the Mormons termed the doctrine of "plural wives" in Utah in the 1850s, in Nauvoo in 1844 polygamy remained a carefully guarded secret among high-level Mormon leaders and a vague rumor among the wider population. Rather, the core problem for anti-Mormons was the way in which Mormonism seemed to threaten American democracy itself, for Joseph Smith could direct the powerful Mormon bloc vote to whichever party he chose, thereby acting as a kingmaker in Illinois.[18] He also appeared to be transforming into something of a monarch in the seemingly theocratic Nauvoo, for he was not only lieutenant general of the Nauvoo Legion, but also mayor of the city and chief magistrate of its municipal court.[19] As a result, by 1844 anti-Mormon vitriol in Illinois had become common, and violence steadily increased between Mormons and anti-Mormons. It looked like the beginnings of another Mormon war.

At this point Mormon leaders turned to the federal government for protection. They had employed this strategy before. In 1839, after the Mormon War in Missouri ended, the Mormons petitioned President Martin Van Buren for redress. Van Buren, however, felt this was a state matter that forbade federal interference—or, at least, that was his justification for refusing to involve the federal government. His quintessential Jacksonian response—"Your cause is just, but I can do nothing for you"—became an infamous phrase among the Mormons, and Van Buren himself became a bête noire.[20] By the time they founded Nauvoo, therefore, the Mormons had come to believe that the United States was a formerly moral and godly nation that had devolved into a "mobocracy" (notably, law-and-order types applied this same term to the Patriots), but they still held out hope for the nation's redemption.[21] In 1843 and early 1844, Smith and other Mormon leaders sent out petitions to various federal and state leaders and legislatures, appealing for aid based on their shared Americannness and playing to the masculinity of these leaders by claiming that attacks against Mormons threatened the chastity of Mormon women.[22] For the most part, the Mormons were met with deafening silence.

Smith and other Mormon leaders likely expected this indifference and used it to rally the Mormon community behind Smith's own newly crafted, highly ambitious—yet carefully hedged—political goals.[23] First, he declared himself a candidate for the 1844 presidential race, publishing a twenty-three-page platform titled *Views of the Powers and Policy of the Government of the*

United States.[24] The document was a curious mix of stunning naïveté and astute political intervention that attempted to find middle-of-the-road policies that could gain both Democratic and Whig adherents. For my purposes here, what is most important about Smith's pamphlet is its definitive reflection of the Texas Moment. Over several pages, Smith charted the history of the United States through its presidents, venerating each in turn, his rhetoric reaching a crescendo for Andrew Jackson's presidency, which he described as the "*acme* of American glory, liberty, and prosperity."[25] But then came the "withering touch of Martin Van Buren!" To Smith, Van Buren's presidency marked the beginning of US decline. He lamented that in the pristine American past there had been "no sound of rebellion in South Carolina, no rupture in Rhode Island, no mob in Missouri expelling her citizens by Executive authority, corruption in the ballot-boxes, a border warfare between Ohio and Michigan, hard times and distress, outbreak upon outbreak in the principal cities," and "a thousand other difficulties."[26] Careful readers could have pointed out that events such as South Carolina nullification and the conflict between Ohio and Michigan known as the Toledo War in fact came during Jackson's presidency, but many would have still agreed with Smith's core argument: put together, these calamities all demonstrated that "the glory of American liberty is on the wane."[27] Winfield Scott, the frequent lamenter of the Texas Moment, could not have said it better.

Noteworthy, too, was Smith's strong support for US expansion; he arrived at an expansionist platform months before James Polk, who had yet to win the Democratic nomination. Smith's elucidation of *how* this expansion would occur was also revealing. He argued that Oregon was rightfully US territory, therefore "when we have the red man's consent, let the Union spread from east to the west sea." He continued, "If Texas petitions Congress to be adopted among the sons of liberty, give her the right hand of fellowship, and refuse not the same friendly grip to Canada and Mexico."[28] The caveats "when" and "if" demonstrate that Smith believed in US expansion as many other Americans did—as a phenomenon that would happen peacefully over an indefinite length of time.

Perhaps, however, expansion could be sped up with Mormon assistance. This was Smith's second political option, a hedge against failing to win the presidency. Perceiving US military weakness and perhaps emphasizing that he personally held the rank of lieutenant general for his command of the Nauvoo Legion, Smith petitioned the US government for the authority to raise a force of 100,000 men. Presumably, these men would be current Mormons and future Mormon converts, although he did not make this explicit. He hoped to use them to protect the western and southern borders from any encroaching foreign power—namely, Great Britain.[29] Here again he combined the fantastical—at no point was he going to raise 100,000 men—with an acute understanding of North American geopolitics. As Smith wrote in early 1844, both Texas and Oregon and, to a much lesser extent, California were prominent topics in US politics, but no one had yet offered a pathway forward for the United States to acquire these territories. Smith's solution was to outsource expansion to individual groups of Americans, which reflected that he was a keen reader of national news, for the federal government had recently employed a similar strategy in Florida during the Seminole War, and some Arkansas politicians hoped to do the same thing with their border with Indian Territory.[30]

Then there was Smith's third political option, which was also indicative of the Texas Moment. If he could not become US president, and if the Mormons could not facilitate US expansion on the frontier, then the solution to the Mormons' political problems must lie beyond US borders—in Texas itself. Smith came to this idea through reading a letter from Lyman Wight, one of the members of the Quorum of the Twelve, the highest leadership body in the church.[31] Wight wrote from the Wisconsin pineries, where he and several dozen Mormons were securing lumber to build the Nauvoo temple. Wight first mentioned the favorable response several Wisconsin Native tribes, specifically the Chippewas and Menominees, had given to Mormon outreach.[32] He revealed that these tribes contemplated moving to Texas, where there was more game to hunt. Wight then made a bold suggestion: the Mormons should do the same. Once in Texas the Mormons could convert Natives and white southerners, making the region the Mormon "gathering place for all the South."[33]

Wight's letter struck a chord with Joseph Smith. The following day he organized the secret Council of Fifty. Unlike the religiously oriented Quorum of the Twelve, this organization would further the political goals of the Mormons—whatever they might be.[34] Confirming the secular nature of the body was Smith's inclusion of several non-Mormons. Although non-Mormons were only nominally represented and neither influential nor dedicated attendees, their inclusion demonstrated Smith's belief that the coming of the kingdom of God on earth was imminent, and it would encompass both Mormons and gentiles (the Mormon term for non-Mormons).[35] Soon the council sent ambassadors to Texas, the United States, Britain, France, and even Russia in order to negotiate for Mormon power somewhere in North America.[36] Over the next several months, the Council of Fifty met regularly to strategize how best to accomplish at least one of Smith's ambitious political goals.

Like all things explicitly political in the Jacksonian era, the Council of Fifty was an all-male body. Yet the gendered nature of the council was more than simply a reflection of the time: the council emphasized an age-based patriarchy and patriarchal authority. During each meeting, council members sat in a circle with the oldest member on Smith's direct right, followed by the second oldest, and so on around the circle, with the youngest finally seated to his direct left. All votes were taken in order of age, moving counterclockwise around the circle with the oldest man voting first and the youngest voting last.[37] That Smith had formalized patriarchy in this way was perhaps no surprise. In the spring of 1844, the same time when Smith was creating the council, he was engaged in what one historian deemed a multiyear "power struggle" with his wife Emma Smith over his secret doctrine of plural wives.[38] As Joseph cemented and expanded the practice among his close confidants— by the spring of 1844, twenty-eight men had taken at least one plural wife— Emma increasingly denounced it, most notably to the more than a thousand members of the Female Relief Society, which she served as president.[39] The Smiths had not arrived at a public breach of their marriage, but it seemed as if matters were coming to a head, for neither one showed signs of yielding. In council meetings, therefore, Smith reasserted the patriarchal authority that seemed to be threatened in his personal life. Among the council members, the practice of polygamy remained unacknowledged, with only fourteen of the fifty having taken plural wives.[40] Nevertheless, all members, whatever their stance or their knowledge about plural marriage, would have clearly understood the council's patriarchal nature.

The Council of Fifty's gendered dynamics were an important undercurrent that buttressed its three explicit political choices: elect Smith president, guard the western frontier, or migrate to Texas. With hindsight, it is easy to disparage each of these three goals as at best impractical, at worst absurd. In 1844, however, all were logical from the Mormon perspective—and in the eyes of many non-Mormons as well. Take Smith's presidential ambitions.[41] The 1844 election occurred at the height of American political partisanship, and Smith's attempt to break down this divide seems quixotic. Yet Smith clearly thought he could depend on this partisanship to help him achieve victory. He combined Democratic foreign policies with Whig domestic politics and offered a moderate stance on slavery, in which he denounced abolitionism while calling for compensation for southern slaveholders if they manumitted their enslaved people. Outside the vehemently proslavery Deep South (where no slaveholder would have taken up Smith's offer), Smith's platform offered policies that could appeal to men across the political spectrum. Smith also tapped into the well-established and highly successful practice of Mormon missionary outreach, turning what had been religious proselytizing into political campaigning. The organizing effort was extensive, with hundreds of missionaries sent out; only in 1895, when there were nine times as many Mormons as in 1844, would the LDS Church again send out that many missionaries at a single time.[42] With such a robust campaign, perhaps Smith could capture the votes of a few states and deny the other candidates an Electoral College majority, leaving the decision to the House of Representatives—where, at least in Smith's eyes, anything could happen. Even if it turned out Smith did not have enough support in the House or the nation at large, perhaps he could extract political concessions from one of the major candidates; once snubbed by Van Buren during the Missouri war, the Mormons would no longer be ignored by the federal government. At minimum, Smith's campaign would raise national awareness for the plight of the Mormons and perhaps force the hand of the next president to intervene in the increasing violence around Nauvoo. Ultimately Joseph Smith, US president, was nearly impossible, yet a presidential campaign could still reap dividends for the Mormons.

Smith's proposal to guard US borders had a similar calculus, although its logic betrayed the Mormons' inflated view of their influence in the halls of Congress. In 1844 the North American West remained in flux. Americans had recently begun migrating in large numbers to Oregon and California, but both of these regions possessed uncertain political futures. By protecting migrants, the Mormons could secure themselves power in this uncertain West with US acquiescence, and perhaps US funding. Indeed, both Henry Clay and Stephen Douglas recommended that the Mormons travel to Oregon as a means of "redress."[43] Smith took steps to make these plans a reality. In February 1844, he proposed sending send men west to explore the possibility of settling in Oregon or California, but too many were at work on his presidential campaign, and he could not find enough volunteers.[44] Yet Smith did not simply want to settle in Oregon or California, but to defend it—particularly from Britain—and it was on this point that Orson Hyde, the Mormon ambassador in Washington, reached an impasse with congressional leaders. While some Washington politicians could support a Mormon settlement in the West, they could not countenance a Mormon defensive force. If the Mormons were seen as US actors, their presence could lead to war with Britain. When Hyde told members of Congress that the armed group of Mormons would be independent from the United States, several senators believed that the American public would view this as favoring the Mormons above other western migrants. Other congressional leaders were even less sympathetic and believed the entire maneuver was simply unconstitutional.[45]

Rejected by Congress, Hyde urged Mormon leaders to lead a migration to Texas or Oregon without the consent of the United States, for a geopolitical vacuum had opened in the West that could only be a sign of divine favor: "There are many powerful checks upon our [federal] Gov. preventing her from moving in any of these important matters [i.e., Texas and Oregon], and for ought I know, these checks are permitted to prevent our gov. from extending her jurisdiction over that territory which God designs to give to his Saints."[46] Yet this opportunity would not last, and the Mormons must move fast. As Hyde wrote, "If the Saints possess the kingdom I think they will have to take it; and the sooner it is done the more easily it is accomplished."[47] Mormon leaders doubted Hyde's efforts and castigated him for not pursuing the Mormon frontier defense force, while Hyde pleaded that Mormon leaders did not understand Washington politics.[48] By June the entire plan was off the table, with Lyman Wight claiming that the idea of Mormon defense of the frontier had been a bluff to "tease" Congress away from intervening in the Mormons' actions elsewhere.[49] Whether true or not, Wight's statement reflected that Mormon leaders had moved on, for they had found marked success with their third plan, the one originally devised by Wight and now endorsed by Hyde in Washington: Mormon migration to Texas.

At the same time as Smith sent Hyde to Washington, he also sent Lucian Woodworth, another Council of Fifty member, to Texas to negotiate with Texas president Sam Houston. Unlike Hyde, however, Woodworth received a warm welcome. He and Houston held preliminary talks about a Mormon settlement in the Nueces Strip, a region on the Texas-Mexico border that both countries claimed.[50] Houston's readiness to negotiate with the Mormons was hardly an offer of humanitarianism, but a calculated geopolitical maneuver. Texas's annexation to the United States was still contested in 1844, as Houston reportedly acknowledged to Woodworth.[51] Indeed, if Clay had won the presidency that fall—as appeared likely at the time—annexation would have been postponed indefinitely. Moreover, Texas was in debt, migration to the republic had stalled, and Mexican leaders refused to acknowledge Texas independence. Therefore, a Mormon settlement in the disputed and remotely settled Nueces Strip would serve as a powerful buffer between Texas and Mexico. The Mormons possessed potential military strength, especially compared to Texas: the Nauvoo Legion in 1844 was four times the size of the Texan army at the Battle of San Jacinto in 1836. Houston explicitly argued for the importance of Mormon military power, reportedly saying that he would welcome the "*Mormon Legion* in Texas as armed Emigrants, with open arms."[52] Importantly, even if—as Houston privately hoped—Texas *was* soon annexed to the United States, both the Texans and the Mormons would still have found a Mormon settlement useful: Texas would have additional frontier protection, while the Mormons would be far away from hostile Americans. Joseph Smith's support for such a plan reflected an important fact: by the spring of 1844, he was willing to give up on Missourians and Illinoisans, but not the mass of Anglo-Americans throughout the continent more generally.

With the failure of Hyde in Washington, Smith's three options for Mormon power became two: a campaign for the presidency or a mass migration to Texas. The former remained the priority. As Council of Fifty member George Miller put it, if Smith were elected, "We would at once establish dominion in the United States, and in view of a failure we would send a minister to the then Republic of Texas to make a treaty."[53] In his diary, Joseph Smith made it clear that going to Texas would mean a decisive turn against the United States: "If Houston will embrace the gospel [we] can mend that constitution and make it the voice of Jehovah and shame the U[nited] S[tates]."[54] Here again, Smith mixed Mormon theology with politics. If the United States were truly irredeemable, then perhaps the kingdom of God would be realized in neighboring Texas. It was, after all, still an American republic and therefore held many of the virtues the Mormons believed the United States had once held. While Smith believed that the government created under the US Constitution was divinely inspired, perhaps the "mended" Texas constitution would become the constitution of the kingdom of God through the influence of Smith and other Mormon leaders. Smith left unmentioned that the antislavery views of the Mormons would be at odds with the slaveholding republic of Texas, but this was not an issue of immediate concern. The Mormons could figure it out if and when they arrived in Texas.

Mormon leaders began laying the groundwork for the Texas contingency if Smith failed at his presidential bid. In April, Smith published a new revelation in which the entirety of North and South America was the Mormon Zion, divulging to all Mormons the real possibility of abandoning Nauvoo—and with it, the United States.[55] Mormon papers printed increased coverage of Texas, while British Mormons contemplated a mass migration from the British Isles to Texas.[56] Lucian Woodworth, the Mormon ambassador to Texas, made it clear to British Mormon leaders that the migration plan must be kept quiet for several months, for they would need to travel to and through the United States for the move.[57] For the time being, therefore, the Mormons must not cause US authorities any concern. In June, Joseph Smith investigated purchasing land from private Texas landowners instead of the Texas government. Smith's exact intentions here remain unknown, but perhaps he was giving second thoughts to settling in the Nueces Strip, where conflict between Texas and Mexico was ongoing.[58] Of course, there was no need to make a final decision about Texas just yet, for the presidential election was still months away.

While all of these plans—Smith's presidential campaign, Mormon ideas of western defense, and the potential Texas migration—were reported outside of Mormon circles, the Council of Fifty was in the midst of a private debate of their own about just what sort of government they hoped to create. To the public, Smith maintained that he desired to create a "theo-democracy," which would presumably preserve American democratic practices while somehow also incorporating the will of God. Yet this was all a facade deliberately crafted by Smith and the Council of Fifty.[59] Privately, Smith and the Council of Fifty sought the creation of a theocracy that would be democratic only if the people followed God's plan, which would be voiced by Smith and other members of the council—and thus, it would not be a democracy at all. As council member Heber Kimball stated, "We must swallow the whole stream and then will have all power." Brigham Young agreed, asserting, "Revelations must govern. The voice of God, shall be the voice of the people."[60] This theocracy would obliterate the wall between church and state that had been erected in the US Constitution, and the council began writing a new theocratic constitution to be implemented once the Mormons gained power, wherever that might be.

Yet despite this radical break with American republicanism and the practices of Jacksonian democracy, the Council of Fifty's theocratic plans remained thoroughly rooted in their Americanness, which is best exemplified in the draft of the Mormon constitution. Despite Mormon disappointment with the corrupt government of the United States, the Mormon constitution still echoed the US Constitution. It opened, "We the people of the Kingdom of God," thus modifying the famed "We the People." Like the US Constitution, the Mormon constitution's second and third articles discussed the executive and judicial branches, respectively. The constitution also echoed the Declaration of Independence (and John Locke) when it defined the "rights of man" as *"life, liberty, possession of property, and pursuit of happiness,"* although it noted that no government of men had yet been able to guarantee these rights—hence the need for a theocracy. Rather than "self-evident truths" and an ambiguous reference to "our Creator," the Mormons were explicit: "God hath created all men free and equal."[61]

The echoes of both the US Constitution and the Declaration of Independence were of course no coincidence. All but one of the Council of Fifty were Americans thoroughly rooted in their country's history and government, as Joseph Smith had demonstrated with his presidential platform. The task to improve the US Constitution was also made explicit. In writing the Mormon constitution, the council resolved that their constitution "should be perfect, and embrace those principles which the constitution of the United States lacked."[62] In a later meeting, Smith was more specific, saying that there were only "two or three things lacking in the constitution of the United States," one of which was a clause that would allow the federal government to enforce "principles of liberty" if they were being taken away.[63] Clearly the Mormons' history in Missouri and Illinois was on his mind. Thus, like Mirabeau Lamar's description of how the Republic of Texas's constitution improved on the US Constitution, the Mormons sought to correct the flaws of US governance. Like the Texans, the Patriots, and, as I discuss below, Cherokee leaders and American migrants in Oregon and California, the Mormons offered an alternative America. Although the Mormon vision was theocratic instead of republican, it remained American nevertheless.

Indeed, the Mormons' inability to get outside of this American paradigm caused them to stop writing their constitution entirely. After the initial text of the constitution was read aloud, John Taylor, who would become the third president of the LDS Church after Brigham Young, rose to voice his concerns. One of the three members tasked with writing the first draft, he stated that his committee was "treading on holy ground." The text of the minutes then described the scene: "In contemplating the situation of nations and our situation, [the committee tasked with writing the constitution] felt placed in a delicate situation. They can[']t refer to any constitution of the world because they are corrupt. [Taylor] referred to the leading article in the document. He said that the chairman might well say that he had appointed them that work that they might learn that they are fools."[64] In essence, the committee had been appointed to write a divinely inspired document, but the "leading article" was actually inspired by the very earthly US Constitution. Taylor was from England, the only Council of Fifty member born outside the United States, and he maintained that in order to write a truly theocratic constitution, they "needed a revelation from God to shew the very principles of the kingdom of God."[65] After Taylor finished speaking, other members of the council added further concerns about the constitution, many demonstrating ambivalence about writing a document supposedly based on God's will. Joseph Smith agreed. At the council's next meeting, he altered course. The committee should stop writing a constitution, he proclaimed in a new revelation, because "verily thus saith the Lord, yea are my own constitution."[66] Now, with the Council of Fifty itself acting as God's constitution, no written document was necessary. Instead, they should turn to Smith's presidential campaign and work to get him elected.

Although Mormon leaders were uncomfortable writing a theocratic document that so obviously mimicked the US Constitution, Smith's plans for the presidency make it clear that he had not entirely given up on the United States or the American people. He believed that a theocracy could still be created *through* the US government with the aid of some gentiles. Indeed, he had already included three non-Mormons on the Council of Fifty. Moreover, while Smith's presidential platform was a public document and therefore catered to American sensibilities, it seems likely that Smith thoroughly believed his own account of US history, in which the republic remained glorious and virtuous until the twin disasters of Van Buren and the Panic of 1837. Countless non-Mormons agreed at the time. Moreover, Mormonism had arisen, spread, and thrived in the United States, and its theology was rooted in an ancient American past, which would make it difficult for Smith to permanently sever all ties to the United States. Even as late as 1844, Smith and most Mormon leaders blamed individuals and groups—Martin Van Buren, Lilburn Boggs, the Missourians—for their plight, not the United States or its people as a whole.[67] The quest for a Mormon theocracy remained a thoroughly American project.

And then disaster struck the Mormons, as local politics intruded on their national and international plans. As Smith's ambitions grew, so did the opposition of anti-Mormons and, even more important, a contingent of former Mormons. Deeming Smith a fallen prophet, several Mormon apostates, led by Smith's former counselor William Law, made plans to publish the *Nauvoo Expositor,* an exposé of Smith's increasingly ambitious worldly plans.[68] They first published a prospectus for the paper on May 10, 1844, in which they called Smith a "SELF-CONSTITUTED MONARCH" and promised to reveal details of Mormon political goals in the first issue and perhaps salacious details about the still-secret but growing practice of plural marriage among Smith's closest confidants.[69] Events then moved fast. Smith convened the Nauvoo City Council, at which it was decided that the *Nauvoo Expositor* was a public nuisance and ought to be silenced. Wielding his power as the mayor of Nauvoo, Smith then ordered the city marshal to destroy the printing press. That night, the marshal set fire to the paper's headquarters. Smith had weathered years of hostility from US citizens, but his decision to attack the cherished right of freedom of the press proved to be his undoing. Within weeks, Smith, his brother Hyrum, and two other Mormon leaders were arrested and taken to the neighboring town of Carthage, Illinois. On the evening of June 27, a hundred-man mob stormed the jail. When the attackers reached Joseph Smith's cell, they proceeded to shoot him six times and Hyrum four times. Within minutes, both men were dead.[70]

Smith's shocking death destroyed hopes for Mormon power in the United States, but Texas remained an option for Mormon settlement. Two weeks after Smith's death, Lucian Woodworth sent a hurried letter to Sam Houston to inform him of the murder. Woodworth then asked Houston to respond if he still considered Mormon immigration "practicable."[71] There is no evidence that Houston ever replied. Even if he did, it would not have mattered. Although nineteenth-century Mormon historians would make it appear as if Brigham Young's assumption of leadership was a divinely inspired development, the truth was much messier.[72] Smith had never designated a successor, and within weeks several factions began to vie for control. This leadership crisis lasted for more than a year, until Young and most of the Quorum of the Twelve managed to gain the following of a majority of Mormons. At no point during this time were the Mormons prepared to migrate to Texas or, for that matter, anywhere else. For a time, it even seemed that a permanent exodus had become unnecessary. The brutality of Smith's murder stunned not just the Mormons but the non-Mormon communities around Nauvoo, causing many people to step back from the brink of open warfare. Yet permanent peace was a mirage. In the autumn of 1845 the violence reignited, and this time Young and the Twelve felt they had only one choice: they had to leave the United States entirely.

However, the Mormons would not go to Texas. The geopolitical situation in the American West had shifted dramatically. As I demonstrate in chapter 7, the US annexation of Texas rapidly moved from the realm of unlikely to possible, and then from possible to accomplished, all within the course of a year. Now a migration to Texas simply meant a migration to another region in the United States, which the Mormons had tried before and which had failed to alleviate conflict. Moreover, even if Texas had remained independent, it is doubtful that Young and the Council of Fifty would have sought refuge there. The pattern of persecution that culminated in Smith's murder made Mormon leaders much more cynical about gentile Americans than Smith had ever been. Wherever the Mormons went, Young believed, they must be the first—and hopefully only—settlers. Only Lyman Wight disagreed, arguing that the Mormons should stick with Smith's Texas plan, which of course had originated with Wight himself. In August 1844, he left for Texas with the 150 men, women, and children whom he had led in Wisconsin. Young did not want to contradict Smith's wishes or the still influential Lyman Wight when Young had not yet fully secured power, and he gave Wight's company his blessing. However, he mandated that anyone else who joined them "will be damned and go to destruction."[73] Wight presumably believed that this order was temporary and that Young would eventually accede to a mass migration. However, after it was clear that Young had no intention to direct any additional Mormons to Texas, Wight broke with Young permanently, believing that Young had betrayed Joseph Smith's divinely inspired mandate. Wight remained in Texas for the rest of his life, dying of illness in 1858.[74]

To Brigham Young and a majority of the Council of Fifty, meanwhile, Texas had become an untenable project that was "wild and visionary."[75] Highly practical, with an acute understanding of realpolitik, Young needed a plan that was not "wild" but achievable. The Mormons would build Zion elsewhere.

The Lamanite Redemption and the Mormon-Native Alliance

In 1844, when Lyman Wight was in Wisconsin and first proposed a Mormon settlement in Texas, he included a crucial second component in his plan: the Texas move should be accompanied by a general outreach to Indians.[76] In fact, Wight noted that several Wisconsin Native peoples—the Menominees, the Chippewas, and the Winnebagos—had given him the idea of Texas in the first place. These people had been forced to live off US government annuities amid dwindling game, and Wight claimed that they looked to Texas—"where game was more plentiful"—as a place to reestablish themselves and their older economic and social practices.[77] However, they stated they would only move to Texas under Mormon leadership for, as Wight explained, "They have great confidence in us."[78] Wight then significantly amplified his proposal. He believed that all Native peoples "bordering on the United Territories from Green Bay to the Mexican Gulf, [were] all crying with one voice. . . . 'Give us an understanding of your doctrine and principles, for we perceive that your ways are equal.' "[79] As the Mormons traveled to Texas, Wight believed, they could send missionaries to the Cherokees and Choctaws, who were also "desirous to have an interview with the Elders of this Church."[80] In Wight's eyes, the southern "gathering" would include vast numbers of converted Native people.

To the Quorum of the Twelve, Wight's Indian references would not have come out of the blue, for Native people represented a crucial component of Mormon theology. According to the Book of Mormon, the descendants of the Israelites who came to America eventually split into two warring peoples, the Nephites and the Lamanites. The Nephites were righteous, and they built great cities and retained their white skin. The nomadic Lamanites, by contrast, were marked with dark skin because of their wickedness. Eventually the Lamanites destroyed the Nephites, and the Lamanites' descendants became the Indians. The Book of Mormon foretold that eventually the Latter-day Saints would redeem the Lamanites, and they would regain glory during the Last Days. Smith took steps to fulfill this prophecy. As early as 1830 he sent a mission to the Wyandots, Shawnees, and Delawares in Missouri, which made white Missourians suspicious and became one of the many reasons they sought Mormon expulsion.[81] During the Nauvoo period, the Mormons maintained disparate connections to various Native groups, although Smith moved cautiously, not wanting to replay the events of Missouri in Illinois.[82]

Mormon missionary outreach differed from typical evangelical missions to Native groups during this period. Because the Mormons believed that the Lamanites would join with them during the Last Days, missionary work held political implications: Lamanite redemption in the future presupposed a more immediate Mormon-Native alliance. Perhaps as early as 1840, and certainly by 1842, Smith expressed a hope to "unite with the Indians" somewhere beyond the Rocky Mountains.[83] At times Smith sent missions to tribes living as far away as Canada, and he received several Native delegations in Nauvoo.[84] In the final months of Smith's life, however, when he was both running a presidential campaign and preparing for a migration to Texas, the Native alliance was only a vague afterthought. If and when the Mormons moved to Texas, then the Lamanite redemption could proceed, but no concrete steps were taken. Nevertheless, the potential of an alliance with Native people continued to hold allure for Smith. Only days before his death, as the crisis surrounding the *Nauvoo Expositor* intensified to the point of no return, Smith predicted that believers would gather in the "strongholds of the Rocky Mountains" with the "red men." These "red men" would become the "strong arm of Jehovah, who will be a strong bulwark of protection for your [i.e., Mormon] foes."[85] It would be left to other Mormon leaders to fulfill this vision.

The idea of the Lamanite redemption was so deeply rooted during this period of Mormon history that several members of the Council of Fifty would go off on their own to attempt to convert Native people, disregarding the orders of the council and, like Lyman Wight, eventually breaking with Mormon leadership altogether.[86] For my purposes here, however, the plans of the Council of Fifty are what is important. In February 1845, Brigham Young convened the body for the first time since Joseph Smith's death the previous June. Still working to solidify his power, Young called together only twenty-five members, deliberately excluding those who had opposed his leadership.[87] The purpose of this first meeting seems to have been making the council a functional and effective body once again. During their meeting, council members discussed a proposal by a non-Mormon named William Richards, who had written to them suggesting they seek a "reserve" of twenty-four square miles in Iowa or Wisconsin, where they could erect a "little commonwealth" that would remain separate from the rest of the United States and the American people. In a follow-up letter in the *Nauvoo Neighbor*, Richards argued that Indian removal in the 1830s was a precedent for such a step: the Mormons would become like removed Indians. Somewhat intrigued, the council nevertheless noted that twenty-four square miles was too small of an area to support the thousands of Mormon converts.[88] Ultimately, however, they had greater geopolitical ambitions than a "Mormon reserve." Their goal was not to become like removed Indians, but to use removed Indians to their advantage.

In the weeks that followed Young's first convening of the council, the Lamanite redemption became the talk among church leaders.[89] This discussion fused with a more vehement and explicit anti-US rhetoric than anything the Mormons had voiced before. Even in 1844, after the Missouri expulsion and during the escalating conflict in Nauvoo, Joseph Smith had moderated his stance toward the United States. In his *Views of the Powers and Policy of the Government of the United States,* he had attacked its current leaders but praised its history and institutions, and he was willing to live among Anglo-Americans in Texas and sought to protect them on the western frontier.

Smith's murder, however, snuffed out any remaining goodwill the Mormons felt toward the United States. The Council of Fifty member Amasa Lyman described the United States as "a damned wrotten [*sic*] thing—, full of lice, moth eaten, corrupt, and there is nothing but meanness about it," while Brigham Young stated his desire to "wipe [the Americans] out of existence."[90] After more than a decade of persecution without redress, Mormon leaders felt no need to proselytize any longer to white Americans. Instead, said Young, "let the damned scoundrels be killed"; the Mormons would now reach out to the Native people instead.[91]

In March 1845, Young convened the Council of Fifty once again, with the primary purpose of organizing the Lamanite redemption.[92] The council appointed several Mormons already familiar with Native missionary work to undertake this task, among them Lewis Dana, the Oneida Mormon convert I described in the introduction. At the same time, Dana was inducted into the Council of Fifty, the first Native to be received into any church body.[93] Also chosen was Brigham Young's brother Phineas. The backgrounds of the men sent on this mission confirm its importance: not only were they experienced with Native outreach, but they were all more than forty years old and members of the Council of Fifty.[94]

There was good reason to send men of experience and prestige: their mission to the Lamanites was not just to convert Natives, but to seek them as political and military allies against the United States. The council made this explicit, Brigham Young most of all. He avowed, "I want to go and convert the Lamanites and dwell with them, and I believe in twenty years the land will be divided off to the Lamanites. . . . The gentiles will be glad to lick the dust of the feet of the Lamanites to get their favor and we will live to see it."[95] Mormon leaders hoped to join with their new Native allies somewhere in the West, although where exactly remained up in the air. W. W. Phelps raised the prospect of settling in Oregon Country. Reflecting the geopolitics of the Texas Moment, Phelps argued, "It is well known the course of the United States is to grasp Oregon but there is not stability enough among them to do any thing."[96] George Miller disagreed, arguing that Mexico would be a better destination. Turning the typical American prejudice against Mexicans on its head, Miller argued that "three fourths of the inhabitants [of Mexico] are Indians and we have nothing to fear."[97] Reynolds Cahoon took the most extreme stance by opposing all emigration plans. He thought that the Mormons should unite the many Native peoples of the region, and together they would defend Nauvoo. Cahoon declared, "And if the enemies do not let us alone we will call out these men of the forest [i.e., the Native people] and they [i.e., Americans] had better leave us alone. . . . I believe we have as good a right to this land as any body and if they won[']t let us have it we will take it. I have no notion of going to the rocky mountains except for amusement."[98]

Where the Mormons would go with their new allies remained uncertain, but they could wait to make that decision. What they needed to decide immediately, however, was which Natives to convert. Brigham Young initially suggested the Comanches. His idea reveals once again how much the Mormons had come to loathe the United States. In 1845, the Comanches were at the height of their power, ceaselessly raiding Mexican and Texan settlements for horses and slaves.[99] Young clearly understood them as a formidable military power that could become the Mormons' potent ally against the United States. As he stated after suggesting the Comanches, "Our time is short among the gentiles, and the judgment of God will soon come on them like a whirlwind."[100] Presumably, the Comanches would help bring this "whirlwind."

As the discussion continued, Jonathan Dunham gently pointed out that converting the Comanches would be exceedingly difficult. He was someone to be heeded in regard to Native affairs, as Joseph Smith had tasked him with numerous Mormon missions to Native peoples in New York, Missouri, and Illinois over the previous two decades, and unsurprisingly he was one of those chosen for the Lamanite redemption in 1845. He did not argue against going to the Comanches because they were immensely powerful and hostile to white encroachment, which testifies to Mormon leaders' confidence in their ability to find Native allies. Rather, Dunham argued that the Mormons would be unable to survive among the Comanches because Comanche lands lacked timber, and therefore the Mormons would have no means of shelter in the winter. Dunham then suggested going to the Cherokees instead, stating, "If we can get the Cherokees to admit us amongst them we can have a place to stay one, two or three years in peace."[101] Living in US Indian Territory among the settled Cherokees was much more feasible than traveling to the Great Plains to live among nomadic Comanche bands.

Dunham's idea inaugurated the prominence of the Cherokees as the primary target of Mormon outreach. This decision made sense for several reasons. The Cherokees were deemed the most "advanced" Native people by many white Americans, and the Cherokee elites' acculturation to American norms would presumably make their conversion easier to accomplish. Moreover, the much-publicized Cherokee removal made the Mormons see the Cherokees above all as a group that also had suffered unjustly at the hands of what they now termed the US "mobocracy."[102] And for both the Mormons and the Cherokees, migration within US borders did not solve the problem with encroaching Anglo-Americans. Perhaps, as Lewis Dana wrote to Brigham Young, the Cherokees, like the Mormons, also wanted to gather away from "gentile oppression" for a second time.[103] Moreover, the Mormons had a history of thinking about the Cherokees. Lyman Wight referenced them, along with the Choctaws, in his original Texas letter, while a few months later Orson Hyde, the Mormon ambassador in Washington, sought a meeting with Cherokee leader John Ross, but it ultimately failed to materialize.[104]

Plans for the Indian mission slowly progressed over the next few weeks, but then Jonathan Dunham came up with a means for fast-tracking the process. Dunham claimed that various tribes were going to hold a grand council at Council Bluffs in Iowa Territory in June.[105] He suggested that the Mormons send emissaries to the council, which would allow them to meet with many different Native peoples at once. He argued that there "must be a union amongst the tribes" before they would convert to Mormonism, and this would ideally occur at the council. It seems that Dunham thought Joseph Smith's murder would act as a catalyst among the Native people. Despite Mormon outreach, no Indian had come to the Mormons' aid as they fled Missouri in the 1830s, but now Smith's death provided additional evidence of the persecution the Mormons suffered. Dunham dreamed of vengeance, arguing that Native support for the Mormons would lead to a moment when "Missouri would be swept clean."[106] He was not the only one who hoped for revenge: a few weeks later, Brigham Young stated that the Mormons could form an "alliance" with the Indians, at which point "we want to supply them as fast as we can with knives, guns and ammunition."[107] In the following days, others echoed their support for arming various Native peoples.[108] The joint Mormon-Native force would defend their two peoples against American encroachment, wherever that occurred.

Whatever the source of Dunham's information about the council meeting, much of it turned out to be incorrect. While Dunham believed the Cherokees were hosting the council, it was in fact hosted by the Creeks, and it was scheduled for May instead of June. Moreover, this council was convened by removed Natives to deal with deleterious Comanche and Pawnee raids, hardly a place to discuss an alliance against the United States.[109] Whether the Mormons would have had any influence at this gathering is debatable, but due to Dunham's dating error, the four Mormon emissaries who left in early May missed the council entirely. They did travel through the lands of several tribes on the way to the council, among them the Stockbridge Mohicans, the Senecas, and the Cherokees, and they reportedly planned to travel to a total of twenty-one Native nations, testifying to their ambitions.[110]

During their journey, a remarkable exchange of letters took place between Lewis Dana and John Brown, a Cherokee chief of the Old Settler faction, members of which had traveled west more than a decade before Cherokee removal and the infamous Trail of Tears. Most likely understanding that Brown would have known little of Mormonism, Dana chose to highlight his identity as an Oneida and fellow Native and did not mention Mormonism at all. He wrote to Brown, "We wish to send a party of our [i.e., Oneida] men, on an exploring tour to the Western part of the continent, or on some water course of the Western Ocean." He then proposed, "Unite with us in exploring the western continent for the purpose of finding some resting place for our [Native] people and rising generation."[111] Writing after the United States had already annexed Texas, Dana still believed in a future in which the West Coast of North America would remain free from US conquest in the near— and, ideally for the Mormons and their Native allies, distant—future. Brown responded to Dana favorably but explained that due to "the present confused state of affairs in this nation," he could not commit; he was likely referring to the ongoing violence among three factions of the Cherokees. Yet, Brown explained, "so soon as this confused state of affairs is settled, and the unfinished business with the Government of the United States is finally concluded, I think you would [have] no difficulty in getting a part of the Cherokee people and other tribes to co-operate with their northern friends & Brothers."[112] In all likelihood, the "part" to which Brown referred was his Old Settler faction, which remained unsatisfied with the dominance of Cherokee chief John Ross and his much larger faction. At the time, the Ross Party was not going anywhere (see chapter 4).

The exchange between Dana and Brown was the apogee of the Mormon mission to the Cherokees. Ultimately, the Mormon emissaries failed, for reasons both in US Indian Territory and in Mormon Nauvoo. In Indian Territory, Mormon dreams crashed against the on-the-ground reality that, as Phineas Young later lamented, "when we got among them, we found that there was not an Indian who ever heard of the word of Mormon."[113] John Brown, it seems, was the most important political leader with whom they were able to make contact, and he was a Cherokee leader of only secondary importance. Thomas Hendrick of the Stockbridge Mohicans was also receptive, but his people were a minority faction of a larger tribe that had remained at their reservation in Wisconsin instead of traveling to Indian Territory. Hendrick's followers would hardly give the Mormons the balance of power in the American West. Yet it is important to note that at the very least, the Mormons found traction among some Native leaders, for good reason. They were a faction of white Americans who seemingly turned the typical Native-white interactions on their head. These whites did not seek Native expulsion, but an alliance against the United States. In a certain way, the Mormons played on the long history of alliances in the Trans-Appalachian West, where Natives had united both with one another and with various European powers until the late 1810s—an era that was within the living memory of both parties. Like these coalitions of old, the Mormon-Native alliance would act as a formidable check on US ambitions.

To exploit this real but minimal traction, the Mormons would have had to follow up their first mission with another, even more extensive one. Yet once again, events around Nauvoo stopped Mormon ambitions in their tracks. Although Joseph Smith's murder in June 1844 had diminished the violence between Mormons and anti-Mormons, this peace was only temporary. In January 1845 the Illinois legislature repealed the Nauvoo charter, and by the summer anti-Mormon rhetoric had reached an all-time high. In September, Mormons from Nauvoo's outlying settlements fled to the city after anti-Mormons repeatedly burned their barns and crops.[114] By October Mormon leaders were furiously preparing their people for an exodus west. Although never definitively abandoned, plans for a Native alliance dwindled in the face of this much more immediate crisis, as had occurred before with the Mormon-Texas negotiations of 1844. In October 1845, Lewis Dana arrived in Nauvoo to meet with Mormon leaders. While there, he married a white Mormon convert named Mary Gont, demonstrating his full integration into the Mormon community.[115] By December, however, Dana was back in the Cherokee Nation. Writing to Brigham Young, Dana stated that the Cherokees hoped he would stay at least three years among them, but he would obey the wishes of the Quorum of the Twelve if they wanted him to return to Nauvoo.[116] They sent for him the following April, and by the autumn of 1846 Dana was involved with Mormon-Native relations in Iowa Territory.[117] Mormon-Native interactions during the exodus, however, would not be concerned with geopolitical alliances but, more simply, with ensuring the Mormons a safe passage across Native lands. Plans for a Mormon-Native alliance were defunct.

Navigating US Expansion

As violence escalated in the fall of 1845, Brigham Young and the Quorum of the Twelve understood that the Mormons would need to leave Nauvoo. Only by promising that the Mormons would evacuate the city did Young avert an all-out war. But where would they go? It was certain the Mormons were not going to Texas, nor were they finding allies among the Natives—at least, not soon enough to prevent their exodus from Nauvoo. Yet the vast North American West seemed open for settlement. Of course, few areas of the West were actually empty. Natives had lived there since time immemorial, and Californios, Nuevomexicanos, British trappers working for the Hudson's Bay Company, and recently arrived Anglo-Americans had settled among them in certain regions. Nevertheless, whatever the barriers to Mormon settlement, in 1846 the western portion of the continent was not yet the US West, and it was the United States from which the Mormons fled. Although their travels would bring them in contact with people who might not share their views, at least a westward migration would take the Mormons out of the United States. Joseph Smith had prophesied such a step perhaps as early as 1840, undoubtedly by 1842.[118] Further, at the first official meeting of the Council of Fifty in 1844, Smith had described its purpose as establishing a "Theocracy either in Texas or Oregon or somewhere in California &c," demonstrating that Texas was not the only possible destination.[119] Thus, by the fall of 1845, when Young and the Quorum of the Twelve decided they had no choice but to lead the Mormons from Nauvoo, they were tapping into a long-established albeit vague idea that anywhere in the West could become the Mormon Zion.

The Mormons had three potential sites open to them. The first was somewhere in the vast Oregon Country, which at the time was jointly claimed by the United States and Great Britain, although in most of the region Natives retained on-the-ground control. After Texas, Oregon had received the most Mormon attention before Smith's death. As noted above, Orson Hyde had weighed the benefits of Oregon versus Texas in letters from Washington, DC, in the spring of 1844, and Henry Clay, Stephen Douglas, and Arkansas governor Thomas Drew advised the Mormons to solve their problems by moving to Oregon.[120] After Young publicly announced the exodus, the Illinois paper the *Quincy Whig* maintained that in Oregon Country, the Mormons were specifically going to Vancouver Island, an assertion that then reverberated throughout the US press.[121] For some observers, the next logical step was a Mormon alliance with Great Britain; they would work together to prevent the

Robert Campbell, *General Joseph Smith Addressing the Nauvoo Legion* (1845). This painting shows how Joseph Smith's power and prestige could be interpreted in two completely different ways. Mormons of the time would have found comfort in the legion's numbers and orderliness and pride in Mormon influence and power. Anti-Mormons, meanwhile, would have been concerned with Smith's growing political and military ambitions. Courtesy of the Church History Museum, Church of Jesus Christ of Latter-day Saints, Salt Lake City, UT.

United States' annexation of Oregon.[122] At times, Mormons themselves contemplated a British alliance. From London, one Mormon leader urged such a step, for he believed Great Britain was poised to decisively defeat the United States if war broke out over Oregon. He based his assertion on the presence of sixty British ships in US waters and the British ability to "arm the slaves and the Lamanites."[123] The Council of Fifty member Peter Haws voiced a similar opinion during one of the discussions about sending missionaries to the Indians, arguing that the Mormons should also partner with the British, for they already had a history of successfully forging Native alliances.[124]

Although a few other council members voiced support, Brigham Young quickly shut this talk down. "If we were to come under the British Government we would not last forty eight hours," Young stated, and he wanted "nothing to do with them." Later he elaborated that the British were powerful enough that they could quickly "break up" any Mormon negotiations with Natives before the Mormons would be able to make any headway toward forging a Native alliance. Others piled on. John Taylor said "he would as soon go to the devil, as under the British government," and George Miller pointed out that "the British government would never do any thing, unless they be satisfied it would result in their own advantage and they would not benifit [*sic*] us."[125] Mormon leaders were taking a page from Joseph Smith, who had attacked the British in the years before his death.[126] That the idea of a British alliance did not receive more support reveals that the Mormons could not help but maintain a semblance of American nationalism. On its face a Mormon-British alliance seemed natural, as many anti-Mormon Americans noted. The Mormons had no concrete reason to dislike the British government, and they had converted thousands of British subjects. By the 1850s, British converts would make up almost half of the Mormon population in the West.[127] Yet in 1846, the still predominantly American Mormon population in and around Nauvoo could not let go of the long tradition of American disdain for John Bull. They were not the only breakaway Americans who saw a British alliance as a step too far: Americans in Texas and Oregon felt the same way. While it might bring concrete benefits, a British alliance would betray each group's American heritage and endanger its ability to remain independent, for the British remained permanently untrustworthy.

While Oregon was no longer an option, it retained importance among the Council of Fifty as a ruse that would hide the Mormons' true destination from the United States and the American public.[128] In public letters and conversations with public officials like Stephen A. Douglas, Mormon leaders maintained that they sought to populate "Vancouver's Island."[129] Such was the extent of the deception that many Mormons outside the church's power structure also believed that Vancouver Island was the ultimate destination as they readied to leave Nauvoo in early 1846. While Young did hope Vancouver Island could become a way station for British Mormon migrants traveling to the new Mormon settlement in the West, he had no plans to make anywhere in Oregon Country a permanent settlement. Wary of US intervention, he and the Quorum of the Twelve hoped to disguise their true destination for as long as possible, and advancing the Oregon rumor served this purpose.

If the Oregon Country was unpalatable, then what about the even more extensive Mexican province of Alta California? In this vast territory were two choices: somewhere along the coast, which at that time was sparsely settled by Californios and roughly a hundred Anglo-American immigrants, or somewhere in the remote interior, which was populated by more than 100,000 Natives at varying degrees of density. Many non-Mormons wrote to

Young, urging the Mormons to settle on the coast, particularly near San Francisco Bay. Often these were New England merchants who believed a Mormon settlement in California could prove useful for their businesses. In their letters, they extolled the climate and location of northern California, while also denigrating Mexico and the Californio inhabitants for their inability to make the region economically prosperous.[130] Illinois governor Thomas Ford echoed them, arguing that the Mormons could establish an independent government in California "subject to only the laws of nations."[131] Like the New England merchants, Ford wrote for selfish reasons: he wanted the Mormons out of his state.

Of the non-Mormons pushing for a Mormon settlement in California, none was more intriguing—or ambitious—than Lansford Hastings. Hastings had led several migrant companies west, and in 1845 he published *The Emigrants' Guide to Oregon and California*, regaling the American public with the economic prospects of California (and not Oregon). Left unsaid in his book was his more ambitious political agenda. Hastings schemed for an independent western republic, presumably with himself as its leader.[132] Hastings was in contact with Samuel Brannan, a Mormon convert in New York. Brigham Young had tasked Brannan with organizing a seaborne migration to California of Mormons who remained in eastern states. While it is unclear just what exactly Hastings planned, he clearly hoped to use the Mormons as allies in his ambitious California scheme, and it seems Brannan was at least aware of some of these plans. Also caught up in the plot were the California promoter and author of the travelogue *Travels in California*, Thomas Farnham; New York merchants Arthur and Alfred Benson; and former US postmaster general Amos Kendall. It remains unclear exactly what each man hoped to get from promoting Mormon migration to the coast of California, but it was probably some combination of money and power.[133] Unfortunately for Hastings and the rest of the schemers, Young sensed something deceitful was afoot and did not take Hastings's bait.[134]

Although Brigham Young ignored Hastings, for a time the coast of California did tempt him and other members of the council. Young mentioned that Joseph Smith had long touted the "commercial advantages" of San Francisco Bay and discussed how, if the Mormons settled there, they could build up a fleet and "send them all over the world" to "preach the gospel to the islands of the sea."[135] As to the fact that California was officially under Mexican sovereignty, some council members foresaw no problem, while others were concerned. Erastus Snow asserted that the "Mexican government is weak," and this power vacuum would allow the Mormons to take whatever land they wanted. He argued, "The spirit of conquest has been burning in our veins for years and all that has kept it from boiling over is our women & children. If we pitch upon California . . . we can take care of ourselves."[136] Orson Hyde, however, foresaw a problem with the local Californio population. As he noted, American Catholics had largely been sympathetic with the Mormons' plight for, like the Mormons, they were despised by a significant number of American Protestants. Yet once the Mormons were among a population that was entirely Catholic, they would "soon show us their power and enmity."[137] To Hyde, as long as the Mormons were a minority, the majority—no matter who they were—would despise them.

While Orson Hyde's words were not decisive in the moment, this general sentiment that the Mormons needed to be in the majority was ultimately the key reason the council decided against coastal California and instead chose the Salt Lake Valley for their destination. As council member George Smith argued, the Mormons needed to become the "old settlers," where they could build Zion without outside interference—especially, if not exclusively, the interference of Americans.[138] Americans had already arrived in both Oregon and coastal California, and many more were on their way. If the Mormons settled in these regions, they would once again become a minority sect; if they went to the remote and inhospitable Great Basin, on the other hand, they would rule the region and could fully implement their theocracy. The fact that so many letters urged the Mormons to go to the area around San Francisco, while none recommended the Salt Lake Valley, would only have made the latter more attractive in Young's eyes. While some Mormons noted the region's dubious agricultural prospects and doubted his decision, Young believed it was worth the risk.[139] Zion would be built in the Salt Lake Valley.

Once again, gender likely played a role in this choice. If Joseph Smith's decision to form the Council of Fifty helped reassert patriarchal power, then Brigham Young's decision to move to the Salt Lake Valley cemented it. Unlike Smith, who had granted his wife Emma a significant amount of power and influence in early Mormonism, notably the presidency of the influential Female Relief Society, Young was dead set against women playing a public part in the faith. In 1845 he suspended the relief society meetings. He was aided by Emma Smith's public break with his leadership, which allowed him to claim that because the relief society no longer had a president, its functions were "deferred."[140] When Young and a majority of the Mormons left for the West, Emma Smith stayed behind in Nauvoo. This meant that arguably the most influential and vocal critic of polygamy in the church never traveled to the Salt Lake Valley. Moreover, as Young and his allies sought to expand plural marriage to increasing numbers of Mormon converts, becoming the "old settlers" would undoubtedly further this endeavor. In the West, no American mob would threaten plural marriage, and women would remain safely and securely under their husband's watchful care.[141] In the Salt Lake Valley, plural marriage—which the church at times called "patriarchal marriage"—could occur without interference, and a patriarchal society could be more fully realized.

Although Mormon leaders knew they were going to the Salt Lake Valley in early 1846, the general Mormon populace did not. Trusting their leaders to guide them, most Mormons were concerned with the day-to-day hardships of procuring food and supplies for the rigorous journey, which would take many of them more than two years. Thus, Mormon diaries and trail journals during this period emphasized the Mormon exodus as an epic tale of survival, a journey into the unknown western wilderness. Of course, Mormon leaders were also primarily concerned with day-to-day survival, but for them the final destination was not unknown; rather, it was quite known. They had read John C. Frémont's reports and Lansford Hastings's *Emigrants' Guide* and had studied the western maps that hung in the Nauvoo Temple.[142] They knew they were leaving the political boundaries of the United States. As one Mormon leader wrote, "It is with the greatest joy I forsake this republic."[143] Their destination was a remote corner of northern Mexico—although it remained to be seen how Mexico would receive them.

Just what Mormon leaders believed they could accomplish in Mexico is guesswork, as the Council of Fifty was largely silent on the matter, only mentioning it once—although this mention is revealing. Council member Erastus Snow argued that because Mexico was weak, the Mormons would have no problem at first, but if Mexico were able to reassert control, it could "torment" the Mormons "much as the United States would if it had the power."[144] In essence, Mexican weakness provided the Mormons with time, something they no longer had in Nauvoo. They could figure out their political status— whether that was outright independence, autonomy, or some other agreement with the Mexican government—once they were safely out of the United States and ensconced in the Salt Lake Valley. But then, for the third time in two years, external events rendered the Mormons' political plans irrelevant. Joseph Smith's death had destroyed the Texas plans in the summer of 1844; anti-Mormon violence around Nauvoo had ended the quest for an alliance with Native people in the fall of 1845; and on May 13, 1846, the United States declared war on Mexico.

Mormon leaders learned of the war in late May, two weeks after it began. Their initial reaction was unsurprising: they hoped that Mexico would reap divine vengeance on the United States. As Mormon diarist Hosea Stout wrote, "I confess I was glad to learn of war against the United States and was in hopes that it might never end untill [*sic*] they were entirely destroyed for they had driven us into the wilderness & was now laughing at our calamities."[145] However, Mormon leaders also knew they were playing a decidedly political game, and they needed to mollify federal officials in case the United States decided to intervene. Before the outbreak of war, as they prepared to move west in early 1846, the Mormons had already made multiple public proclamations of their loyalty that belied their true feelings, even claiming they traveled west to "sustain the claim" of the United States to the region.[146] Once they learned of the war, they did not change their western plans or their professions of loyalty to the United States. They could not control who won on the battlefield. Their primary objective remained to travel safely to the Salt Lake Valley, and only when they arrived would they assess the larger geopolitical situation—and judge how to best maintain and expand Mormon sovereignty.

CHAPTER FOUR

The Cherokee Nation and the Quest for a Native Republic

In June 1843, between 3,000 and 4,000 Natives gathered at the Cherokee Nation's capital, Tahlequah, in US Indian Territory. They represented reportedly eighteen different tribes: Cherokees, Creeks, Chickasaws, Seminoles, Pottawatomies, Osages, Shawnees, Iowas, and others not listed in the sources. For two weeks they socialized with one another, and then the official proceedings began, the highlights of which were speeches by Cherokee chief John Ross and Creek chief Roley McIntosh. Such was the spectacle that one white missionary observed that the Great Council, as it became known, was the "largest and most imposing of its character probably that was ever convened."[1] At the end of the speeches, the Great Council produced eight resolutions that provided for "perpetual" peace among the tribes. The fourth resolution stood out for its defiance: "We hereby solemnly pledge ourselves to each other, that no Nation, party to this compact, shall, without the consent of the other parties, cede, or in any manner alienate, to the United States, any part of their present territory."[2] By standing united against any further US attempts to take Indian lands in the West as it had done in the East, the Great Council defiantly asserted Native sovereignty.

Or, at least, some of the Great Council did. In the end, only three of the eighteen tribes signed the resolutions: the Cherokees, the Creeks, and the Osages. That only the Cherokees and the Creeks—of the countless northern and southern tribes forced west in the 1820s and 1830s—signed the resolutions reflected the particular geopolitics of US Indian Territory in the early 1840s. Most of the Native peoples that the United States had removed to the region numbered in the hundreds or a few thousands, were dependent on US supplies for their sustenance, and remained militarily impotent. The Cherokees and Creeks, on the other hand, each had populations close to 20,000, which gave them very real geopolitical power. Moreover, the Cherokees especially possessed advantages that allowed them to navigate the frequently hostile world of Jacksonian politics with both knowledge and skill. Because they had explicitly based both their written legal code and their republican government on American models, and because their leaders had been educated in American schools, they were able to cultivate allies among influential missionaries and reformers in the Whig Party. They also possessed a military force, the Cherokee Light Horse, that guarded the borders and inhabitants of the Cherokee Nation. Cherokee leaders like John Ross had fought removal tooth and nail in the East, but once forced west Ross and his allies recognized that while removal was a tragedy of colossal proportions, it also was a geopolitical opportunity. On the far western edge of US jurisdiction, Indian Territory remained a borderland over which the federal government possessed little control—and the Cherokees, perhaps with other Native allies, tried to take advantage.

The Cherokees' struggle for sovereignty in the West began at the same time as the Patriot War raged along the northern border. While these struggles occurred thousands of miles apart, they ran together. After the Patriots went underground in early 1838, peace seemed to return to the northern frontier, so the Van Buren administration sent the indispensable Winfield Scott from New York to Georgia to oversee Cherokee removal. Just as he mistrusted the militia along the northern border, Scott also mistrusted the local Georgia militia, for white Georgians wanted Cherokee land and cared little for ensuring the Cherokees' survival. He requested federal troops, but— as at first along the northern border—none were available, and he had to make do with the untrustworthy militia. By the summer Scott's forces had succeeded in forcing the Cherokees into camps, but then Scott was called back to the northern border to deal with the resurgent Patriots. Scott's departure meant the Cherokees were left to the mercy of the Georgians, leading to the Trail of Tears, during which more than 4,000 Cherokees died of exposure, disease, and starvation. Scott's journey from Canada to Georgia and back to Canada epitomized the Texas Moment on one level: the United States simply did not have enough troops to control its borders and the movement of peoples within them.[3] No wonder Cherokee leaders saw a chance to reclaim sovereignty in the West.

As I have discussed, the Mormon Council of Fifty saw the same opportunity, and they sent emissaries to the Cherokee Nation and to the greater US Indian Territory to find Native allies who would join them against the United

States. That the Mormons saw the Cherokees in such a light made sense: both groups were simultaneously *of* and *outside* American society and culture. The Mormons were white Americans whose religion made their loyalty suspect; the Cherokees were Natives whose predominantly mixed-race leaders had decided to wholeheartedly embrace American cultural, legal, and religious norms in the 1810s and early 1820s, but their race continued to make their loyalty suspect. Unlike the Mormons after the death of Joseph Smith, however, the Cherokees did not seek to entirely extricate themselves from the larger umbrella of US sovereignty. They still possessed influential white allies in the United States, and they and their allies had proven far better at navigating the halls of Congress than had Mormon emissaries like the flailing Orson Hyde. Indeed, their cause had been victorious at the Supreme Court in *Worcester v. Georgia*, although Andrew Jackson infamously refused to abide by the decision.[4] Moreover, the Cherokee elite also owned several thousand enslaved people, and this elite hoped to continue to practice plantation agriculture after removal. Rooted in the United States through politics and economics, the Cherokees had no need to look to California or Oregon: US Indian Territory would do just fine.

In the late 1830s, Indian Territory existed as an ill-defined political and legal anomaly, inhabited by roughly 100,000 Natives.[5] It was not a state; it was not an official US territory as stipulated under the Northwest Ordinance; and according to the 1835 Treaty of New Echota, which led to Cherokee removal, the Cherokee Nation would never be put under state or territorial jurisdiction. As the Committee of Indian Affairs stated in 1836, Indian Territory was fundamentally meant to be *"outside* of us, and in a place that will forever remain an *outside."*[6] Yet the Treaty of New Echota also allowed for the continued existence of Fort Gibson on Cherokee land and for the future erection of "military roads and forts" if the United States deemed them necessary.[7] In their new home, the Cherokees would be "protected from interruption and intrusion from the citizens of the United States," although how exactly this was to be accomplished—legally, politically, and militarily— remained unclear. The Cherokees were also entitled to a delegate to the House of Representatives. To make matters even more uncertain, John Ross and his allies—known as the Ross Party—who commanded the allegiance of a majority of the Cherokees, argued that this treaty was fraudulent and illegal. Ultimately, Indian Territory in general, and the Cherokee Nation more specifically, existed, in the words of one historian, as an ambiguous "military protectorate."[8]

The geopolitical ambiguity of Indian Territory does not fit neatly into the typical binary narrative of Native sovereignty in lands that would be claimed and conquered by the United States in the nineteenth century. The latter story sees Native sovereignty with a distinct before and after: before US conquest, in which Native sovereignty was absolute, and after US conquest, when Native sovereignty was effectively erased.[9] Thus, at least from this geopolitical perspective, the story of the Cherokees ended with removal. Yet just as white Americans living on and beyond US borders lived with an uncertain political future, in which the United States could but did not have to expand and the Republic of Texas or the Republic of Upper Canada could arise as a "sister republic," Native peoples living at the margins of the United States also lived with their own uncertain political future. The United States' power was just as sporadic and unimpressive when it came to Native peoples as it was for white Americans, and just because the Cherokees and other removed Natives were no longer entirely independent did not mean they were subservient. The range of sovereignty options between total independence and absolute obedience was vast—and, for more powerful Native peoples like the Cherokees, this range presented a window of opportunity, particularly if Indian Territory forever remained a borderland at the far edge of US territory.

From the perspective of the first half of the nineteenth century, there was nothing remarkable about the vague geopolitical parameters of Indian Territory, as the United States—or, for that matter, any European state—had not yet completed what one historian labeled "territorialization," the process of defining borders and the sovereign spaces within them.[10] If one looks for parallel political relationships that existed in US history at the time, the most appropriate was across the Atlantic Ocean. Like Indian Territory, the African American settlement of Liberia was a product of white Americans' "benevolent racism" of the 1810s and 1820s, which asserted that African Americans and Native people could become "civilized" by modeling themselves on US society, but this could not be done amid a white American population.[11] For black freedpeople, the solution was colonization; for "civilized" Natives, it was removal. Liberia and Indian Territory possessed many other geopolitical similarities. The Americanized inhabitants in both regions were unwelcome by the existing indigenous populations on their respective frontiers: the Comanches, Kiowas, and other "wild Indians" (as removed Natives termed them) on the western edge of Indian Territory, and the Dey, Grebo, Bassa, and Kru peoples that surrounded the small Liberian coastal settlement. Both projects were aided and, at times, directed by Anglo-American missionaries.

Both removed Natives and black Liberian settlers were simultaneously protected and supervised by the US military—the US Army in and around Indian Territory, the US Navy along the Liberian coastline. Like in Indian Territory, Liberia's legal and political situation remained uncertain, to such a degree that the British asked the United States to clarify if Liberia was an official possession in 1843.[12] The major difference between them, of course, was their geographical locations: Liberia was separated from the United States by the Atlantic Ocean, while Indian Territory was contiguous with the states of Arkansas and Missouri, and thousands of white settlers lived directly across this border. This difference would decide the fate of these two anomalous American territories.[13]

The Cherokee Nation and Liberia also shared a profound irony: even though it was white Americans who had forced the Cherokees and African Americans from US borders, once they arrived in their new homeland, both groups embraced many aspects of Anglo-American society and culture. Indeed, in some ways, the Cherokee Nation that the Ross Party hoped to create was the breakaway America most like the actual United States, for it did not model itself on an idealized—and largely fictional—version of the United States, but on the one that already existed. Once in the West, Cherokee leaders followed the lead of the US South, in particular white southern plantation owners: they further institutionalized slavery, further entrenched patriarchy, further integrated themselves into the market revolution, and embraced a system of vigilante justice. Crucial differences remained between the Cherokee Nation and the white southern plantocracy—particularly, the Cherokees' effective social safety net—yet these differences could not hide a profound truth. The reestablished Cherokee Nation in Indian Territory was more southern, and more thoroughly American, than anything that the Cherokees had created in the East.

To be clear: the Cherokees would never have defined themselves as Americans. No matter how Americanized their leaders were, they remained a Native nation and self-identified as Cherokees. Like the Mormons after 1845, the Cherokees—of any era—would have absolutely rejected such a moniker. But their leaders did not reject the American practices of plantation agriculture, slaveholding, Protestantism, republicanism, or the English language. Historically, therefore, the remade Cherokee Nation in the West was a breakaway America. Ironically, while the Cherokee Nation was a breakaway America, there were two Cherokee minority factions that were in fact breakaway Cherokee nations, both of which actually sought closer connections to the United

States. As a majority sought both further Americanization of their society and further independence from the United States, a second group longed for more US involvement and intervention. The Cherokee Nation itself was sundered by breakawayism.

Competing Understandings of the Cherokee Nation

Cherokee removal was in many ways a culmination of the many tragedies of the Cherokee people. They had done everything the United States had told them to do. Cherokee elites had adopted American political, social, and economic customs, and they and their white missionary allies supported this acculturation for the remaining majority of Cherokee society. They had allied with the United States against the Creeks during the War of 1812. Since then, they had remained at peace with neighboring whites, despite continuous harassment by both individual white settlers and Georgia's state government. Their cause had even achieved victory in the US Supreme Court. Ultimately, however, none of these achievements allowed the Cherokees to remain in their homeland, and the Trail of Tears killed 4,000 men, women, and children. Yet the tragedy was not over, for removal did not bring relief, as the Cherokees remained fundamentally divided over the Treaty of New Echota, which had ceded all Cherokee land in Georgia. The signers of the treaty, most notably Major Ridge, his son John Ridge, the *Cherokee Phoenix* editor Elias Boudinot, and Boudinot's brother Stand Watie, believed removal was inevitable, so they had signed the treaty, arguing that they had secured the best deal possible. However, John Ross and his supporters, representing a majority of the Cherokee people, still resisted removal and believed that the Treaty of New Echota was a fraudulent betrayal of both Cherokee sovereignty and majority rule, as stipulated in the 1827 Cherokee constitution. When they too were forced west by the terms of the treaty, they blamed the treaty signers. The stage was set for instability and violence in the western Cherokee Nation.

Once in Indian Territory, John Ross's supporters constituted two-thirds of the roughly 18,000 Cherokees who now resided in the nation. Countering the Ross Party (also known as the Patriot Party or the National Party) were 4,000 members of the Treaty Party or the Ridge-Boudinot Party, who had voluntarily left for the West several years before the Trail of Tears. Two thousand Old Settlers were a third faction. When a majority of Cherokees either embraced American norms in the 1810s and 1820s or at least acceded to the leadership of the Americanized elite, this faction had dissented. Hoping to avoid white encroachment and prevent acculturation to American society, they left for the West and became known as the Old Settlers.[14] Although they welcomed their fellow Cherokees as refugees, the Old Settlers feared losing political control of the Cherokee Nation now that the arriving Ross Party heavily outnumbered them. The Treaty Party, meanwhile, agreed to live under the continued governance of the Old Settlers, thus bringing those two parties together as allies against the Ross Party.

The divisions among these three factions were not based on social or religious differences—although they existed as well since the Cherokees were divided between a Protestant minority and a majority who either practiced traditional beliefs or syncretized them with Christianity.[15] Instead, the political rift over the Treaty of New Echota outweighed social differences, and Christians and traditionalists could be found on both sides of the Ross Party–Treaty Party divide. In general, the leaders of both sides possessed significant white ancestry (only one of John Ross's great-grandparents was fully ethnically Cherokee), spoke English as their predominant language, and were Protestant. These leaders were also the wealthiest of Cherokee society, and most owned slaves. By contrast, most of the traditionalist and largely poor Cherokee majority did not.

Underlying the divisions of race and class was the Cherokees' kinship system, which was based on seven matrilineal clans. Until the late eighteenth century, these clans organized the basic structure of Cherokee society, regulating family life, personal relations, marriage and incest (no person could marry within his or her clan), and homicide via the principle of blood revenge, or the "law of blood." If a clan member was killed by a person from another clan, the clan of the deceased was required to kill a member of the offending clan, regardless of whether or not the original death was purposeful. When the killing was carried out, harmony returned to both clans. Yet beginning in the 1780s, this law proved problematic as the Cherokees tried to enforce their borders, which were increasingly transgressed by white American encroachers, for it allowed clans to kill offending whites without any larger oversight. This action, in turn, enflamed other white Americans, putting Cherokee sovereignty fundamentally at risk. The Cherokees gradually curtailed blood revenge, first prohibiting it against white Americans in 1785, and then in 1810 against other Cherokees if the original death was accidental. This shift was part and parcel of Cherokee political centralization and the nation's movement away from a matrilineal kinship system to one based on patriarchal nuclear families. Nevertheless, clan identity and kinship were never fully abandoned, even if in national affairs these relationships retained only a secondary importance.[16]

In 1839, without John Ross's knowledge, his supporters murdered Major Ridge, John Ridge, and Elias Boudinot. The murderers justified their actions by invoking another facet of blood revenge, which held that any Cherokee who illegally sold tribal land could be punished with death by any "citizens of the Nation . . . in any manner most convenient, within the limits of this Nation, and shall not be held accountable for the same."[17] In practice, the law "had been [in] existence for many years," but it had also been officially passed by the government in 1829, thus surviving the transition from the traditional Cherokee Nation of the late eighteenth century to the Americanized one of the 1820s.[18] Indeed, the murders demonstrated that kinship continued to play a part in Cherokee society. In the secret meeting that was reportedly held to plan the killings, all seven Cherokee clans were represented, and members of all seven voted to carry out the law of blood.[19] These clan members also vowed that no one from the victims' clans would invoke blood revenge in the aftermath of the murders. Thus, while kinship still mattered in the Cherokee Nation, the politicization of the nation now mattered even more. The Cherokees' political divisions, not its clans, would define Cherokee history over the ensuing decades.

The murderers also targeted Boudinot's brother Stand Watie, but because he had not been home when they arrived at his door, Watie survived. Like the Ridges and Boudinot, Watie was Christian, multiracial, and a slaveowner, and his family ties and social position immediately made him the de facto leader of the Treaty Party after the deaths. He sent his murdered brother's family to safety in Connecticut and vowed to take revenge on the perpetrators. After the murders, political strife and endemic violence convulsed the Cherokee Nation, as the Ross Party fought the Treaty Party in a low-level civil war.

John Ross and Stand Watie, the leaders of the two parties, also demonstrated that the fault lines of this struggle were fundamentally political, for Ross and Watie possessed similar backgrounds and worldviews. Both men were of mixed-race ancestry, both came from influential Cherokee families, both were educated by white Protestant missionaries (Ross by Presbyterians, Watie by Moravians), both were slaveowners, and both assumed positions of leadership in the 1820s, although Ross wielded more influence. Ross became the most important Cherokee delegate in Washington due to his virtuoso understanding of US law and the Constitution, while Watie published articles in his brother's influential newspaper, the *Cherokee Phoenix*. In other circumstances, Ross and Watie might have been lifelong allies, yet Watie's support for the Treaty of New Echota permanently ruptured any potential collaboration. The two men led their irreconcilable sides against one another for the next three decades.

The stakes of the conflict between the Ross Party and the Treaty Party were, ostensibly, which faction would govern the Cherokee Nation, but at a deeper level the struggle revolved around just what type of sovereignty the Cherokees would possess as a "domestic dependent nation" within US borders, as Supreme Court justice John Marshall famously put it in *Cherokee Nation v. Georgia*.[20] The Treaty Party and the Old Settlers, as the minority factions, essentially emphasized the "domestic" and "dependent" in this formulation. They frequently employed rhetoric that they hoped would be well received among white US officials, who wanted little to do with an intra-Native conflict occurring at the margins of the United States. In 1839, for example, the Old Settlers wrote to US authorities that they were "thrown into the hands of the United States."[21] A few years later, the Treaty Party beseeched the federal government, "In the name of humanity turn us not away!"[22] To a significant degree, these words reflected reality: as they often admitted, the Treaty Party and their Old Settler allies needed the United States to sustain them, or they would be swamped by the numerical strength of the Ross Party.[23]

When there still seemed a chance that the Cherokees would be able to remain in the East, the Ross Party had used similar piteous and pleading language in order to cultivate white allies, deeming the Cherokees "weak and dependent" like an "unfortunate child."[24] Yet John Ross and his allies thoroughly abandoned this strategy after removal became a certainty. In a series of resolutions made at the Aquohee Camp in Tennessee, the final meeting of the Cherokees before undertaking the journey west, the Cherokee National Council forcefully maintained that, first, the Cherokees still possessed the rights to their land in the East; second, their removal was illegal; and third, Cherokee sovereignty was inviolable, and therefore the Treaty of New Echota was fraudulent. Furthermore, the United States was entirely to blame for removal, and thus "all damages and losses, direct or indirect, resulting from the enforcement of the alleged stipulations of the pretended treaty of New Echota, are in justice and equity, chargeable to the United States."[25] This newly assertive rhetoric demonstrated that Ross and his allies understood a crucial fact even before they left Georgia: location mattered. For the Ross

Party, removal was a colossal political defeat, but opportunity could be found in tragedy. They knew that once in remote Indian Territory, the United States' ability to force its will on the Cherokees would be significantly curtailed.

The assertions of sovereignty escalated even further once the Ross Party arrived in Indian Territory. When the United States tried to broker peace between the Cherokee factions, the Ross-led Cherokee National Council maintained that US interference was "utterly inappropriate and uncalled for . . . a violation of the rights and liberties of the Cherokees."[26] At times the Ross Party portrayed the United States and the Cherokee Nation as political equals in a manner more akin to international diplomacy than to relations between a supposedly conquered people and their conqueror: "We think it our duty to say plainly that no finessing to impose an unwelcome government on us will succeed. No intrigue to dismember our possessions for the reward of individuals will be tolerated by the Cherokees."[27] In the spring of 1846, in perhaps the most remarkable statement of Cherokee sovereignty, John Ross even defended the Ridge and Boudinot murders as entirely legal due to the law of blood, although Ross maintained his innocence in the proceedings.[28] And because the killings were legal, Ross suggested that the US government stop worrying about finding and prosecuting the murderers who, seven years later, remained at large. From a legal perspective, Ross may have been correct, but it was a stunning statement nonetheless, as most observers (both then and now) believed the murders were brutal and horrifying.

Many US authorities were stunned by the Ross Party rhetoric. Commissioner of Indian affairs Thomas Crawford protested that the Cherokees' assertions of sovereignty were "totally inconsistent with the supreme power of this nation." To Crawford, the Cherokees were no different than any other Indians, and thus, "the constitution and laws of the United States extend over all . . . and they must command obedience."[29] Indian agent Matthew Arbuckle was more succinct, writing, "The United States must and ought to dictate the terms [of peace to the Cherokees]."[30] Yet enforcing this perspective was a different matter for, unlike in Georgia, neither the US federal government nor any state government possessed a monopoly of force in Indian Territory. On the contrary, federal power was quite limited, although the United States had two forts within the Cherokee Nation. Fort Gibson was considered the most important fort in the West, yet it only housed several hundred troops, it remained dilapidated until 1845, and disease frequently plagued its soldiers.[31] In 1838 the US Army built Fort Wayne, but it was situated on swampy land that was soon perceived as disease-ridden, and it was rebuilt two years later in another location. Yet in 1842, this fort too was abandoned.[32] Clearly, amid thousands of potentially hostile Cherokees, the United States was not in a particularly strong military position. As commissioner of Indian affairs C. A. Harris bluntly acknowledged in 1838, "The present force which the United States has on that frontier is not sufficient to hold the Indians in check."[33] Moreover, small forts could be liabilities rather than assets, as observer Major Ethan Allen Hitchcock explained in 1842: "The presence of a garrison here [in the Cherokee Nation] has thus made and not found excitement and diffi-culty, and its continuance here will not have the slightest influence in pre-venting outrage in the future, but is calculated to invite it."[34]

The United States' limited power was not something federal authorities wanted to admit, but at times they could not hide the truth. In 1840, after several years during which John Ross had been able to fend off US attempts to depose him, Secretary of War Joel Poinsett lamented to Fort Gibson com-mander Matthew Arbuckle, "[the] Government regrets . . . [the] inability to carry into full effects the principles its desiring of establishing." To Poinsett, the future would be different, for the period had "arrived when the active interference of the government has become necessary."[35] Expanding on a plan first voiced by his predecessor Lewis Cass, Poinsett hoped to establish a line of forts along the United States' western border, all linked by a military road to facilitate easy transport. In theory, these forts would provide a check on all parties: Plains Indians bent on invading US territory through Indian Territory, removed Natives causing trouble in US borderlands, and white Americans preying on the vulnerabilities of removed Natives.[36] This view reflected a long-held belief that the United States' western border would become a permanent "Indian barrier."[37] Yet little came of Poinsett's vision. With US coffers empty due to the depression, the federal government built few forts and actually reduced the US Army by a third—and this army re-mained busy in Florida, where it was trying, and at first failing, to defeat the Seminoles.[38]

Unlike Washington officials, the white Americans who lived in or just out-side Indian Territory recognized the on-the-ground limits of federal power. Cherokee agents, in particular, knew firsthand that their authority was largely dependent on the goodwill of the Ross Party. Often given orders by higher authorities to curb John Ross's influence, they invariably responded that ei-ther they were powerless to do so, or if they did it would lead to disastrous consequences.[39] They even sympathized with Ross. Pierce Butler, Cherokee agent from 1840 to 1846, quickly came to the belief that Ross was a "modest and good man" privately, and "as a public man [he] has dignity and grace."[40] Not surprisingly, neighboring whites in Arkansas profoundly disagreed. Unlike the many white Americans in the rest of the country who viewed Cherokee removal as a problem finally solved, Arkansans believed that the federal government had simply moved the problem to their backyard. Indeed, they thought removal had made the problem worse, for now the Cherokees would want revenge. The *Arkansas Gazette*'s warning in 1839 was typical: "The policy of concentrating on our borders large bodies of armed and hostile Indians, smarting under a sense of recent injury, was generally supposed to be rather dangerous to the quiet of the frontier; and a war that may arise, will probably last as long and prove as expensive as the Florida war."[41] Moreover, the Cherokees' perceived status as the most "civilized Indians" was something to be feared, not applauded, for it rendered them particularly suited to forge an alliance with other Natives that would lead to a "common constitution" and "one state government."[42] The numbers involved in this alliance would be formidable: according to some estimates, the Cherokees possessed "4,000 fighting men" who could command "26,000 warriors" from other tribes, creating an intertribal alliance of anywhere from 72,000 to more than 100,000 Natives.[43]

Arkansans who cited these inflated numbers had a purpose: to obtain federal aid for the defense of the western frontier. They understood intuitively that a few hundred soldiers at Fort Gibson could not protect the long, defenseless Arkansas border, and they wanted the federal government to send more soldiers and build more forts.[44] Arkansas senator William Fulton hoped to create a buffer zone between Indian Territory and Arkansas by granting armed settlers free land on the frontier in return for their willingness to protect the state.[45] While the federal government would pass just such a proposal to protect Florida from the Seminoles (the 1842 Armed Occupation Act), nothing came of Fulton's desire for a similar policy for Arkansas.[46] Ignored by the United States, Arkansans responded by verbally lashing out. Asked the *Arkansas Intelligencer*, "What have the military done on this frontier during the few past years? Nothing. We do not want more troops to do nothing. But we want more troops to do something, to be actively employed. If we are not to have protection from the Army, we want it disbanded—the expense saved—and we will defend ourselves."[47] As Arkansans saw it, eastern politicians had spent federal funds to remove Native peoples from their own lands, but now, "secure from the apprehensions of midnight attack, and the startling war-whoop, savage yell, and nocturnal conflagrations," they refused to spend further money. They could not "imagine . . . the slumbering volcano upon which we repose."[48]

Much of this rhetoric was inflated and had a self-serving financial motive: federal soldiers and forts brought more federal dollars to the region.[49] It also reflected a long tradition of white Americans' obsession with Native violence—what historian Peter Silver termed the "anti-Indian sublime."[50] At no point did the Ross faction ever contemplate the Cherokees attacking white Americans wholesale or forging a vengeful alliance of Native peoples. But observers of the Cherokee Nation, like anti-Patriot Americans living along the northern border or anti-Mormons in Missouri and Illinois, believed that the Ross faction of the Cherokees were on the verge of creating a new political entity, perhaps only remotely under the umbrella of US sovereignty. The "volcano" of Cherokee power was neither as violent or hostile nor as imminent as Arkansans maintained, but the rhetoric did possess a certain degree of truth. John Ross and other Cherokee leaders *were* attempting to create a new quasi-independent polity: a sovereign republic with very real military, legal, and political power.

Reestablishing and Remaking the Cherokee Nation

It is tempting to read the Cherokee Nation in the early 1840s through the lens of the inevitability of US western expansion less than a decade later, which led to white Americans' encirclement and eventual dismemberment of Indian Territory. By the 1870s and 1880s, Natives who lived in Indian Territory were at the mercy of a federal government that could—and did—remove various facets of Native sovereignty on a whim. The post-removal Cherokee Nation, so this reading goes, was from its inception a postcolonial canton that existed neither within nor outside the United States.[51] Using the lens of the Texas Moment, however, requires not looking ahead to what became, but understanding the geopolitics of North America as they existed at the time. During this decade, the potential for a robust, regionally powerful Cherokee Nation—and, perhaps, a larger Indian Territory—that could wield effective sovereignty was quite good, as the Arkansans understood well. Federal officials believed that the land directly west of Indian Territory was unsuitable for settled agriculture, and thus the United States had little incentive to continue to push in that direction. On the contrary, to many federal officials, it made sense to keep Indian Territory reserved for Natives, for its presence reaped geopolitical advantages for the United States. It acted as a buffer between white Americans to the east and the Comanches and Kiowas to the west, a region that one 1841 map simply deemed "Hostile Ground."[52] Thus federal officials ensured that it would be removed Natives who would bear the brunt of Comanche and Kiowa incursions, which would hardly cause the same outrage among white Americans as it would if fellow white Americans were being attacked.

The Comanches and Kiowas were not the removed Natives' only problem. Another was the new independent republic to their south. Texas under President Mirabeau Lamar had little regard for Native sovereignty of any kind, even if Indian Territory was officially a part of the United States. As John Ross noted, Texas was "made up of many of the old foes of the Indians," who would undoubtedly cause trouble.[53] He was right: Texan forces crossed the US border with impunity, raiding into Indian Territory and at one point even being expelled by US soldiers.[54] To the Cherokees in the United States, the Texans were only a nuisance, for the Cherokee Nation did not share a border with Texas. However, to the much smaller group of Cherokees who had resided in Texas since the 1820s, Texan policies were disastrous (see below).

Compared to the governments of all of their neighbors—other removed Natives, Anglo-Americans, and Anglo-Texans—the apparatus of the Cherokee state was rather robust. Before they had been forced from their lands in the East, the Cherokees had created and extended various forms of centralized state power. These structures blended social services that were based on the connections and obligations of the Cherokees' traditional matrilineal kinship system with practices that followed US precedent, such as a constitution ratified in 1827 that echoed the US Constitution ("We, the Representatives of the Cherokee Nation, in order to establish justice, ensure tranquility, promote our common welfare, and secure to ourselves and our posterity the blessings of liberty"), a court system, and a police unit.[55] To be sure, the deaths, diseases, and social trauma of the Trail of Tears meant that this potential power was in tatters once the bulk of the Cherokees arrived in Indian Territory in 1839. However, the memory and institutionalization of such practices were there to be recalled, and state power could be brought back to the fore—and the Ross Party would do just that.[56]

The first and most visible manifestation of this power was military force. As violence escalated, Ross Party leaders restored the Cherokee Light Horse as the Cherokee Nation's police unit. The Light Horse had been formed in the late eighteenth century to patrol the borders of the Cherokee Nation and protect it from encroaching white settlers from Georgia, which enraged both distant white observers like Andrew Jackson and the would-be settlers themselves.[57] In the West, Ross Party leaders reorganized this unit into a body of 200 men, which was then split into eight squads of 25.[58] The Light Horse's job was ostensibly to enforce law and order in the Cherokee Nation, which included catching fugitive slaves, crushing potential rebellions of enslaved people, and arresting those inhabitants of the Cherokee Nation (both Cherokee and non-Cherokee) who broke Cherokee law. As John Ross explained to Brigadier General Zachary Taylor, who was in command of the portion of the US Army assigned to the western border, "[The Light Horse's] best efforts are still used to ferret out and bring [outlaws] to justice."[59] Here Ross echoed the arguments of countless American Whigs, who supported the creation of police companies in US society to enforce law and order. This similarity made ideological sense, for Ross and his allies possessed a generally Whiggish outlook, and they passed other state-building measures in the Cherokee Nation, including the creation of a national school system and social welfare services for orphans.[60]

However, Ross's defense of the Light Horse did not match the Light Horse's actual conduct. This body may have caught fugitive slaves and arrested lawbreakers, but it also harassed and intimidated Treaty Party members, at times arresting them without charge or making them flee across the border of the Cherokee Nation for self-preservation. What the Ross Party called law and order was to the Treaty Party "tyrannical power and oppression."[61] In response, they sought help from the federal government, but authorities like Cherokee agent Pierce Butler remained helpless in the face of the Ross Party's assertion of power. Butler and several other agents tried to broker a meeting between the leaders of the Ross Party and the Treaty Party, but when the agents arrived at the meeting place they were stunned to see Light Horse companies roaming the area, at which point they left in protest. Remonstrating against Ross Party leaders after the fact, the agents argued that "the display of these companies . . . was too well calculated to inspire the fears of the parties called together. . . . There is no doubt in our minds, that, in coming from distant parts of the Nation to this place on this occasion, the array of the Cherokee force has had a decided influence upon the minds of the complaining [i.e., the Treaty] party."[62] It was unsurprising, the agents noted, that no one from the Treaty Party showed up in the face of such intimidation.

Few documents exist that describe Light Horse actions in the words of the volunteers themselves, but those that do also suggest that this force took liberties with the law in order to defeat the Treaty Party. Light Horse colonel Ross Brown described how a Treaty Party man was "arrested by some young men (of the *police company*) on their own authority, without orders."[63] At another point, Treaty Party men killed the Ross Party leader Isaac Bushyhead, and in retaliation possibly 500 Ross Party men—several hundred more than the official number of Light Horse volunteers—scoured the country for the murderers.[64] At moments like these the Light Horse essentially transformed into a Ross Party army designed to crush Treaty Party resistance. Even when the Light Horse existed as it was supposed to, in eight groups of 25 men, it blurred the lines between a legal police force implementing law and order and a group of paramilitary vigilantes bent on achieving victory for the Ross Party. In this way, the Light Horse resembled the newly created Texas Rangers operating south of the border of Indian Territory, who frequently employed violence and broke the letter of the law in order to enforce its (supposed) spirit.[65]

Brown's description of the volunteers as "young men" points to some gendered aspects of the Light Horse, which epitomized the role of gender in the Cherokee Nation more generally. The rapid acculturation of the Cherokee elite to American customs and culture in the 1820s had altered the roles of both men and women in the Cherokee Nation. Gone was a culture that proved masculinity through martial prowess. In its place, Cherokee men proved their manliness by their education, acculturation to American norms, and property ownership. At the same time, the imposition of a constitution based on free male citizenship eroded the influence of Cherokee women, undermining matrilineal kinship, the importance of clans, and the town council government, all of which had given women a significant voice in Cherokee politics.[66] During the Trail of Tears, this powerlessness was augmented by trauma, as Cherokee women were frequently assaulted and sometimes raped by both white militiamen and traders.[67] The ordeals of Cherokee women in turn created a crisis of masculinity for Cherokee men, who were helpless to protect their families from brutality and humiliation.[68] Cherokee men's embrace of US law and American customs had backfired, for US law failed to prevent removal and then failed to prevent tragedy on the journey west. As one white missionary remembered, the migration to Indian Territory initiated a "year of spiritual darkness."[69]

Once in the West, however, the conflict between the Ross Party and the Treaty Party offered Cherokee men a chance to reassert the older, martial version of Cherokee masculinity of the pre-constitution era. Legally, the Ridges and Boudinot did deserve death.[70] The manner of death—extrajudicial murder by a band of armed Cherokee men rather than public execution following a guilty verdict in court—harked back to earlier decades when blood feuds were a key part of justice in the Cherokee Nation. The murders proclaimed to the Cherokee Nation that an older era had returned, one in which men would take the law into their own hands and enact the "right to vengeance," rather than have disputes adjudicated in an American-style courthouse.[71] To the murderers, the case had already been decided, as members of all seven clans had approved of the killings beforehand and willingly relinquished any right to blood revenge in their aftermath.[72] Although John Ross publicly deplored the murders, he at least tacitly accepted the violent actions of his followers. He never made an effort to uncover the perpetrators and at times explicitly defended their actions.[73] Moreover, the rapidity with which Cherokee men periodically congregated into armed bands following the more famous murders of the era (the Ridges and Boudinot, James Foreman, Isaac Bushyhead) suggests an eagerness to undertake—even perform—violence. Cherokee men asserted the entwined notions of vigilantism and honor that had taken root in the US South during the same era, in which men of local communities violently upheld their power irrespective of the law.[74] Certainly, too, the Cherokee Light Horse was never at a loss for volunteers, and the Cherokees asserted their military power far more aggressively in the West than they had done in the East.

Like the Ross Party, men of the Treaty Party also performed violence and thus asserted their masculinity. Stand Watie demonstrated the military leadership for which he would eventually become famous fighting with the Confederacy during the Civil War. At one point his Treaty Party soldiers gathered in defense at the abandoned Fort Wayne, vowing to avenge the deaths of his family. For a time, his followers renamed it "Fort Watie." At other moments his band acted as a guerrilla force, which attacked or intimidated Ross Party adherents and then fled for refuge across the Arkansas line.[75] These actions did not fit Watie's profile as a Moravian convert who had never previously committed violence. In the aftermath of the murders of his family, however, he was seen as a Robin Hood by his allies and as a bloodthirsty outlaw by his enemies. He even murdered one of his Ross Party nemeses, James Foreman, in cold blood. His Treaty Party allies invoked their masculinity explicitly, remarking that if they had to die at the hands of the Ross Party, they would "perish like men" in battle rather than be captured.[76] He did not need to choose this path. Instead, Watie and his band could have sought refuge in Fort Gibson and appealed to the US Army for protection as some of his Old Settler allies did.

The Light Horse also reflected the class dynamics of Cherokee society. Although no muster roll has survived to reveal who exactly volunteered, all evidence points to middle- and upper-middle-class Cherokee men, who were drawn from a population of the roughly 4,000 middling Cherokees (out of 18,000 total) who arrived in Indian Territory. The reason for this assumption is simple: while the Trail of Tears decimated all segments of the Cherokee population, it wreaked the most havoc on the traditionalist Cherokees who had practiced subsistence farming in the East and would resume doing so in the West. Unlike the wealthier mixed-race Cherokees, this mostly poor population simply did not have the means to weather the hardships encountered on the brutal journey, and those who reached Indian Territory alive remained impoverished.[77] For the next decade, they focused on simple survival. Moreover, it remains uncertain how the Light Horse was outfitted, but if, like the Texas Rangers, volunteers needed to supply their own horse and gun, then only middle- and upper-class Cherokee men could afford these expenses. If wealthy men like Lewis Ross, brother of John Ross and owner of the largest store in the Cherokee Nation, outfitted the Light Horse, then they would have been more willing to give supplies to those who ran in the same cultural and class circles.[78]

Beyond the entwined missions of enforcing law and order and subduing the Treaty Party, the Light Horse's class dynamic points to their third reason for existence: to act as a slave patrol. The Cherokees had forced approximately 3,000 enslaved black people to travel with them on the Trail of Tears, and while a majority of Cherokees did not own slaves, it had become an embedded practice among the Cherokee elite. In Indian Territory, roughly 300 Cherokee families, comprising 8 percent of the population, each owned between 25 and 100 slaves.[79] Slavery had to be violently enforced in the East, and it was the same in Indian Territory—even more so. Having witnessed the powerlessness of their owners during the removal process, many enslaved people decided to take advantage of the disorder of the Cherokee Nation to run away to any number of destinations that seemed to offer freedom—north to Kansas, west to California, or to other removed Natives.[80] Of the latter, the most welcoming were the Seminoles, who continued to harbor fugitive slaves in Indian Territory as they had done in Florida. Indeed, the significant number of free black Seminoles who settled in the West challenged Cherokee authority over their enslaved people by simply existing.[81]

In the face of these multiple avenues for resistance, the Cherokee National Council tasked the Cherokee Light Horse with ensuring that enslaved people remained enslaved. In 1841, the national council passed a law that authorized patrol companies to find and punish any enslaved person "strolling about . . . without a pass" and to identify any enslaved person who possessed weapons of any sort.[82] The passage of this law proved prescient, for only a year later people enslaved by the Cherokees mounted their strongest show of resistance yet, when somewhere between 21 and 200 enslaved people from several plantations imprisoned their owners, procured weapons and horses, and as a group fled to Texas. On their journey south, several of the runaways killed two slave catchers—one white, the other Delaware. In response, the Cherokee National Council paid Light Horse captain John Drew and a 100-man posse to capture them, which they did only seven miles from the Texas border.[83] Ultimately most of those who had escaped were returned to their owners, including a few to neighboring whites in Arkansas. Although the Ross Party and Arkansans were frequently at odds, in the case of enforcing black chattel slavery the two groups remained united.

The authorization of slave patrols was part of a much larger shift toward the racialization of the Cherokee Nation. Before removal, the multiracial Cherokee elites had already taken steps to self-consciously identify themselves as fundamentally separate from and biologically superior to all black people, but this trend accelerated in Indian Territory.[84] Upon arrival, Cherokee leaders established a written black code that was significantly stricter than anything that had been enforced in the East.[85] Free black people who had not been emancipated by their Cherokee owners had to leave the nation, while Cherokee owners who did emancipate their slaves were now held responsible if the newly freed misbehaved. While the education of enslaved people had been a common practice in the East, it now became prohibited in the West. The new Cherokee constitution of 1839 mandated that any resident who had a black or mulatto parent could not become a citizen, and it prohibited marriage between Cherokees and African Americans. A year later, the Cherokee National Council prohibited enslaved people from owning property.[86] These measures pointed toward the Cherokee Nation's increasing alignment with the racial policies of white southerners, who had increased the surveillance and regulation of African Americans, both enslaved and free, in the aftermath of Nat Turner's 1831 rebellion. By moving outside the borders of the white South, the Cherokee Nation had become more like it.

Of course, the southernization of the Cherokee Nation had begun years before removal, and it was precisely this development that had spurred the Old Settlers to move west. Yet in the East, this transformation had always been partial. Women's power stemming from the matrilineal kinship system was eroded, but not erased; slavery was further institutionalized, but enslaved people still possessed more rights and privileges than existed in most southern states. Once in the West, however, elite Cherokee men gained the opportunity to further southernize their nation, enshrining their own status at the expense of Cherokee women and enslaved African Americans. This trend was clear in the 1839 constitution, which mandated that only "free Cherokee male citizens" were eligible to be elected to the Cherokee National Council—thus making gender discrimination explicit more than two decades before the United States did in 1868 via the Fourteenth Amendment.[87]

While the Ross Party's attempt to create a patriarchal and slaveholding Cherokee republic echoed developments in the US South, two crucial differences remained. First, unlike white Georgians and Andrew Jackson, who had negated Cherokees' landholding based on their Native ethnicity, Cherokee leaders did not assert the same racial bias. White men could live and own land in the Cherokee Nation, marry Cherokee women, and even become Cherokee citizens. To the Ross Party, these men had "expatriated" themselves from the United States and thus were under the Cherokee Nation's jurisdiction (an issue that caused conflict with the United States, as I discuss below).[88] While this policy seemed to offer a back door to allow white Americans to infiltrate the Cherokee Nation and gradually obtain Cherokee land, the 1839 constitution provided the means to prevent this development. The very beginning of the constitution stated, "The lands of the Cherokee Nation shall remain common property." While the nation's individual citizens would own the improvements on the land, they "shall possess no right or power to dispose of their improvements, in any manner whatever, to the United States, individual States, or to individual citizens thereof."[89] With all inhabitants of the Cherokee Nation prevented from selling land, the nation would remain intact. Land would not be worked communally, but it would be owned communally, a remnant of the matrilineal Cherokee society that existed before the Cherokees' American acculturation. For Ross Party leaders, this practice would ensure the Cherokee Nation's permanent sovereignty.[90]

The second exception was Cherokee leaders' continued support for a series of social welfare services that significantly surpassed those of most US states, even the most reform-oriented ones in New England. As the historian Julie Reed documented, even during the height of the Ross Party–Treaty Party conflict, Cherokee leaders implemented a national education system and provided for the many orphans and disabled people living in the nation—

the preponderance of such groups yet another tragic legacy of the Trail of Tears.[91] Ultimately, then, John Ross and his allies' vision for the reestablished Cherokee Nation in the West blended the new and the old to create a unique republican experiment. Patriarchy, slaveholding, racial hierarchy, American culture, and—for the segment of young men who joined the Light Horse—vigilante justice were solidified and expanded. All of these were core aspects of southern society in the United States. Meanwhile, the practice of communal landholding and an expanded social welfare system were areas where the nation significantly broke with southern practices. The Cherokee Nation confronted an uncertain future as a novel Native polity on the United States' western border.

Just what the thousands of poor Cherokees, male and female, thought of this remade Cherokee Nation is difficult to determine. Constituting three-quarters of the Cherokee Nation, most of these men and women did not speak English and could not write in either Cherokee or English. Of course, even if they could, most were simply trying to survive the hardships of settling in a new land, without the labor of enslaved people that allowed the Cherokee elite to rapidly reestablish themselves upon arrival.[92] For years this population remained destitute, some even lacking the basic tools to undertake subsistence farming.[93] Judging by events of the late 1850s, when this class of Cherokees would assert themselves against the multiracial elite's continued attempts at southernizing the Cherokee Nation—in particular, the support for slaveholding—discontent may have simmered below the surface. Nevertheless, a substantial majority of poor Cherokees continued to support John Ross and his allies in the years following removal. One reason for this support is obvious: most Cherokees of all classes continued to blame the Treaty Party for removal, and many supported the Ridge and Boudinot murders as legally justified revenge. Added to this was the fact that Ross was a particularly skilled politician, to which his almost four decades (1828–1866) of serving as principal chief attest. Even his enemies in the United States reluctantly acknowledged his political talents. His popularity among the Cherokees was such that agent Pierce Butler noted that his arrest was impossible, for the entire Cherokee population would rise up in bloody revolt.[94]

It is also likely that Ross and his allies' attempts to further racialize and masculinize the Cherokee Nation helped maintain the support of poor Cherokee men. Mirroring similar social dynamics in the US South, most Cherokee men may have been poor and powerless when compared to the Cherokee elite, but they retained—and expanded—their prestige in relation to both enslaved black people and Cherokee women. Like poor southern whites, they supported a system that guaranteed them a place of social superiority, both at home with their wives and in the broader society when they came into contact with enslaved people, whether or not they owned any personally.[95] Thus, the ideological parameters of the remade Cherokee Nation entrenched the power of Cherokee men. Most may have been impoverished patriarchs, but they were patriarchs nonetheless.

By 1845, due to both popular support and the effective use of the Light Horse, the Ross Party was on the verge of victory over the Treaty Party. While the Light Horse's power was never overwhelming, after several years it had worn down the ability of Treaty Party partisans to resist. As one Treaty Party member described to Stand Watie, "The Ross party are out and adoing. They state that their intentions are to make every sacrifice of every respectable citizen belonging to the Old Settlers & Treaty Party they may fall in with and their Police parties are all the time on the alert and doing mischief of considerable magnitude." The writer then described how 150 Treaty Party men, women, and children had sought refuge across the Missouri state line, where they relied on the US Army's rations to prevent starvation.[96] Over the previous months, the Light Horse had successfully stormed one Treaty Party fort, which then caused the Treaty Party to abandon a second one. While Arkansas and Missouri continued to offer Treaty Party members safe havens, this would only stave off defeat for so long. One Treaty Party member wrote to Watie, who at the time was in Washington desperately seeking federal support, that he needed to obtain this aid at all costs, or "there is no telling what the consequences might be."[97]

By this time, the Ross Party had grown even bolder in its defiance of US officials. The party had been temporarily bolstered by an 1844 US commission that for the first (and only) time sided with the Ross Party against the Treaty Party as to who bore primary responsibility for the violence. When officials requested that Ross disband the Light Horse, he replied that the Cherokees had every right to police their own land.[98] In fact, he countered, it was the US Army that ought to leave the Cherokee Nation—a request he had long made privately to Cherokee agents, but in 1845 became a public outcry.[99] That year, a Cherokee man got into a drunken brawl with several US soldiers, and the soldiers reacted by assaulting the man's family.[100] In response, the Ross Party held a public meeting that issued a series of resolutions condemning the army's presence and demanding that Fort Gibson be abandoned. This was no small request, as Fort Gibson was the preeminent fort of the western frontier. Clearly, the Ross Party was confident in its ability to defeat the Treaty Party—and, by extension, stand against the United States. It remained to be seen whether the United States would—or even could—counter the Ross Party's increasingly strident moves toward independent sovereignty.

The Geopolitical Opportunities of Indian Territory

The Cherokees' journey to Indian Territory in the late 1830s was unique in its compulsory nature (during the Jacksonian era, no other Native tribe was forced into concentration camps and literally moved at gunpoint, although other Natives would suffer similar treatment in later decades) and its appalling mortality rate, but it was not novel in regard to the overall process of migration among the Cherokee people. For decades, groups of Cherokees had chosen to leave the borders of the Cherokee Nation in the East for various locales in the American West.[101] The first migration occurred in the early nineteenth century, when the group that would become the Old Settlers traveled west. However, once in the West, pressure from both migrating whites and hostile Osages triggered some of these Cherokees to migrate again. Led by a Cherokee chief named Duwali, this group of roughly 300 traveled south to the Red River valley in Mexican Texas, where they joined other migrant Natives— Shawnees, Chickasaws, Choctaws, Kickapoos, Creeks, and Seminoles—in a loose confederacy. Cherokee migrants continued to join this group over the next decade, increasing their number to 800.[102] Unfortunately, the Indian-hating president of Texas, Mirabeau Lamar, sought their extermination, and after defeat at the hands of the Texans in 1839 most of the Texas Cherokees fled to US Indian Territory.

With this history of migration and resettlement, it is not surprising that at various points in the removal process, Ross Party leaders contemplated moving somewhere else besides US Indian Territory. In 1835, a few years prior to removal, Ross attempted to contact the Mexican government, hoping Mexican authorities would allow the Cherokees to settle within their borders.[103] The Mexican government never seems to have responded, and nothing came of this. Perhaps this Mexican precedent was what John Ross's brother Lewis had in mind when he pondered in early 1838, as the removal process began, whether "it may be possible that we may find a Country out of the United States which we may live in."[104] This discussion continued intermittently after the Cherokees arrived in Indian Territory. In 1841 rumors arose among both Cherokees and non-Cherokees that it was Ross's "design to cross the Rocky Mountains."[105] As already mentioned, Mormon leaders certainly hoped this would be the case, for they wanted to join with Natives against the United States. Moreover, the federal government did not possess the means to prevent a Cherokee exodus—nor, perhaps, did it possess the inclination. After all, many white Arkansans would have been overjoyed to see the Cherokee "threat" disappear from their border, although some of the more perceptive authorities recognized that the Cherokees, along with other removed Natives, provided a buffer between the Comanches and the US western frontier.[106]

After removal, some Cherokees revived the idea of migrating to Mexico, which was a much for feasible journey from Indian Territory than it had been from the Cherokee Nation in the East. This time, however, the idea arose not with Ross Party leaders, but among Cherokees opposed to the Ross Party's dominance, in particular Chief John Brown. Brown was a recalcitrant Old Settler who refused to come to an agreement with the Ross Party, and he hoped to lead an exodus of Old Settlers to Mexico. He even contacted Mexican officials and found them receptive. Once in Mexico, he hoped, the Old Settlers would join with the small numbers of Texas Cherokees who had fled Texan aggression by going south rather than following the majority north to US Indian Territory. Unfortunately for Brown, few Old Settlers were interested, although one of these was the eminent Sequoyah, creator of the Cherokee alphabet. In 1843, Sequoyah sought out the small Cherokee band in Mexico to try to reunite them with the rest of their people, but he died upon his arrival. Nevertheless, his fame meant that the Mexican possibility soon became widely known among the Cherokees in US Indian Territory.[107]

Yet most Cherokee leaders from both the Ross Party and the Treaty Party ignored the proposed migration completely, despite the Treaty Party having considered it prior to removal. These elites believed that the path to prosperity lay with slaveholding and market access. While the Cherokees could not grow substantial amounts of cotton in Indian Territory (the region was slightly too far north), they could still raise lucrative crops via slave labor—wheat, corn, tobacco, and hemp—which would then be sent to the Mississippi River via the Arkansas River. This trade quickly created a booming riverboat operation. Some wealthy Cherokees, like Lewis Ross, opened prosperous mercantile businesses to cater to elite needs, while others became steamboat owners to capitalize on the growing river trade, adapting slave labor to the new needs of the economy in Indian Territory. No wonder, then, that Cherokee leaders possessed little desire to move to the northern reaches of Mexico, where the market was more distant and slavery was prohibited. Moreover, the removal process itself had taught these elites that any further migration would put their slaveholding in peril, for significant numbers of enslaved people were able to use the chaos of the journey to escape bondage.[108] While some Cherokees who resisted American acculturation had willingly migrated to Arkansas, Texas, and Mexico, Cherokee slaveholders were, as one pro-Cherokee writer to the *Arkansas Gazette* put it, "anchored by their interests" and would remain in Indian Territory.[109]

The economics of slave labor were not the only reason that Indian Territory seemed the best option. As a geopolitical space, Indian Territory also had much to offer. As I have mentioned, it existed at the margins of US control, which would allow the Ross Party to assert power—not just in the Cherokee Nation against the Treaty Party, but beyond the Cherokee Nation's borders. These other regions were, first, its eastern border with the United States, which needed to be secured from any white encroachment; second, Indian Territory's western and southern borders, which abutted the territories of the Comanches and Kiowas; and third, the border with Texas. Securing these boundaries meant erasing another set of borders: the physical and ideological borders between the various removed Natives of Indian Territory.

For the Ross Party, the Cherokees' border with Arkansas was a cause of daily concern, which was a feeling many white Arkansans shared. The border assumed such importance that both Cherokees and Arkansans simply deemed it "the line."[110] The term unintentionally highlighted the major issue: not based on any geographic barrier, this border was nothing more than an imaginary line, allowing both Cherokees and whites to cross with ease. Legally, however, this imaginary line mattered a great deal, for it created two entirely different jurisdictions, which led to an unsustainable legal situation.[111]

Initial problems arose over the issue of alcohol. Both the federal government and the Cherokee Nation prohibited selling alcohol in Indian Territory, but Arkansans easily avoided the restriction by setting up "grog shops" that straddled the line.[112] On the Arkansas side, merchants distilled whiskey, which was then brought into Indian Territory via pipes, thus avoiding the illegality of selling whiskey on a technicality. Presumably, Cherokee consumers handed over money to the distiller in Arkansas and then received the whiskey in the Cherokee Nation, thereby separating money from product and allowing distillers to claim that no whiskey was ever sold in the Cherokee Nation. While the situation may have been absurd, it also demonstrated the very real legal power of the line, for neither Cherokee authorities nor US soldiers at Fort Gibson felt they had the right to shut down the shops directly. Without the ability to stop whiskey sales, alcohol continued to devastate portions of the

Cherokee population, particularly those who remained destitute in the aftermath of removal.[113]

Beyond the problem of alcohol, the line potentially represented a crucial legal discrepancy over the meaning of citizenship in the United States and its relationship to citizenship in the Cherokee Nation. In 1841 the US Congress passed a law stating that the United States possessed jurisdiction over the Cherokee Nation and other polities of Indian Territory, with the exception of crimes of one Native person against another. The parameters of this law were put to the test in 1845, when the United States brought William Rogers to trial for the murder of Jacob Nicholson.[114] Although they were both white, Rogers and Nicholson had lived in the Cherokee Nation for years, and each had married a Cherokee woman. Rogers argued that the court had no jurisdiction over him, for both he and Nicholson had assumed the mantle of Cherokee citizenship, meaning that Rogers's trial should be held in the Cherokee Nation. To Judge Ben Johnson of the Arkansas District Court in Little Rock, this argument was persuasive. A few days earlier, Johnson had ruled in a similar case that a white counterfeiter who had moved to the Cherokee Nation and married a Cherokee woman could not be brought to US court, for he had "expatriated" himself years ago.[115] Unluckily for Rogers, however, Supreme Court justice Peter Daniel was making the rounds for appellate cases and was also present in Little Rock at the time. Daniel disagreed with Johnson, arguing that it was not the Cherokee Nation's decision whether or not Rogers was a Cherokee citizen. It was the decision of the United States: if federal authorities wanted to try Rogers, they had the right to do so. The two judges' disagreement meant that no verdict was rendered, and the case automatically went to the Supreme Court.[116]

Both the Cherokees and neighboring whites recognized the implications of this case, and unsurprisingly they came down on different sides of the issue. For the *Cherokee Advocate*, the Ross Party organ and lone newspaper of the Cherokee Nation, if the Supreme Court ruled against Rogers, then "bad disposed whites" who resided in the Cherokee Nation would break the law with "impunity," understanding that the Cherokee Nation no longer had the right to put them on trial.[117] This decision would create "disastrous consequences" as Cherokee authority on the ground would become hollow.[118] To the editor of the *Arkansas Gazette*, however, the Cherokee Nation's attempt to try "expatriated" whites was absurd, for it was not a "foreign, independent nation." If the court ruled for Rogers, then "it would be an encouragement for our worthless citizens to harbor among [the Cherokees], for the purpose of freeing themselves of the rigor of law of the United States."[119]

That both sides used the term "expatriation" was revealing. The word harked back to discussions over Americans leaving US borders for Texas in the 1820s and 1830s and for Canada in the late 1830s. As the US Circuit Court asked the US Supreme Court, did becoming a citizen of the Cherokee Nation entail transferring allegiance away from the United States to another "government, State, or community"?[120] The failure of the circuit court to even define the status of the Cherokee Nation—was it a "government," a "State," a "community," or something else?—reflected the Cherokee Nation's geopolitical ambiguity. No wonder the *Rogers* case was so important to both sides.[121] If the Cherokee Nation possessed jurisdiction over Cherokees only, then whites possessed effective immunity, and Cherokee sovereignty was minimal. If, on the other hand, the Cherokee Nation possessed jurisdiction over all of its inhabitants, then it could potentially wield substantial local legal, political, and military power.

The case also had demographic implications. Many Native peoples had long histories of adopting nontribal members—of any background or race, including white—into their tribe, and the Cherokees were no exception. But was adoption the same as naturalization? If so, then the Cherokee Nation and other removed Native peoples could augment their population—and power—through adopting not just other Natives, but white Americans, who would then fall under the jurisdiction of not the United States but the Cherokee Nation. Certainly, the Cherokees believed that, at least from a legal perspective, adoption equated to naturalization. William Rogers and Jacob Nicholson may have been ethnically white, but they were Cherokee by history, custom, and law. While at the moment this question would hardly change local demographics, the implications for the future were substantial. After all, north of the Cherokee Nation, thousands of Mormons were searching for similar legal protections, although they knew nothing of this specific case.

The *Arkansas Gazette*'s fear that the Cherokee Nation would become a haven for white criminals could not have been more wrong: it was not "worthless [American] citizens" in the Cherokee Nation, but Cherokee outlaws and their white allies in Arkansas who caused the major problems on the line. Arkansas, not the Cherokee Nation, was the criminal haven. The Cherokee Nation's court system was sophisticated and effective, and the Light Horse successfully enforced the law within Cherokee borders.[122] Over the line, however, both of these institutions were powerless, thus allowing suspected outlaws to use Arkansas as a refuge. At first, most of these outlaws were petty criminals, but as Cherokee violence escalated to a low-level civil war in the early 1840s, Arkansas became a shelter for the Ross Party's enemies, including political refugees like Stand Watie's guerrilla band and genuine criminals like the infamous Starr Gang.[123] Because the Cherokee Light Horse could not pursue its enemies over the line, Watie and his allies were able to continue and escalate their opposition to Ross and his allies, even though they possessed fewer numbers and resources. Without the line, either there would not have been a Cherokee civil war or the Ross Party would have won it in its first year.

There was even greater ambiguity when it came to the Cherokee Nation's southern and western borders, which abutted the other polities of Indian Territory. Were the borders within Indian Territory as hard as the border of Indian Territory with the United States? Could a Cherokee expatriate himself to, say, the Choctaw Nation, or a Choctaw to the Cherokee Nation? No one knew the answer. Also ambiguous was the relationship between removed Natives and what they termed the "wild Indians" farther west, such as the Comanches, Wichitas, and Kiowas. These nomadic peoples of the Great Plains raided the lands of removed Indians for material goods and slaves, and deemed them effete for their sedentary lifestyle and acculturation to American norms. At the same time, they were willing to trade with removed Natives and treat with them under the right circumstances, and thus their relations with Indian Territory mirrored their relations with Mexican, American, and Texas settlements in the Southwest. For their part, removed Natives believed that people like the Comanches were savage, heathen, and violent, but nonetheless traded with them when it suited their interests.[124]

The solution to both of these ambiguities was the Native council. The council had long been a practice of Native diplomacy, but it was not until 1837 that removed Natives employed the custom in their post-removal lands in the West. The men who called these councils sought to reestablish ties among removed tribes that had once existed in the East, while also creating diplomatic openings that would solve the incursion of the Plains Natives to the west. In general, councils held in eastern Indian Territory prioritized the former, while those held in western Indian Territory, in close proximity to the Plains tribes, emphasized the latter. It was the Old Settler faction of the Cherokee Nation that initiated the first intertribal council in 1837, and subsequently the Cherokees continued to attend them. As one of the two most populous removed tribes (the Creeks were the other) and seen—by themselves and others—as the most "civilized" tribe by other removed Natives, their leadership and participation were crucial to any council's success.[125]

Thus, when John Ross called for a Native council in 1843, he was building on both a short history of councils in Indian Territory and a longer tradition that dated deep into the Native past.[126] As in prior councils held in Indian Territory, Ross hoped to unify removed Natives by adopting "international laws" that they could all follow, such as a settlement of boundaries, the extradition of criminals, and establishing parameters on trade.[127] Unlike previous councils, Ross gave little attention to the Plains Natives to the west. This council faced East, not West; it was designed to focus on the relationships among removed Natives and, in turn, their collective relationship with the United States. Perhaps, too, it was an attempt by Ross to elevate his reputation in wider Indian Territory and restore his credibility among some Cherokees, for he had recently failed to secure a more favorable financial settlement with the United States than the one dictated in the Treaty of New Echota.[128] Ross and several other Cherokee leaders convened with Creek chief Roley McIntosh in January 1843 in a meeting facilitated by Cherokee agent Pierce Butler. Butler's presence attests to the peaceful intention of the proposed council—although, as usual, neighboring whites in Arkansas assumed the council's intentions were hostile.[129] After a preliminary discussion, Ross and McIntosh invited twenty-one other removed tribes to convene at the Cherokee capital of Tahlequah in June.

Their proposal found a ready reception. Between 3,000 and 4,000 Natives representing eighteen tribes attended the Great or International Council, which lasted for more than four weeks.[130] Following historical Native practices of treaty making, the tribes first engaged in rituals of gift giving and smoking of the calumet, thereby establishing trust and providing for the renewal of ties that had once existed in the East. In general, the Cherokees and the Creeks took the lead in the proceedings, as both Ross and McIntosh gave extended speeches explaining their reasons for holding the council. Missionary William Goode observed the proceedings, and he described how each speech proceeded with "deliberate slowness," for the speaker needed to pause after every sentence to allow his words to be translated into multiple Native languages. Goode may have found this tedious, but it allowed him to record each speech verbatim for posterity.[131] In Goode's assessment, every speech covered the same topics: "[the Natives'] lingering love for their former homes, respect for their ancestry, a cautiously expressed sense of the injustice done

John Mix Stanley, *International Indian Council (Held at Tallequah, Indian Territory, in 1843)* (1843). This painting of the Great Council argues for the continuing influence and power of removed Natives, while also revealing, in the isolated figure of Zachary Taylor at the center, the seeming irrelevance of US power in the West. Accession number 1985.66.248,934B, Smithsonian American Art Museum, gift of the Misses Henry.

them by their removal, a reluctant resignation to their fate, and a desire to cultivate the arts of peace and to provide for their offspring."[132] Goode's transcriptions of the Native speeches certainly support his assessment, for these common themes arose again and again, with good reason: seeking to open up intertribal dialogue, the speeches were purposefully weighted toward generalities.

Yet Goode had a blind spot. Contrary to his assertions about the attendees' repetitive expressions of "reluctant resignation" and nostalgia, his transcriptions provide evidence for much more provocative statements that pushed the rhetorical boundaries of Native sovereignty. In a preamble to eight concluding resolutions, the council stated that the "lands we now possess shall be the undisturbed homes of ourselves and our posterity forever."[133] Even more remarkable than this assertion of sovereignty was another resolution that stated: "We hereby solemnly pledge to each other, that no Nation, party to this compact, shall, without the consent of all other parties, cede, or in any manner alienate, to the United States, any part of their present territory."[134] Here the Cherokee National Council's law of communal landholdings was confirmed by other tribes, many of which also held similar notions of shared property. Just as the Cherokee law prevented any individual Cherokee from selling his land to a white intruder, now no tribe could cede land to the United States or any other entity without the authorization of all other removed Natives, thus providing a powerful check against any individual tribe that looked for immediate financial gain over long-term Native autonomy. In the future, the United States would have to deal with Indian Territory as a unified polity and with removed Natives as a unified people. The Cherokees knew all too well how important unity was, for it was the removal of their Creek, Choctaw, and Chickasaw neighbors that proved a key turning point on the road to Cherokee removal. Once their neighbors were gone, the Cherokees became isolated and were more easily preyed on by covetous whites.[135] Also remarkable, if more vague, was Ross's statement that he had pursued relationships with many more Native peoples to the north and the south, demonstrating a considerably broader geographic scope than the already noteworthy assemblage at the Great Council.[136]

In pledging its participants' collective refusal to sell land to the United States, the Great Council echoed a famed moment of pan-Indianism from an earlier era. In the early 1810s, the Shawnee leader Tecumseh and his brother the prophet Tenskwatawa had forged a Native alliance among tribes of the Old Northwest and had inspired similar resistance in the South, particularly among a faction of the Creeks known as the Red Sticks. Key to the brothers' influence was their message that Native land cessions to the United States were a betrayal of all Native people. This was stressed to such an extent that at first the brothers criticized these seeming Native allies of the United States more than the United States itself.[137] In 1811 Tecumseh traveled south and addressed the Creeks directly, with some Cherokees in attendance. Thus, thirty years later, there were almost certainly Creeks and Cherokees living in the West who had once heard Tecumseh speak, although whether they attended the council or possessed any influence is impossible to determine.[138] Neither Ross, Roley McIntosh, nor any other leader at the Great Council invoked Tecumseh or Tenskwatawa by name, which made sense for two reasons. First, invoking these names would have alarmed any attending US delegates; and second, it was Americanized Cherokees—like the Ross Party leaders—who had been the most skeptical of Tecumseh's message decades before, as they instead had hoped to preserve Cherokee independence through their embrace of American culture and institutions. Nevertheless, even without naming Tecumseh, their emphasis on a collective Native refusal to cede land demonstrated that the Great Council's purpose was not simply to foment goodwill between tribes, but to inspire resistance to any further US encroachment.

As the missionary William Goode recorded the proceedings, John Mix Stanley sketched. Stanley was a painter from New York who had decided in 1839 that his ticket to prosperity lay in painting Indians. In 1842 he set up a studio at Fort Gibson, and in 1843 he traveled with Pierce Butler to the Great Council. From his sketches and perhaps his daguerreotypes, he eventually produced the painting *International Indian Council*, which offers in a visual medium what Goode supplied in words. In the foreground of the painting, about a dozen Native men, all wearing different clothes and holding different positions, are engaged in various discussions. Beyond them are scores of other Native people: their faces are less clear, but their heads extend beyond the confines of the large, open-air building that housed the council proceedings. The scene exudes both vibrancy and seriousness. This is not a "vanishing race," but a respectable, numerous, and dynamic people planning for the future. Most telling is the lone non-Native figure in the painting: Zachary Taylor, who, as the commander of the western frontier, also attended the council. He stands in the center of the proceedings alone—and thoroughly ignored. Taylor, scowling, with his right hand at his waist, seems displeased with this state of affairs, but no Native cares. The message is clear: the United States retained a presence in Indian Territory but little more.

There are more signs that Ross and his allies intended that the Great Council would mean something different than prior councils. The location of the gathering was significant. Tahlequah was no compromise meeting point or neutral ground, but the Cherokee Nation's capital and the site of the Cherokee National Council. By successfully bringing many other tribes to the Cherokee Nation, Ross and the Cherokees asserted their preeminence among removed Natives. Indeed, Goode reported that after the council's end, "some of the tribes spent three months or more in going, staying, and returning."[139] Tahlequah had become, for all intents and purposes, the capital of not just the Cherokee Nation but Indian Territory, if only for a brief period of time. Moreover, at the conclusion of the council, some "wild" Cherokees engaged in a dance that gave Goode a "shivering sense of horror," startling him after what had been a Sunday of "good order" that demonstrated respect for the Christian Sabbath.[140] As Goode explained, this behavior simply was not normal: the Cherokee National Council never ended their meetings with dances. This council, however, "had brought together an assemblage of spectators too large and too rude to submit to control."[141] Combined with the provocative resolutions and the choice of meeting place, the dances demonstrated an assertion of Cherokee power and a bid for Cherokee leadership of the region's Native peoples.

Yet while Ross succeeded in convening the Great Council and asserting Cherokee power, he was much less successful in its outcome. Whatever the goodwill among all the Natives who attended, only three tribes ultimately signed the provocative Great Council resolutions: the Cherokees, the Creeks, and the Osages.[142] The Cherokees and Creeks were the two most populous and powerful of the removed tribes, and the lack of signatories to the resolutions demonstrated some of the dilemmas of the different Native peoples. Less populous tribes that attended the council, such as the Pottawatomies, were significantly more dependent on the US government and took seriously the warnings of both US officials and American missionaries to avoid signing such a provocative document. They also did not want to cede the little autonomy they still possessed to their much more populous Native neighbors.[143] In contrast, the Cherokees and Creeks had large enough populations—and therefore potential military power—that they could sign such bold statements, understanding that the United States would not (and could not afford to) intervene over provocative language alone.

From one perspective, Ross's inability to facilitate the greater political unity of Indian Territory demonstrated that the Great Council was a failure. In future dealings with the United States, removed Natives would not present a united front as he and Creek chief Roley McIntosh had planned. Yet this assessment is only true in hindsight, with US expansion assumed. By 1848, Indian Territory had become a curious internal autonomous polity surrounded by official US territory and—soon—Anglo-American citizens, mirroring the situation of the Cherokee Nation in the East before removal. But from the perspective of 1843, this picture changes. That eighteen tribes and up to 4,000 Natives responded to Ross's overtures had shown that Cherokee diplomacy and his personal influence carried great weight in the West, for these numbers were far higher than had attended prior councils. All Ross and his allies needed was time. With time, Indian Territory could be united into an effective polity of 100,000 Natives with effective courts, a powerful police force, and a robust slave-based economy, with goods traded with white Americans to the east and Plains Natives to the west. As it appeared in 1843, the Great Council was a remarkable success, for it was a first step on the road toward this larger Native confederacy, which would maintain its sovereignty on the western edge of US territory—in the words of the council—"forever."

CHAPTER FIVE

The Seigneurial Republic of California

The Mormons were not the only Anglo-American contingent that sought to seize a portion of Mexican Alta California in the spring of 1846. In June of that year, thirty-three Anglo-American men captured the sleepy frontier town of Sonoma in what has become known as the Bear Flag Revolt. Although few in number, the Bear Flaggers' deeds have since become lore among Americans, Californians in particular, and the revolt has been given at least a cursory description in most US history textbooks. From the perspective of historical accomplishment, this attention makes little sense. The Bear Flaggers captured a single, tiny frontier town; they did not fight a single significant battle; and their military struggle and the cause of the Bear Flag Republic were quickly subsumed by the United States. The Bear Flaggers learned in early July that the United States had declared war on Mexico, making their republic immediately defunct.

That the Bear Flag Revolt continues to live in historical lore stems from a combination of three factors. First, something about the bear flag itself has clearly charmed the public, as the apparel one can purchase in California airports makes clear. Indeed, when late nineteenth-century historian Hubert Howe Bancroft and his aides interviewed former Bear Flaggers in the 1870s and 1880s, they spent more time asking about what the Bear Flag looked like than what actually happened.[1] Second, the Bear Flag has provided California and its millions of inhabitants—particularly Anglo-Californian inhabitants—with a romantic founding narrative that helps bring the state's history to the level of Texas. The Bear Flag Revolt was no Alamo or San Jacinto, but it was at least *something*.[2] Third and most important, the event solidifies the typical portrayal of Manifest Destiny, in which grasping white Americans asserted their power on behalf of the United States and the Anglo-Saxon racial order.

Indeed, the Bear Flag Revolt is Manifest Destiny on overdrive. In Texas, Americans took a decade to revolt against Mexico and another decade to join the United States. In California, Americans took only a few years—and for some Bear Flaggers, only a few months—to revolt against Mexico and only a month to join the United States.

Yet to most Americans who traveled overland to California in the early 1840s, the United States' conquest of California hardly appeared destined. On the contrary, compared to Texas, Oregon, and perhaps even Canada, it was the least publicized and least enticing target for US expansion, which is why only a few thousand Americans made the difficult overland journey. For these Americans, California did entice, but not because it was ripe for US conquest. Rather, the American men who traveled to California were drawn to the accounts of life there, in particular those of the elite Californios who governed vast ranchos and oversaw the countless dependents who lived on them. These patriarchs lived lives of seeming ease and simplicity, apparently without the toil of individual work and without the moral baggage of plantation slavery. California, in essence, offered a vision of an idyllic seigneurial life that did not exist in the United States. When American overlanders arrived in California, they were quite willing to cooperate with the Californios, so long as they could achieve the same social and economic status. Thus, the Bear Flag Revolt was not a culmination of Anglo-American migration, but a disruption.

Alta California before the American Overlanders

In the mid-1830s, Alta California remained a remote and economically marginal region of Mexico, a status largely unchanged since the first Spanish settlement in California in 1769. The vast territory had approximately 5,500 Californios living on the coast between San Diego in the South and Sonoma in the North, and there were tens of thousands of unconquered Natives in the interior—an interior that stretched as far east as the Salt Lake Valley, at least officially. Most of the Californios were mestizo descendants of Spanish soldiers and Native women.[3] Their lives revolved around raising livestock on ranchos: these vast estates were once part of the California mission system and had only been secularized in the 1820s and early 1830s. Californio society was family-oriented, hierarchical, and traditional; one scholar labeled it a "seigneurial" system, and I also use that term.[4] At the top were the dons, a class that dominated California's social and political world in a manner reminiscent of feudal lords. At the apex of a patriarchal pyramid, these men ruled over many dependents, which included their wives and children, middling Californios, and dozens or even hundreds of Native laborers effectively bound to the rancho. Numbering around fifty, elite Californios controlled California's local politics and the regional economy.[5] Almost all of these families were related to one another by either intermarriage or godparentage. Thus, while Californios frequently quarreled with one another and at times went to war against each other, these conflicts rarely resulted in significant violence, for they did not want to be responsible for the deaths of their own extended family members.[6]

Below these dons was a middling class composed of smaller rancho owners and those who rented land from the dons. Both upper and middling Californios relied on former mission Natives to provide the bulk of the rancho labor force, paying them in food, clothing, and perhaps a few cattle hides. In the feudalistic society of the Californios, Natives were the serfs. Although most Californios were mestizos, possessing significant Native ancestry, they drew a clear distinction between themselves and their workers. Natives living among the Californios could not and would never be allowed to ascend beyond their serf-like status—unless they fled to join the unconquered Natives in the interior. While this system was not the same as chattel slavery in the US South, California's economy was also based on unfree labor.

Much of California society in the 1830s was paradoxical. Californios, particularly the younger generation that came of age in the years surrounding Mexican independence from Spain in 1821, were committed to liberalism and republicanism, but also to the patriarchal society that had existed since the late eighteenth century. They wanted a free and democratic society—as long as they remained its masters.[7] Moreover, while Californio families were united by generations of intermarriage, California society was riven with frequent political and military squabbles, especially between the autonomous northerners (*norteños*) based at Monterey and the southerners (*sureños*) in Los Angeles, who were more closely tied to Mexico. Finally, Californios were insular and disdained Mexicans and the Mexican government, but at the same time they welcomed foreigners into their ranks as long as they adopted Californio culture. Foreigners could become, like the Californios, *gente de razón* (people of reason), which was defined as Spanish-speaking, Catholic, and willing to work for the benefit of the community.

Natives, by contrast, were seen as *sin razón* (without reason)—whether they were former mission Natives now working on ranchos or they were living unrepentant and independent lives in the California interior. Although the Native population had been decimated by disease and warfare in the decades since the Spanish arrival, more than 100,000 Natives remained in the mid-1830s, outnumbering the Californios twenty to one.[8] Although Native power in the interior would never fundamentally threaten Californio authority on the coast, Native raids on the ranchos were relentless and deleterious, and they increased with the secularization of the missions in the 1830s, as former neophytes now joined the raids. Mostly seeking horses and cattle to trade with Nuevomexicanos farther south, Natives destabilized Californio society at its margins.[9] Because of the specter of Native attacks, Californios hesitated to become aggressive when confronted with other threats to their precarious autonomy, whether this threat came from Mexico, Anglo-American immigrants, the United States, or fellow Californios.[10] Thus, while most Natives played little part in Mexican California's major military and political events of the 1830s and early 1840s, they remained an all-important psychological factor.

In the 1820s, New England and European merchants, lured by the lucrative hide and tallow trade, began settling in California's coastal towns. Seeking profits above all, these men readily acculturated to Californio society by converting to Catholicism, marrying into prominent Californio families, learning Spanish, and eventually becoming Mexican citizens. The Californios clearly accepted these new arrivals.[11] By the mid-1830s, these maritime immigrants had become an integral part of Californian politics and society. Thomas Larkin, who was born in Massachusetts and arrived in California in 1832, estimated in 1845 that three-fifths of the town *alcaldes* (mayors) and two-sevenths of the legislature were foreigners.[12] Of these men, Larkin was the exception to the rule, for he refused to give up his US citizenship and, following his appointment as US consul in 1843, continuously sought a peaceful means for California to enter the American union. While other American merchants were not necessarily opposed to US annexation, they were content with any political system that would continue to guarantee their profits.[13] Many would remain uninvolved in the international conflicts that intruded on insular California in the early 1840s.

In contrast to these well-established maritime immigrants, a new and—for Californios—more worrying group of immigrants began to arrive in the 1830s. These were American hunters and trappers who had crossed the Sierra Nevada, some coming to stay permanently, many others enjoying a respite before returning to the continental interior. Sparse records make it impossible to pinpoint these men's numbers and long-term goals.[14] Even Isaac Graham, who became the most infamous, is impossible to locate for the three years prior to his arrival on California's political stage in 1836.[15] These men intermingled with another group of seemingly shiftless vagrants: American and British seamen who abandoned their ships upon arrival in California, most of whom had no desire to return to the harsh discipline and hard months at sea that characterized the life of a common sailor.

There were probably fewer than a hundred mountain men and seamen, but their presence outweighed their numbers, for elite Californios perceived them as unruly, vulgar, and dangerous. Unlike poor Californios or wealthy New England and European merchants, these foreign vagrants could not be easily integrated into the extended system of patriarchy that had developed over several generations. Marriage tied Californios to one another and to foreign merchants, but these shiftless mountain men and seamen, by contrast, remained permanently single and thus subject to permanent distrust.[16] Ultimately, Californio authorities reluctantly followed the Mexican policy and grudgingly issued this population passports. They then watched warily.

By the 1830s, Californios, Natives, maritime immigrants, mountain men, and former sailors lived under a Mexican sovereignty that existed in name only. Since Mexican independence in 1821, the Mexican government had mostly ignored California, and in turn, California ignored Mexico.[17] The hide and tallow trade had reached its most lucrative point, and traders easily disregarded the Mexican law that dictated that all California trade must be conducted through the California capital of Monterey. Moreover, while the Mexican government appointed the governor, Californios ran the day-to-day affairs through their own political organization of town councils (ayuntamientos) and regional representative bodies (*diputaciones*), both of which were dominated by the powerful dons. When Californios clashed with the appointed governor—which they often did—it was the governor who was expelled, taking the form of a (mostly) bloodless coup. Thus, Mexican California, like its neighboring territories of Texas and New Mexico, possessed a great deal of autonomy, whether its residents desired it or not. Nevertheless, California remained nominally Mexican territory, and thus, in 1836, when centralists seized power in Mexico City, the event reverberated to distant California.

Rifleros Americanos and the Californios' Seigneurial Republic

In October 1836, Alta California, like Texas, New Mexico, and Yucatán, revolted against the centralists who had recently seized power in Mexico City.

Led by a young Californio liberal from Monterey named Juan Alvarado, the California rebels aimed to oust the centralist governor, Nicolás Gutiérrez.[18] Previous rebellions had arisen over largely personal grievances, but this time more was at stake.[19] Alvarado aimed to overthrow not just the governor, but the new centralist constitution—and with it, Mexican sovereignty itself.

Alvarado commanded seventy-five fellow Californios and a few dozen American mountain men and ex-seamen, who were led by trapper and whiskey distiller Isaac Graham. The Californios called this contingent the *rifleros Americanos* (American riflemen). These Americans joined Alvarado for two self-interested reasons. First, in exchange for their support Alvarado likely promised them land, which they had been unable to obtain because they were not Mexican citizens.[20] Second, the rifleros may have been motivated by the Mexican governor's increasing hostility toward foreigners, and they saw Alvarado as a natural ally against him.[21] During the rebellion, the rifleros' superior marksmanship gave Alvarado the edge. With Graham's contingent taking the lead, Alvarado and his force overwhelmed Gutiérrez in the Monterey presidio without any loss of life. Alvarado and his allies forced Gutiérrez to return to Mexico and then turned their *diputación* into an official congress "that shall pass all the particular laws of the country."[22] They then declared California a "free and sovereign state."[23] An independent California was born.

But it was a tentative independence, for there was a key caveat in the declaration: California was free and sovereign but only "until the federal system of 1824 should be reestablished."[24] This proviso reflected the myriad divisions and anxieties of California's inhabitants. Californios disdained centralist Mexico, but they feared Mexican retaliation. They also believed they might require Mexican aid if confronted with a large-scale Indian attack. Moreover, whether it was Mexicans or Natives who might invade California, Californios understood that their small numbers precluded international ambitions.[25] The ambivalent declaration also reflected a regional tension between norteños and sureños. Closer to Mexico and with more recent settlers from Mexico, sureños were less willing to declare complete independence. Even more important, both sureños and norteños feared domination by the other. In 1836, after Alvarado's norteño rebellion, it was sureños who felt wary.[26]

To assuage the sureños, Alvarado, fifty Californio soldiers, and Graham's riflemen journeyed to Los Angeles. After a productive meeting with sureño dons, Alvarado returned to Monterey and disbanded his army. He did so too soon, however, as he quickly learned that the sureños had affirmed their commitment to the centralist constitution and welcomed the new commissioner from Mexico, Andres Castillero. Castillero, however, had come alone, for Mexico had no army to spare for marginal California while countering rebellions in Texas and New Mexico. With Alvarado unable to enforce his rule in the South, Castillero powerless to assert Mexican sovereignty in the North, and the South caught between the North and Mexico, a political compromise emerged. In exchange for disavowing independence and taking an oath to the centralist constitution, Alvarado kept his power and became California's governor, while Castillero returned to Mexico and promised to keep Mexican troops out of the territory. By July 1837 California was once again officially under Mexican sovereignty.[27]

The divisions in California society reflected the major impediment to independence in 1836. Californios were confident about whom they were not—they were not Mexicans, Indians, or Americans—but they struggled for a positive group identity. They were united by blood, Catholicism, and a vague dedication to liberalism, but there was no newspaper or state education system that would forge a wider sense of California nationalism.[28] Thus, Californios were willing to throw out Mexican governors, but not yet embrace full independence—which, with only 6,000 non-Native inhabitants, was a perilous undertaking. This lack of nationalism revealed itself upon Alvarado's capture of the Monterey presidio. Before the attack, Alvarado's soldiers used the password "California libre" (Free California) to identify each other. Once the rebels captured the presidio, they promptly took down the Mexican flag. Yet soon they realized they had no acceptable replacement, and the following day they reraised the Mexican flag.[29] *California libre?* The Californios were undecided.

Alvarado and his fellow rebels did have one other flag option besides that of Mexico: a Texas-inspired lone-star flag. Likely prepared by some of Isaac Graham's American riflemen, it represented a full embrace of independence, Texas style.[30] Alvarado and his Californio allies may have revolted for similar federalist reasons as those of Anglo-Texans and Tejanos, but they did not want to become another Texas. After all, the Republic of Texas was not just a federalist victory, but one that came at the hands of recently arrived Anglo-Americans, who quickly assumed dominance of the fledgling state. Elite Californios like Alvarado may have hoped for a restoration of the federalist constitution, but not at the expense of becoming inundated with American settlers—at least, not settlers like the itinerant, uncouth, well-armed rifleros Americanos.

Californios' dislike for American mountain men and seamen was not readily apparent in 1836, when Alvarado relied on Graham's forces in his rebellion. By 1840, however, these men had made themselves unwelcome. The ostensible problem was their drunk and disorderly behavior, which reached the point of insulting Alvarado personally in the streets of Monterey.[31] Yet this behavior was only an outward manifestation of the larger problem: these shiftless men ruptured the order of California's seigneurial society and highlighted a clash between the values of Mexican California and Jacksonian America. Both societies were based on representative government for white men (with Californios ignoring their Native ancestry). In California this representation was filtered through a system of patriarchy that was based on marriage, godparentage, patronage to dependents, and deference to superiors. In Jacksonian America, by contrast, the ideology of white male equality overrode any pretense of deference and civility. Moreover, in California in particular, Jacksonian Americans were armed, rootless, outspoken, and often inebriated. The drunken insulting of a public official was not an action to be lauded in the United States, but it was a normal manifestation of American politics; indeed, the infamous drunken revelry at Andrew Jackson's first inauguration made this clear. In California, the same action threatened the societal order itself.

To solve this social crisis, Alvarado manufactured a political crisis. He accused Graham and other foreigners of plotting to overthrow the government and declare California independent. He then ordered California authorities to arrest all foreigners without passports, with the exception of those who had married Californio women or were engaged in honorable professions, thereby excluding all Anglo-American merchants from arrest. Indeed, merchants such as Thomas Larkin approved of Alvarado's actions, and many of those arrested believed that Larkin and other wealthy foreigners were part of Alvarado's conspiracy.[32] Initially Alvarado arrested a hundred foreigners, forty-five of whom he sent to Mexico for a lengthy imprisonment; half of those were American and the other half British.[33]

According to their later accounts of the Graham affair, as it became known, in Mexico the prisoners experienced a version of the Spanish Black Legend: they were imprisoned in a hot, confined space without water or sufficient air for an extended period of time.[34] Like much of the incident, the allegations are impossible to prove. The prisoners likely did suffer, but whether they were actually mistreated more than other prisoners in Mexico or, for that matter, Americans jailed in the United States remains uncertain. When it was all said and done, the Graham affair made California, briefly, an international subject. The arrests outraged the US and British governments, and both protested the incident to the Mexican government. Graham became something of an American hero through the writings of Thomas Jefferson Farnham, whose 1844 work, *Travels in California*, portrayed Graham as a Tennessee rifleman à la David Crockett.[35] Farnham was also largely responsible for the Black Legend spin that reverberated throughout the US press. However, the United States never escalated the matter beyond haphazard diplomatic protests. Indeed, one American observer of the incident lambasted the United States for its complete lack of presence in California, in contrast to the ever-present Britain and France, whose ships constantly sailed the coast.[36] Graham's arrest did not provide an excuse for US intervention in California, nor did it make California a subject of sustained interest in the US press.[37] With the exception of the wealthy New England traders, the Americans who lived in California were still on their own—but not for long.

American Visions of a Seigneurial Republic

As the Graham affair ran its course in Monterey and Mexico, two events of immense importance for California's future occurred on the territory's northern frontier. First, in 1839, Swiss immigrant John Sutter (originally Johann Suter) received Governor Alvarado's blessing to construct a permanent inland settlement on the Sacramento River. Although Alvarado balked at Sutter's idea to become an empresario like Stephen Austin in Texas, in which Sutter would foster further immigration, Alvarado believed that Sutter could be a useful bulwark against Indians.[38] In his discussions with Alvarado, Sutter concealed an unending thirst for power and influence behind a magnanimous and gregarious facade, which clearly helped sway the governor. Aided by several Hawaiians in his employ and after forging trade alliances with Native peoples in the Sacramento Valley, within two years Sutter made New Helvetia a power center. By the time he purchased Fort Ross from the Russians on credit that same year, Sutter had become the master of the northern California frontier. When his newfound power was threatened by potentially hostile Californio authorities, he threatened to establish an "independent republique" if they did not accede to his wishes.[39] Although this was bluster, he clearly felt secure enough in his power that he could make such claims with-

Joseph Warren Revere, *Sutter's Fort—New Helvetia* (1849). This print portrays Sutter's Fort as it would have appeared to the American migrants who claimed land in the Sacramento Valley in the early 1840s. Notice the seemingly endless expanse of land to the right. Courtesy of Special Collections, University of Texas at Arlington Libraries, Arlington.

out effective Californio retaliation. Sutter was right: the Californios backed down, recognizing that Sutter was a problem that would not go away easily.

November 1841 witnessed a second significant event—and a second problem for the Californios—when a bedraggled group of 33 Missourians (31 men, a woman, and a child), who would eventually be known as the Bidwell-Bartleson Party, arrived in northern California. Without passports, the immigrants were illegal—and, as a matter of policy, the Mexican government refused to grant them the right to stay, for officials feared that the events of the Texas Revolution would replay themselves in other regions.[40] Yet Commandant General Mariano Vallejo, the largest California landholder, guardian of the northern California frontier, and uncle of Alvarado, was unwilling to enforce Mexican law. Vallejo did not want to send the migrants on a return journey that would likely kill them, but his decision was not just about humanitarianism. He believed that these new immigrants, unlike the previously arrived mountain men, were industrious and could prove as useful to California society as the New England merchants had become.[41] Lying to distant Mexican officials that he needed 2,000 troops to expel the 33 Missourians, he issued them passports and let them stay.[42] For two years, these American overlanders were an anomaly. No other overland group arrived in California in 1841 or 1842. Then, in 1843, 38 more Americans arrived, followed by 53 in 1844. In 1845, the number increased substantially to 260, and in 1846 roughly 1,500 Americans made the journey. A trickle had become a flood.[43]

This American influx is difficult to explain. Little had been written about California in the US press. The US region most connected to California was not Missouri, from which a majority of the migrants hailed, but New England, through the trade and communications facilitated by the merchants who had settled along California's coast. Neither was there a collective American presence in the region—certainly nothing like Austin's settlement in Texas, nor even something akin to the more modest migration of Protestant missionaries who traveled collectively to Oregon Country in the late 1830s. California was a distant Mexican territory, and so Americans had no right to its land. No wonder, then, that by 1845 more than 5,000 Americans had traveled to Oregon, which the United States jointly claimed with Great Britain, whereas only 384 had traveled to California. Expatriation to any region in the early 1840s was risky, but California was the riskiest destination of all.

But 384 is not zero and still requires an explanation, which is this: while there may have been a guarantee (or, at first, at least a strong likelihood) that free land was available in places like Oregon and Texas, there was much *more* free land *potentially* available in California. With greater risk came greater reward. There are hints of this calculus among the Bidwell-Bartleson Party. John Bidwell was the most enthusiastic supporter of migration to California and remembered he had heard about California's potential from two sources. The first was a personal conversation with fur trapper Antoine Robidoux, who described California as a "perfect paradise, a perpetual spring. . . . Cattle and horses ranged there in the greatest abundance."[44] The second source was the personal letters of John Marsh, a ranchero in northern California. Marsh was a Harvard graduate and had journeyed to California via the Santa Fe Trail in 1836, fleeing both personal and business failures in the East.[45] By 1841 he was likely the only wealthy American in the territory who had come overland and made his fortune in the interior, in contrast to the New England merchants who lived along the coast. Marsh had written to acquaintances in Missouri, and the letters were subsequently shared. Marsh praised California as the "finest country" with the "finest climate" and then stated, "I have as much land here as I want."[46] Both Robidoux and Marsh noted that neither California's government nor the Californios themselves were a threat to settlement. On the contrary, Robidoux enthusiastically described the Californios as exhibiting "unbounded" hospitality.[47] Marsh was less sanguine, noting that California "lacked a good government," but because of this he had "no apprehension of being molested."[48] Bidwell had recently claimed 160 acres of land in Platte County, Missouri, but another squatter had jumped his claim. He had no legal recourse for its return, for he had not improved the land nor was he twenty-one, the legal age for landownership. No wonder, then, that after hearing from Robidoux and Marsh, the young, adventurous Bidwell jumped at the chance of a paradise of limitless land in a place where it seemed no one could take it from him.[49]

Bidwell and a few fellow enthusiasts created the Western Emigration Society to foster California migration, and it boasted 500 members within only a few months. The initial enthusiasm, however, gave way to trepidation: at this point Thomas Farnham's account of the Graham affair appeared in newspapers, which recounted the mistreatment of Graham and his fellow prisoners and portrayed California's authorities as nefarious and cruel. The Western Emigration Society fell apart; the 33 who remained enthused about California became the Bidwell-Bartleson Party. In the years that followed, word began to filter back from California to US western states that abundant land remained available and the Mexican authorities were no threat. Some of this information came through word of mouth from members of the Bidwell-Bartleson Party who returned east. It also came in writing. Unbeknown to Bidwell, his journal account got back to Missouri and was published in 1843, 1844, and 1845—thus becoming the first unofficial California trail guide.[50] In it, he described how "one Spanish league (this is about 6½ sections or square miles) is considered a farm. This I believe is the smallest grant which the Spanish Government gives and 11 leagues the largest."[51] The US preemption law promised only a quarter square mile for a fee and Oregon only one square mile. A quarter mile versus one mile versus a *minimum* of more than six square miles: here was the crucial incentive to go to California. Soon, early guidebooks supplemented the word of mouth and Bidwell's unofficial account.[52] Only in this distant Mexican territory could Americans acquire land that measured, in the words of one observer, "leagues in extent."[53]

Yet it was not just the amount of land that was important to California migrants, but the way of life this land promised. Needless to say, obtaining thousands of acres of land did not create the life of a simple yeoman farmer, but allowed a man to become a powerful, influential, largely carefree patriarch—as the lives of the few dozen Californios sitting atop California society exemplified. Indeed, the few accounts of Mexican California that existed prior to the US-Mexican War consistently described the easygoing lives of these patriarchs in detail. In his published journal, Bidwell described how a "Spaniard will not do anything which he cannot do on horseback—he does not work perhaps on an average one month in the year—he labors about a week, when he sows his wheat, and another week, when he harvests it. The rest of the time is spent riding about."[54] One of the early guidebooks echoed Bidwell: "The Spaniards do not . . . often engage in laborious exercise. They are generally content with merely living; and in a country possessed of so mild a climate as California has, it requires very little exertion to live."[55] Lansford Hastings, whose *Emigrants' Guide to Oregon and California* was the catalyst that turned a few hundred migrants to California in 1845 to more than a thousand in 1846, described how the small group of Americans in California "all have fine herds of cattle and horses, with farms, under a good state of cultivation, they grow a great abundance of wheat, corn, oats, and flax, as well as a great variety and superabundance of vegetables, and that too, with very little labor or expense."[56] The message was clear: if you managed to obtain land in California, then your life would become idyllic.

Of course, even if California's climate was sublime and its soil fertile, manual labor still had to be done, and guidebooks and letters made it abundantly clear who would do it: Native people. Just as Natives labored for the Californios, so too would they labor for Anglo-Americans. Bidwell noted, "You can employ any number of Indians by giving them a lump of beef every week, and paying them about one dollar for same time."[57] Hastings echoed: "Indians are readily employed, and, in any numbers, at the trifling expense of merely furnishing them such clothing . . . and with such food as meat alone, or whatever else you may feel disposed to furnish them; for any thing . . . would be preferable to the crickets and grasshoppers, upon which they have formerly subsisted."[58] In an 1846 letter to Lewis Cass, John Marsh was more succinct: "Throughout all of California Indians are the principal laborers; without them the business of the country could hardly be carried on."[59]

In certain ways, Native "employment" in California was akin to chattel slavery in the US South, for both were manifestations of unfree labor. This fact was not news to those who provided eyewitness accounts in the early 1840s, which routinely compared Native laborers to enslaved people. Hastings wrote that the Native people were "in a state of absolute vassalage, even more degrading, and even more oppressive than, that of our slaves in the South."[60] Another guidebook described how Indians were "little else than slaves," for they were employed for only "nominal compensation."[61] John Sutter echoed these statements but tried to separate Native labor from slavery: "We can hire Indian laborers very cheaply. They make slavery wholly unnecessary here, and may be employed for all field and house work. In harvest I have frequently employed at least 400 Indians."[62] In essence, Natives could be put to work *like* enslaved people, but to Sutter that meant that they were *not* slaves. Perhaps these semantics were necessary for the image Sutter hoped to project of himself, for if they were in fact enslaved, then Sutter was the most notorious and brutal slaveholder in northern California, an inconvenient blow to Sutter's self-defined benevolence.[63]

Considering that almost all guidebooks and letters from Mexican California at least mentioned the pervasiveness of Natives' servitude, American migrants certainly knew the broad tenets of the system, and many embraced this forced labor system immediately after they arrived in California.[64] Indeed, Natives' servitude was likely one of the major attractions that drew certain Americans to California instead of Oregon. This was certainly the case for a Texan named Sam Kinney. Kinney did not try to hide his intentions when he encountered a Native person on the Overland Trail, stating, "I am going to capture that Indian, and take him as a slave."[65] As a Texan, Kinney was clearly comfortable with slaveholding in a way most migrants were not, and no other migrant stated so explicitly the desire to profit from Native forced labor. Yet when these migrants arrived in California, they showed no hesitation in embracing such labor. Some, like John Bidwell, followed a path of racist yet paternalistic benevolence. Bidwell spent several decades advocating for Native rights, including the right to vote in the 1849 constitutional convention, while still reaping profits from Native labor. Others, like the brothers Benjamin, Andy, and Sam Kelsey, became notorious Indian slave traders.[66]

American migrants were no doubt attracted to the seemingly easy life that the combination of Native labor and the ownership of immense amounts of land promised. Yet the gulf that separated Bidwell from the Kelseys when it came to the treatment of Native people demonstrated an additional attraction to Natives' servitude: its ideological flexibility. These Americans had emigrated from a United States that was increasingly divided on the issue of black chattel slavery. By the early 1840s, northern abolitionists rigorously attacked slavery, and they were met by an equal rigorous defense from proslavery southerners. Throughout the country, increasing numbers of Americans who abhorred these extremist positions had come to believe that a half-slave, half-free republic could not last forever. To solve this issue, breakaway

Americans created polities that eliminated ambiguity: Mirabeau Lamar's Texas promoted itself as a haven for slaveholders; Oregon migrants created a white yeomen's republic that outlawed both slavery and all free black migrants (see chapter 6). California offered a third way where a white man could reap the material benefits of slaveowning—accruing vast profits, forgoing manual labor, wielding patriarchal power—without its supposed ideological burdens: paternalism and the need to morally justify slavery. In an 1847 description, California pioneer Robert Semple gave the best account of the benefits of this system: "A farmer who is fitted with sufficient teams and farming utensil[s], may employ as many Indians as he pleases, for nothing but their victuals, and that very cheap, and about two shirts and a pair of pantaloons of the coarsest kind. He may keep them while he wants them, which is only at seed-time and harvest, and then send them to their villages again for the remainder of the year. They are about half as good as the negroes of Missouri, with good looking after. So that a farmer with a capital of four or five hundred dollars, can raise and gather as much grain as the Missourian with forty negroes."[67] A potential migrant could read this passage in two ways: either he could gain the profits of slaveholding without actually owning any people, or he could become a profitable slaveholder of Indians. In either case, it would take little capital: purchasing forty black enslaved people cost more than $20,000 in the early 1840s, meaning a migrant could attain a similar lifestyle in California for one-fortieth the price.[68] The end result would be a life of patriarchal authority and daily leisure.

The pull of patriarchy was infused with issues of masculinity. The Bidwell-Bartleson Party was overwhelmingly male (31 men, 1 woman, 1 child), as was the next major overland group, the 1843 Walker-Chiles Party (30 men, 6 women). These groups of mostly single men had been inspired by the letters of other single men, notably wealthy patriarchs like John Sutter and John Marsh, both of whom left their families behind when they traveled to California. By 1844, as California became more well known among the American public, the gender ratio on the Overland Trail started to balance out, yet California still remained a place for single men, many of whom were willing to employ violence to achieve their aims. At times this violence was directed at Natives, while in 1845 and 1846 it took the form of rebellion against authorities. Thus, the names of California's first pioneers—John Sutter, John Marsh, Benjamin Kelsey, Lansford Hastings—still emit a whiff of notoriety for their audaciousness and ruthlessness, a reputation not matched by the first American migrants to Texas in the 1820s or to Oregon in the early 1840s.

Once in California, American overlanders could follow one of three avenues to gain thousands of acres of land: become naturalized Mexican citizens, marry a Californio woman, or make a land claim more than twenty-five miles from the coast. Demonstrating their identity as white Jacksonian Americans, no overlander married a Californio and only a few became Mexican citizens. They all took advantage of the third path, settling in the Sacramento Valley almost a hundred miles from the coast.[69] Early migrants claimed tens of thousands of acres, portions of which they then granted to later migrants. John Bidwell laid out the strategy in a letter to pioneer John Townshend, who had arrived in 1844: "Obtain a grant of land in the San Joaquin, say of 18, 25, 30, or even 50, leagues on such conditions that if you put on the same land, [a] certain number of families, within one or two years, and then if you should not in that time fulfill the requisition, to have your obligations null, leaving you free from all responsibility, I would heartily approve of the measure."[70] In a follow-up letter, Bidwell showed that he was not helping Townshend out of selflessness alone, noting that if Townshend would allow him, he would be glad to help sell some of Townshend's land to incoming overlanders.[71] This process of securing land from the Californios and then selling it to other Americans provided men like Bidwell with not only significant monetary compensation, but also a degree of social compensation: bestowing land yielded a form of patriarchal power over the region and its new settlers.[72] Bidwell wanted to solidify himself as one of the scions of American-settled California—an endeavor at which he and many other early Americans were largely successful.[73]

Thus, through the literature they read, the motivations they voiced, and the actions they took when they arrived, the small group of American migrants in California looked to create, in essence, a seigneurial republic. They wanted more power and prestige than yeomen had, but they did not want the moral and material baggage of chattel slaveholding. As former inhabitants of the Jacksonian United States, they remained dedicated to democratic practices when these concerned interactions with one another. In this sense, they did not want to emulate the feudalistic practices of Sutter, who would come to dislike these immigrants for their leveling tendencies. At the same time, they hoped to become patriarchs living on huge tracts of land, overseeing their various dependents—their wives, their children, and their Native workers. They hoped, essentially, to emulate the practices of the elite Californios.

Yet their desire to emulate the Californios only went so far. In their search for land and patriarchy, these early migrants mirrored the actions of the

American empresarios in Texas in the 1820s, but becoming Texas-style empresarios was not their ultimate goal. Neither did they want to follow the path of the American merchants who had arrived in California in the 1820s and 1830s. Both the early Anglo-Texans and early Anglo-Californians had acculturated themselves to the local society and culture: they learned Spanish, married Tejano and Californio women, and converted to Catholicism (at least officially). Some, like Stephen Austin, even praised Mexican federalism.[74] Perhaps most obviously, but also most important, both of these early groups were willing to live alongside and interact with the existing non-Native population. Not so with the 1840s migrants to California: they remained thoroughly breakaway *Americans*. They congregated in the Sacramento Valley, far from Californio authority and military power. They continued to revere the Fourth of July, and they showed no inclination to learn Spanish or convert to Catholicism.[75] The single men among these immigrants married the daughters of their fellow American immigrants or, more heinously, satisfied their sexual urgings by raping Native women. They did not marry Californio women. Like all breakaway Americans, the settlers in the Sacramento Valley were carving out their own ideal version of an American society, one that would remain a world apart from that of the Californios and foreign merchants living along the coast.

Of course, no American migrant voiced his desires in such a coherent manner, partly due to human nature: migrants made decisions based on whims, gut feelings, the advice of friends and fellow migrants, and the travel literature they had read. Only when all of this is added together does a consistent ideology emerge. Yet in California, it was not just human nature that kept this ideology subsumed, but immigrants' prejudice toward the Californios. In a profound irony, American men hoped to become like the people they were supposed to (and often did) despise. Indeed, at the same time as writers like Lansford Hastings and John Marsh extolled the virtues of California and the prosperity that migrants could achieve there, they denigrated the work habits of the Californios. As Hastings described, "A Mexican [i.e., Californio] always pursues the method of doing things, which requires the least physical or mental exercise, unless it involves danger, in which case, he always adopts some other method."[76] In an addendum to the second edition of Hastings's overland guide, Robert Semple agreed with Hastings, claiming that Californios were "thieving, cowardly, dancing, lewd people, and generally indolent and faithless."[77] For Semple—and many others—Californios' laziness (and dancing?) explained the seeming backwardness of the territory.

In this way, American promoters of California engineered a mischievous bait-and-switch, although they were probably unaware of what they were doing. They used the supposed indolence of the Californio population as the primary reason that white Americans deserved to populate and eventually dominate California. In many ways, they employed a trope similar to one that white Americans had employed toward Native peoples for centuries: Californios did not deserve the land because they did not get full use out of it. But what would Americans do once they populated the territory? Why, they would live easygoing, carefree lives that required little labor or sustained effort! Thus, the "slothful" lives of the Californios became lives of "very little labor or expense" for American migrants.

No American migrant would admit that, in reality, they simply wanted to emulate the Californios. Outsiders, however, could be more honest. In 1847, a midshipman in the US Navy visited California, and he hit on familiar themes in a letter to his father: "Fortunes can and are amassed here [in California] in five or six years—but the inhabitants [i.e., Californios] have no life or enterprise in them and foreigners [i.e., Americans] are the only ones that carry on the larger business." But then he frankly added, "And even they become enervated after a stay of several years."[78]

Re-creating Texas on the Pacific

As overland immigration from the United States slowly increased from several dozen in 1841 to several hundred in 1845, Californio authorities' anxiety also increased. Mexico had sent neither troops nor funds since Alvarado's rebellion in 1836, and neither seemed to be returning any time soon, forcing the Californios to confront the American influx on their own. When they considered what American immigration foretold, they naturally thought of Texas. As already mentioned, a Texas flag had been present during Alvarado's 1836 revolt, and Alvarado had arrested Graham for trying to create another Texas in 1840. The lesson of Texas was seemingly simple: a trickle of American immigrants would soon become a flood, and eventually these immigrants would seek to assume control. In the context of the early 1840s, when the Republic of Texas was an independent country, the lesson was not that American immigrants would pave the way for US annexation. On the contrary, in the early 1840s the United States remained mostly a nonentity in California, and authorities rarely referred to the United States when voicing their concerns. Instead, Californios feared that American immigrants would create an Anglo-dominated Republic of California. Tellingly, they rarely deemed the overland immigrants "Americans." Instead, immigrants were either "Missourians" or *estrangeros* (foreigners).[79]

In hindsight, Californios' lack of attention to the United States appears naïve with the era of Manifest Destiny looming, but in 1841 it was a logical reading of North American geopolitics: Texas was an independent republic, whose president, Mirabeau Lamar, wanted to avoid US annexation and expand Texas borders. California residents knew of these developments.[80] Authorities in Mexico agreed with this assessment, and they warned Californios of an immigration process like the one spearheaded by Stephen Austin, in which the American migrants' peaceful overtures hid more insidious political designs.[81] They did not warn of US intervention. To avoid Texas's fate, Californio authorities needed to counteract American immigration, not the US state. The two were not related—at least not yet.

Even Thomas Larkin, who was appointed California's US consul in 1843, believed that the United States had little role to play in the region for the foreseeable future. More than most maritime immigrants, he maintained an interest in US politics and hoped the United States would eventually acquire California peacefully. Yet in the early 1840s, he and other Americans in California knew US expansionism was at a standstill, as the country was still suffering from economic depression and political dysfunction. As Larkin's cousin wrote to Larkin a few months after the unexpected death of William Henry Harrison, "The political horizon is overhung by shadows & clouds of fearful uncertainty."[82] Other Americans in California also understood that the United States remained a nonentity in the territory. As mentioned above, overlanders had learned of California's potential from word of mouth, a few letters printed in western papers, and the unsanctioned publication of John Bidwell's diary, not because of some mass movement building in the United States for increased California migration or increased US interest in the territory. Such was the ignorance about California in the United States that Larkin felt he needed to awake Americans to its merits, and thus in 1843 he started promoting California in letters to New York papers. Only in 1845, however, did editors encourage Larkin in this endeavor. For the two years prior, he was writing to an unreceptive audience and was often unsure if his letters had even reached their destination.[83] Further, Larkin, with his many contacts as US consul, was unaware of US designs on California, as were his Californio friends and acquaintances, most of whom also followed international developments closely.

Of course, simply because California residents did not fear US objectives for the territory did not mean the United States was entirely irrelevant. In 1841, the US Exploring Expedition led by Charles Wilkes sent an overland party south from Oregon through northern California, which then rendezvoused with Wilkes's fleet in San Francisco Bay. Although in retrospect the expedition seemed to portend growing US power in California, Wilkes did not think so, maintaining that California would one day join with Oregon and form a "powerful maritime nation" that would "control the destinies of the Pacific." While Wilkes believed that this Pacific nation would undoubtedly be controlled by the "Anglo-Norman race," it would not be US territory.[84]

One year later the United States was again involved in California, although this incident became more infamous. Commodore Thomas ap Catesby Jones of the US Pacific Squadron interpreted several Mexican newspapers erroneously and came to the conclusion that the United States was at war with Mexico. He further believed that Great Britain was going to seize California in order to preserve the territory's autonomy, and to preempt the British Jones seized Monterey on behalf of the United States. Within a day Jones learned of his mistake, withdrew his ship, and sheepishly traveled to southern California to apologize to the new governor, Manuel Micheltorena.[85] Internationally, this event did have some repercussions, ending preliminary negotiations among the United States, Mexico, and Britain for, among other things, the US acquisition of California. Yet President John Tyler's aborted push for California had never been sincere, but had been used as a means to stall the British on an Oregon compromise.[86] Tyler had never thought these negotiations with Mexico would lead anywhere; he simply wanted to keep the British guessing. Authorities in Mexico City, meanwhile, viewed Jones's mistake as part of a secret US plot, while newspaper reports in the United States awakened Americans—slightly—to California's existence.[87] However, the Californios did not have the same reaction as their Mexican counterparts, and they were more disgusted at Mexico for leaving California in such a defenseless state than they were at Jones's actions or at the United States more generally.[88] If anything, Jones's actions represented a US attempt to enforce the Monroe Doctrine by preventing European interference in the Americas, rather than a prelude to US expansion.[89]

Meanwhile, American overlanders who had reached California had geopolitical ideas of their own. In a few cases, their beliefs justified Californios' concern over their arrival, for a handful of immigrants did indeed hope to wrest California from the Californios and establish a Texas-style republic. The most famous—or infamous—of these would-be revolutionaries was the aforementioned Lansford Hastings, the writer of the famous travelogue who had sought to use the Mormons to achieve his own geopolitical goals. Published in 1845, the title of his book, *The Emigrants' Guide to Oregon and California*, concealed his larger thesis: California offered much better prospects than Oregon, for California promised thousands of acres of land and dependent Indian laborers, whereas Oregon offered the difficult life of a yeoman farmer.[90] Hastings believed that once he persuaded thousands of migrants to travel to California, they would "revolutionize" the Californio-led government and establish a California republic—with, presumably, Hastings as its president.[91] Under his guidance, Hastings believed, California would become a second Texas.

Hastings was joined in his revolutionary plans by a host of past, present, and future California residents, among them Thomas Farnham. Like Hastings, Farnham was a lawyer, western traveler, and author; he had described the Graham affair in *Travels in California*. As I have discussed, his narrative worked against migration to California in the short term by portraying Californios as hostile to Americans, but by 1845 Farnham was on board with Hastings's plan to foster immigration and seize the territory from the Californios.[92] Hastings and Farnham seem to have eventually worked as a team, with Farnham acting as a promoter of immigration in the US East and Hastings filling the role of guide who would lead immigrants west.

In the summer of 1845 Farnham gave a letter to Hastings to deliver to John Marsh, in which he proclaimed that the "Republic of California" would "arise," and "neither Europe nor the United States are prepared for the event."[93] Marsh, of course, had encouraged American immigration as early as 1841, although by 1845 he had largely given up his efforts as hopeless.[94] Whether Marsh knew of Hastings's and Farnham's revolutionary plans before Hastings arrived in California in 1845 is uncertain, but clearly they recognized him as a tailor-made co-conspirator. There was reason for this: that year, Marsh and Charles Weber, a German who had migrated to the United States in 1836 and had been a member of the Bidwell-Bartleson Party in 1841, had made efforts to organize immigrants in the territory for defensive purposes.[95] Weber even hinted to Marsh that Marsh could become the George Washington of California, if he so desired.[96] Hastings and Farnham's other conspirators included Sam Brannan, the Mormon convert discussed in chapter 3 who would bring the first ship of Mormons to California in 1846. They even possibly included the Hudson's Bay Company's chief factor, John McLoughlin, who hoped to maintain the HBC's power in Oregon by pushing

American overlanders to California.[97] Even John Sutter, who would come to dislike American immigrants for their refusal to obey his orders, was likely privy to some of Hastings's plans, for Hastings and most other overlanders made New Helvetia a prominent meeting place to discuss California affairs. Thus, although this revolutionary conspiracy was still inchoate in 1845, it nevertheless connected a wide spectrum of influential people.

It is all too easy to impugn Hastings and company's ability to establish an independent California republic. In hindsight, declaring California independence based on the continued migration of Americans looks simultaneously delusional and vainglorious. Yet the geopolitical reality of California before 1846 was different than the reality after. While James Polk's election in 1844 had restarted momentum toward the United States' annexation of Texas and thus potential war with Mexico, western geopolitics remained fluid through the spring of 1846, when the United States actually declared war. As I showed in chapter 1, during these years both Whig and Democratic papers believed that an independent California republic was a likely political outcome in the short term. They just disagreed on whether it would join the United States in the long term.

Moreover, the would-be revolutionaries could boast of some real accomplishments. Both Hastings and Farnham had traveled to Oregon, California, and Mexico, and both wrote best-selling accounts of their journeys. John Marsh had become a wealthy California ranchero. John Sutter's fort dominated the Sacramento Valley. Sam Brannan had thus far accomplished little, but he would start San Francisco's first newspaper, and thanks to the gold rush, he would become one of California's wealthiest residents. It is true that all of these men were, in the words of one historian, "scoundrels," for they were all unlikable and obnoxious. Contemporaries saw all of them at various points as manipulative, arrogant, overly ambitious, and reckless; historians have added to this portrayal by pointing out their anti-Native and anti-Mexican racism.[98] Yet notwithstanding their immense flaws, they were proven leaders. Hastings is a case in point. Despite his poor grasp of geography, Hastings was elected as the head of his overland party to Oregon in 1842, guided another group of migrants from Oregon to California in 1843, and led a final group to California in 1845. Although Hastings's prediction that 20,000 migrants would come to California in 1846 was a vast overestimation, 1,500 still came, six times as many as the previous year, all largely due to his *Emigrants' Guide* and promotional tour. Hastings's marketing efforts made 1846 the only year prior to the California gold rush during which more migrants chose California over Oregon. In the contemporary understanding, Hastings and the rest of these men practiced the Jacksonian ethos of "go ahead"—and when they did, some Americans followed.

For other Americans in California, like John Bidwell, revolution brought a lot of risk with little reward. Bidwell had acquired 17,000 acres of land, and while he had not yet transformed his holdings into a functioning rancho, he had demonstrated an ability to successfully navigate California's legal system. He had established enough connections with Californio authorities and knew enough rudimentary Spanish that his future prospects looked good.[99] Bidwell was in the minority, for many more immigrants possessed no legal title, but even these men had been able to seize the land they wanted in the Sacramento Valley, for the Californios had no presence in the region and therefore no ability to stop them. Would-be revolutionaries needed to look to a third group: the most recent arrivals and a few others who had not been able to gain land either legally or illegally. This group remained rootless and made a living on California's northern frontier by hunting, trapping, and working for John Sutter. Like Graham and his compatriots imprisoned in 1840, this population was the most volatile and remained the most threatening to Californio power. No wonder Hastings felt the need to exponentially increase migration in order to facilitate his revolution. Not only would this give him much greater numbers, but it would also bring Americans to California who, unlike established men like Bidwell, had no stake in preserving the status quo.

Thus, the questions of political allegiance and political decision-making were fundamentally and permanently entwined with the issue of land. Whoever guaranteed American immigrants land rights could guarantee their loyalty. Conversely, whoever called into question these land rights would guarantee rebellion.

Hints of a Multiethnic California Republic

After the arrival of the Bidwell-Bartleson Party and its portent of even more American immigrants, Californio authorities like Alvarado and Vallejo asked Mexican president Santa Anna for increased Mexican oversight. In response, in December 1842 Santa Anna dispatched Brigadier General Manuel Micheltorena to California with 300 Mexican soldiers. Micheltorena was a veteran of Santa Anna's Texas campaign and a personal friend of Santa Anna.[100] He was, in essence, the type of governor whom federalist Californios should have distrusted as a centralist hostile to their autonomy. However, many Californios believed that Micheltorena would provide needed stability to a territory wracked by internal divisions, American immigration, potentially hostile Natives, and the growing power of John Sutter.[101] Considering that the Mexican state had been absent from California for five years, it is not surprising that Californios failed to take seriously the threat Micheltorena posed to their autonomy. At best, they hoped Micheltorena and his troops would provide the order they craved. At worst, Micheltorena's presence would be irrelevant and California would maintain its status quo. The Californios would quickly be proven wrong.

Micheltorena did little to solve California's ongoing problems. Rather than provide stability, he made things worse. Not only did he permit the presence of American overlanders, but he formed political ties with none other than John Sutter. Yet it was his Mexican troops that caused the most problems. Labeled "cholos" by elite Californios, these troops were mostly penniless Mexican convicts who quickly turned to petty theft to obtain food.[102] First at Los Angeles and then at Monterey, Micheltorena's troops succeeded in antagonizing practically all of the Californio population, uniting both norteños and sureños against their presence.[103] Like Graham and his mountain men in 1840, the cholo soldiers particularly offended the sensibilities of the elite—including, once again, Juan Alvarado—and they needed to go. In November 1844, the Californios rebelled.[104]

Unlike Alvarado's previous opponents—Gutiérrez in 1836, Graham in 1840—Micheltorena possessed a sizable (albeit undependable) army and had potential allies at his disposal. At first Micheltorena acceded to the demands of Alvarado and his co-conspirator José Castro, a fellow Monterey don, former California governor, and future commandant general. Micheltorena agreed that his soldiers would leave California within three months, although he would remain as governor. Yet this was a false promise, for Micheltorena was in contact with John Sutter and hoped to enlist Sutter in his cause. In December 1844, Micheltorena made Sutter an extraordinary offer: in exchange for Sutter's aid in suppressing the rebellion, Micheltorena would grant Sutter the ability to legally grant land in the name of the Mexican government.[105] Although Sutter had previously run into conflict with Mexican and Californio authorities—recall his threat in 1841 to establish an "independent republique"—Micheltorena's offer was tailor-made for Sutter's inflated ego. Sutter above all craved power and legitimacy, and he jumped at the chance to aid Micheltorena.[106] Promising he could now legally grant land to all settlers, Sutter induced many American immigrants to join his military contingent. On New Year's Day 1845, Sutter's army—composed of 100 Natives, 40 Californios, and, most remarkably, roughly 100 American immigrants—left New Helvetia to join Micheltorena.

Thus, in early 1845, with the United States' annexation of Texas accomplished and war with Mexico only a year away, 100 American men joined the army tasked with upholding Mexican sovereignty in California. Of course, their willingness to support Micheltorena had nothing to do with their affection for Mexico, but rather came from pure self-interest. Fighting with Micheltorena and Sutter could guarantee their legal right to a significant amount of land, which had been their primary goal for leaving the United States in the first place. Moreover, many may have calculated—and Micheltorena may have pointed out—that they could trust Micheltorena's promises more than they could trust the Californio rebels. After all, the Graham affair had occurred under Alvarado's governorship.[107] Indeed, Isaac Graham himself readily joined Micheltorena to get his revenge. John Bidwell also volunteered with Micheltorena, for in the moment upholding Mexican sovereignty seemed to best protect his landed interests. For all of the Americans who joined Micheltorena, their political allegiance followed whatever would give them economic prosperity, and if this meant fighting for Mexico, so be it. They were following their own destinies, not the destiny of the United States.

Sutter's heterogeneous militia joined Micheltorena's Mexican army at Monterey, and their combined forces then marched south, as the now-outnumbered Californio army retreated toward Los Angeles. Micheltorena had more than 400 men at his command, thus far the largest army ever seen in California, while Alvarado and Castro's army dwindled to 100, giving Micheltorena overwhelming numerical superiority. Yet over the course of the march south, Micheltorena's American contingent started to make trouble. They showed a tendency to drink and a desire to loot, especially as the long journey started to wear on their clothes and supplies.[108] Although Sutter largely was able to limit both problems, he could not prevent the Americans' Jacksonian tendency to engage in local democracy, which included voting on their leaders, publicly discussing their strategy, and questioning the course of the war. Sutter was unused to any challenge to his authority, and this moment marked the beginning of his disillusionment with Americans in general.[109]

When Sutter's force passed John Marsh's rancho, Sutter tried to persuade Marsh to join him. As a California resident since 1837, Marsh understood the transitory nature of the power of the Mexican state, and he argued that the

Americans' decision to aid Micheltorena was a poor long-term strategy.[110] Sutter then forced Marsh to join the expedition anyway or face imprisonment, but the move backfired. On the march south, Marsh sowed dissension among the American volunteers, the first of several seditious elements in the American ranks.

Trouble continued after Micheltorena's army left Santa Barbara, when José Castro's Californio lancers captured fourteen Americans who had strayed too far from the rest of Micheltorena's force. William Streeter, an American dentist in Castro's employ, persuaded Castro that instead of killing or imprisoning them, he should treat the captive Americans well, explain the Californio cause, and release them after they pledged to no longer take part in hostilities.[111] Castro agreed, and the captured Americans immediately accepted his offer. Streeter then accompanied them back to Micheltorena's army, where this group tried to deter the remaining Americans from fighting. Fearing growing dissent, the elected leader John Gantt, a mountain man who had many years of experience hunting on the California frontier, staged an elaborate Alamo-style motivational speech, drawing a line in the sand and asking all men who had decided to abandon the cause to cross it. At first, twenty-four stepped across the line—the fourteen former captives and ten others. Gantt tried a second speech and drew a second line. No Alamo heroics here: this time, fifty Americans crossed. Micheltorena had lost half of his American contingent.[112]

Meanwhile, in Los Angeles, the Californios were marshaling their defenses. The composition of Micheltorena's army induced sureños to rally to Castro's largely norteño army. Despite their differences, prominent Californios in both the North and South believed that Micheltorena had demonstrated a "black intent" by enlisting Natives, Mexican convicts, and American "adventurers" into his force, essentially a who's who of the groups that elite Californios disliked and distrusted.[113] With Micheltorena camped at the outskirts of the city, the Los Angeles assembly declared Micheltorena's governorship at an end. All Californios, as well as foreigners who lived around Los Angeles, believed that Micheltorena's army presented a radical threat to their property and way of life. As American merchant and San Diego resident Abel Stearns wrote, "I am no friend of revolusions [sic]."[114] While Stearns himself did not fight, he did help muster fifty Americans and other foreigners who lived around Los Angeles to serve in the Californio army. With these additional sureño and foreign volunteers, the Californio force now stood equal in numbers to Micheltorena's army. When the armies faced each other on

February 19, 1845, outside Los Angeles, it appeared to be the makings of the largest battle in California history.

Yet appearances were deceiving, for the Battle of Providencia did not come anywhere close to a cataclysm.[115] As both sides lobbed shells over each other, the Americans fighting with the Californios met with the remaining Americans in Micheltorena's army. Although the details remain murky, the Californio-allied Americans persuaded the Mexican-allied Americans that Micheltorena's promises were meaningless, for the Mexican state had no ability to permanently control California. Even if American immigrants received land from Micheltorena, so the argument went, he and his soldiers would eventually leave California, and the land grants would vanish with them. Therefore, the only sensible thing was to side with the Californios. Eventually the Californio-allied Americans summoned to the meeting Pío Pico, who was a sureño don and the senior member of the Los Angeles ayuntamiento. When Pico arrived, he promised the Mexican-allied Americans that although he could not legally grant land to any non-Mexican citizen, he would not disturb their current occupation of it.[116] He further explained that if the Americans eventually chose to become Mexican citizens, he could then legally grant the land. Ultimately most Americans abandoned Micheltorena and withdrew from the battle, giving numerical superiority to the Californio rebels. Whether the Americans on the Californio side continued to fight remains disputed, but this debate is largely semantic, for the entire battle consisted of a long-range, casualty-free artillery duel.[117] During its course, Sutter was quickly captured; forsaken by his men, this was likely by his own doing. On the day after the battle, Micheltorena asked for surrender terms, which the victorious Castro granted. Within months Micheltorena and his soldiers had returned to Mexico, and California was once again free of Mexican forces.

The successful revolt against Micheltorena represented the apogee of California's independent sovereignty. Norteños, sureños, and Americans had come together—albeit circuitously—to expel the Mexican governor and his army. With Americans once again aiding the Californios (or at least not fighting against them), it was in some ways a reiteration of the 1836 Alvarado revolt, but with two important differences. First, although both rebellions were casualty-free, the 1845 rebellion was waged on a much larger scale, with significantly more soldiers traversing far greater distances. It was, essentially, a popular revolt, compared to Alvarado's glorified coup. Second, the involved Americans were not Graham's coarse trappers of 1836, but many who were becoming California's most influential and prosperous residents: Abel Stearns,

John Bidwell, and John Marsh all played a part. In fact, the roughly 150 Americans who took part in the campaign represented more than 20 percent of the American population in California at the time and a far greater percentage of the adult male population.[118] Clearly, the American population in California was invested in the region's political future.

Of course, many or all of these Americans did not fight in the climactic battle, but their commitment to the cause had hardly been marginal. They committed months of their lives to marching hundreds of miles across the entire span of coastal California. More important, the bloodless settlement between the American forces and the decision by a majority of Americans to sit the battle out did not represent a rift between them and the Californios; rather, it was an acculturation of Americans to Californio-style warfare. The Californio way of war was defined by long campaigns, violent threats, expectations of violence—and then nothing. Once they could assess which side had the upper hand, Californios ratified the status quo without significant bloodshed in order to concentrate on what they considered more important matters: Native threats, personal business, and family affairs.[119] Indeed, family played a key part in this repeated pageant: elite Californios were so intricately bound to each other through marriage and godparentage that there were always family members on the other side of the battle. Americans at the Battle of Providencia may have not had family members on the other side, but they recognized that Americans in California, like elite Californios, were bound by the common interests of land, blood, and culture. Ultimately, they imitated what Californios had done for decades, and the Californios and Mexicans followed suit the next day.

In the aftermath of Micheltorena's surrender, elite Californios and many Americans recognized that their self-interests coincided. Californios had always disliked Mexican rule, and now so did most Americans, even those—or especially those—who had joined Micheltorena's Mexican army. Also like the Californios, American immigrants disdained and feared Natives, prompting Californio leaders to contract with John Marsh, John Gantt, and other American participants in the Battle of Providencia to undertake retaliatory expeditions against Natives for prior raiding. In return, the Americans received a total of 500 cattle and half of all they recovered.[120] In this way, Californios began to bind the more rootless Americans (along with Marsh, who was quite established) to California society, giving them a stake in supporting the status quo. In another area of mutual self-interest, Californios had long detested John Sutter's arrogance and power, and now so did many Americans, who felt it was Sutter's manipulations that had misled them into volunteering for Micheltorena's army.[121] Abandoned by his American allies, Sutter returned to New Helvetia chastened and significantly more isolated. The American and Californio interests seemed so aligned that Californio authorities acquiesced to the growing American presence on the frontier by agreeing to extend "all the guarantees they may desire for establishing themselves in this department, and for living securely in the exercise of their respective occupations."[122] In essence, the Californios were not willing to allow American landownership on a grand scale, but they recognized and accepted the permanence of American settlements. With the knowledge that they could benefit from one another, there seemed to be the makings of a fledgling Californio-American alliance.

It is important, however, to not overstate the strength of this alliance: it was tenuous, and both sides recognized that it could fracture. Perhaps this would come via the clash of legal traditions, as immigrants quickly became frustrated with the paternalistic and—as they saw it—largely ineffectual Mexican legal system.[123] Moreover, Americans were still without legal titles to their land, and they recognized this could produce conflict down the road. Revealingly, John Marsh and Charles Weber put out a "call to foreigners" in March 1845, urging representatives to convene in San Jose on July 4 for the purpose of uniting their political interests.[124] The date was significant, for meeting on the Fourth of July demonstrated Americans' cultural and social unity—a unity that they did not share with Californios. Thirty years later Charles Weber would remember this as an attempt to turn northern California into an independent Texas-style republic, although more likely the meeting was designed to avoid a replay of the Micheltorena rebellion, during which immigrants joined both sides; in future conflicts, Marsh and Weber recognized, they needed to remain united.[125] Whatever its purpose, it seems unlikely the meeting was ever held. Nevertheless, its planning demonstrated that certain immigrants perceived that their interests could be opposed to the Californios in the future, even if their interests aligned for a time.

Despite the ongoing uncertainty of the Californio-American relationship, it is worth pausing to consider a different political future for California, one that briefly revealed itself in the first half of 1845. The Mexican state was clearly powerless in California, as most California residents fully recognized.[126] Therefore, the residents were on their own. For ambitious Americans like Lansford Hastings, who at the time of the rebellion against Micheltorena was promoting his guidebook throughout the western United States, this meant

California could be seized by Americans and run as an independent republic. By contrast, in the eyes of Californio leaders such as José Castro and Pío Pico, and perhaps immigrants like John Marsh, Charles Weber, and John Gantt, independence could be created via an alliance between the two peoples. New England merchants had fully assimilated in the 1820s and 1830s. While the more overtly American immigrants of the 1840s were hardly going to embrace Californio culture in the same fashion, there was no reason that they could not build up Californios' trust. Indeed, one established American trader in San Diego believed that an American-Californio alliance was imminent, which presaged dramatic political developments: "[Californio commandant José Castro's] object was to unite the Californians and foreigners and then declare the *Country independent of Mexico*. That will no doubt be the case soon."[127] The letter writer did not anticipate what for most California inhabitants was also completely unforeseeable: the arrival of the US state.

The Changing Meaning of the "Texas Game" in California

As the revolt against Micheltorena reached its conclusion in the early months of 1845 in California, events with much larger geopolitical ramifications had been taking place in the United States. James K. Polk had secured the Democratic nomination for president over Martin Van Buren thanks to Polk's embrace of US expansion into Texas and Oregon. His subsequent election in the fall of 1844 had drastically altered the geopolitical trajectory of North America. With Texas annexation looming—it was probable by March 1845, but not finalized until the end of the year—the very meaning of Texas had changed. No longer did it designate a separate North American republic created by expatriates from the United States, but a mode of US expansion in which the United States intervened to aid supposedly beleaguered American settlers beset by a hostile foreign power. By May 1845 some pro-expansion US newspapers were already calling for the "Texas game" to be replayed in California, by which they meant American settlers should declare an independent California republic and then seek admission to the United States.[128] In this manner, these editors hoped, American settlers would soon make California a part of the union.

Rumors of Texas annexation had reached California before. In the summer of 1844, Governor Micheltorena had heard that the US annexation of Texas was imminent following a treaty negotiated between Secretary of State John C. Calhoun and Texas commissioners. In response, Micheltorena had planned to implement a new militia system, in which all Californios and naturalized foreigners would drill on Sundays and become "Defenders of the Nation" to protect California against a US attack.[129] However, the US Senate rejected Calhoun's treaty, and Micheltorena's plans lapsed by the end of the summer. Nonetheless, clearly even rumors of Texas annexation caused consternation in California.[130]

During the summer of 1845 California residents again heard reports of the US annexation of Texas, which resulted in a Mexican directive to—yet again—completely prohibit American immigration.[131] Californio officials did take small steps to strengthen the territory against American immigrants and other potential enemies. To obtain desperately needed funds, the new governor, Pío Pico, accelerated the sale of the last nonsecularized mission property. Reminiscent of Micheltorena's pronouncement in 1844, Pico also called for all residents to protect California if war came.[132] Yet overall, Californio officials were either unwilling or unable to enforce the ban on foreigners. Even after Pico sold off the final missions, the California government remained poor. It also remained divided, as José Castro began forming a norteño coalition against the sureño Pico. Moreover, many—although not all—prominent Californios were not entirely opposed to increased American immigration. In the same pronouncement in which he urged all California residents to protect the territory, Pico also ordered that under no circumstances should foreign residents be bothered or suspected of disloyalty.[133] In Sonoma, the town closest to the majority of American settlements, Mariano Vallejo privately longed for further immigration and peaceful annexation by the United States, although publicly he continued to declare his desire to prevent immigration. Continuing his pattern from 1841, Vallejo quietly allowed Americans to keep settling along the northern frontier.[134] Thus, although it prompted small changes, Texas annexation did not change the fundamental dynamics of California politics.

The intrusion of the Texas issue did cause some California residents, especially Americans in tune with international affairs, to speculate on the territory's political future. In general, most observers agreed that California would soon break from Mexico for good. As John Marsh wrote, the Californios "cared about as much for the Government of Mexico as that for Japan."[135] Yet even with rumors of the "Texas game" and possible US annexation, there was no consensus among Americans in California that the United States would ultimately assume sovereignty over the territory. One American echoed the Whig argument that the United States simply could not take on more territory, for it would become "so overgrown and unwieldy that he [i.e., the

United States] would sink under such Ponderosity."[136] Many believed that California would instead become an independent country, although its existence could prove unstable due to the continuing antagonism between norteños and sureños. As one New England merchant in San Diego wrote, "A house divided against itself cannot stand."[137] Considering the dysfunction of California politics, some observers predicted it was more likely that American immigrants in Oregon would join with those in California and form a Pacific republic, with a capital on San Francisco Bay.[138] The trouble brewing between the United States and Britain over Oregon buttressed this belief, for the assumption was that neither country would gain control of the region. Even US consul Thomas Larkin, who longed and worked for US annexation, wrote in the summer of 1845 that he was certain California would eventually be dominated by "millions" of Anglo-Saxons "under a happy government speaking the language we speak," but "under what flag I can not say nor when."[139] He too believed that Oregon and California would soon join together as an "independent nation."[140] Six months before US conquest, California's political fate remained fluid.

However, in December 1845 a new figure arrived in California who did fundamentally alter the dynamics of California politics: US captain John C. Frémont, the head of a contingent of sixty men of the US Army Corps of Topographical Engineers. Frémont had already led two expeditions west, one of which had crossed into unsettled portions of Alta California far from Californio settlements, and his accounts had become best sellers among a US public newly eager for accounts of the region. On this third journey, in the first months of his arrival near settled California, Californio authorities greeted his presence without a great degree of alarm. They agreed that as long as Frémont and his men avoided coastal towns, as he had in his previous journeys, they could resupply and remain in California for the winter. In late February 1846, however, Californios' nonchalance turned to panic when Frémont and his men left camp at San Jose and, instead of marching north toward Oregon as expected, marched south toward Monterey.

In the year following the revolt against Micheltorena, a degree of calm had developed across the American settlements in the Sacramento Valley. But no longer. John Bidwell ably described the rapid transition:

> In past years rumors of threats against Americans in California had been
> rather frequent, several times causing them and other foreigners to hasten
> in the night from all places within one or two hundred miles to Sutter's Fort,

sometimes remaining a week or two, drilling and preparing to resist attack. The first scare of this kind occurred in 1841, when Sutter became somewhat alarmed; the last in 1845. But in every case such rumors had proved to be groundless, so that Americans had ceased to have apprehensions, especially in the presence of such an accessible refuge as Sutter's Fort. And now, in 1846, after so many accessions by immigration, we felt entirely secure, even without the presence of a United States officer and his exploring force of sixty men, until we found ourselves plunged into a war.[141]

The newly long arm of the US state had finally reached California.

CHAPTER SIX

The White Yeomen's Republic of Oregon

More than 500 miles north of the escalating tension between California's American settlers and the Californios, a second contingent of American settlers was engaged in a seemingly much less dramatic affair: establishing Oregon's first newspaper. On February 5, 1846, the first issue of the *Oregon Spectator* appeared in print; it had been funded by seven prominent Oregonians and a public campaign offering $10 shares. Although six of these seven were members of the Oregon provisional government, the newspaper stated explicitly that no column would be allowed to "discuss politics" in any manner whatsoever.[1] In the midst of an era of extreme partisanship, this stance was out of touch with prevailing American sentiment, but the reason for it was simple. The editors believed that the settlers of Oregon had created a remarkably contented and prosperous society already, and they did not want partisanship to break apart their quasi-utopian experiment. As the newspaper stated, the Oregon provisional government had "but one interest to represent, and that interest [is] the welfare of Oregon and the citizens unanimously."[2]

The lack of drama in Oregon's only newspaper is part and parcel of the seemingly unique status of Oregon in the era of Manifest Destiny. While various military and/or political clashes erupted across the continent in the early 1840s—in Texas and California, among the Mormons and the Cherokees, in eastern cities, and in the halls of Washington, DC—Oregon remained mostly free of conflict. Certainly, from a diplomatic standpoint, the United States and Great Britain engaged in increasingly bellicose rhetoric in the mid-1840s over how the territory would be divided, but there is a disconnect between this history and that of Oregon itself, where American settlers, British employees of the Hudson's Bay Company (HBC), and even the Native peoples of the Willamette Valley mostly got along with one another, with a few minor exceptions, until 1847. The agreeable nature of Oregon certainly registered with Lansford Hastings. He sought to create an independent Oregon in 1842 but found few who were willing to take such a risk, and he promptly departed for what he hoped was the riper territory of California. Without men like Hastings, who were willing to rock the political boat, Oregon remained an undramatic place: first it was peacefully infiltrated by the HBC, then it was peacefully settled by Americans, and finally it was peacefully annexed by the United States. As one historian of US expansion wrote, Oregon was the "cleanest and least dismaying" of all the United States' continental acquisitions.[3]

Although this history is downplayed in national accounts of the era, local historians, family genealogists, and Oregon's historical societies have amply filled the void for two good reasons. The first is human beings' general desire to celebrate their family heritage, and in this Oregonians are no different. Yet theirs is not simply any heritage, but a *heroic* heritage epitomized by the image of the hardy Oregon pioneer and the epic journey over the Oregon Trail.[4] Indeed, the story of early Oregon reads like a blueprint for a certain trope of American exceptionalism. In the 1840s, Oregon promised free land to all white settlers while at the same time prohibiting slavery, and as such enshrined ideals of freedom and equality. The first Americans in Oregon were Protestant missionaries, followed by resilient pioneering families, two groups that white Americans could laud without hesitation. As evidenced by the nonpartisan stance of the *Oregon Spectator*, Americans in Oregon seemed united in creating a just and equitable society, and they did not let politics or self-interest get in the way of their goals. Even the brutality of Oregon's Indian wars in the late 1840s and 1850s could be downplayed, for they were inaugurated by the tragic 1847 Whitman massacre, in which nonviolent missionaries were killed by several Cayuse Natives who believed the missionaries had purposefully caused an outbreak of disease: in essence, it was all a big misunderstanding. Early Oregon thus allows white Americans to tell a story about themselves that they want to hear. Such is the seeming innocence of the Oregon story that it was marketed to third-graders in the classic 1980s computer game *The Oregon Trail*. Early Oregon pioneers also possessed this self-conception, and they continued to celebrate their past feats in the later decades of the nineteenth century.

To give the pioneers' historical conception of themselves credit, there was a significant degree of truth in how they understood their past. In many ways, they did create a white yeomen's haven in Oregon, at least for a few years. Yet this image masked two complicating factors. First, it downplayed or ignored some of the unseemlier aspects of this society, particularly its racist underpinnings. Oregon's American settlers were at times quite prejudiced toward the employees of the Hudson's Bay Company who also lived in the territory, particularly toward the Native women and Métis children, who constituted a majority of the population. More blatantly, white Oregonians passed an infamous anti-black exclusion law that tried to maintain racial purity by literally the power of the whip: any free black person who remained for more than six months in Oregon would receive at least twenty lashes. Second, Oregonians created their yeomen's utopia not to mimic US society, but to create an alternative. Oregon was not an outgrowth of the United States, but a reaction against it, for such a haven did not then exist in the United States. This ideological stance led to important geopolitical ramifications: because Oregon pioneers expatriated themselves as a reaction against US society, once they arrived in Oregon they did not act as US nationalists upholding the United States' right to the territory. On the contrary, very few settlers were willing to fight the British in Oregon to establish US control; many were rather ambivalent about US annexation; and a minority even hoped to create an independent Oregon republic. Oregon, therefore, was not the supreme example of the United States' Manifest Destiny, but a demonstration about how tenuous that destiny truly was.

Oregon before Overland Migration

In 1818, the United States and Great Britain agreed to the "joint occupation" of the vast Oregon Country, which stretched from the northern border of Spanish California to the southern border of Russian Alaska. The countries renewed this agreement in 1827, essentially allowing time to sort out the Oregon boundary for good. Until the early 1840s, time seemed to be on the side of the British, in the form of the Hudson's Bay Company and its chief factor, John McLoughlin. In 1824 McLoughlin assumed control of Fort Vancouver, situated on the north side of the Columbia River on today's Oregon-Washington state border, a few miles north of modern Portland, and within several years the HBC had created nothing less than a fur empire in the Pacific Northwest. By bringing in a multinational group of workers and forming lasting trading partnerships with the Native peoples of the region, the HBC dominated the international fur trade and effectively shut out all US competition. While the HBC's power rested on trade, it also facilitated settlement around Fort Vancouver, where former HBC employees created a small agrarian community. This community, as well as relations within the HBC as a whole, was based on the intermarriage of French Canadian men and Native women, including McLoughlin and his Métis wife, Marguerite, whose mother was Cree and father was French Canadian.[5] While the community's race relations were fluid, its incipient class relations were not, as McLoughlin ran Fort Vancouver and its environs in a strictly hierarchical manner. By the mid-1830s, Oregon Country, particularly the fertile Willamette Valley, was practically McLoughlin's private fiefdom, and any intruder into the region had to navigate his rule.

But McLoughlin's talents could not prevent the spread of infectious diseases among Oregon's Natives. The thousands of Kalapuya and Chinook people in the Willamette Valley had prospered in loosely organized villages, but in 1831 an "intermittent fever"—probably malaria—first spread into the region. Typical of European infectious diseases, it affected but did not devastate those of European background, but it utterly ravaged the local Natives and did so for the next several years. By 1841, the Kalapuya and Chinook peoples had lost more than 90 percent of their populations.[6] Beyond the tragic loss of thousands of lives, these yearly epidemics had two other effects. First, while the Métis community living in the vicinity of Fort Vancouver was largely unaffected, the deaths of so many surrounding Natives left the French Canadians isolated and potentially vulnerable, for they no longer had the ability to find substantial Native allies in case of conflict.[7] Second, the Willamette Valley now lay open for settlement, for the remaining Natives had no way to resist any significant population incursion. Unlike California, where tens of thousands of Natives from the interior continued to threaten Californio and American settlements, the Natives of the Willamette Valley would be irrelevant as geopolitical players in the power struggles to follow. Beyond the Willamette Valley in the larger Pacific Northwest, Natives remained powerful, but it was not to these places that most Americans would travel.

In 1834, the Methodist missionary Jason Lee journeyed overland to Oregon. Lee was born in Quebec, close to the Vermont border, but as a teen he left for the United States, where he attended school and became a Methodist—yet another small example of the porousness of North American borders at the time. He was the first of a series of Methodist and Presbyterian ministers from the United States who hoped to convert Oregon's Natives to Protestant Christianity. McLoughlin welcomed Lee, directed him to settle near the French Canadians in the Willamette Valley, and provided him with supplies to get the first mission off the ground. McLoughlin would eventually regret his decision, but initial relations between the HBC and the missionaries were hospitable. By 1840 missionaries had opened more than a dozen stations, both Methodist and Presbyterian. Spread as far as north as Puget Sound and as far west as Walla Walla, all of these missions ministered to local Native people, many of whom welcomed the needed supplies and care in the aftermath of each yearly epidemic. Yet the number of stations did not translate to successful conversion; although many Natives took part in some mission activities, few adopted Christianity and its "civilized" life wholesale. Because of their failure, Lee and his cohort over time assumed the role more of secular colonizers than of Christian missionaries, and their participation in commerce and politics quickly made them important players in Oregon's local affairs.[8]

The missionaries also awakened Americans in the United States to Oregon's economic and political potential. There had been a few haphazard efforts to induce American settlement previously, but only with Jason Lee's return to the United States in 1838 did American interest become self-sustaining.[9] Lee returned primarily to recruit missionary reinforcements and to secure his leadership role—at that point under question by both missionaries in Oregon and the Methodist Missionary Board in the United States—but his speeches reached a broader audience. By 1839 potential settlers formed the Oregon Provisional Emigration Society, "Oregon fever" engulfed western states, and the small Peoria Party made its journey to Oregon, the first of its kind (preceding the Bidwell-Bartleson Party's journey to California by two years).[10] These developments led to a mutually reinforcing cycle: the more Americans who arrived, the more reports on Oregon were sent back to the United States, which in turn led to more American migrants. Oregon residents of all backgrounds recognized that the dozens of American arrivals would soon become hundreds, and eventually hundreds would become thousands.

In 1838, two Catholic missionaries also journeyed to Oregon. Since 1834 the French Canadian community had petitioned for Catholic priests in order to form their own parish. The French Canadians were not necessarily reacting to the arrival of Methodist and Presbyterian missionaries, with whom they largely got along. Rather, they simply wanted to create a religious community of their own.[11] However, the priests' subsequent missionizing efforts toward Natives quickly put them at odds with the Protestants. Protestant missionaries' resentment only increased in the early 1840s, as they perceived that Catholics were "penetrating" the country and winning the battle for Native souls.[12] To counteract this development, the Protestants believed they would need to rely on the influx of American settlers they knew was coming.[13]

Facing East and West from Missouri

In 1840 and 1841, a few dozen Americans arrived in Oregon, and more than 100 arrived in 1842, but it was in 1843 that overland immigration truly swelled. That year, 875 Americans traveled to Oregon as part of the Great Migration. They were followed by 1,475 migrants in 1844 and 2,500 in 1845.[14] All of these people were leaving US borders and, like migrants to Texas and California, were in effect expatriating themselves from their native land. Indeed, Jason Lee referred to Oregon as "this expatriated country," reflecting Oregon inhabitants' ongoing uncertainty about the region's political future.[15]

Of course, while Oregon's political future remained unknown, it was more defined than other western regions in the early 1840s. It seemed certain that the United States would acquire at least *some* of Oregon Country. In this regard Oregon differed from California, which was under Mexican sovereignty, was governed by the Californios, and had much of its territory still under Native control—characteristics that attracted a significantly smaller number of migrants, many of whom were ready to use violence to achieve their ends. In contrast, prior to Oregon annexation in 1846, the much larger group of Oregon immigrants remained at peace with the HBC, the British government, the Natives of the Willamette Valley, and one another. While these migrants took substantial risks in crossing a continent, they proved much more reticent to take bold political action once they arrived in Oregon.[16]

While migrants possessed a multitude of reasons for risking the overland journey, for most of them economics was the primary driver. Specifically, migrants were responding to the Panic of 1837, whose effects did not reach some western states until 1841. From these western states most migrants came—from Missouri above all, but also from other states in the western Upper South (Arkansas, Kentucky, Tennessee) and the Old Northwest, all of which suffered during the depression.[17] During the early 1840s, wheat prices fell by more than half across the Midwest.[18] Moreover, many families simply could not get their agricultural goods to market, for they farmed land distant from major rivers and roads since land speculators had already purchased all the prime real estate.[19] In certain western regions, even specie was hard to come by. Thus, for many in the western states, the economic situation had become untenable. As one migrant noted, "I realiz[ed] my limitations in that then well settled country."[20] Most migrants traveled as families, and it cost $125–$150 to outfit each family member for the journey. Clearly, migrants possessed at least some resources and were not drawn from the most destitute portion of the population.[21] However, after spending most of their money to reach Oregon, many arrived in dire straits. As one settler noted, "The people which have emigrated here are mostly poor and in want of everything."[22]

To migrants, however, being penniless in Oregon would only be a temporary problem, for Oregon offered free land—and the United States did not. In 1839, awakened to Oregon's potential by Jason Lee, Missouri senator Lewis Linn proposed a bill granting 640 acres in Oregon Country to any man who made the journey. Linn hoped to rapidly populate Oregon with Americans, thereby giving the United States a better claim to the territory. Although Congress largely ignored the bill, westerners did not, and many seized on the 640 acres as a basis for their migration. The earliest migrants simply claimed land for themselves because they were the first to arrive, but soon Linn's proposed law in Congress became an actual law in Oregon: in 1843, the Oregon provisional government enshrined the 640-acre promise in the Law of Land Claims.[23] As long as a claimant made improvements to his land within six months of making the claim and then resided on it within a year, he gained legal title.[24]

This liberal land policy stood in direct contrast with the land policy of the United States, which had favored speculator over squatter since the nation's founding. While there always existed "empty" land (since most Americans disregarded Natives' prior claims), until 1841 acquiring land was prohibitively expensive for all but the wealthiest. The federal government consistently emphasized accruing revenue above populating the West.[25] This policy changed somewhat when Congress passed the Preemption Act of 1841. Known as the Log Cabin Bill, it allowed squatters to purchase 160 acres of land on which they had previously settled for the price of $1.25 an acre. Symbolically, this law was an important break from the conservative policies of the past, but even $1.25 per acre was too expensive for many westerners during the depths of the depression, as many were already in debt.[26] Indeed, there is some evidence that the Preemption Act may have even exacerbated inequality. When squatters were unable to buy their land, they had two options: they could borrow money from loan sharks at usurious interest rates, which they were often unable to repay, or they could become tenants under the speculators who purchased the land that the squatters had coveted. Thus, by midcentury more than half of all midwestern farmers were tenants.[27] Meanwhile, in Oregon, migrants could obtain four times as much land for free. Recalled Missouri pioneer Peter Burnett, "[The Oregon] land would ultimately be able to pay [my debts.] There was at least a chance. In staying where I was, I saw no reasonable probability of ever being able to pay my debts."[28] Thousands of other Americans agreed.

Migrants' desire for land also possessed ideological roots. Free land in Oregon promised not just financial gain, but a specific way of life. By acquiring substantial holdings, men would be able to bestow their many sons with land of their own. This practice had once been the norm, but the increasingly market-driven United States made it significantly less feasible.[29] Thus families could now reassert this tradition beyond US borders. Moreover, many yeomen farmers had become disillusioned with the increasingly capitalistic US economy, with its rampant speculation, boom-and-bust cycles, and growing commercialization of agriculture, which was at odds with their values and customs. They hoped the excesses of capitalism could be avoided in Oregon. An Oregon resident wrote to his brothers in the United States that one benefit of Oregon's economy was that "there is no money here at present. . . . Our wealth consists in herds of cattle, horses, and hogs, etc., which we can exchange for all the necessisaries [*sic*] of life."[30] Another memoir emphatically stated of life in Oregon: "NO breaking each other up for debts."[31]

In essence, Oregon migrants sought a return to the ideal of the agrarian yeoman, prosperous but not wealthy, unbeholden to neither man nor market. Alva Shaw, an Oregon pioneer from Ohio, summarized this attitude best: "[In Ohio], you are a slave to your property, your labor is principally spent for [others], while here [in Oregon] a man's property will support him."[32] Moreover, Oregon promised a society of much greater equality than that found in the East. As another pioneer remembered, "All was on an equality. . . . there was no upper class, no middle or lower, but all was on the same plan[e?]."[33] Oregon was not just a solution to individual economic hardship, but a solution to a broader socioeconomic world with which migrants could no longer identify.

To be more precise: this was an ideal of the *white* and *male* yeoman farmer, since the ideology of the yeoman was rooted in issues of race and slavery, gender and family. In regard to the former: with a few rare exceptions, slaveholders, even those who hailed from states like Missouri and Arkansas, did not migrate to Oregon in the early 1840s. There were two reasons for this. First, slaveholders were better able to navigate the depression, for their enslaved people were an asset on which they could fall back in hard times, selling or using them as collateral to gain access to capital.[34] They had no need to travel to Oregon in the first place. Second, Oregon's 640 acres of free land represented a free soil ideal. Oregon migrants chose Oregon because slavery was absent. Either these migrants came from the Old Northwest and brought their free soil ideology with them to Oregon, or they were non-slaveholders in slaveholding states and thus had little attachment to a system that had plainly not benefited them.[35] One Oregon resident argued that slaveholding made whites inherently lazy, which a free soil Oregon would prevent.[36] Another stated that slavery was one of the "great evils" of the United States and other countries, which Oregon would avoid.[37] Unsurprisingly, the Oregon provisional government explicitly outlawed slavery in 1844, mandating that all owners free their enslaved people once they arrived.

Oregon offered American migrants a refreshingly clear picture as to its stance: unlike the increasingly divided half-free, half-slave republic they had just left, Oregon would be entirely committed to free soil. In this sense, Oregon acted as the converse to Mirabeau Lamar's explicitly proslavery Republic of Texas. Like Texas, Oregon would eliminate ambiguity, only in reverse: just as no future Supreme Court case or federal law would eliminate slavery in Texas, no case or law would ever force slavery on Oregon.

Yet Oregonians paired this commendable antislavery law with a brutal racist corollary that also eliminated ambiguity: while enslaved people would be free upon arriving in Oregon, they—and all other black people, for that matter—had to immediately leave the region or suffer twenty to thirty-nine lashes. What became known as the Lash Law would solve the issue not only of slavery, but of race. This stance was not unique to Oregon. Many northern US states, particularly those of the Old Northwest, attempted to maintain lily-white populations by passing Black Laws of varying levels of severity against their local African American populations, which included restrictions on settlement, migration, labor, and citizenship. On a comparative level, they successfully prevented the number of black people living in the Northwest from ever reaching the number that lived in the Northeast. On an absolute level, however, the Black Laws failed to expel black people from the Old Northwest or even prevent their population growth. These laws also failed to prevent radical abolitionism and its principle of racial equality from slowly infiltrating the region, as black and white activists continued to battle against the Black Laws through the Civil War.[38] Oregon, presumably, would have none of these problems. The Law of Land Claims stated that only white men would receive free land, which would discourage black people from migrating to Oregon. And for the few that still did, the Lash Law would force them to leave. Oregon would be, as one settler noted, "superior" to the eastern states because it would avoid the evil of "mixed races."[39]

The notorious Lash Law and Oregon's more general attempt to prevent the mixing of races stemmed from two incidents in 1844 involving James Saules, one of Oregon's very few black residents. In the first, which was eventually known as the Cockstock affair, Saules disputed ownership of a horse with a Chinook man named Cockstock. Eventually their disagreement led to violence among Cockstock, Saules, and several other Oregon settlers, in which Cockstock and two white Oregonians were killed. Two months later, Saules was arrested for reportedly joining with several Natives to assault a white Oregonian who, revealingly, was one of the few migrants who hailed from the South and espoused vehement proslavery views.[40] Due to a dearth of unbiased sources, many of the details of these two incidents—including whether they were connected and Saules's guilt or innocence—will forever remain unknown. Clearly, however, white Oregonians saw Saules as a threat simply because he was black. His very existence in the Willamette Valley shattered its promise of racial purity, and following a sham trial, Saules was expelled from the community. The Lash Law was passed only a few weeks later. Ultimately, it seems, the law was never actually enforced, but it provided a clear message to potential migrants: Oregon was for white people only, and to a callously extreme extent, black people were not welcome.

The yeoman ideal was also predicated on gender. Oregon promised incoming male migrants that they could achieve a version of masculinity that seemed increasingly difficult to attain in the United States. Landless men had been attracted to the promise of free land in Canada during the Patriot War, and now landless men were attracted to Oregon for the same reason—although this time the promise was fulfilled. In classic republicanism, landownership secured a man's personal independence and his virtue, the bedrock qualities on which American society was built.[41] In more concrete terms, this meant a log cabin, a modest farm, and a few cattle, all of which provided for a man's family. Letters and memoirs from Oregon painted just such an idyllic picture, even to the point of describing the actual home. Charlotte Mathery Kirkwood, who came to Oregon as a young girl, remembered how her father purchased a house from a Methodist missionary, and she described it: "It was a good house, built of logs. The doors and windows had been shipped around the horn. It had one of the old fashioned brick chimneys coming down the middle with a fireplace on each side. It was a fine farm."[42] In many ways, she painted a portrait of the quintessential nineteenth-century American dream, which appealed to thousands of American men who longed for land and a home of their own. And for these men, it was much easier to fulfill this dream beyond US borders than within them. The 1841 Log Cabin Bill in the United States rarely generated an actual log cabin, but Kirkwood's memoir makes it clear the Oregon land law did.

In the idealized version of the yeoman farmer, the nuclear family assumed an important role. Men were supposed to watch over their wives, sons, and daughters in a caring, paternalistic manner. It was no coincidence that migration to Oregon was largely a family affair. As a letter from Oregon printed in the *St. Louis Gazette* proclaimed, "Come to Oregon, and make your children rich and live happy yourself."[43] The order was clear: first "your children," then "yourself." The emphasis on family was eventually enshrined in Oregon law. While the 1843 land law promised 640 acres to white men, later manifestations emphasized the entire family, promising married men 640 acres but single men only half that. However, if a man arrived single in the territory, he could still claim 640 acres if he married within a certain period of time, creating what one early settler remembered as a "mad rush for a wife."[44] Moreover, the law provided for a son to inherit this claim if his father died and also gave 120 extra acres of land to him in his own name (or 320 acres if he was married).[45]

Temperance was key to this yeoman ideal. A moral father and husband avoided liquor. Unsurprisingly, Oregon society was predicated on temperance. This attitude originated with the first American missionaries in the region, who sought to prevent "spiritous liquors" from infiltrating and potentially destroying Native societies.[46] The missionaries also influenced early migrants, and both groups mentioned Oregon's temperance stance in letters to their friends and families in the United States. As one early overland guidebook stated, because there were no "intoxicating liquors" in Oregon, "there is more harmony in society than we have ever known or heard of, in any part of the world."[47] Temperance likely acted as a pull to a certain type of migrant who valued order, concord, and morality. By 1844, Oregonians made temperance the law of the land, as the Oregon provisional government passed an order that prohibited the importation, sale, or distilling of all alcohol.[48] In many ways, therefore, Oregon offered white migrants a quasi utopia—"quasi" because, unlike utopian communities like the Owenites or Fourierists, its promise remained grounded in traditional, real-world practices of landownership, labor, and the family.

There were, of course, other reasons to be pulled to Oregon that were not grounded in economics and ideology. For some, the primary motivator was health: Oregon supposedly offered a disease-free climate at a time when "ague" (malaria) routinely erupted in the Mississippi River valley.[49] Some migrants had the propensity to move from place to place, and Oregon was simply their next destination. Others, above all the minority group of single men, were simply yearning for adventure.[50] Each of these motivations, however, could combine with the economic and ideological prospects of Oregon society. Rarely did a single factor induce migration.

These myriad factors did not, however, include patriotism. Whatever their reasons for traveling to Oregon, migrants were not "winning" the region for the United States—despite what many later claimed in their memoirs. In many memoirs, migrants recalled that they left for Oregon with distinctly patriotic intentions. For example, one migrant said he made the following claim upon leaving US borders: "Well, I allow that the United States has the best right to that country, and I am going to help make that right good."[51] While a few Oregonians argued for their patriotism immediately following Oregon's annexation to the United States in 1846, this attitude only became truly ubiquitous in the second half of the nineteenth century. By then, "saving Oregon" became the keystone of the Oregon "pioneer tradition," and former migrants celebrated their accomplishments in annual meetings of the Oregon Pioneer Association.[52] However, in the diaries and letters written before 1846, the United States was largely a nonentity. No migrant lamented leaving US borders, and before 1845 no migrants expressed a desire for US annexation prior to their departure on the Overland Trail. Ultimately Oregon migrants were matter-of-fact expatriates looking for more secure lives in the Pacific Northwest, concerned more with gaining free land than with that land's future political fate.

Nevertheless, migrants' elevation of pragmatism over patriotism does not mean they were opposed to US expansion. On the contrary, compared to the other two groups of western overlanders—the anti-US Mormons and the volatile, grasping men who went to California seeking patriarchal power—future Oregonians were far more concerned with US interests. While migrants were clearly dissatisfied with their current economic prospects and with aspects of US society more generally, they were not shedding their American heritage when they left US borders. In Oregon, the Fourth of July remained an important day. Some residents reverentially remarked on the anniversary in their diaries, and the community routinely chose this date as an opportune time to hold important meetings.[53] Moreover, Americans in Oregon remained staunchly committed to republican government. And more than any other breakaway Americans discussed in this book save perhaps those who went to

Texas to fight Mexico in the mid-1830s, a majority unambiguously supported US annexation.

Yet as with the Anglo-Texans, many of whom embraced Texas independence after the United States scorned their bid for annexation, other breakaway Americans could change their minds. This potential was always present in Oregon. Most migrants supported US interests not out of some abiding affection for the United States as a political entity, but for the same pragmatic reasons they had chosen to migrate to Oregon in the first place: land. They believed that with US annexation would come the passage of Linn's Oregon bill in Congress, which would legally guarantee them the holdings they had acquired by occupation. Thus US annexation became a more enticing scenario once they were in Oregon than it had seemed prior to their leaving US borders. Yet support for US annexation was never unequivocal. Moreover, pro-annexationists faced a minority who hoped for a different future: Oregon's complete independence.

The Defeat of Oregon Independence, Part I

Despite its brief duration and the small population over which it governed, the history of the Oregon provisional government is surprisingly complex, for each year brought a new set of migrants, which meant hundreds or even thousands of new voters, some of whom possessed new motivations and new ideas. Thus, the decisions made in the spring and summer of one year were often completely overturned by the spring of the following year. This fluidity of population meant not only that the government structure was constantly in flux, but also that there were never any official political parties around which to organize. Oregon's political "parties" were simply loose factions that rarely cohered for an extended period of time.[54]

The political beginnings of Oregon started with the death of Ewing Young in 1841. Young was an American mountain man who had become the wealthiest Oregon settler by virtue of his early 1834 arrival. When more migrants arrived, his well-developed land claim assumed the roles of marketplace, store, bank, and factory.[55] Because many Willamette Valley settlers were either Young's creditors or debtors, the community decided that Oregon required a probate court to administer Young's estate after he died without a will. Therefore, in February 1841, both Americans and French Canadians gathered to arrange the matter. At first they also discussed drafting a constitution and creating a more organized government. However, as one participant remembered, this idea "died away" because the population was still so small (perhaps 150 people), and the "peace and harmony of the community could be preserved without it."[56] Ultimately the settlers decided to simply appoint a probate judge and several administrators.

In these early years of settlement, there was a second reason that both the French Canadians and Americans saw little need to form a more substantial government: both put their faith in larger political entities. For the French Canadians, this was the HBC, which they had long worked for and trusted. For Americans, it was the United States. Not only were they encouraged to go to Oregon because of Lewis Linn's land bill, but several times in the early 1840s the United States made its presence known in Oregon, thereby providing further hopes that US annexation was imminent. The first instance was the arrival of the US Exploring Expedition led by Charles Wilkes, which traveled up the Columbia River in early 1842. As one American missionary remembered, "The arrival on the coast of Oregon of so extensive an armament produced a very great excitement in the community, and but little was heard of but the Exploring Squadron during its somewhat protracted stay."[57] Americans' excitement may have been amplified by the British attempt to counteract American immigration with settlers of their own. Earlier in the year, the HBC had facilitated the migration of twenty-five families from the Red River Colony in Canada to Oregon, which would prove to be the only substantial British migration to the contested territory.[58] Wilkes's arrival allayed American settlers' fears that they were outnumbered, and it proved to them that the United States cared for their plight.

Their hopes were soon dashed. Wilkes paid the settlers little attention, for he had concerns of his own. While in Oregon, one of his vessels hit a sandbar and sank at the mouth of the Columbia River. No lives were lost, but Wilkes needed to arrange transportation and supplies for the stranded sailors, which meant he depended on McLoughlin and the HBC and needed to stay on McLoughlin's good side. He was not supposed to interfere in continental geopolitics anyway. The US Exploring Expedition's mission in the Pacific was twofold: gain as much scientific knowledge as possible for the United States and act as a protective ally for US shipping to China, Hawaii, and other Pacific nations.[59] Thus, he trod softly when the expedition moved toward the HBC-dominated Pacific Northwest, ensuring McLoughlin's acquiescence as Wilkes surveyed the region.[60] When he spoke to Oregon settlers, he remained silent on the subject of US annexation.[61] Personally, he doubted Oregon would ever become part of the United States. He predicted that Oregon and California would eventually join together to form a "powerful maritime nation" that would "control the destinies of the Pacific." While he believed that nation would be controlled by the "Anglo-Norman race," it would not be part of the United States.[62]

Wilkes's lack of interest in Oregon politics, as well as what migrants perceived as a haughty attitude, frustrated the American settlers in Oregon.[63] As one missionary wrote, "I am sorry to perceive that the Commander of this expedition, thinks himself too *important* and *dignified* . . . to give that attention and consequently to impart additional influence that he might to American settlers, and American missionaries, as I believe they are entitled to."[64] Americans' dashed hopes for Wilkes's support were representative of their general feeling of vulnerability in the early 1840s, when they were still outnumbered by the HBC-affiliated Métis families, who favored Great Britain. They could not predict certain developments that historians now take for granted. They could not predict, for example, that the British would never again succeed in facilitating migration to the region. For all they knew, the Red River settlers were the first of many. They also did not know that fur trade profits were declining and that HBC's dominance would soon be at an end. Thus, it is no wonder that these Americans saw US annexation as a solution to their vulnerability, and they dramatized this vulnerability to gain the federal government's attention. In 1838, 1840, and 1843, various groups of American settlers sent petitions to Congress that pleaded for US annexation and a territorial government. As the 1840 petition warned, if the United States did not soon extend its jurisdiction into Oregon, American settlers would be "exposed to be destroyed by the savages around them, and *others that would do them harm.*"[65] This statement played on a common assumption in the United States that McLoughlin and the HBC (the "others that would do them harm") were permanently in league with Oregon's Natives, and together they could destroy the small American settlement at a moment's notice.

The petitions reflected a palpable feeling among American settlers that Oregon was slipping away to the British in the early 1840s. For Protestant missionaries, this feeling had a theological bent, for they associated any Catholic success as a victory for British sovereignty. Their belief was quite irrational, for Britain had long been a bastion of Protestantism, and Parliament had only recently repealed centuries of anti-Catholic legislation. To Protestant missionaries on the ground in Oregon, however, the two went together. As Presbyterian missionary Marcus Whitman stated, "I think the papal effort is designed to convey the country over to the English."[66] This "papal effort" was twofold: increased Catholic immigration and Catholic success in missionizing the Native people.[67] While the 1841 Red River settlers were the only Catholic migrants of the period, Catholicism did take hold among Oregon's Natives to a much greater extent than did either Methodism or Presbyterianism, both of which continued to fail at finding converts. Protestants directed much of the vitriolic blame for their failures at John McLoughlin personally, for he was a combination of all their fears: he was a Catholic, the chief factor of the HBC, and a British subject. In Jason Lee's eyes, McLoughlin "would rejoice to have the whole country under Catholic domination."[68] Gone were the days when Protestant missionaries valued McLoughlin for his life-saving supplies.

McLoughlin's business was another source of contestation. The Methodists disputed McLoughlin's claim to the potentially valuable Willamette Falls, located in Oregon City. Missionary Alvan Waller built a sawmill alongside the falls, arguing that McLoughlin had never improved his claim, and thus the land was open for the taking. Waller's argument was disingenuous, for he was ignoring local land claims and betting on international developments. If the United States gained jurisdiction over the Willamette Valley, the recently passed 1841 Preemption Law would go into effect, part of which stated that American claims took precedence over foreign claims. No wonder Waller and his missionary allies longed for US annexation.[69] Waller went so far as to petition the chief justice of the US Supreme Court, Roger Taney, to grant him permanent rights to the disputed land, but as the United States had no official jurisdiction over Oregon, the letter was ignored.[70] Moreover, beyond Waller's specific dispute, many newly arrived Americans resented McLoughlin's prosperity and the monopolistic dominance of the HBC—doubly so, because they remained dependent on McLoughlin's supplies.[71]

All of the fears and frustrations of Oregon settlers reflected a larger truth: in the early 1840s, there existed in the Willamette Valley an "other"—whether defined as Great Britain, Catholicism, John McLoughlin, or Oregon's Natives. Of these threats, Britain loomed the largest: it was Britain that stood behind the influence of the HBC and the power of John McLoughlin; it was Britain that would supposedly incite Native attacks on American settlers; and it was Britain that supposedly supported Catholicism. That the British were a legitimate presence in Oregon by treaty fostered the American settlers' continued attachment to the United States. Certainly, American settlers, both missionaries and overlanders alike, exaggerated the British threat (at least as it existed on the ground), but considering the rampant anglophobia and anti-Catholicism of many Americans, their attitude was unsurprising. And while they did inflate the power of their enemies, Americans in Oregon were indeed a rather weak and powerless group. They were still outnumbered by British-allied settlers in Oregon, and they still depended on HBC supplies for survival. Thus, when US Indian agent Elijah White arrived in the Willamette Valley in late 1842 with a hundred American settlers, Americans already living in Oregon celebrated. Wilkes and the US Exploring Expedition may have disappointed them six months prior, but White's arrival, they believed, presaged greater US involvement in Oregon.[72] After all, White was a representative of the US government (although whether he had any jurisdiction in Oregon was a matter of doubt). Adding White's arrival to their knowledge of Lewis Linn's and Thomas Hart Benton's continued agitations for Oregon annexation in Congress, it is no wonder that American migrants in Oregon once again believed that US annexation was imminent.[73]

Despite their faith in US action, American men in Oregon also understood that the community was growing at a rapid pace, and it required a formal government to provide order. Many of the HBC's French Canadian men agreed that, at the very least, the subject should be discussed, although they remained wary of the Americans' ultimate intentions. Thus, in 1843, both groups met several times at the village of Champoeg to discuss just what structure this government should take. Because these meetings resulted in the formation of the Oregon provisional government, the Champoeg story has become a key component of early Oregon lore. While the details are in dispute, the general outline is not. The first meeting started somewhat inauspiciously in March 1843, when Oregon settlers convened at Champoeg to discuss predatory wolves that were attacking livestock. During these wolf meetings, they once again discussed creating a formal government for the community, but unlike after Ewing Young's death or Wilkes's arrival, this time the discussions proved productive. Informal talks then continued among the settlers until May 2, when, once again meeting at Champoeg, they officially founded the Oregon provisional government.

According to the traditional narrative, these debates and the final vote reflected the ethnic divide of the community. On one side were the French Canadian men affiliated with the HBC. Once willing to engage in discussions about forming a government, after hearing from the Americans at Champoeg they were now adamantly opposed, for presumably any fledgling government would interfere with their allegiance to the quasi government of the HBC and Great Britain more generally. On the other side were American settlers. They desired a government that would act for US interests and serve as a placeholder until the United States officially gained control of the territory. In the famous meeting in early May 1843, the American settlers won the day by a narrow margin of 52–50, after two French Canadians switched their votes and allied with the Americans. Thus, the Oregon provisional government was formed; Oregon's Organic Laws (as the code was termed) were written; and Oregon Country was "saved" for the United States.[74]

Yet the traditional Champoeg story is subject to doubt. It was based on the account of William Gray, a cantankerous Methodist layman and vociferous opponent of the HBC who was present at Champoeg. Gray's *A History of Oregon* was one of only two detailed accounts of the government discussions, and it conflicted entirely with the account of Robert Newell, an American mountain man who had settled in Oregon in the late 1830s and also present at Champoeg. Although it is impossible to prove definitively which is correct, Newell's account lines up much more with the other prevailing evidence on Champoeg, and it should be taken as the more likely scenario. As described by Newell, Gray, rather than desiring US annexation, was "determined upon the act of secession."[75] Newell's continued use of the word "secession" reflected that he wrote his account in 1867, only two years after the Civil War. In reality, in 1843, Oregonians had nothing to secede *from*. Gray's actual goal was Oregon independence, and a minority of the attendees of the Champoeg meeting, some of whom were also American, supported him.[76] One of these supporters was none other than Lansford Hastings, the soon-to-be California booster and schemer of California independence. Hastings had journeyed to Oregon in 1842 and upon his arrival worked as McLoughlin's lawyer in the Waller-McLoughlin land dispute. At Champoeg, Hastings was likely voicing an early version of his Pacific republic dreams.

Moreover, the Champoeg debate revolved around not *whether* to form a government, but what *type* of government it would be. Gray, Hastings, and others who supported full independence desired a strong and active government. They wanted, for example, a single executive officer possessing legitimate power and a legislature that had the ability to tax. In contrast, supporters of US annexation wanted to keep the government weak, with a three-man executive committee and a legislature that had no power to tax. This government would serve simply as a caretaker until Oregon was, in the words of the pro-annexationists at Champoeg, "brought as soon as practicable, under the jurisdiction of our mother country."[77] Because the government would hold so little power, it would never obstruct US annexation. It also would ensure that even those settlers ambivalent about the United States as a polity would still desire US annexation, if only to have a more effective government.

Conflicting feelings of vulnerability and confidence played into the divide among American settlers debating Oregon's future. Throughout his life Lansford Hastings exhibited boundless (and often foolhardy) ambition, and he always believed in his leadership abilities. Although there is no account of what Hastings said at Champoeg, it would have been very unlike him to fear the HBC, Catholicism, or McLoughlin; he was, after all, McLoughlin's lawyer. However, most Americans in Oregon did not share his confidence in the future. To them, the easiest way to combat their perceived enemies was US annexation. In the end, the latter were in the majority. The pro-annexationists got their wish, creating an Oregon provisional government that would only exist, as the preamble explicitly stated, "until such time as the United States of America extend their jurisdiction over us."[78] Although defeated in his ambitions, William Gray remained in Oregon, served as a legislator in the provisional government, and eventually wrote his version of early Oregon history to cover his now-embarrassing and seemingly traitorous behavior. Indeed, there is circumstantial evidence that Gray or one of his allies even doctored the minutes of Champoeg to hide their "secessionist" tendencies.[79] While Gray remained in Oregon, Hastings left for California to continue his pursuit of an independent republic. When he published his guidebook a few years later to facilitate this goal, he extolled the virtues of California while denigrating Oregon, making the disingenuous claim that Oregon's agricultural prospects were poor.

After Champoeg, independence sentiments continued among portions of the American community in Oregon, although no longer via the method that Gray and Hastings had argued for. The vote at Champoeg had defeated an active push for independence, but it did not defeat a second method for achieving the same goal: simply awaiting continental developments that could lead to independence down the road. Instead of relying on US annexation to solve their vulnerability in Oregon, Americans could depend on the continued immigration of even more Americans. Additional immigration would not put Oregon under US jurisdiction, but it would invariably put Oregon under *American* jurisdiction, for Americans would dominate the region demographically. The missionary P. L. Edwards, for example, noted that Oregon already possessed a "moral, religious, and industrious population." With an increased population, he believed, Oregon could be "perchance the germ of a powerful State."[80] Whether Edwards meant "state" as in one of the United *States*, or "state" as in an independent nation, is unclear, for both definitions were used at the time.[81] Perhaps his ambiguity was deliberate, and immigration would decide the issue. The missionary David Leslie was more forthright, writing of Oregon, "There is a nation being born in a day, the future eminence and greatness of which needs not a prophet to predict."[82] Leslie did not argue explicitly for Oregon independence, but neither was he envisioning immediate US annexation. Like Edwards, he believed that Oregon's destiny rested with future migrants. Edwards's and Leslie's statements reflected a growing confidence among some settlers that Oregon's future was promising as long as more Americans continued to arrive—regardless of whether the United States annexed Oregon in the near future. And in 1843, arrive they did, in the form of the Great Migration.

The Defeat of Oregon Independence, Part II

The 875 immigrants who arrived in Oregon during the fall of 1843 outnumbered the entire existing population of the Willamette Valley. Induced by the exhortations of Presbyterian missionary Marcus Whitman, their journey became known as the Great Migration, and their arrival presaged the decline of missionary influence in Oregon. For the rest of their lives, members of the Great Migration argued that their arrival "saved" Oregon for the United States. This narrative was decidedly false. As the historian Frederick Merk observed, American settlers had almost nothing to do with the 1846 Oregon Treaty.[83] Yet it makes sense that—well after the fact—migrants argued for their patriotic importance. They were the first to leave US borders for Oregon after the United States and Britain signed the Webster-Ashburton Treaty in August 1842, which concentrated solely on the New Brunswick–Maine border and left the fate of Oregon unresolved. They also departed after February 1843, when Congress failed to pass Senator Lewis Linn's 640-acre land grant bill for all Oregon migrants.[84] In essence, they departed the United States when, after several years in which Oregon annexation seemed to be gaining momentum in Congress, the prospect again had dropped precipitously. In retrospect, their arguments that the United States was able to annex Oregon only a few years later *because* of their arrival had logic.

Yet the 1843 migrants, like migrants from every other year, made no mention of their patriotic goals, and looking back, their migration takes on a whole new meaning. In all likelihood, the 1843 migrants cared the *least* about the US annexation of Oregon, for they left when the prospect for annexation was at a nadir—even though, in hindsight, this nadir was only temporary. Seen in this light, their actions upon their arrival in Oregon were eminently rational: they sought to make the Oregon provisional government strong and functional, for they had no faith that the United States would any time soon "extend their jurisdiction over us," as the original Organic Laws stated. To the members of the Great Migration, the deliberately weak government created at Champoeg was simply untenable. Not only had rapid US annexation become more unlikely, but the Great Migration more than doubled the population of the Willamette Valley. The region now possessed a burgeoning community of many different interests: newly arrived American migrants, Protestant missionaries and American settlers from earlier years, Métis families affiliated with the HBC, and the Hudson's Bay Company as a corporate entity. Such a community required something more than a caretaker government.

When the Cockstock affair had ensued in February 1844, it acted as a further catalyst. Confronted with the (mistaken) belief that violence between the settler community and Oregon's Natives was imminent, Americans, both the recently arrived and the more established, saw the necessity for a stronger, more active government. They made their new demographic power known in May, when the Oregon provisional government held its first elections under the original Organic Laws. The now-dominant 1843 migrants elected mostly their own: seven of the nine members of the legislative committee were part of the Great Migration. Led by Peter Burnett, a participant in the Great Migration and a future California governor, these newly elected officials set out to drastically revise the original governmental structure. To strengthen the government's power, they hoped to eliminate the three-man executive and replace it with a single governor. They wanted to give this government the ability to tax, and anyone who refused to pay taxes would be disqualified from voting and excluded from the protection of the Organic Laws. Ideologically dedicated to the practices of Jacksonian democracy, they believed that any new government required popular approval via new elections, and therefore the government they were planning in 1844 could only be implemented after the next elections in the summer of 1845. They did, however, make more immediate changes. Responding to the Cockstock affair, they established a militia system, although it would exist mostly on paper until the 1847 Cayuse War. Moreover, by agreeing to respect the rights of the French Canadians and not send any more petitions to the US Congress, the newly elected officials induced the French Canadian settlers to participate in the government. For their part, the French Canadians recognized that the substantial population influx made their involvement necessary to protect their rights and property. While McLoughlin and the HBC still refused to participate, Oregon was on its way to a functional, active government.[85]

Such was the alteration of Oregon's government from 1843 to 1844 that one historian deemed the newly elected officials the "independent party."[86] The name does not reflect their sentiments as to Oregon's political future; they did not necessarily seek political independence. But they were pragmatic enough to realize there was no guarantee for US annexation, and they needed to act *independently* to create a functional government. After all, many had left US borders when quick annexation seemed defunct. During the first legislative session in June, the provisional government even acknowledged a potential future in which Oregon would never join the United States. As part of its instructions tasking the Legislative Committee with strengthening the Organic Laws, the Executive Committee referred to the original 1843 laws: "At the time of our organization it was expected that the United States would have taken possession of the country before this time, but a year has rolled around, and there appears little or no prospect of aid from that quarter, consequently we are left on our own resources for protection. In the view of the present state of affairs . . . we would recommend to your consideration the adoption of some measures for a more thorough organization."[87] It is impossible to determine whether this message was obliquely referring to the failure of Linn's Oregon bill in Congress, the lack of attention to Oregon in the Webster-Ashburton Treaty, or both, but undoubtedly the new leadership felt that a stronger Oregon government was necessary as the United States continued to dally.

Six months later, with US annexation not any closer, the Executive Committee used even stronger language that hinted at future independence in its instructions to the Legislative Committee. Among its recommendations was convening a constitutional convention in order to write an official constitution for the government of 1845. The use of the word "constitution" was significant, for it demonstrated a permanence that the Organic Laws did not. So too did the concluding paragraph of the proclamation: "And we sincerely hope that Oregon, by the special aid of Divine Providence, may set an unprecedented example to the world, of industry, morality, and virtue. And although we may now be unknown as a State or Power, yet we have the advantages, by uniting efforts of our increasing population, in a diligent attention to agriculture, arts and literature, of attaining, at no great distant day, to as conspicuous an elevation as any State or Power on the continent of America."[88] The message concluded that all Oregon citizens, regardless of whether they were of American or British origin, should "cultivate kind feelings, not only of our native countries, but of all the Powers or States with whom we may have intercourse."[89] While this message was not necessarily anti–United States, the change in language since 1843 was notable. No longer was Oregon desperate for US oversight. Indeed, the continued use of "State or Power" indicated an ambiguous but confident future for the region, in which Oregon—whatever its political formulation—would be a powerful and prosperous polity.

This message coincided with a growing sentiment among Oregon settlers, many of whom had once hoped for annexation to the United States, that now independence was the best course to pursue.[90] As Indian agent Elijah White reported to the US government, "Such sentiment[s] . . . are more favorably listened to this year than last."[91] Unfortunately, all sources are sparse as to the specifics behind this growing support for independence. There are no records of more detailed political speeches, particularly because no Oregon newspaper existed until 1846. In all likelihood, Oregon settlers brought up the subject of independence in places where politics were discussed: small meetings at the various missions (which remained community hubs in spite of the missionaries' diminishing influence), dinners at houses of friends made on the wagon train, and the stores of Oregon City.

Counterintuitively, the growth of support for independence coincided with the growth of the American community in Oregon. In 1843, the independence movement had been led by a minority of ambitious schemers like Lansford Hastings. For the more moderate Americans at the famed Champoeg meeting, their fears had overridden their ambitions. One year later, however, these fears had greatly diminished, largely due to the results of the Great Migration. While the American population was at best equal to the HBC/French Canadian population in 1843, in 1844 it greatly exceeded it. Pro-British settlers were now a small percentage of the community, and everyone knew this percentage would only grow smaller over time as American immigration continued to increase. There were also no signs that the British were facilitating any more settlements of their own. The Red River settlers increasingly appeared to be an anomaly. Thus, American demographic power would easily overwhelm whatever advantages the British had once possessed. In this sense, the developments in Oregon in 1844 and 1845 mirrored those in Texas in the late 1830s under the presidency of Mirabeau Lamar: continued migration and increasing demographic dominance proved to American settlers in both polities that US annexation was not necessary in the immediate future—and perhaps never would be.

John McLoughlin, the dominant figure in the Pacific Northwest for more than two decades, realized he was now on the defensive. When the HBC governor, George Simpson, voiced frustration with McLoughlin for supplying provisions to the arriving Americans, McLoughlin defended himself by claiming, "If we had not assisted them [Fort] Vancouver would have been destroyed."[92] Whether American settlers would have actually attacked HBC holdings was dubious, but McLoughlin's larger point was valid: the influx of new migrants gave Americans the balance of power in the Willamette Valley. In response, the HBC decided to move its headquarters from Fort Vancouver in the valley to Fort Victoria on Vancouver Island. American settlers also understood this new dynamic. In 1845, members of the Oregon provisional government solicited McLoughlin and the HBC to enter into the government as full participants, and McLoughlin accepted. This action would have been unthinkable several years before, when Americans disliked McLoughlin's influence and power. With the Great Migration, however, the British specter no longer haunted Oregon's American community, and McLoughlin's participation was once again valued—now that he was no longer a threat.

As American fears of the British diminished, their frustration with US inaction over Oregon increased. According to several commenters, this frustration was the root cause for the increased support for Oregon independence. As Peter Burnett wrote, "The people here are worn out by delay [of US annexation], and their condition becomes everyday more intolerable."[93] What exactly was "intolerable"? John McLoughlin gave the answer: "The Settlers are anxious that the Boundary Line should be drawn so as they may get titles for their Lands; some say if it is not soon settled they will propose to declare themselves independant [*sic*]."[94] Both Burnett and McLoughlin referred to the original reason Americans had traveled to Oregon in the first place: the 640-acre land grant originally proposed by Senator Linn, which had failed to pass the US Congress, but which the provisional government had enacted into Oregon law in 1843. Significantly, however, this was an action by the Oregon *provisional* government, its temporariness enshrined in its very title. And because the government was temporary, so potentially were all Oregon land claims. As one settler later remembered, Oregonians were "weary of *quasi*-independence."[95] If the United States refused to annex Oregon in the near future, then only full independence would render the land claims permanent.

Taking such an action, however, did not mean that a fully independent Oregon would be a permanently independent Oregon. As demonstrated by Texas annexation in 1845, an independent republic could join the union under rather generous terms. After annexation, Texas still retained control of all of its public lands, and because it entered the union as a state, it was left to write its own constitution, which did not require congressional approval. And, of course, the Texans received US military protection paid for by the federal government.[96] Oregonians knew of events in Texas and the ongoing politics of Texas annexation in the United States. Some Americans in the United States reported on Texas annexation in letters to their Oregon friends and family, and in 1846 the newly founded *Oregon Spectator* printed news of Texas regularly.[97] The thousand-plus migrants of 1845 departed the United States after presidential nominee James Polk announced his joint Texas-Oregon platform, which deliberately put the two issues together, and the migrants would have informed earlier settlers about this upon arriving in Oregon.

There were clearly benefits for Oregonians if Oregon mimicked Texas. If an independent Oregon joined the United States as a state, then Oregon's laws—including, above all, the 640-acre land grant—would remain in effect. Certainly, Oregon independence and/or statehood required many more settlers, but every Oregonian knew they were coming. With increased population and then a declaration of independence, Oregon could join the United States on its own terms. Indeed, one Oregonian later remembered that the best situation for Oregon would have been for the United States to inform the region's settlers that they were on their own for ten years. Then, after they created a "useful and permanent system of legislation . . . Oregon would have been ready to enter the American constellation as one of the brightest stars in it."[98] Ten years was the same duration as Texas's independence.

If some Oregonians hoped to use independence as a means to bring about an advantageous connection to the United States, others disdained any sort of connection for several reasons. First, American settlers in Oregon had traveled for months over inhospitable terrain and through hostile Indian territory (or so they claimed—in reality, there was minimal violence).[99] The United States was now very far away, which would hinder US governance over Oregon. The US capital of Washington, DC, was simply too remote to administer Oregon effectively.[100] Moreover, if the United States did annex Oregon, it was more likely Oregon would become a territory than a state. This would be a step backward. Oregonians already governed themselves, but territorial status would necessitate ceding their self-governance to the United States until statehood could be achieved.[101] Finally, joining the United States would also reopen the slavery debate, which Oregonians believed they had solved with their laws prohibiting both slavery and all black settlers.

In hindsight, it may appear naïve, even ludicrous, that some settlers believed that Oregon could exist and even thrive as an independent nation, yet for Oregonians in 1845 the future was promising. The Willamette Valley community was flourishing. Oregon was by no means a paradise, but it did fulfill many of the hopes that migrants possessed when they first left the United States: most white men were able to claim their 640 acres, the region was at peace, the land was bountiful, Oregon's republican government functioned as effectively as a provisional government could, and relations with Oregon's Native peoples were generally good—the Cockstock affair notwithstanding.[102] As one observer noted, Oregon already "outstrips any position of the [United] States."[103] Future American migrants would presumably add to this dynamic community and help Oregon take its place on the international stage.

Crucial to this belief was that Oregon would not stand alone on the Pacific Coast, but would join with the other significant American settlement in the region: California. At times Oregonians discussed such a possibility.[104] Their belief in a Pacific republic was eminently logical, particularly because most Americans in Oregon already knew Americans in California from their shared time together during the early months of the overland journey. As I mentioned earlier, Americans in California also discussed a Pacific republic, and the regions remained connected via trade and migration, as dozens of Oregon migrants migrated to California, while a few California migrants migrated to Oregon.[105] Moreover, Americans in both regions, like all Americans, were steeped in the hagiography of the American Revolution, which served as proof that an infant republic could make rapid strides on the world stage. If Oregon joined with California, then Oregon independence was hardly a flight of fancy, but a reasonable and rational response to both Oregon and California immigrants' knowledge of American history and the current geopolitics of the region.

For a select few, there was another reason to support Oregon independence: naked ambition. As US Indian agent Elijah White described in a letter to the Office of Indian Affairs, "Already demagogues are haranguing in favor of independence, and using the most disparaging language regarding the measures of our government as a reason for action. These are but the beginnings."[106] Oregon politician J. Quinn Thornton did not call them demagogues, but simply "persons . . . respectable for their character and influence."[107] For these ambitious few, the calculus was simple. They had achieved some sort of political and/or social power in Oregon, which would be greatly curtailed if Oregon became a US territory and subject to a federally appointed territorial governor. In a US Oregon, they would forever remain local politicians. On the other hand, if Oregon became independent, whether alone or with California, then their future held the possibility of election to some high office. Unfortunately for us, neither White nor Thornton provided the names of these "demagogues." This hole in the historical record is unsurprising. After Oregon annexation, and even more so during and after the Civil War, any pro-independence Oregonian would have appeared a fool at best, a traitor at worst. As American Patriots had done after their struggle failed, those who supported Oregon independence would have likely destroyed any relevant correspondence and hid their former involvement in a now-discredited movement.

While there were practical and not so practical reasons for supporting Oregon independence, it is important to state unequivocally: a majority of Americans in Oregon still supported US annexation. Letters such as those from McLoughlin and Burnett that acknowledged the growing support for independence also acknowledged that a majority of settlers still supported a US Oregon.[108] These pro-annexationists were divided into two camps: the Ultra-Americans (or simply the Ultras) and the moderates. The Ultra-Americans were rabidly patriotic and were frustrated with the provisional government's seeming lack of US nationalism and attention to US interests.[109] Described by one HBC employee as "unprincipled fanatics," the Ultras continued to see the British bogeyman behind any personal setback.[110] In one example, an Ultra lost an election to an HBC fur trader for a government office, and the losing candidate subsequently tried to get the winner disqualified by desperately arguing that the Oregon provisional government only applied to Americans.[111]

This settler did not prevail, for the Ultras were a minority of the pro-annexationists and were opposed by a larger contingent of moderates. While the moderates also desired US annexation, they respected John McLoughlin and generally did not let their pro-US stance affect the practical concerns of their daily lives and of the larger Oregon community. And, in an important sense, supporting US annexation was the most moderate and least risky course to take. All settlers knew that the United States claimed a portion of Oregon, and it had a particularly strong case in regard to all territory south of the Columbia River, which included the Willamette Valley. Oregon independence, whatever its enticements, would still require negating this long-established claim. For most Americans, it would be much more reasonable to await the likely scenario of US annexation, which hopefully would come in the near future.

Such was the preponderance of pro-annexationists that 1845 witnessed a backlash against the "independent party," even though members of that party did not necessarily oppose annexation. Nevertheless, many Americans in 1845—including another 1,500 migrants who had arrived in late 1844—feared what the much smaller group of Americans had feared at Champoeg in 1843: creating too strong a government would put them on the slippery slope toward independence. In their view, this is exactly what members of the 1844 government had done. The moderates and the Ultra-Americans voiced their disapproval in the June 1845 ballot. This was the first election under the laws of the stronger provisional government, in which settlers would elect one governor instead of a three-man executive. Because members of the independent party had essentially made these changes without a public vote, they now sought popular approval for their actions. In addition to the regular election of candidates, the ballot asked a question: should Oregonians call a convention to write a constitution for Oregon, thereby making the new structure of the provisional government more official? The answer was a decisive no, as Oregon men rejected the measure by a vote of 283–190. A few weeks later, however, they voted to uphold the Amended Organic Laws over the original Organic Laws. This vote demonstrated that Oregonians did support the stronger government structure that the independent party had created, for the only difference between the Amended Organic Laws and a potential Oregon constitution was the word "constitution." The word was the crux of the matter, however, for a constitution implied potential independence.[112]

During this election, the scanty evidence suggests that the few hundred moderates rejected the constitutional convention by a ratio of three to one. A much smaller number of Ultras—likely fewer than a hundred—also rejected the convention overwhelmingly, to no one's surprise. Men of British origin, numbering between 125 and 150, supported the convention.[113] These numbers establish that most of Oregon's community was, essentially, moderately pro–United States. Unsurprisingly, the newly elected provisional government of 1845 once again petitioned for US annexation, something the 1844 independents had never done. Concerned about a lack of military protection in case of attacks by Natives and about continued dependence on the HBC for supplies, the petitioners "pray[ed] the national congress to establish a district territorial Government, to embrace Oregon and its adjacent sea coast."[114] As one historian noted, the emphasis of the 1845 provisional government was once more back on the "provisional."[115]

But moderation, by definition, is predicated on rationality and an ability to assess all sides of a debate. Moderates in Oregon could contemplate another future besides US annexation, even if most supported such an outcome. At the end of the day, these men were not primarily concerned about securing US sovereignty over Oregon, but they were pragmatically looking out for their own interests. Their moderation was revealed palpably in their actions during the final year and a half before US annexation. During this time the possibility of war between the United States and Britain greatly increased, as President Polk belligerently argued against any compromise that did not give the United States most or all of the vast Oregon Country—which became the infamous call of "Fifty-four forty or fight."[116] Now back in the United States, US Indian agent Elijah White believed that Americans in Oregon would support Polk's stance and follow him to war if need be. Writing to the Washington *Daily Union*, White claimed that Oregonians were "true to the American eagle" and would "defend our flag" in the territory.[117]

White's statement was thoroughly incorrect, and it demonstrated how divorced events in the United States were from those in Oregon. Oregon officials had welcomed the HBC into the provisional government months before White wrote his letter, and Americans citizens and British subjects seemed to be getting along just fine.[118] The provisional government even had implemented an oath of office in which officials promised to support the Organic Laws "so far as they are consistent with my duties as a citizen of the United States or a subject of Great Britain."[119] Although McLoughlin noted that the Ultra-Americans were upset with what they perceived as an antipatriotic oath, they were outnumbered by "respectable Americans in the Settlement" who supported the binational wording.[120] And as war hysteria increased in the United States, Oregon remained at peace. In 1846, one letter writer to the *Oregon Spectator* likely voiced the sentiments of most Oregonians as to their best approach to a US-British war: "As the main war would be on the Ocean, I see no use of our fighting here. . . . let our provisional government stand, and those who wish to stay at home and cultivate their farms, be permitted to do so without censure or molestation."[121] The seal of the Oregon provisional government attested to the region's moderation. There was no symbol on the seal that gave away Oregon residents' political preference—no stars and no

Seal of the Oregon provisional government,
1845. Simply picturing three bundles of
wheat and a salmon, the seal demonstrates
the modest ambitions of Oregon's settlers.
Without US or British symbols, it also
demonstrates the lack of nationalism in the
region. Courtesy of Oregon Historical Society.

stripes of any kind. Instead, the seal pictured three bushels of wheat and a salmon. The message was clear: Oregonians' primary goal was to farm and to fish.

Clearly Americans in Oregon were not "winning" Oregon for the United States, as they later remembered. After all, if they actually had wanted to win Oregon from the British, they could have done so: by 1845, thanks to continued migration, Americans outnumbered pro-British settlers by more than ten to one. The British knew this. In 1844, as talk of war over Oregon increased, a British ship had arrived in the region to protect its subjects and to investigate whether it would be feasible to bring a British army overland from Canada if war in fact did break out. However, when officers from the ship visited the extensive American settlements in Oregon, they realized they had little chance to conquer the now thoroughly Americanized territory, and McLoughlin himself protested their arrival as interrupting the business and harmony of the community. It was evident to everyone involved: the Willamette Valley was irreversibly an American territory—although it remained to be seen if it were also a US territory.

The moderation of the majority of Americans also implied an ability to change their minds according to the circumstances, particularly about Oregon independence. Recall that, of the moderates, approximately a quarter had voted to hold a constitutional convention in the summer of 1845. Clearly some moderates saw logical reasons for taking such a step, even if they were not trying to force independence by doing so. Their vote suggests that other moderates might change their minds about a constitution—and therefore independence. And what could have changed their minds was, above all, continued US neglect, meaning continued impermanency to all Oregon land claims and, more generally, a continued inability to plan for a still ambiguous political future. Even the pro-annexation 1845 provisional government implicitly voiced this frustration in its petition to the United States: "We, as citizens of the United States . . . are forced to the enactment and execution of laws not authorized, *and for what we know*, never will be sanctioned by our Government."[122] Frustration bred a search for a solution, and the solution in 1846 remained the same as in 1844: independence.

A long letter to Oregon citizens in the *Oregon Spectator* in April 1846 best demonstrates how this discussion had evolved over the previous few years in the Willamette Valley. Written by "A Friend to Oregon," the letter noted that the subject of independence was "one of great moment to this people, and one which seems to be engaging considerable attention." The writer went on to argue that US annexation was a much more preferable option than independence, naming several specific reasons. First, Oregon was too poor to stand on its own and could benefit from US expenditures on the territory. Second, echoing James Madison in Federalist No. 10, he said that as a small republic Oregon would be plagued by faction, but factionalism would be mitigated within the extended republic of the United States.[123] Third, Oregon could simply not survive on the international stage among other great powers. Ultimately, the writer argued, "We see that the home government has more effectual means, more extensive jurisdiction, to promote the general welfare than can possibly be anticipated to fall to our lot, as an independent Oregon." If Oregon joined the United States, it would "become entitled to all the privileges and immunities of the older states." The writer then asked, "Ought not then the government of our birth to become more deeply an object of regard and reference, or attachment and pride?"[124] Perhaps he believed that Americans in Oregon were not as attached to the United States as they should be.

Even though "A Friend to Oregon" supported US annexation in 1846 just as many of his fellow settlers had in prior years, the contents of the pro-annexation argument had changed markedly. No longer was the argument based on emotional concern about protection from attacks by Natives and "others that would do [Americans] harm," as the 1840 petition to the United States had stated.[125] Gone were fears of HBC influence and British might. Now the argument against independence was based on an assessment of long-term geopolitics and a calculated gesture toward Madisonian constitutional theory. In a certain sense, by using rational arguments to oppose Oregon independence, the letter writer also legitimized the rational reasons for Oregon independence. The letter writer's intellectual arguments revealed that Oregonians did not feel panic over their future prospects, for the writer would have employed those fears—as Americans had done until 1843. Oregon was no longer a peripheral, endangered settlement of a few hundred subsistence farmers on the edge of civilization, but a flourishing agricultural community of several thousand people. Oregon settlers no longer needed to beg the United States for its protection. Instead, they could calmly assess the positives and negatives of US annexation versus Oregon independence. "A Friend to Oregon" may have favored the former, but he did not find the latter option ridiculous. When he published his views in April 1846, it remained to be seen whether the United States was as "attached" to Oregon as this particular Oregonian was to the United States.

The End of the Texas Moment

By 1844 the Texas Moment had flowered across North America as pockets of white Americans and removed Natives asserted their right to create independent—but still thoroughly Americanized—polities. In the United States, the effects of the Panic of 1837 continued to reverberate. States continued to default on their loans through 1843, and Congress continued to reduce spending on items as seemingly vital as the US Army.[1] Violence and disorder persisted in places like Philadelphia, where the economic crisis helped fuel nativist riots; in New York, where the Anti-Rent Wars still simmered; and in Illinois, where a second Mormon War appeared at hand. Yet for many Americans, there were also signs of hope and reasons for optimism. On both the southern and northern fronts, US borders were more secure: in Florida, the United States had finally emerged victorious in the Second Seminole War, and the 1842 Webster-Ashburton Treaty had put the simmering controversy over the Maine border to rest and quelled Patriot agitation in the Great Lakes region for good. And while the US economy had nowhere near recovered its mid-1830s heights, at least the depths of the depression had been weathered in most states. The United States, in fits and starts, was on the mend.

Meanwhile, in the second American republic, Texas, President Mirabeau Lamar's dreams of empire had collapsed. His planned conquest of New Mexico, known as the Santa Fe Expedition, had ended in catastrophe as Mexican forces captured all 321 soldiers who had embarked on the mission. Lamar had more success pursuing brutal wars against Natives, but these battles bankrupted the revenue-strapped Texas government. Mexico could not yet mount a proper invasion of Texas due to continued political instability, but its forces did capture San Antonio de Béxar twice in 1842. The Texas constitution mandated that Lamar could not run for a second term, but even if he could have, Texans were tired of his failed policies. In 1841 they voted to return to the more conservative approach of San Jacinto hero Sam Houston. It was now up to Houston to find a way forward for an increasingly wobbly Texas republic.

Houston understood all too well the many weaknesses of Texas, and he did what many statesmen of weak countries have done in precarious geopolitical situations: he searched for a more powerful ally. Realistically he had only two options: the United States and Great Britain. The United States was the most logical choice and the one favored by most Anglo-Texans, who by this point constituted 90 percent of the republic's population. The John Tyler administration seemed a willing partner, but Houston understood the difficult path a treaty would face in the US Senate, and so at the same time he put out feelers to Britain. For their part, British officials were intrigued with Houston's overtures for two reasons. First, they hoped to contain the United States' continental ambitions, and preventing the US annexation of Texas would greatly serve this goal. Second, abolitionist statesmen in Britain saw Texas as a prime target for their emancipationist goals. Perhaps, some British leaders hoped, the Texans would accede to gradual emancipation in return for international protection of their independence. Eventually Texan and British officials worked out the parameters of an agreement: Britain would intercede with Mexico on Texas's behalf and broker a peace treaty that would guarantee Texas independence; in exchange, the Texans would forgo annexation to the United States.[2]

As Houston later admitted, his overtures to Great Britain were primarily designed to pressure the United States toward annexation, although Houston took the British alliance seriously as a credible backup plan if the United States failed to act. Whether a substantial number of Anglo-Texans would have gone along with a British alliance is debatable. Anglo-Texans were, after all, breakaway Americans, and as Americans, many harbored an intense dislike for Great Britain, particularly if they were slaveholders. Luckily for them, Houston's gambit worked. Prominent southern Democrats in the United States had long feared a British-backed emancipationist Texas on the country's southwestern flank. The proslavery Tyler administration amplified its outreach to the Texas government in an effort to counter British antislavery imperialism, thereby beginning the drive for US expansion that would culminate under James Polk.[3] Yet, crucially, fears of abolitionism and British imperialism depended on a third fear, one often neglected by historians: breakaway Americanism. British imperialism and abolitionism could only be activated if Texas remained an independent republic on the continent.

Ostensibly, of course, expansionists in the United States celebrated Texas independence in 1836, and they wished their sister republic success in the years after. Whatever Houston's manipulations, most white Americans believed that the overwhelming mass of Anglo-Texans supported annexation to the United States. But what if this majority were not in control of events? What if the will of the majority was about to be thwarted by self-interested Texas politicians? As in Oregon, Texas leaders had a personal stake in remaining independent, for annexation to the United States would curb their power significantly once Texas became a US state or—heaven forbid—a territory. Although Houston had reached out to Britain, Americans largely gave him a pass due to his friendship with Andrew Jackson and his previous support for annexation. His successor, Anson Jones, elected in 1844, did not share that support. The New Orleans *Times-Picayune* suspected Jones of engaging in a "secret intrigue [with Britain] in order to defeat the popular will."[4] Jones and his pro-British allies were, in the words of Andrew Jackson, "ambitious aspirants," and Jackson worried their numbers would grow if annexation did not occur swiftly, as Britain offered more and more inducements for Texas to remain independent.[5] To both the *Times-Picayune* and Jackson, Jones's pro-British stance was illegitimate, for it was thwarting the democratic will of the people of Texas. Hidden in this criticism was an important but unsettling implication: Jones was a popularly elected president of an internationally recognized state, and thus any diplomacy he conducted with Great Britain *was* perfectly legitimate. In this way, an independent Texas provided lawful means for Britain to enter into continental affairs.

Even more worrisome for anglophobic Americans, Texas could be just the beginning of British meddling. If other breakaway Americas arose, they too would provide means for the British to sink military and diplomatic roots into the continent. The *Richmond Enquirer*, for example, was stunned at Daniel Webster's assertion that Oregon would become a "great Pacific republican nation." If this occurred, the paper argued, it would be "subject to the intrigue and influence of English policy. . . . Such a concession would but encourage her to new aggressions."[6] The *New York Herald* went further, painting a grim portrait of the future of the United States: "We believe, indeed, that we are now in a most important crisis connected with the destiny of republican government, and the independence of the United States on this continent. There is every reason to believe that the powers of Europe have been weaving a web of subtle policy, for the purpose of arresting the progress of this country, and of encompassing it with *governments under their control*."[7] Here was the crux of the matter: the British may have held the balance of power in the Americas, but Americans did not believe they would undertake a massive military invasion alone. Rather, they could only assert their power through influencing, manipulating, and bullying weak states. This fear had merit. At the same time as Americans debated Texas annexation, the British navy was ensuring the survival of the Uruguayan independence movement, laying the groundwork for Britain's "informal empire" in South America. By allying with Texas or any other breakaway America, Britain would lay the groundwork for an informal empire in North America as well.

For most who were concerned with British (and, in a few cases, French) intrigue on the continent, it was the British who were the true enemy, for they were trying to corrupt Texas's leaders and subvert its democratic government. In a few cases, however, observers expressed concern that the problem went deeper, to the very character of the Americans who chose to leave US borders. After all, as one correspondent from Texas stated, corrupt officials could only be elected by an electorate of "contemptible . . . citizens."[8] Migrants to Oregon and California were also suspect. Noting that soon many "adventurous men" would travel to Oregon, the *Milwaukee Weekly Sentinel* hoped they would be "of better character, and for better purposes than many in Texas have had."[9] In a widely reprinted editorial, the *St. Louis New Era* took this concern to another level, noting that the very nature of migrants led them to take bold political action: "The opinion is very freely expressed by persons who have lived in Oregon and California that the emigrants already look forward to separate independence. . . . The bold restless spirits who have gone to Oregon and California are the very sort of men who are disposed to set up a new government."[10] The Mormons, of course, were even more suspect. The *Sangamo Journal* of Illinois stated the case succinctly: "[The Mormons] are said to number 18,000, are bitterly hostile to the Government of the United States, and many of them are Englishmen, and are likely . . . to act in concert with the British and all of their designs."[11] The *Platte Argus* of Missouri had little doubt that the Mormons would facilitate a British Oregon, writing that once the Mormons arrived, "it is easy to guess whether the interests of the United States or those of Great Britain would suffer by such a state of things."[12] Thus, American migration would not pave the way for US expansion, as vocal expansionists like John L. O'Sullivan claimed. On the contrary, it would inhibit it, for the flawed characters of these expatriates made their settlements predisposed toward becoming independent republics, which in turn would lead to geopolitical openings for the British.

Texas, Oregon, California, and the Mormons: when all of these movements were added together, it seemed like the British were trying to enclose the US borders and thus prevent US expansion. As the *Public Ledger* of Philadelphia ominously warned, the British were trying to "surround us, like a scorpion, with a circle of fire."[13] This paranoia could be found in the highest levels of government. In the House of Representatives, Illinois Democrat John McClernand sought to awaken his fellow congressmen to the British threat by displaying a series of "beautifully colored maps" of the potential British cordon around the United States, which prompted "numerous members" to crowd around the maps in excitement.[14]

At the heart of the relationship between US expansion and breakaway Americanism were several troubling questions that few Americans sought to ponder in any depth, for they called into question breakaway Americans' loyalty to the United States. Could the United States really cite the Monroe Doctrine and try to prevent British influence on the continent if people on the ground—most of whom were American migrants—*asked* the British for aid? Did not these American migrants have a right to do so by the very tenets of Jacksonian democracy? Anglo-Americans of all backgrounds and political affiliations had long celebrated demography as destiny, but what if the demographic explosion of Americans actually worked against the geographical expansion of the United States? At the very least, as things stood in the mid-1840s, demography did not aid US expansion. Breakaway Americans had either voluntarily left the United States or they were forced from the United States. Neither situation engendered confidence in their future loyalty.

This was not the way things were supposed to happen. On the contrary, demography and geopolitical expansion were supposed to be wedded together. This was the fundamental premise at the heart of the Texas game, which foresaw American migrants taking control of foreign governments (peacefully or not) and then seeking US annexation. The Texas game was supposed to make US expansion natural and easy—or, as the *Democratic Review* averred, it was supposed to be "manifest destiny."[15] But now, to Americans in the United States who examined continental geopolitics closely, it seemed that instead of facilitating US expansion, the Texas game actually inhibited it. Instead of seeking US annexation, the American-dominated Republic of Texas was seeking British support. If Oregon or California declared independence, their inhabitants could also look to Great Britain—or, at the least, reject US annexation. Thus, the Texas game needed to be prevented—something Polk understood all too well in 1845. Unlike most Americans, Polk could take action against breakaway Americanism because he had been elected to the highest office in the land—but this was something that almost no one could have predicted during the height of the Texas Moment.

The Improbable Road to an Expansionist President, 1837–1846

At times, the course of history is determined by enormous, structural forces—social, economic, political, demographic. At times, however, history is determined by a stroke of improbable luck—or several.[16] Such was the case with the election of James Polk to the presidency in 1844. In the mid-1830s, Polk, a Tennessee Democrat, was the speaker of the House. In the aftermath of the Texas Revolution in 1836, Polk wrote and spoke little of Texas. While he had family members, friends, and acquaintances who chose to move to Texas and who supplied him with firsthand news, for someone who would make US expansion the primary plank in his presidential platform in 1844, in the late 1830s he did not publicly support annexation.[17] In this, Polk was typical. Between 1837 and 1843, Texas annexation was hardly discussed among prominent politicians or in major newspapers.[18] Even in 1844, after President John Tyler resurrected the issue, a meeting of pro-annexationists in St. Louis urged the rest of the country to awake from its "slumber on the subject."[19] But lack of discussion did not mean lack of support, and annexing Texas almost certainly remained a popular issue among large swaths of Americans, particularly southern and western Democrats. However, it was not worth discussing when it was politically impossible, as politicians from both parties and all sections realized. It was the economic depression that drove politics during these years, not geopolitical expansion.

Indeed, the depression swept William Henry Harrison into the White House and a Whig majority into both houses of Congress in 1840. At the state level, Whigs also seized control of a majority of governments. Before Harrison's election, such a sweeping political realignment had only been seen once before in US history, during the triumph of Jeffersonian Republicans in the "revolution of 1800." The 1840 Log Cabin campaign has long been treated as remarkable for two reasons: its turnout rate of 80 percent of eligible voters and the seemingly issueless tactics both sides used to turn out the vote, including campaign songs, famous slogans ("Tippecanoe and Tyler Too"), and drunken rallies. Yet behind these tactics lay the deep-seated anxiety of thousands of Americans concerned about the future of a depression-laden United States. A convincing majority of these Americans yearned for a decisive shift in the priorities of both the national and state governments, and they voted Whig. The election results seemed to portend a new Whig-dominated political era.[20]

And yet in their triumph the Whigs inadvertently sowed the seeds of their future defeat, although no one could have foreseen the series of contingent disasters that would lead to it. These disasters were threefold: first, the Whigs nominated William Henry Harrison over Henry Clay, thanks to Harrison's greater support among northern constituents. If Clay had been nominated, he almost certainly would have won the 1840 election; despite Whig fears that Clay had too many enemies, in 1840 Van Buren had many more.[21] Second, the Whigs balanced Harrison's northern appeal by nominating for vice president the Virginian John Tyler, a candidate who believed in few Whig ideals other than an abhorrence of Andrew Jackson. Third, after famously speaking for hours in the bitter cold during his inauguration, the elderly Harrison contracted pneumonia and died. Remarkably, in order for Tyler to become president, all three of these events needed to occur—and all three did. Tyler's nickname, "His Accidency," seems too quaint to do justice to the unlikelihood of his presidency.

The consequences of John Tyler's ascension to the White House were profound. From a political standpoint, Tyler's refusal to allow congressional Whigs to pass their economic policies bred voter disillusionment, which in turn cost the Whigs numerous state elections in the early 1840s. More important for my purposes here, if, instead of Tyler, a more traditional Whig had been nominated vice president and then had become president following Harrison's death, Texas would have remained on the political backburner. To a man, both northern and southern Whigs opposed Texas annexation, and with a Whig majority in Congress, they would have spent time implementing their economic and political agenda—and not debating US expansion.[22] Southern and western Democrats might have continued to support Texas annexation, but they would have been powerless in the face of Whig dominance. The issue would have been consigned to an extended period of oblivion, meaning the Texas Moment would have continued for an unknowable period of time.

As it happened, Texas annexation remained in oblivion for only five years. Its reemergence was due almost solely to the machinations of President Tyler. As an advocate of slavery's expansion, Tyler had always supported Texas annexation, and in the first months of his administration he asked Secretary of State Daniel Webster whether northerners could be reconciled to it.[23] Webster thoroughly rebuffed him. Although frustrated, Tyler could not afford to replace Webster, for he was integral to the delicate negotiations with Britain over the northeastern boundary, which culminated in the 1842 Webster-Ashburton Treaty.

Two years later, however, both continental geopolitics and Washington domestic politics had changed. The Texas government now looked to the intercession of Great Britain as a way to secure Mexican recognition of its independence, which augured well for the future emancipation of enslaved people in Texas. To a select number of proslavery politicians in the United States, particularly Tyler and his new secretary of state, Abel Upshur, this development portended disaster.[24] In order to prevent British interference in Texas, Tyler reopened the annexation issue, directing Upshur to undertake secret negotiations with the Texas government.[25] A president without a party, Tyler also hoped his efforts would invigorate his reelection chances by forging a new coalition of supporters.[26]

When these secret negotiations became public in early 1843, reactions among US politicians varied. Missouri senator Thomas Hart Benton later remembered that it was like "a clap of thunder in a clear sky. There was nothing in the political horizon to announce or portend it."[27] This news was indeed a bombshell to many politicians, so close had Tyler held his cards on the issue. Yet, although surprised, few believed that these negotiations would lead to any game-changing political developments. Henry Clay thought Texas was simply Tyler's desperate political gambit to find a new political constituency and would come to nothing, writing, "I do not remember to have heard lately a solitary voice in favor of or against Annexation. Let Mr. Tyler recommend it, if he please, and what of that? The whole world will see the motive, and impotency of the recommendation." To Clay, Tyler was a "despicable traitor" to the Whig Party, and Texas was his "last move."[28] Longing to win the presidency in 1844, Clay had reasons to believe (and hope) that Texas was a dead issue, but even someone like the Tennessee representative and ardent annexationist Aaron Brown shared Clay's assessment. Writing to his confidant James Polk, Brown maintained that Tyler was only bringing up Texas in order to buttress his political popularity, and Brown thought nothing would come of it. Most Whigs and Democrats, Brown maintained, would quickly let the issue "die away."[29]

Polk did not write or say anything significant on Texas in 1842 and 1843, nor did he respond to Brown's letter. On its face, Polk's silence is surprising, for US expansion would be his winning campaign issue in 1844. Yet Polk's silence was logical in 1842–1843, considering his political fortunes at the time. In 1839 Polk had left the House of Representatives to run for the Tennessee governorship, which he won. In his bid for reelection two years later, however, he lost narrowly to Whig James C. Jones, and then he lost again in 1843. By that year, Whigs had become the dominant party in Tennessee politics, leaving Polk facing the potential end of his political career. Polk was a staunch, lifelong Democrat and a supporter of the expansion of both US borders and the institution of slavery, and it is likely he wanted the United States to annex Texas. But this was not an issue that would resurrect his fortunes in politics in the state of Tennessee (indeed, Polk lost Tennessee during his presidential election).[30]

Meanwhile, John Tyler and his small cadre of pro-annexationists did not want to let Texas annexation "die away," and during the first few months of 1844 they skillfully brought Texas back into the national consciousness. As Secretary of State Abel Upshur continued his secret negotiations with the Texas government, pro-annexationists launched a publicity campaign supporting their position. Most noteworthy was Pennsylvania senator Robert Walker's series of pro-annexation letters in the Tyler administration's organ the *Madisonian*, in which Walker argued that annexation would provide a safety valve for the United States' excess enslaved population.[31] Walker's letters laid the groundwork for some northern Democrats to jump onto the Texas bandwagon by claiming that annexation would weaken slavery, thereby appeasing their constituents who had been hesitant about embracing slavery's expansion.

Yet while contingency had benefited pro-annexationists by improbably making John Tyler president, contingency then handed anti-annexationists a window of opportunity, although it came with tragedy. In February 1844, Tyler and much of his cabinet were on board the USS *Princeton* when one of its massive guns exploded. While Tyler was safely below deck, Abel Upshur and five other men were killed. As Tyler's lead negotiator with the Texas government, Upshur's death threw a wrench into Tyler's annexation plans. Knowing that Upshur had frequently discussed the issue with John C. Calhoun, Tyler promptly nominated Calhoun to replace Upshur—and Calhoun promptly made a mess of things. After reading Upshur's diplomatic correspondence, Calhoun became convinced that the British sought Texas independence solely in order to foster the abolition of slavery in Texas. He then wrote a letter to the British minister Richard Pakenham, in which Calhoun defended slavery as a benign institution and tied Texas annexation to the preservation of slavery in the union.[32] Calhoun's Pakenham letter had the reverse effect of Robert Walker's carefully argued safety valve letters, cooling northern Democrats on Texas annexation. Momentum toward annexation collapsed. In June, when Tyler finally brought a treaty of annexation to the Senate, some northern Democrats joined with all but one Whig to overwhelmingly defeat it by a vote of 35–16. Since a treaty required two-thirds support to pass, this vote represented a crushing defeat for the annexationists.

The stage was set for the dramatic and unexpected presidential election of James Polk in 1844, which in many ways was just as subject to whim and contingency as Tyler's presidency. Only days after Calhoun's Pakenham letter, Martin Van Buren and Henry Clay, the presumptive contestants for the 1844 presidential election, published separate letters opposing the immediate annexation of Texas. Clay was adamantly opposed thanks to his Whig anti-expansionist ideology, although in a follow-up letter designed to mollify expansionists, he argued that annexation could occur in the medium-to-distant future if everything aligned accordingly.[33] Van Buren also equivocated, maintaining he would accede to annexation once the Mexican government consented, but everyone knew this consent was not coming any time soon. Democratic expansionists were horrified with Van Buren's stance, but he still remained the presumptive favorite going into the Democratic convention in May. Clay's nomination on the Whig ticket was practically certain, for he commanded overwhelming party support.[34] Thus, as of late May, it seemed that two men who opposed immediate Texas annexation would face each other in the fall. Immediate annexationists were left without a candidate.

Little, it seemed, had changed since 1837. Despite the substantial political efforts of southern and western expansionists, Tyler and Calhoun above all, Texas annexation was no closer than it had been seven years before. There were simply too many political factions arrayed against it: northern Whigs led by Daniel Webster and John Quincy Adams, southern Whigs led by Henry Clay, northern Democrats led by Martin Van Buren, and even some western Democrats such as Thomas Hart Benton. Other than the intransigent northern Whigs, all of these factions could be persuaded to support annexation under the right circumstances, but these circumstances had not yet arrived— and perhaps they never would. The Texas Moment, it appeared, would become the Texas era, as two (or more) Anglo-American republics would continue to exist side by side into the foreseeable future.

H. Bucholzer, "Matty Meeting the Texas Question" (1844). This political cartoon shows the Democratic Party being torn apart by Texas, which is depicted as an ugly hag bearing chains that represent Texas slaveholding. While Van Buren does not want to address the issue, Polk is watching in the background, saying to vice presidential nominee George Dallas, "She's not the handsomest Lady I ever saw but that $25,000 a year [the salary of the president]. Eh! It's worth a little stretching of Conscience!" Like many other observers of the 1844 presidential election, this cartoonist did not think Texas was a winning issue but was harming the Democratic Party. Courtesy of the Library of Congress, Prints and Photographs Division, Washington, DC.

And yet, only weeks later, the Democrats nominated the ardent expansionist James K. Polk over Van Buren, a stunning turnaround for a man recently facing the end of his political career and for a party concerned with suppressing its sectional tensions. Polk then defeated Clay in the presidential election, permanently shifting the trajectory of US politics. The crucial development in Polk's improbable victory was the introduction of Oregon as an expansionist goal. By grafting the "reoccupation" of Oregon onto the "reannexation" of Texas, Polk and his allies desectionalized expansion, thereby creating a new Democratic center. For the fervent expansionists in the party, Oregon always remained a minor issue. Even in the Old Northwest, where the issue loomed the largest, Oregon was scarcely discussed.[35] Rather, Oregon acted as a counterweight to Texas by proving that expansionists were not bent on expanding slavery. Instead, they argued, they were simply hoping to enlarge the area of freedom for all white Americans, a core Democratic ideology since the party's inception.[36] Moreover, wedding Oregon to Texas allowed anglophobic Democrats to resurrect the British as a specter haunting Americans everywhere, not just—as Calhoun's Pakenham letter argued— slaveholders in particular. While Polk did not originate the Texas-Oregon pairing (it seems that Cave Johnson, one of his campaign managers, first gave him the idea), he clearly understood its potential, and he allowed his supporters at the Democratic Convention to rapidly embrace it.[37] Even then, his appeal was limited; he was, after all, a seemingly failed politician. Ultimately, however, his allies at the convention were able to thread a small political needle, supporting Van Buren until it was clear he would not win the nomination and then bringing together the disillusioned pro–Van Burenites, who remained thankful for Polk's prior support, with the anti–Van Buren men to support Polk's candidacy.[38]

While Polk was relatively unknown nationally—Whigs famously derided his candidacy by asking, "Who is James Polk?"—his Texas-Oregon expansionist platform mitigated his lack of fame and charisma, electrifying Democrats throughout the country and providing a convenient means to paper over the party's sectional and economic disagreements.[39] Rather than expansionism driving partisanship, partisanship drove expansionism. Certainly, tens of thousands of Americans had long supported Texas annexation specifically and US expansion more generally. Yet, as I have shown, their ideas remained undeveloped and diverse, and expansionism remained an amorphous subject that hovered in and around US politics rather than being a core campaign issue. Polk, in effect, activated Texas as a new symbol for the Democratic Party, turning what once had been a term that reflected independent American republics to one that reflected US continental dominance, which, crucially, would only occur if the Democrats won the election.[40] As one anonymous anti-annexationist writer complained, Texas annexation had nothing to do with actual continental affairs, but was an "affair of party."[41] Democratic meetings unwittingly demonstrated this dynamic by their rhetoric. Predicted one Indiana Democrat, "The prairies of the whole west *will* ring with loud shouts for Polk and Texas, Dallas and Oregon."[42] A Democratic meeting in Illinois proclaimed, "We assure the public, that all of us have the *Young Hick-*

Edward Williams Clay, "Going to Texas after the Election of 1844" (1844). This cartoon predicts that the Texas issue will lead to a Democratic loss in 1844. Sitting on a horse, James Polk and his running mate, George Dallas, leave for Texas while Andrew Jackson bids them farewell. To their left, John Tyler looks forlornly at the ground, lamenting his "treachery" and "unscrupulous efforts," and to his left Henry Clay celebrates from the White House. Courtesy of the Library of Congress, Prints and Photographs Division, Washington, DC.

ory, Texas, and Oregon fever!—It is very *contagious*."[43] In both of these statements, Democrats viewed expansionism as something novel and energizing that had diffused from the party's leadership to its voters.

Oregon's inclusion in this rhetoric highlighted one more piece of luck that helped Polk immeasurably: the American migration to Oregon or, as Americans in the West termed it, "Oregon fever." Polk and his allies were able to graft Oregon to Texas because of these Oregon migrants, even though they would play practically no role in Polk's blustering diplomacy with Britain that followed. Here again, unintended consequences bore fruit for the Democrats, in that Polk depended on an issue to which neither he nor US politics more generally had any relation. The Great Migration to Oregon occurred in 1843, which prompted Democrats to argue for the first time that the United

States needed to gain control of Oregon to protect the migrants. If the Great Migration had occurred only one year later, expansionist Democrats would have been unable to fuse Texas with Oregon and thus unable to mitigate slavery as the primary goal of expansion. In an ironic twist, migrants had journeyed to Oregon because of their unhappiness with their prospects in the United States, but this ultimately allowed US politicians to justify Oregon annexation.

Of course, for all of the good Texas and Oregon did for the unity of the Democratic Party and for the enthusiasm of its supporters, Polk still had to win the 1844 election. He did win—but barely. As the oft-told narrative goes, Henry Clay would have won the election if he had won New York, which he lost to Polk by roughly 5,000 votes. For those looking for a logical and explainable drift toward the Civil War, this result has much to offer. According to this argument, Clay's ambivalence on slavery, and slavery's relationship to Texas annexation, cost him both proslavery votes in the South and antislavery votes in the North. If Clay had captured only a third of the abolitionist Liberty Party's tally of 15,000 votes in New York, he would have won the presidency. That he did not, that Polk won the presidency and initiated an expansionist agenda, which in turn initiated the countdown to the Civil War, has therefore a certain logic to it: slavery and its relationship to US expansion led to disunion, for these were the issues on which Americans voted.[44]

And yet, as the historian Michael Holt has analyzed meticulously, this logic does not hold up to scrutiny. Clay's ambivalence toward slavery did not swing New York to Polk. On the contrary, it helped drive Whig turnout in New York, for most Whigs appreciated his moderation in contrast to the radical abolitionism of the Liberty Party. Like Clay, most Whig voters in 1844 wanted to suppress slavery as a political issue, not abolish its existence in the South. Moreover, Polk's narrow victory in New York had nothing to do with Texas annexation but was caused by an influx of newly naturalized Irish and German voters, who were motivated by a clumsy, belated Whig attempt to rally nativists to its ranks.[45] The New York results also may have been influenced by the lingering effect of the Patriot War along the state's northern border. In 1840, American Patriots and their mostly Democratic supporters were disgusted with Van Buren's anti-Patriot actions, so they had stayed home on election day. In 1844, Polk engendered no such feelings, so Democratic Patriots voted.[46] In the end, it was not expansion that decided the presidential race, but a bevy of local issues.

Thus, Polk won the presidency, which gave the lame duck Tyler a (supposed) mandate to push Texas annexation through Congress via a joint resolution. Although this method possessed dubious constitutional legality, it was the only way forward for annexationists, for they still could not achieve two-thirds support in the Senate for a treaty. Only after Polk's election did Texas annexation become a foregone conclusion in US history. Indeed, until the election of Polk, countless Americans believed that Texas would *not* become a matter of national importance in the near future. Even many of those who favored annexation believed it could wait years, even decades.

Certainly, Polk's election was not based entirely on contingency. Polk and his allies deserve political credit: when opportunities arose that allowed them to reignite the issue of annexation, they seized the moment. However, that these opportunities arose was the result of a remarkably improbable series of events. It is no wonder, then, that John Quincy Adams believed that the issue of Texas annexation was resurrected by an inimical proslavery conspiracy, part of "one great system" in which the United States would also attack and occupy British Oregon, attack Mexico, and seize California.[47] How else to explain such an unlikely series of events? How else to explain developments that the entire Whig party and Democratic stalwarts, such as Van Buren and Thomas Hart Benton, opposed? Adams was wrong; slavery and expansion were intimately related, but slavery did not simply beget expansion. There was no vast conspiracy, but rather a sequence of unlikely contingencies. For Adams—and, indeed, for a small but now growing number of antislavery northerners—conspiracy seemed a more satisfying explanation, because it offered a rationale that was both coherent and consistent. Bad luck did not.

Incentivizing Expansion:
From Breakaway Americans to Agents of US Empire

In a single year, the Texas Moment ended. Acting with unprecedented speed and aggressiveness, Polk facilitated federal intervention in various guises in Texas, in Oregon, in California, in the Cherokee Nation, and with the Mormons, who were traveling to a remote area of California.[48] By the end of 1846, every breakaway America had entered the union, although it would take two more years and the invasion of Mexico City to make Alta California officially US territory. For Americans who supported US expansion, it was a remarkable achievement. Breakaway Americans, on the other hand, were more ambivalent.

In some ways, Polk's predecessor, John Tyler, shared Polk's continental vision. He was, after all, an ardent expansionist and specifically focused on foreign policy during his presidency after it was clear that neither party would support his domestic agenda.[49] Tyler involved the United States in diplomatic disputes in California, Texas, the Maine–New Brunswick border, and even Hawaii. In each case, he pursued US expansion, but always carefully, through diplomatic rather than military means. For example, during the Aroostook War, in which Americans from Maine and Canadians from New Brunswick almost came to blows over disputed territory, Tyler worked to cool the on-the-ground passions of Americans while pursuing diplomacy with Britain. The result, the Webster-Ashburton Treaty, gave the United States more territory than Britain received. Tyler also worked for two years behind the scenes to negotiate the annexation of Texas to the United States, and while he disregarded Mexican objections, he nevertheless hoped to avoid war. When it came to Oregon, Tyler argued that the best course was to wait until more Americans arrived in the territory, which would strengthen the US claim. For Tyler, expansion did not need to be hurried, because the Texas game would play out as planned. Demography would soon be destiny, which one Democratic congressman deemed the "American multiplication table."[50]

After Polk became president, Tyler believed that Polk should follow the course that he had pursued—expansionist but diplomatic, firm in the pursuit of US interests but not confrontational.[51] Unlike Tyler, however, Polk thought that nothing about US expansion was destined, and he ramped up US aggression—to Tyler's dismay. Polk believed not only that the British were bent on securing footholds across the continent, but—crucially—that these actions would be legitimized by the policy-makers in actual and would-be breakaway Americas, who were not necessarily gravitating toward the United States. His concern stemmed not from a distrust of breakaway Americans themselves, but he feared that their polities would be too weak to prevent British meddling. They would act as geopolitical soft spots that would invariably open up the continent to British interference and even conquest. Polk also feared delay on both political and partisan levels. Because he had pledged himself to one term, he had a finite amount of time to accomplish his stated goals, and he needed to do so in order to maintain Democratic control of Congress. Here again, partisanship helped drive expansion: the only means to ensure Whig defeat in 1846 was to annex both Texas and Oregon before the congressional elections.

Polk's concerns about breakaway Americanism were most prominent in regard to Texas. His prioritization of Texas was understandable, for it was already an independent republic and thus had greater room for geopolitical and diplomatic maneuvering than other breakaway Americas had. Moreover, Texas had already been tied to Polk's own political future: if the republic had rejected annexation prior to the 1844 election, the news would have ensured Polk's defeat—which he knew all too well.[52] Once elected, Polk worked behind the scenes to ensure that annexation proceeded as fast as possible. Standing in his way was the Missouri senator Thomas Hart Benton, who proposed that the United States reopen negotiations with the Texans instead of accepting annexation terms that he believed would make war with Mexico all but assured.[53] Benton had the allegiance of many western Democrats, and his proposal offered an alternative for more conservative-minded expansionists, who desired Texas but only if war with Mexico were avoided. To Polk, however, reopening negotiations would be disastrous. Writing a few months after these events, he explained, "If [Benton's] alternative had been chosen, I think we have now abundant evidence to prove that Texas would probably have been lost to the union. If negotiations had been opened by commissioners great delay would necessarily have taken place, giving ample opportunity to *British* and *French* intrigue to have seriously embarrassed, if not defeated annexation."[54]

His belief that annexation had reached a now-or-never condition rested on information from the many letters he received from agents he had sent to Texas as president-elect, all of which portrayed Sam Houston, Anson Jones, and a majority of the Texas cabinet as welcoming to British overtures—which was rooted in some truth.[55] As to why Texas would prefer Britain over the United States, most of Polk's correspondents emphasized the cunning of the British. A few, however, also cited annexation's implications for Texas officials, who "conceive[d] that their own importance may be diminished by the transformation of that territory from a *primary* to a *secondary* position."[56] Here Polk's correspondents shared the assessment of some other observers— including Polk's mentor Andrew Jackson—that Texas officials would thwart the will of the Texan people for the sake of their own power. These observers were not wrong: as late as 1845, a majority of the Texas cabinet and the Texas Congress opposed annexation to the United States, although most of the members were ultimately unwilling to buck the choice of the vast majority of Anglo-Texans, who desired US annexation.[57]

In the end, Polk's and Tyler's allies in Congress wrote a joint resolution on Texas annexation that gave the president the choice of whether to reopen negotiations or not. Needing the support of Benton and his allies to pass the resolution, Polk gave Benton the impression that he would reopen negotiations once he became president, thereby ensuring that Benton and his followers would vote yes. At the same time Polk urged Tyler to not reopen negotiations and proceed with annexation, betraying his promise to Benton. While Polk's machinations opened an irreparable rift between Polk and Benton, Polk had accomplished his primary goal: Texas was annexed.

There was some irony in Polk's yearlong anxiety about Texas annexation: the United States of America (population 17 million) had found itself at the diplomatic mercy of the officials of the Republic of Texas (population 125,000), a weak and isolated, albeit independent, international state. In 1837, Texas had courted the United States for annexation. In 1844, the situation was reversed, as the United States waited for Texans to make up their minds. Texas had essentially held out for a better deal: it would join the United States as a state rather than a territory, and it would retain control of its public lands.[58] Even after the Texans agreed to annexation, Polk remained concerned that they would change their minds and pursue the British option if the United States failed to ratify the annexation terms. And if the Texans did so, Polk would have little recourse to stop them; at no point would Americans countenance a war to conquer an Anglo-American sister republic, even if that republic were underwritten by British dollars and diplomacy. Here was the core risk with allowing the Texas game to be played: US expansion was left to the voters and politicians of breakaway Americas, not the will of the voters and politicians of the United States.

The question was, then, how to incorporate breakaway Americas and the breakaway Americans who inhabited them while simultaneously deferring to the principle of self-determination, all while the US state had a relatively modest reach. The answer lay in what the historians Paul Frymer and Laura Jensen have pointed to when explaining the success of a weak US state: the incentivizing of Anglo-American populations in the borderlands.[59] Breakaway Americans left US borders due to various degrees of unhappiness with the United States, and thus they needed various incentives to not only reattach themselves to the United States, but act as agents of US empire. Depending on which breakaway Americans were being courted, these incentives could come in the form of political power (usually a guarantee of political autonomy) or economic prosperity (usually a guarantee of landownership). Further, for Indian-hating Democratic officials, alongside incentivizing whites was the need to *dis*incentivize Natives to maintain independence. This was particularly necessary for removed peoples like the Cherokees, who were carving out their own autonomous space in Indian Territory. Carrots for white Americans would be matched with sticks for Natives.

Yet incentivizing could not come through federal policy, as it had in the past via measures such as the Armed Occupation Act, which Congress passed in 1842 in order to facilitate settlement of the Florida frontier. Because breakaway Americas were either entirely independent of the US government or at least autonomous, the federal government needed to incentivize through diplomats and army officers, which meant, by extension, executive action. Polk used the power of the executive to send out diplomats and secret agents, who in turn attempted to incentivize breakaway Americans on the ground. Only in Oregon could Polk avoid dealing with breakaway Americans directly, for the joint agreement with Great Britain allowed him to supersede the input of Oregonians by maintaining that Oregon had always been partially controlled by the United States.

Part of this strategy rested on the bedrock Americanism of breakaway Americans. As I have shown, breakaway Americans may have been unhappy with their prospects in the United States, but they did not seek to abandon the American principles they continued to hold dear—which, of course, varied greatly among such ideologically diverse populations. Politicians in Washington and US agents on the ground could appeal to American values, American history, and often white racial solidarity to help bring breakaway Americans back into the fold of US empire and perhaps even act as US expansionists themselves. There was an early incarnation of this phenomenon during the Patriot War, when American Patriots were willing to counter the US state in various ways, but they were never willing to fight the United States itself. They may have wished to create a second American republic in Canada, but not to the point of attacking the original American republic from which they hailed. In this way, the flexibility of American nationalism allowed breakaway Americanism to take root, but it also allowed breakaway Americans to be reintegrated into the US state.

Polk's (and, in this case, also Tyler's) incentivizing began with Texas. The generous terms of Texas annexation provided a series of enticements for Anglo-Texans to willingly give up their independence—but, crucially, not their autonomy, as they would enter the United States as a state instead of a territory. The latter was a dreaded status that all Americans hoped to avoid. With state status, Texas officials did give up some of their power, but they still retained much of it. Sam Houston was no longer the president of an international state, but within a year he would be giving a speech in Washington, DC, as one of only fifty-eight senators—with much less political anxiety hanging over his head. Texas would also retain control of its public lands, which the government could sell in order to pay off its substantial debts. Meanwhile, Texas sovereignty was now guaranteed by the US Army, dashing Mexican hopes to retake the territory. Ultimately, for Anglo-Texans, annexation brought many incentives and few pitfalls.

Employing this same incentivizing strategy, Polk and his Democratic allies ensured that no other North American region that they coveted would follow the Texas model, which had taken initiative out of the hands of the United States and given it to a smaller republic. The Texas game could not be played again. If a legitimate—Anglo-American and republican—government arose in any of these regions, Polk could not allow that government to remain independent for long. Of course, in 1845, with the United States risking war with both Mexico and Great Britain, Polk would not say that. Instead, he had to pay lip service to the principle of self-determination, as he did in his 1845 inauguration, when he stated that "the people of this continent alone have the right to decide their own destiny."[60] He then claimed that if people wanted to form an independent state or join the United States, that was their concern, but Europe should not interfere. In this manner, Polk employed the Monroe Doctrine to justify US involvement in the affairs of other North American regions.[61]

Revealingly, later in Polk's presidency, after the acquisition of California and Oregon, he became more open about the danger that breakaway Americanism posed to US expansion. In an 1847 message to Congress, Polk maintained that the United States needed to keep the vast amount of territory it had conquered from Mexico, because if it did not, it would leave behind independent or autonomous regions ripe for interference from an outside power. As Polk stated, no North American people, whether "inhabitants or foreigners," could be allowed to form an independent government: "Such a government would be too feeble to long maintain its separate independent existence, and would finally become annexed to or be [the] dependent colony of some powerful state."[62] Breakaway Americanism now needed to be snuffed out before it could take root—and, as president, Polk believed it was his responsibility to take aggressive measures to ensure such. With Texas safely in the union, he set his sights on other people and places that seemed to offer trouble: the Mormons, Anglo-Americans in California and Oregon, and the majority Ross faction of the Cherokee Nation.

The Mormons

By early 1846 Mormon leaders had decided that their people would move to a remote region of Mexican California, where they believed they could carve out their own independent empire. This stunning ambition made the Mormons the most hostile to US expansion of all breakaway Americans. Yet they were able to keep this ambition hidden from most US policy-makers, Polk included. For someone who consummately thought in geopolitical terms, Polk was blind to the Mormons' objectives and gave them little thought during the first year of his presidency. When he initially learned of their emigration, he refused to take action, arguing that "absurd" religious beliefs did not countenance presidential intervention.[63] Left to their own devices, a majority of the Mormons by early 1846 had arrived in Iowa Territory, from where they planned to send out a smaller party to scout their final destination in the Great Basin. As already mentioned, when Mormon leaders learned of the US declaration of war in May, they privately wished for a Mexican victory but publicly stayed silent. They could not be bothered with international geopolitics in the moment, for they were in the midst of coordinating the safe travel of thousands of their followers hundreds of miles across North America's most inhospitable regions.

Events might have continued in this vein, with Polk and the Mormons largely ignoring one another, if not for the intervention of Mormon leader Jesse Little and Mormon sympathizer Thomas Kane. In January 1846 the Quorum of the Twelve had appointed the New Englander Little to head the Eastern States Mission, replacing Samuel Brannan, who was on a ship to California. The Quorum of the Twelve urged Little to go to Washington and seek tangible assistance for their move west—although it would be another futile request.[64] Little soon struck up an acquaintance with Kane, a Philadelphian with connections to the Democratic Party and the Polk administration. Kane urged Little to write a letter to Polk, and Kane probably suggested playing on typical American fears of Mormon hostility to get Polk's attention. Little wrote to Polk that the Mormons were "true hearted Americans, true to our country, true to its laws, true to its glorious institutions—and we have a desire to go under the outstretched wings of the American Eagle." These (false) professions of loyalty may have put Polk's mind at ease, until he read the unmistakable threat in the next sentence: "We would disdain to receive assistance from a foreign power—although it should be proferred—unless our government shall turn us off in this great crisis and will not help us, but compel us to be foreigners."[65] By this time, the United States had already declared war against Mexico, and possible war with Great Britain over Oregon loomed, awakening Polk to the Mormon threat. Now this "absurd" sect represented a potentially hostile force traveling into lands that Polk coveted. Indeed, Little's statement aligned precisely with Polk's paranoia about how breakaway Americans would create openings for British interference. After receiving this letter, Polk wrote in his diary that he needed to "conciliate" the Mormons and "prevent this singular sect from becoming hostile to the U.S."[66] The Mormons and the US government would strike a deal.

After days of backroom discussions, the Polk administration and Jesse Little came to an agreement: in return for federal aid, several hundred Mormon men would enlist in the US Army and assist in the conquest of California. Eventually deemed the Mormon Battalion, this contingent would endure the longest journey of any armed force in US history and make an imprint on the West as road builders, peacekeepers, and, for a few, gold finders. The battalion's creation was not a gesture of goodwill on the part of President Polk, nor was it an expression of patriotism by the Mormons, although both sides outwardly expressed such lofty sentiments. Rather, the Mormon Battalion resulted from a calculated realpolitik on both sides. For fighting with the United States—and, perhaps more important, not against them—the Mormons received several tangible benefits: the United States would permit them to settle temporarily on and travel through Indian Territory on their journey west; those who enlisted would be moved west at US expense; and the battalion's pay would help finance the westward journey for the rest of the Mormon populace.[67] More symbolically, to Mormon leaders who had long feared potential US hostility, the creation of the Mormon Battalion ensured that the US government would not only not interfere in the Mormon exodus, but endorse it. Thus, Polk incentivized the Mormons to become agents of US expansion, rather than bulwarks against it.

With the deal struck, Little and several US Army officers traveled separately to take the news to Mormon leaders, most of whom were now in Iowa Territory. When the officers arrived before Little, such was the state of Mormon-US relations that several Mormons believed that the US troops had arrived to destroy them or, at the least, were spies meant to keep watch over them.[68] Yet when the commanding officer spoke with Brigham Young, Young instantly responded favorably, even before Little arrived to assure Young of the details of the offer. Young understood the immediate, tangible benefits of what was in reality a calculated Mormon-US alliance. Knowing the hostility with which most Mormons viewed the United States, Young then engaged in a speaking tour of the Mormon encampments to persuade men to volunteer for the battalion. Eventually the ranks filled, the Mormons accepted the US offer, and the Mormon Battalion became a reality.

By agreeing to Polk's offer, Young foreclosed two other actions the Mormons could have taken toward the United States. The first was neutrality. The Mormons could have avoided taking sides with the hope that their settlement in the Salt Lake Valley would present the Mexican War's victor with a fait accompli. The second option was perhaps riskier but had great potential if it succeeded: an outright alliance with Mexico. Certainly, before the United States' declaration of war against Mexico, some Mormons believed they could cultivate Mexico as a valuable ally in the West. Quorum of the Twelve member Orson Hyde, for example, wrote a letter to Brigham Young in which he maintained that Mexico would allow the Mormons to settle in California, if in turn the Mormons would combat the "scapegoat mobocrats" (i.e., American settlers) who were pouring into the territory.[69] Three weeks after Hyde's ruminations, Polk declared war on Mexico, leading whoever received it to cross out this part of Hyde's letter. That person clearly understood that the calculus had changed: an alliance with Mexico would also mean war with the United States.

At least one Mormon believed this alliance was still worth making. William Pickett was not a member of the Quorum of the Twelve or the Council of Fifty, but he was prominent enough that in the summer of 1846, he was tasked with overseeing the final evacuation of Nauvoo by the last few hundred Mormon inhabitants.[70] In a letter titled "A Concise View of the Policy of the Latter Day Saints in Reference to Their Emigration to California," Pickett welcomed war with the United States. He knew about the US enlistment of the Mormon Battalion, but felt there was no reason to trust Polk's offer: "This government has been notorious for making promises during war, and breaking them at pleasure, as soon as it saw fit to do so—witness how the U.S. in the Algerine War in 1804, broke faith with a Barbary prince . . . also its broken promises to the Canadians during the last war—inducing hundreds of them to join the American standard, under the promise of protection, and then shamefully left them to the mercies of British anger, when they had finished using them." Pickett worried that if the United States conquered the West, new American immigrants would arrive, and eventually the anti-Mormon depredations would begin again. His concluded his letter adamantly: "*Our safety is to leave this government.*"[71] He maintained that, once in the West, the

Mormons could contract with Mexico to become empresarios of California. Mexico would be happy to have them, for the Mormons would be able to keep the disloyal Californio population in line and maintain Mexican sovereignty over the territory.

Brigham Young never responded to Pickett's proposal. Ever practical, Young believed that the immediate and tangible benefits of the Mormon Battalion outweighed any distant hope of a Mexican alliance. He also understood that with the onset of war, the Mormons' geopolitical calculus had changed. He may have loathed the United States, but its war against Mexico meant that the Far West would be deluged with US soldiers and, eventually, statesmen. Thus, the Mormons needed to tread softly—at least for the time being. Once they were safely ensconced in the Salt Lake Valley, they would be able to reassess their geopolitical options.

California

From the outset of his presidency, Polk had his eyes on Mexican California. Unlike his focus on Texas and Oregon, which stemmed from domestic politics, Polk's attention to California was almost solely due to geographic, economic, and political concerns. It had little to do with public opinion. Certainly, increasing numbers of Americans were starting to pay attention to the region, and in 1846 more than a thousand migrants traveled there, largely due to the circulation of Lansford Hastings's *Emigrants' Guide*. Yet most Americans continued to believe that the acquisition of and migration to California lay in the medium-to-distant future. John L. O'Sullivan himself, in his famed Manifest Destiny essay, "Annexation," predicted that California would join the union "in the fast hastening year of the Lord 1945!"[72]

However, presidents with an eye toward global trade had coveted the territory, particularly the San Francisco Bay region, for some time. In the mid-1830s, Andrew Jackson had sought to purchase the region from Mexico, and John Tyler had feigned interest in the 1840s in order to manipulate Britain over Oregon Country. Polk, too, understood California's potential and worked toward its acquisition even as the public remained indifferent.[73] In 1845, he ordered his secretary of state, James Buchanan, to investigate ways in which the United States might annex the territory, which led Buchanan to write to the US consul in California, Thomas Larkin, that if the oft-rebellious inhabitants of California chose to create, in Buchanan's words, a "Sister Republic," the United States would celebrate their accomplishment. While Buchanan noted that the United States would welcome California into the union if its inhabitants so desired, he also stated that the Polk administration would gladly accept a California republic as a permanent ally on the continent. What the United States could not abide, Buchanan warned Larkin, was if California opened itself to British influence—note again the obsession with a breakaway state being used as a foothold for British power—and he instructed Larkin to make the utmost effort to prevent such an occurrence.[74]

Buchanan was preaching to the choir, for Larkin had long feared the machinations of the British in California, especially those of British consul James Forbes. Larkin did not know that the British had largely abandoned all efforts to dominate California, and he promptly set out to steer California politics away from an imaginary threat. As soon as he received Buchanan's letter in April 1846, he wrote confidential letters to fellow wealthy New England traders in San Diego, Los Angeles, and Yerba Buena (soon to be renamed San Francisco). In the letters, Larkin warned his confidants to be prepared for war between the United States and Mexico, for they had "much at stake . . . in the coming events." If war did not come, he anticipated that California would join Britain, France, or the United States. Larkin then relayed his argument as to why the United States was the best choice: only in a republic could all California residents (Californio, American, and European) find "fellow feeling."[75] He concluded by asking his confidants to inform him of any Californio political maneuvers.

Larkin then wrote a public letter to all Californios in which he voiced similar sentiments, albeit in a manner less obviously insisting on US annexation. He claimed that the United States would never actively try to conquer the territory, but it would readily accept California as an equal state in the union. In a nod to the class interests of elite Californios, he noted that real estate values would greatly increase with US annexation, and "persons and property" would be significantly safer. His most forceful statements, however, did not involve the United States but addressed the British involvement in California, which would "sow the seeds of future war," for then the United States would be forced to intervene based on the principles of the Monroe Doctrine.[76] Ultimately, he urged, Californios must avoid British influence and either join the United States or become a sister republic on the continent.

Larkin was not fundamentally opposed to an independent California republic. He favored California joining the United States immediately, as long as it happened peacefully and with minimal disturbance to California society. If war broke out between the United States and Mexico, he saw his primary duty as keeping the peace on the ground in California. Yet if war did not ensue and California declared independence, Larkin believed its entrance into the union would be deferred for a little while.[77] In his view, a California republic, with all its internal weaknesses, would eventually, invariably request US annexation.

President Polk did not share Larkin's assessment. A sister republic of California would invite British meddling. Moreover, a California declaration of independence could prevent US conquest, for Mexico would then have no right to cede the territory to the United States, whether through purchase or the results of war. To force the issue, he turned to the same clandestine method he had used in his previous dealings with an independent Texas—he found a secret agent. At the same time as Buchanan sent his letter to Larkin, Polk dispatched Lieutenant Archibald Gillespie to California on what Polk described as a "secret mission."[78] Gillespie carried a copy of Buchanan's letter to Larkin, but he was also given verbal "secret instructions" to relay to both Larkin and John C. Frémont. At the time Frémont was leading another US exploring trek to the Pacific Coast. After a nine-month journey, Gillespie reached California and consulted with Larkin. He then traveled in pursuit of Frémont, who was currently in far northern California.

Gillespie was intervening in what was already a delicate situation, for Frémont had been making trouble. In prior weeks, he had taken his army much farther south than had been previously agreed with Californio leaders, leading Mexican commandant general José Castro to demand Frémont leave California immediately. Frémont refused and asked for an apology. He then moved his force to Gavilan Peak, raised the US flag, and prepared for Castro's impending assault. Frémont's actions caused panic among Californios, particularly *norteños* who were significantly closer to the potential conflict.[79] As Thomas Larkin desperately wrote letters trying to calm both sides, Frémont declared that if attacked by Castro, "we will die every man of us under the Flag of our country."[80] Soon, however, Frémont realized that Castro's force was more than double his own, and he recanted his bravado by abandoning Gavilan Peak and retreating north, ostensibly leaving for Oregon. On the way, Frémont learned from several American immigrants that Natives were planning to attack their settlements. Perhaps stinging from his humiliation at the hands of Castro and wanting to take his aggression out on someone, Frémont and his men located a village of Wintu people and massacred them, murdering hundreds of men, women, and children. Their bloodlust satisfied, Frémont and his men once again turned north, until Gillespie arrived.[81]

Gillespie gave Frémont the same letter that Buchanan had sent to Larkin, as well as letters from Frémont's wife, Jesse, and his father-in-law, Thomas Hart Benton. He then relayed Polk's verbal "secret instructions," which still remain unknown. Whatever Gillespie told Frémont, he was encountering a man who had already made several rash decisions in the midst of a volatile situation. True to character, Frémont responded to Gillespie with further hot-headedness. He promptly turned his force around and headed south, once again threatening the Californios with military action—a decision that would soon precipitate the infamous Bear Flag Revolt.

What exactly did Gillespie tell Frémont? Historians have been debating the contents of the "secret instructions" for more than a century and still have not arrived at a definitive answer (and probably never will).[82] It seems unlikely that Gillespie told Frémont to take such a bellicose stance toward the Californios, for these were not the methods of James Polk. Polk had sent Zachary Taylor's force to the disputed Texas-Mexico border, hoping that Mexico would take rash action and therefore appear to be the aggressor. There is no reason to expect he would have reversed this course in California. It is more likely that Polk wanted Frémont to remain in California indefinitely and intervene if he learned that the United States and Mexico were at war. What Polk did not bank on, and what he could not control across the continent, was Frémont's difficult-to-manage personality, which combined impulsivity, arrogance, and panache—not traits suited for secret missions and backdoor diplomacy. Thus, even if Gillespie urged tact and a wait-and-see approach, Frémont was unable to contain himself, particularly after his humiliation at the hands of Castro.

Frémont's actions reverberated on several fronts. In northern California, where Frémont's presence caused a more direct stir, the norteños convened a meeting of prominent military and civil officers in Monterey to discuss California sovereignty and debate their political strategy. What the Californios defined as a junta met at Thomas Larkin's house, demonstrating that, though he was the US consul, Larkin remained trusted as a fellow elite.[83] One by one Californios and acculturated foreigners rose to offer solutions for California's future. José Castro recommended putting California under French protection, citing the shared Catholic culture. Others wanted to make California a British protectorate, maintaining that Britain could prevent slavery from spreading into the territory and could mediate between American Protestants and Californio Catholics. A few Californios proposed complete independence, proclaiming "California libre, soberana, y independiente" (free, sovereign, and independent California).[84] Mariano Vallejo believed that independence was certainly possible from a military standpoint. He cited the Republic of Texas as an example, arguing that it had maintained its sovereignty for a decade despite being much closer to hostile Mexico than California was. Therefore, he reasoned, if Texas could remain independent, so could California. But Vallejo then recommended an alternative solution: seek US annexation. Vallejo cited Californios' and Americans' shared republican values and the ability to enter the union on equal footing with all other Americans: "When we join our fortunes to hers, we shall not become subjects, but fellow-citizens, possessing all the rights of the people of the United States and choosing our own federal and local rulers."[85] Despite Vallejo's eloquence, the junta was unable to decide, and the meeting eventually dissolved pending communication with the South.

Meanwhile, Frémont's presence also had a decisive effect on the northern California frontier, where it reverberated among American immigrants in the Sacramento Valley. To these migrants, Frémont's presence offered military protection from their real or potential enemies, a fact that seemed even clearer after he followed his massacre of the Wintus with yet another attack on a Native people, this time the Klamaths, in early April.[86] As Frémont made his way north, rumors circulated among Americans who had settled in the Sacramento Valley that the Californios would expel them from their lands. There was some factual basis for these rumors: the Monterey prefect had issued an order to all the California town justices, instructing them to inform immigrants that they had no right to own land in California and could be "expelled from [the land] whenever the government finds it convenient."[87] Yet what was reported among American settlers became something quite different: "Notice is hereby given, that a large body of armed Spaniards on horseback, amounting to 250 men, have been seen on their way to the Sacramento valley, destroying the crops, burning the houses, and driving off the cattle."[88] American immigrants petitioned Frémont to intervene on their behalf against the Californios and attack the northernmost Californio garrison at Sonoma. At first he demurred, but by early June the ever-impulsive Frémont had changed his mind: while he would not yet join the would-be insurgents, he would at least tacitly approve their actions.

Thus, the events that would lead to the Bear Flag Revolt were set in motion: thirty-three American immigrants raided Sonoma, imprisoned Mariano Vallejo and his family, and declared the independence of the Republic of California. Much of what occurred during the revolt remains contested and ultimately uncertain, but one aspect is undeniable: Frémont and Gillespie, as representatives of the US state, changed the dynamics of the entire region. Frémont had begun the process with his journey far into the boundaries of Mexican California and his defiance at Gavilan Peak, and then Gillespie had exacerbated the situation when he prompted Frémont to turn south once again.[89] All of these actions were avoidable. Frémont had traveled through northern California previously, but neither Americans nor Californios had raised a stir because he remained far in the interior. When he and his force arrived again in late 1845, Americans and Californios once again took it in stride—until Frémont aggressively confronted Californios and attacked Natives. These actions incentivized the Americans in the Sacramento Valley to rally to his side for various reasons. Some likely acted in the belief that it was their patriotic duty to the United States, others acted on sheer bloodlust and racism toward nonwhites, and others supported him simply because the neutral middle had collapsed, for now Californios deemed all American settlers to be hostile. While the original Bear Flaggers only numbered thirty-three men, the later California Battalion, also composed of American immigrants, numbered 190. In all cases, it was Frémont's arrival that prompted Americans to act. As one former Bear Flagger remembered, "Disputes about land and personal property were the first causes of bad feeling [between Americans and Californios], but the appearance of Frémont west of the Rocky Mountains . . . made the 'foreigners' bolder and the Californians suspicious."[90] John Bidwell, who joined the insurrection several days after it began, was more succinct, maintaining that all the Bear Flaggers were looking for was a "wink from an American in uniform" to begin their revolt.[91] Once again the US state had incentivized breakaway Americans to act as agents of US empire.

The Bear Flag Revolt, however, was hardly popular. Despite the perception—then and now—that most recently arrived migrants were, in the words of one historian, "hothead pioneers" looking for a fight with the Californios, only thirty-three men initially attacked Sonoma.[92] A majority of these men were in their late teens or early twenties, had arrived in California the previous year, and were "unsettled"—that is, they did not yet possess land and made a living by hunting, trapping, and working for John Sutter.[93] Ezekiel Merritt, a leader of the revolt and one of the few men over forty, had allegedly been whipped by Vallejo's brother in a dispute and desired revenge on the Vallejo family. Peter Storm, at forty-seven the oldest participant, had been imprisoned during the Graham affair in 1840 and may also have wanted revenge. Two participants had previously fought in Texas and thus had experience—and success—with overthrowing Mexican rule.[94]

Clearly, the initial Bear Flaggers were not a representative sample of American immigrants, many of whom had gained access to land and had little inclination to disturb the status quo. While most migrants did not legally possess the land, their claims were at least tacitly accepted by the Californios. Tellingly, three times as many Americans—drawn from a significantly smaller number of settlers—had volunteered for Micheltorena's Mexican army one year prior. Americans who volunteered for Micheltorena constituted more than fifty percent of the existing American population, in contrast to less than ten percent who volunteered during the Bear Flag Revolt.[95] Here is the ambivalent US patriotism of many breakaway Americans: while some, and eventually most, Americans in the Sacramento Valley rallied to the US flag, it took several months and various developments to bring the majority into the US fold. This ambivalence stemmed from the original impetus behind breakaway Americanism: breakaway Americans made choices based on their perceived self-interests. In 1845, Micheltorena promised land, and more than a hundred Americans joined his cause. The Bear Flag Revolt promised nothing but an uncertain future, for even if every single American man in California volunteered, this force would still be too small to actually conquer California from the Californios. No wonder so few volunteered. If the Bear Flag Revolt was an example of the Texas game, then few Americans wanted to play it.

And yet, these few did see themselves as reenacting Texas. To them, the Texas Revolution exemplified moral righteousness and legality: an aggrieved people rising up against a despotic government and declaring independence only because they had no other choice. William Ide, one of the Bear Flag leaders, was particularly concerned to appear in such a light, for he did not want the Bear Flaggers to be perceived as ruffians (which, in most ways, they were). In the initial days of the revolt, Ide wrote and circulated the rationale behind the Bear Flaggers' seemingly rash actions, in what was essentially a declaration of independence.[96] Ide's background differed from most Bear Flaggers. Originally from Vermont, where his father had served in the state legislature, Ide had converted to Mormonism in the early 1840s and served as a delegate to the 1844 Mormon convention that nominated Joseph Smith for president. Whether he was still a practicing Mormon is uncertain, but Ide had a background in constitutionalism.[97] Once Frémont gave up his US Army commission and officially joined the Bear Flaggers, he too wanted to demonstrate the fiction that a new sovereign California republic had been created, to the extent that he requested that John Sutter fly the Bear Flag over his fort.[98]

Although most of the Bear Flaggers cared less than Ide or Frémont did about the legality of their actions, they understood the importance of Texas when they created the Bear Flag itself. The flag was a re-creation of the Texas flag. One participant remembered that the Bear Flaggers first had mimicked the Texas lone star on their own flag, and then they realized they needed "some other device to go with it."[99] However, when the Bear Flaggers learned of the US-Mexican War only weeks after their rebellion, they took down the Bear Flag and raised the Stars and Stripes. Many were relieved to be backed by US power, but many were also annoyed by how quickly US officers and officials dismissed their role in the conquest of northern California. They assumed that by forming a republic and then attaching it to the United States, they were entitled to some benefits—military commissions, financial compensation, public praise—for this is what had happened in Texas upon US annexation.[100] For them, Texas had become a language demonstrating both the legality of rebellion and the personal benefits that accrued from it.

The Bear Flag Revolt racialized and nationalized both American immigrants and Californios, initiating a discourse that had been largely muted in California. The relationship between the two had always been strained, but it had never been hateful. Now, however, Californios associated all American migrants with the thirty-three Bear Flaggers and deemed them traitorous agents of the United States.[101] This understandable reaction to the Bear Flag Revolt forced many Americans into the Bear Flagger ranks in order to protect their families and property. According to John Bidwell, when the "unsettled" portion of the American immigrants initiated the rebellion, the "settled" portion "was compelled to carry out the war in self defense."[102] One Bear Flag leader even remembered that "there were a great many of the American settlers who would have [di]vulged the plan to the Mexicans."[103] Most American migrants had always believed that the Californios were dissolute and duplicitous, but now they went further, challenging the Californios' right to govern their own land. In the years that followed, Americans gradually stripped Californios of their property, despite their possessing legal titles that the Treaty of Guadalupe Hidalgo mandated must be recognized.[104] In a profound sense, therefore, Frémont's arrival in California and the subsequent Bear Flag Revolt actualized the process of Manifest Destiny so prevalent in US history textbooks and syntheses, in which Americans acted on behalf of US expansion. By the summer of 1846, they were doing just that—but the road to this choice had always been winding, and it had never been inevitable.

Oregon

Unlike the federal interventions in Texas, with the Mormons, and in California, there was little on-the-ground drama in the months leading up to the Oregon Treaty. Undoubtedly there was diplomatic drama: the Polk administration's blustering almost led the United States into a war with Great Britain at the same time as the country was already fighting Mexico. Polk's risk taking was, on the surface, perplexing. He had little reason to resort to such confrontational tactics. The Willamette Valley in Oregon was already American, if not yet possessed by the United States. The strategy of "masterly inactivity" was working. John McLoughlin and the Hudson's Bay Company, once dominant in the region, had agreed to join the Oregon provisional government, essentially acknowledging their loss of control. In all likelihood, future years would bring even more American migrants, giving the United States an even better claim on the most valuable parts of the vast territory.

Part of the reason for the Polk administration's aggressive rhetoric was, of course, politics. Polk's 1844 platform had promised a US Oregon as far north as 54°40′ latitude—the famous call of "Fifty-four forty or fight." As president, he felt he needed to deliver on his promise, particularly because gaining Oregon would assuage northern Democrats who wanted to offset the annexation of slaveholding Texas with a free territory. But something more was also at work. Recall that Polk in 1844 and 1845 felt that Texas annexation needed to happen as fast as possible, for soon Texans would give up on joining the United States for good, and Texas would be forever "lost to the Union." By 1846, Polk had inklings that Oregon, too, might begin pulling away from the United States.

To be clear, Oregon hardly necessitated the same rapid response as independent Texas or quasi-independent California. Polk never sent any of his agents to Oregon. Unlike Texas or California, the United States already possessed a legitimate international claim to the territory, having shared it with Great Britain since 1818 (their agreement, of course, did not recognize Native sovereignty). And, as discussed above, the majority of American inhabitants in Oregon desired US annexation. Perhaps most important, unlike in Texas or California, American settlers in Oregon saw Great Britain as a potential threat to their rights, not as a possible solution to their precarious potential independence. Polk acknowledged this attitude in his first annual address, praising them as "ever ready to defend the soil" for the United States.

Yet a careful reading of Polk's first annual message also reveals that he worried what Americans in Oregon would do next. Because the United States had not yet extended jurisdiction over Oregon, Polk mentioned how Oregonians had been forced to create their own government, and they had "just cause to complain of our long neglect." In response, he argued, the federal government should make "liberal grants" of land to Oregon settlers to reward them for making such a difficult overland journey. Additionally, Polk recommended that the federal government erect a series of blockhouses and raise a regiment of riflemen to protect future overlanders from attacks by Natives, and he sought to create an Indian agency in Oregon to manage Native-Oregon affairs.[105] The implications of Polk's statements were subtle but clear: despite Polk's claim that Americans in Oregon were "ready to defend the soil," some of them might require incentives to do so. After all, if they were already fully committed to the United States, why would they have "complain[ts] of . . . neglect"?

Polk's assessment was correct. The United States' neglect of Oregon had frustrated its inhabitants, and by 1844 they began at least discussing an independent republic. How much Polk knew of these on-the-ground developments is unclear. While he did not have any secret agents or contacts in Oregon itself, he read the papers, some of which maintained that Oregon settlers were getting restless. Indeed, the newspaper of Polk's own administration, the Washington *Daily Union*, printed just such an article in October 1845. The paper maintained that there may be "little men" in Oregon as there had been in Texas. These men cared more about their personal gain than they did the good of the American people, and the story insinuated that they would work against US interests to preserve their power. If Oregon declared independence, then "many difficulties would be created [for annexation] which do not now exist."[106] The implicit message of the article was clear: Oregon annexation needed to happen sooner rather than later.

In Oregon itself, events that portended US expansion—Polk's election, Texas annexation, and the US-influenced Bear Flag Revolt—helped reignite support for US annexation, which had seemed stalled in 1844. As one settler wrote in 1845, "Polk is elected and Texas annexed. . . . *The patriots will be reinforced from this place.*"[107] The pro-annexation *Oregon Spectator* printed articles that celebrated Texas's addition to the "great confederacy" that was the United States.[108] The paper's take on the US conquest of California in 1846 followed similar lines, although it took the argument one step further by maintaining that California's independence—a development many in Oregon had once predicted—was an absurdity. Due to a lack of resources, the *Spectator* contended, "California can never be an independant [*sic*] country."[109] Left unwritten was an obvious additional point to those who had once argued Oregon could join with California to form a Pacific republic: if California could not be independent, neither could Oregon.

Of course, for the United States, a solution to the Oregon question required diplomacy with Great Britain, but Polk's various suggestions regarding on-the-ground issues demonstrate that he and his federal allies wanted to keep Americans in Oregon loyal to the United States and prevent them from taking any steps toward further autonomy or independence. To do so, he employed two carrots and a stick. By promising "liberal land grants," Polk affirmed the Oregon provisional government's policy of freely granting 640 acres to all adult white males. The second carrot was Polk's promise of raising a contingent of riflemen to guard the overland route, and there is little reason to doubt that Polk sincerely desired to protect overlanders from supposedly hostile Natives (even though actual attacks were exceedingly rare). By diminishing the risk on the overland journey, this measure would also facilitate greater American migration, thereby giving the United States an even stronger claim in its diplomacy with the British.

Yet the ever-manipulative Polk likely had a secondary reason for raising such a force: it would be the stick that would tether Oregonians to the United States. If, as Polk noted, Americans in Oregon were complaining about US neglect, then there was an underlying unhappiness in the fledgling settlement. A rifle contingent would serve as a powerful demonstration of US power on the journey to Oregon, as would his third promise of the creation of an Indian agency within the territory. The rifle contingent would essentially proclaim to Oregon settlers that the United States was watching over them—a reassurance and a warning at the same time. Of all measures related to Oregon, Polk cared about this rifle contingent the most, writing about it in his diary five times over a seven-month period.[110] Thus, while Polk publicly voiced that Americans in Oregon would defend US interests, he seemed less sure in private. Perhaps even pro–United States Americans in Oregon needed to be lightly and deftly encouraged into acceding to US annexation.

In the end, the US government never needed to bring any of these plans to fruition. Hoping to avoid wars against Mexico and Britain at the same time, Polk backed down from his aggressive 54°40′ rhetoric, which allowed diplomacy to proceed with Britain. By mid-June, the United States and Britain signed an agreement that divided Oregon at 49° latitude. Whether Americans in Oregon would have ever truly pursued permanent independence was a question that no one needed to investigate further. The *Oregon Spectator* celebrated, "We can look forward now with faith, and congratulate one other that we are again citizens of the United States."[111] Oregon provisional governor George Abernethy agreed, writing that he sincerely hoped the "star spangled banner may forever wave over this portion of the United States."[112]

The Cherokees

While the federal government provided incentives for white breakaway Americans to voluntarily reattach themselves to the United States and, in some cases, violently fight for US empire in the process, the Cherokees provide the converse example in regard to nonwhite breakaway Americans—or, more accurately, breakaway Americanized Natives. Although the Cherokees' state apparatus was far more robust than that of most other breakaway Americans, even providing the United States with an effective buffer with the Plains peoples to the west, no Democratic official wanted the Cherokees to become autonomous agents of US empire. Rather, they were supposed to be wards of the federal government—and the federal government would dictate to them as such. The Cherokees would not be incentivized to ally with the United States but be forced to bend to its wishes.

For years, Democrats had disdained the John Ross faction of the Cherokees, which worked against removal and now sought autonomy in the West. Although President Polk spoke and wrote little about the Cherokees, it is almost certain he felt the same way. By the time of his presidency, the Ross Party was largely winning the low-level Cherokee civil war.[113] As the Cherokee Light Horse turned to vigilante justice, arresting and executing its enemies without trial, 750 Treaty Party Cherokees fled across the Arkansas border.[114] There they found the sympathy of Arkansas governor Archibald Yell, one of the few men whom the mostly friendless Polk actually counted as a friend. For years, Yell had been distraught over the potential power of the Cherokees and other removed Indians, warning Polk and anyone else who would listen that the US government had effectively placed thousands of hostile Natives on the undefended Arkansas border.[115]

Yell was not the only person who warned Polk about the Cherokees. Georgia senator Wilson Lumpkin, who had served as Georgia's governor during Cherokee removal, described Ross's power in the West to Polk: "The officers . . . of the U.S. have yielded quite too much to the assumptions of Ross. And if his life is spared, & his assumptions permitted to progress, we shall yet see trouble with our Indian population."[116] Although Polk did not share Lump-kin's assessment that Ross needed to be killed, it is clear that he bought what Lumpkin and Yell were selling. In his longest diary entry on the Cherokees, Polk explained, "[The Ross Party] constituted the majority of the Nation, and since their removal West have pursued and persecuted the Treaty party. . . . Many murders have been committed among them."[117] In terms of numbers Polk was correct: thirty-four Cherokees had died violently over the previous year.[118]

Potential hostilities with both Mexico and Great Britain amplified the dangers of Cherokee autonomy. In case of war, 20,000 hostile Cherokees sit-uated to the rear of US forces would pose an unacceptable military threat to the United States.[119] Moreover, many Americans believed that the Cherokees were natural Mexican allies, for they saw the Mexicans as "mongrels" with Native ancestry.[120] Indeed, in the first months of the Mexican War, rumors cir-culated in the US press that Mexico was "tampering" with the Cherokees.[121]

The British also seemed suitable allies for the Cherokees. John Howard Payne, who had lived with the Cherokees in the 1830s but was now the US consul in Italy, warned Polk of such a possibility in early 1846: "[England] has usually been more on the alert in these matters than the United States. . . . She could win the red men to her interest. . . . She has felt that kindness, at-tended even by a degree of deference, will render them effective friends. I do not believe, in the event of a war, that she will be unmindful of the use which may be made of their enmity, if it can be provided in rendering their border a scene of awful havoc."[122] Not only could the Cherokee Nation ally with Mex-ico or Britain, Payne believed that their role as (in his eyes) the most "civi-lized" Natives would allow them to forge an alliance with their "wilder breth-ren" to the west.

Polk never responded to these correspondents who warned of Cherokee power, but circumstantial evidence suggests that he and his Democratic allies took the Cherokee threat seriously. A key part of this evidence is the progres-sion of events in the spring and summer of 1846. First, in March, the Roger Taney Supreme Court finally delivered its decision on *Rogers v. United States*, the case that asked whether the Cherokees had jurisdiction over any white person who had "expatriated" himself from the United States by moving to the Cherokee Nation. Written by Taney, the court's decision could not have been more unequivocal: the United States still had jurisdiction over the ex-patriated William Rogers, for the Cherokees only occupied their land "under the assent of the United States, and under their authority."[123] This decision broke from judicial precedent and was a crucial blow against Cherokee sovereignty, for it diminished the ability of the Cherokee Nation to govern those within its borders. Indeed, the *Rogers* decision initiated the legal erosion of Native sovereignty in federal courts more generally, as US courts began to use *Rogers* as a precedent to interfere in various disputes within Indian reservations.[124] It also curtailed the Cherokees from doing what they and many other Native peoples had done for generations: adopt others—including whites—into the tribe, thereby amplifying their population and, with it, their geopolitical power. When it came to who deserved citizenship in the Cherokee Nation, it was no longer up to the Cherokee National Council but determined by the race of the potential citizen: Natives could still be adopted and naturalized, but white Americans would forever remain white—and American.[125]

Rogers was a decidedly atypical Supreme Court case for its time. The defendant, William Rogers, had died before the case reached the court, and thus there was no legal need for the court to reach a decision. Moreover, at a time when the Supreme Court often took a year to decide a case, in this instance the court rendered a decision only one week after hearing arguments.[126] These facts point to pressure from the Polk administration to deliver a speedy verdict for expanded federal authority and against Native autonomy. As he would do again in the 1857 *Dred Scott* decision, Taney was willing to both adjudicate to the needs of the particular moment and discuss the case with the executive in order to make his decision.[127]

Polk then intervened against the Cherokees in April, when he asked Congress to permanently separate the Ross Party from the Treaty Party and the Old Settlers.[128] In effect, he wanted Congress to create two Cherokee nations. Without mentioning the *Rogers* decision, he also urged Congress to expand its power not just over whites in Indian Territory, but over Natives themselves. Citing the Cherokee situation, he noted that Indian law was simply ineffective in bringing criminals to justice, and therefore the federal government needed to step in. As part of this attack on Cherokee power, Polk removed Pierce Butler as Indian agent to the Cherokees; Butler had long defended John Ross as an upright leader. Polk may have written or said little on the Cherokees, but when it came to action, he and his administration waged a full-scale assault on Cherokee sovereignty.

Polk's suggestion of permanently splitting the Cherokee Nation endangered Ross's ongoing struggle to keep the Cherokees unified. To Ross, the division of Cherokee sovereignty would be the first step toward its final extinction. Polk had discovered the threat that would make the Ross Party capitulate—and capitulate it did. Long opposed to recognizing the Treaty of New Echota, the Ross Party now argued for the indivisibility of the Cherokee Nation based on the terms of the hated treaty.[129] Most important, Polk's threat of division forced the Ross Party to the negotiating table in a way no administration had done before. Over the summer of 1846 John Ross sat down with Stand Watie in Washington under the supervision of the federal government. By August, the parties had come to a conclusive agreement. To the relief of the Ross Party, the Cherokee Nation remained unified, and the United States recognized the Ross-led Cherokee National Council as the Cherokees' official government.[130] However, on many other points the Ross Party was forced to yield, including recognizing the validity of the Treaty of New Echota, the rights of the Treaty Party, and the claims of the Old Settlers. Significantly, the Ross Party also agreed to abolish the Cherokee Light Horse. On August 7, inveterate enemies John Ross and Stand Watie shook hands at a treaty-signing ceremony in the US Senate. Peace was secured. Cherokee sovereignty—at least as envisioned by the Ross Party—was not.

John Ross later tried to put a positive spin on the agreement. After the Cherokee National Council ratified the agreement in November, Ross proclaimed a day of national thanksgiving, stating, "The tempest is hushed, and peace and security are restored to our country. Our National rights are placed upon a just and permanent basis, and a broad foundation is laid, for making rapid advances in those improves which go to constitute an intelligent, virtuous and prosperous people."[131] He was no doubt relieved that the violence had ended. He and his allies were also relieved that finally the United States had agreed to distribute the per capita payments promised in the Treaty of New Echota—claims that had not yet been fulfilled due to the Cherokees' internal divisions. Yet beneath this relief was an underlying tone of defeat. Gone were Ross's stringent assertions of Cherokee sovereignty, and so too was his defiance in the face of US injustice. He now spoke solely of Cherokee "improvement." The pro-Ross *Cherokee Advocate* could only defend the treaty with the uninspiring phrase "the best that could be obtained under the circumstances."[132] These words reflected the new reality of Cherokee sovereignty. While the Cherokees still possessed a degree of self-government, thanks to the *Rogers* decision they had no jurisdiction over any intruding whites. While they possessed the rule of law, they no longer had the Light Horse to enforce it. The Cherokees possessed sovereignty over their nation, but only by the leave of the United States.

Behind Ross's capitulation lay the new geopolitical reality of Indian Territory. The 1845 US annexation of Texas had converted Indian Territory from a borderland on the edge of US territory to an internal region circumscribed by it. With removed Natives isolated, frontier whites no longer feared their potential connections to Mexico or Great Britain.[133] When the United States declared war against Mexico, the soldiers garrisoning Indian Territory departed for the front, replaced by volunteers from Arkansas.[134] After almost a decade of panic over the seemingly defenseless western border, this news should have given paranoid Arkansans fits. However, the muscular military stance of the United States in the war against Mexico seems to have quieted these fears. One week after the *Arkansas Gazette* announced Zachary Taylor's victories at Palo Alto and Resaca de la Palma, the newspaper issued a call for more volunteers to go to Mexico, maintaining that they were no longer needed in Indian Territory. The paper noted, "[The Natives] show no disposition to engage in war with us. It is true there are heart-burnings between themselves, but we do not apprehend that they will materially affect the amicable relations existing between us."[135] Manifest Destiny, it seems, had quieted their fears.

Meanwhile, Cherokee leaders were practically silent on the US-Mexican War. When the United States declared war, the *Cherokee Advocate* announced the news in one short paragraph.[136] Two weeks later, the paper pleaded with the Cherokees and all other removed Natives to avoid getting caught up in the war frenzy and instead cultivate themselves at home.[137] This relative silence about the US-Mexican War was at odds with the *Cherokee Advocate*'s regular discussion of world events. Perhaps the US conquest over and around Indian Territory was simply too painful to print. The post-1846 Cherokee Nation and Indian Territory more generally entered a new geopolitical world—one where there was no longer any geopolitics to play.

In their failure to secure effective sovereignty, the Cherokees were victims of geography, unlike African Americans in Liberia, who provide a counterexample. In the late 1830s, the depression in the United States had led both the Cherokees and African Americans in Liberia to seize more autonomy—the Cherokees because the US state's presence in Indian Territory was minimal, Americo-Liberians because the American Colonization Society no longer had funds to support the colony. Liberia declared itself a commonwealth in 1839, the same year as the majority Ross Party arrived in Indian Territory. In the early 1840s, both groups were effectively autonomous but not independent, with both the Cherokees and Americo-Liberians living in ambiguous geopolitical situations. Officials of the US government clearly saw the parallels. In 1843, the House Committee of Commerce suggested that the United States' relationship with Liberia was akin to that of its relations with "Indian tribes which have been placed beyond the limits of the States, on the purchased territory of the Union."[138] It then suggested that the United States make Liberia's situation a little less ambiguous by declaring it an official US colony, thereby aligning it more closely with Indian Territory's supposedly dependent status.

The Polk administration disagreed. To Democrats like Polk, continental expansion differed from overseas empire. Thus, Cherokee sovereignty needed to be curbed, while Liberian sovereignty could be ignored, allowed, and even encouraged. After this decision, the fates of the Cherokee Nation and Liberia irrevocably diverged. Living far from white Americans in a land almost no white American sought to claim, the breakaway America of Liberia declared independence in 1847.[139] While the United States would not officially recognize the Republic of Liberia until 1862, Liberia became a geopolitical reality that would not go away. Living in close proximity to white Americans in lands many of them coveted, the breakaway America of the Cherokee Nation was forced to cede its on-the-ground military power and much of its sovereignty. Only time would tell if the Cherokees could maintain any autonomy at all.

Conclusion

The forces of contingency that aligned in 1844 to hand Polk the presidency and a Democratic majority to do his bidding ran out by the end of his term. Despite his seeming triumphs on behalf of the United States, neither his contemporaries nor historians have given Polk much credit—for good reason. By 1848 the Whigs were resurgent, the Democratic Party had temporarily torn itself apart as disaffected northern Democrats formed the Free Soil Party, and the United States' conquest of Mexico remained in doubt, if not for the last-ditch diplomatic efforts of Nicholas Trist and Winfield Scott. Polk loathed both men, and he wanted to reject the Treaty of Guadalupe Hidalgo, which he had no hand in crafting, but he realized he had no choice but to agree to its terms. Almost immediately, the seeming expansionist triumphs of the treaty eroded and eventually destroyed sectional harmony, leading inexorably to southern secession and the Civil War. At the heart of all of these issues was slavery: Polk, a committed slaveholder, had reopened the politics of slavery that had long remained dormant, at least superficially. By the end of his presidency the workaholic, humorless Polk had become worn down by the

N. Currier, *James K. Polk—President Elect of the United States* (1844). This lithograph of Polk ably depicts his aggression, determination, and humorlessness. Unlike images from the final years of his presidency, Polk here is youthful and vigorous, not yet worn down by the job. Courtesy of the Library of Congress, Prints and Photographs Division, Washington, DC.

political infighting and backlash against his expansionist achievements. Having previously committed to one term, he stepped down in 1848, replaced by the Whig and US-Mexican War hero Zachary Taylor who, ironically, had been made famous by Polk's actions. Within months, the utterly exhausted Polk was dead.

Forgotten in Polk's tragic legacy is his crucial insight into continental geopolitics: demography was not destiny, and history did not stop in the far-off regions of North America. On the contrary, the clock was ticking, as the break-away Americans were not invariably waiting for US expansion. They needed to make choices about the future, and as US expansion stalled, the choice of a future outside the United States seemed better and better. This belief fit with their worldview. They had initially traveled beyond US borders, some voluntarily and some not, because the United States no longer promised prosperity. To contemplate a different future—an independent Texas, a Pacific republic, an autonomous Native nation, a Mormon empire—was hardly a stretch of the imagination.

Thus, to wonder why Polk and his allies failed to foresee that expansion would increase sectionalism and that sectionalism would invariably destroy the union is to miss the concerns of the immediate moment. Civil war was not the future over which Polk and other expansionists fretted. Rather, in their dystopian future, the United States was beset from all sides by hostile forces. Underwritten by British funds and now part of Britain's informal empire, a revamped Republic of Texas embraced gradual emancipation and expanded west at a rapid rate, pushing Texas's Natives into US territory. North of Texas, the removed Natives of Indian Territory gradually coalesced around the leadership of John Ross, quickly transforming it into an autonomous, virtually independent Native zone. Supported by the British navy, Californios declared an independent republic, their rule buttressed by new American immigrants who gained land in exchange for political loyalty. Some of these Americans were Mormons, who settled as a powerful community in remote areas of Alta California, thereby providing a bulwark against US expansion. Frustrated by US dalliance, Oregon settlers declared an independent republic, granting free land to any white American settler who would travel overland and join their experiment of a yeomen's republic. Canada remained a steadfastly loyal member of the British Empire.

Hemmed in on all sides, the US economy stagnated, and its people became increasingly discontent. This, not civil war, was what Polk and his allies feared. They understood what so many failed—and continue to fail—to see: Manifest Destiny was not a chimera only because it concealed the violent conquest of westward expansion, but because it assumed that Americans and the United States were one and the same.

Epilogue

On April 15, 1846, Sam Houston rose to speak in the Senate on the Oregon question.[1] Only recently arrived from newly annexed Texas, Houston was now a Texas senator. He wanted to voice his full support for President James K. Polk's intention to abrogate the current Oregon Treaty with Britain. Americans in Oregon, Houston claimed, had migrated there only because they believed that the United States would soon acquire it. To not do so soon would be fundamentally betraying their trust. Refuting those who wanted to slow down Polk's aggressive diplomacy, Houston argued that it would be repugnant to offer protection to settlers "gradually" over several years. On the contrary, promptly repealing the Oregon Treaty would pave the way for Oregon annexation and the protection of American settlers. Thus, Houston wed American settlers in Oregon to the US state and saw them as mutually reinforcing US power in North America.

Then Houston transitioned to Texas, for "allusion ha[d] been made" between the two, and he wanted to "correct any errors" in regard to Texas's recent history. Here he flipped the narrative. Unlike Americans in Oregon in the 1840s, Americans who had migrated to Texas a decade before were not relying on the US federal government for anything. It was their initiative alone that created the sovereign republic of Texas. Houston then described how this republic had transitioned from a disastrously weak polity in 1836 to a respectable, even ascendant republic in 1845. He related how Texas had created a stable currency, reestablished peace with Native people, restored law to the region, imposed order on the land, kept the seas free from invasion, and gained international recognition. Houston concluded that, in acceding to annexation to the United States, Texas "was not a suppliant. She came into this confederacy as a sovereign and independent state. . . . If she did not make her advent with all the paraphernalia of bridal array, she brought a nation for her dowry, and the hearts of freemen for her jewels."[2]

Few seemed to listen to Houston's ramblings. The speech received little press and garnered minimal reaction from those assembled. Houston later admitted that the speech was hastily written, and he was sick when he gave it. Yet in retrospect, Houston's words mark a crucial transition in the history of US expansion, a hinge point that demonstrates how the expansion of *Americans as a people* became irrevocably wedded to the expansion of the *United States as a state*. Houston's speech described both phenomena. His description of Texas's short but glorious independence was a history of the former: Anglo-American migrants paved the way for the Texas Revolution and Texas independence, and these people had made the fledgling republic strong, dynamic, and sovereign. Annexation to the United States came out of not necessity but convenience. In contrast, his description of Oregon demonstrated the expansion of US borders via diplomacy and possibly war, with decisions made in the halls of Washington, DC, instead of in distant Oregon. Indeed, in Houston's retelling, in Oregon Anglo-Americans remained helpless against British might and thoroughly dependent on the US state.

I have demonstrated, of course, that Houston's accounts of both Texas and Oregon rested on countless spurious assertions. The Texans were never as strong nor the Oregonians as helpless as Houston described. The importance of Houston's speech lay not in these many factual flaws but in the stunningly contradictory blind spot at the heart of his larger argument. If Texas could begin its independence in such a precarious state but then emerge prosperous and united a decade later, then why could Oregon not do the same thing? As in Texas, so too in Oregon: weakness could beget strength, particularly because both populations consisted of (in Houston's eyes) hardy, industrious, dynamic, and fertile white Americans.

By acknowledging the supposed vitality of the Republic of Texas during its independence and then placing Texas alongside Oregon (and finding the latter wanting), Houston demonstrated the precariousness of the US expansionist project. While Houston may have been supporting Polk in his speech, expansionists who listened closely would have rightly been concerned that Houston was actually giving other Americans beyond US borders ammunition for creating their own sovereign, independent polities. After all, if the Texans could do it, why could not other breakaway Americans?

And yet it seems that expansionists were not listening closely, or if they were, they were focusing only on Houston's account of Oregon. In that story, white American settlers and the US state expanded side by side, united toward the same goal, each needing the other to fulfill the United States' Manifest Destiny. This blind spot in Houston's argument—and other Americans' failure to recognize that blind spot—demonstrates the rapid transition in the narrative Americans told themselves about the unprecedented expansion of the United States in the mid-1840s. Houston's defense of Texas's former independence was adamant, but for most Americans, Texas's decade as a republic could be largely ignored and its annexation assumed as preordained. Instead, Houston's Oregon argument became the dominant trope of US *and* American expansion. Oregon's annexation was soon understood as an inevitable result of the superiority of the United States and the American people— the state and its demographics fundamentally entwined to the point that they were now seen as one and the same. Inevitable, too, was the United States' conquest of California and New Mexico and its defeat of Mormon and Native autonomy.

In essence, if we are to understand the actual messiness of US expansion, we should look to the history of Texas. However, if we are to understand how expansionists thought the process should work, we must look to Oregon, where American migrants and the United States marched side by side toward continental domination. Together, these two forces were unstoppable, and thus expansion became seen as inevitable to such an extent that it no longer needed to be explained. For most Americans, this story was easy to understand, and by 1848, it seemed to be over. Breakaway Americans, by contrast, were still living out the story's conclusion. By 1848 they confronted a very different geopolitical world, as they found themselves once again within US borders and under the umbrella of US sovereignty. Considering their diverse goals and actions during the Texas Moment, it should come as no surprise that their reactions to its end varied widely. The Texas Moment splintered.

The Mormons had always been the breakaway Americans who most desired independence and most loathed the United States. The creation of the Mormon Battalion represented a temporary alliance between the Mormons and the US federal government, but it did not last. In the aftermath of the US-Mexican War, Brigham Young and other Mormon leaders realized that political independence was no longer feasible, but statehood in the union would still bring a significant degree of autonomy and self-government. Thus, they sought statehood for what they called "Deseret," a term from the Book of Mormon that means "honeybee." Deseret's proposed borders demonstrated continued Mormon ambitions, for they ran as far west as Los Angeles and encompassed territory twice the size of modern California. The federal government, however, remained wary of Mormons' intentions and refused to support Deseret—both its borders and its statehood. Instead, they created the much smaller Utah and, even more alarming to Mormon leaders, gave it territorial status. The Mormons found themselves governed by federally appointed officials. Immediately, they defied this encroachment on their sovereignty, expelling these officials and refusing to abide by their pronouncements. The stage was set for the Utah War of 1857. In the early 1840s, Mormon leaders desperately but futilely sought powerful allies against the United States, and the Utah War demonstrated why this had been such a preoccupation of first Joseph Smith and then Brigham Young. In 1857, the Mormons were thoroughly isolated, their efforts at recruiting Ute and Paiute allies having failed. Left with no recourse, the Mormons were forced to back down, largely giving way to federal demands.[3]

Unlike the Mormons, the Cherokees had never sought complete independence from the United States, but they did desire to wield effective sovereignty within the borders of the Cherokee Nation. After 1848, however, Indian Territory was fully circumscribed by US territory, and the federal government had succeeded in forcing the Ross Party to yield much of its power. In the 1850s, Cherokee diplomats in Washington worked to stop any further erosion of the Cherokee Nation's now precarious sovereignty. At various points, they fought against the federal licensing of white traders in the Cherokee Nation, the imposition of military garrisons, the use of federal courts to try Native-white crimes (as enshrined in *Rogers v. United States* in 1846), and the desire of some federal authorities to make Indian Territory an official US territory.[4] In a few areas, the Cherokees achieved some measure of success; in others, they met unrelenting federal hostility and thus worked to postpone the issue rather than suffer immediate legislative defeat.[5] Meanwhile, John Ross and other Cherokee leaders did little to further the intertribal diplomacy that Ross had initiated in 1843. No new Great Council was convened.[6]

Within the Cherokee Nation itself, the underlying divisions reemerged in full force. After more than a decade in which multiracial, slaveholding Cherokee leaders had sought to further southernize the Cherokee Nation, the non-slaveholding majority took a stand. They organized the secret Keetoowah Society, whose membership was limited to non-slaveholding Cherokees of unmixed ancestry who spoke Cherokee as their first language. They dedicated themselves to preventing the further erosion of Cherokee culture, above all by curbing the power of slaveholders. The struggles between the Keetoowah traditionalists and the slaveholding, Americanized elite and their followers continued through the Civil War—and after.[7] To this day, the Cherokees living in Oklahoma remain bitterly divided between the United Keetoowah Band and the Cherokee Nation of Oklahoma. The United Keetoowah Band traces its roots to the Old Settlers and holds stricter membership requirements (one-quarter Cherokee by the measurement of blood quantum), while the larger Cherokee Nation of Oklahoma only requires a direct ancestor from the late nineteenth century.

The thousands of Anglo-Americans who had moved to Texas, California, and Oregon had a variety of individual goals, which also splintered after 1846. A certain segment of men had always been drawn to breakaway Americanism out of personal ambition, pursuing some combination of military glory, political power, economic success, and adventure. Luckily for these types, the US-Mexican War gave these motivations added life. Upon the outbreak of the war, thousands volunteered for US forces with great enthusiasm, seeking fortune and glory in an exotic land.[8] When the war ended, the aspirations of men like these did not, and the 1850s became the decade of the filibusters. Filibusterism was, in a sense, a reemergence of breakaway Americanism—but only for the most violent and ambitious breakaway Americans who were guided by what the historian Amy Greenberg called an ideology of "martial manhood."[9] With the American West now closed to the formation of independent polities, filibusters set their sights on more distant places in the hemisphere: Cuba, Nicaragua, and Mexican Sonora. While their goals may not have been different from the Lansford Hastings types a decade earlier, their methods were. Unlike Hastings and his ilk, the filibusters of the 1850s never believed that their political power would be buttressed by thousands of Anglo-American settlers, who possessed the more modest goals of land and personal independence. Without this additional population, American filibusters remained isolated amid foreign, largely hostile people. No wonder filibusterism failed time and again.[10]

The situations of those migrants with more ordinary ambitions—namely, landownership—who had traveled to the Republic of Texas, Mexican California, and Oregon Country differed depending on which of these places they called their new home and how quickly those sites were able to achieve statehood. Texas's experience demonstrated why this status was so important. Because Texas entered the union as a state, it rapidly assumed a place alongside other states of the Deep South. Like Mississippi, Alabama, and Louisiana, Texas's economy was based on cotton and chattel slavery, and in the 1850s Anglo-Texans relentlessly defended their "peculiar" practice in lock-step with their southern neighbors. Although key differences remained, for all intents and purposes Texas became simply another member of the US Deep South, despite the fact it only had joined the United States less than a decade before.[11]

In California, both its Anglo and Californio inhabitants recognized that they too would greatly benefit from statehood, particularly after the experience of military governance in 1846 and 1847. Thus, forty-eight of California's leading Anglos and Californios drafted a constitution in the hopes that Congress would grant statehood. The resulting document demonstrated their elitist priorities. The constitution outlawed chattel slavery, but at the same time it provided the means to continue the unofficial practice of enslaving Natives. The ranchos would continue to be run as patriarchal fiefdoms. Yet at the same time, the constitutional convention represented the beginning of the end of the dominance of Californio and Anglo-American patriarchs. In 1849, the gold rush brought tens of thousands of migrants to northern California, transforming the social composition and political dynamics of the region. The rapidly urbanizing California of the 1850s, particularly its northern half, was no longer the same place as the sparsely settled (by non-Natives) patriarchal world of the 1830s and 1840s, as Thomas Larkin recognized. Now residing in San Francisco, he lamented to his friend Abel Stearns in Los Angeles that the simplicity of life he had once enjoyed was lost in the new California: "Times are hard here—becoming harder—I begin to yearn after the times prior to July 1846 and all their honest pleasures. . . . Halcyon days they were. *We* shall not enjoy there [*sic*] like again."[12]

Unlike Texas and California, Oregon remained a territory until 1860 and therefore subject to federal jurisdiction. This status caused considerable consternation among Oregonians, particularly around the question of whether Congress would pass a version of the land law that had been enacted by the Oregon provisional government in 1843. If Congress failed to act, then it would render all Oregon men propertyless and, in the words of Oregon's delegate to Congress, "would work utter ruin and do gross injustice on the settlers in Oregon."[13] To counter this potential catastrophe, Oregonians responded with what became known as the "saving Oregon" narrative, in which they claimed that it was their migration that had saved Oregon from British domination. As one settler wrote in 1850, "Who does not know that the British gov. never would have given up this country as they did, if we had not been here."[14] Less than five years after the Oregon Treaty, pre-1846 migrants were already claiming that they had traveled west due to their patriotic love for the United States. The ideology of Manifest Destiny, in which Americans are conflated with the United States, had already run roughshod over the more complicated facets of local history.[15] In 1850 the federal government finally passed the Oregon Donation Land Act, allaying settlers' fears.

Oregonians were unhappy not just with their territorial status, but with the state of Native relations, a sentiment shared by Californians and Texans. Whatever trepidations these former breakaway Americans possessed about US annexation, they all believed that it would bring one important benefit: federal power in one form or another would defeat the remaining Natives and confiscate their land, which would then be bequeathed to white American settlers. Yet whites were sorely disappointed with federal inaction. In the 1850s, they stepped up their own efforts to take Native land, hoping for support from the US Army. Throughout the West, they initiated countless wars with Native peoples, often far more brutal and wide-ranging than the periodic violence of the 1830s and 1840s. Yet the US Army did not come to the rescue, and it struggled to defend the scattered American settlements spread across the West.[16] When the army did arrive, it was often ineffectual or—much worse in settlers' eyes—pro-Native.[17] Faced with the ineffectiveness of US regulars, settlers in Texas, California, and Oregon took matters into their own hands, forming unapologetic vigilante groups who sought, quite simply, to kill Indians.[18] Thus the 1850s demonstrated that the seeming robustness of US power that lay at the heart of the Manifest Destiny creed was an easily disproved fiction. American western settlers were still very much on their own, and it seemed that "no territory" Whigs like John Quincy Adams and Daniel Webster had been proven correct: US power was far too weak and spread far too thinly to govern a transcontinental nation.

Nevertheless, these settlers' unhappiness with the US state did not translate into movements for independence. For most breakaway Americans, their breakawayism had always been flexible and pragmatic, and proactively countering the United States was nothing of the sort. Many Americans in the West may have been displeased with federal oversight, but they were not going to rebel against their native country. They were still dictated by pragmatism—and they were too busy. Panning for gold, clearing forests, and plowing fields took precedence over weighing the benefits of US sovereignty.

Yet the general idea of an independent western polity still hovered around western politics, for the simple reason that Washington was just too far away to govern the region effectively. Easterners, including none other than US president Zachary Taylor, joined westerners in this assessment. During the journey to his inauguration in 1848, Taylor casually told the outgoing Polk that he believed that distance made a western republic likely, which stunned Polk as "alarming opinions" from an "old man" who was "uneducated" and "exceedingly ignorant of public affairs."[19] Polk was rightfully concerned, for both California and Oregon had been his presidential projects, and now Taylor was calmly dismissing all of Polk's work.

The situation changed dramatically during the Civil War, when US sovereignty in the West collapsed entirely. President Abraham Lincoln and his Republican administration were too concerned with the secession of the South to concentrate on distant places like California or Oregon. As US sovereignty receded, the Texas Moment reemerged in full force. In Utah, the United States pulled troops out of the territory to reassign them to more needed areas, at which point Brigham Young promptly reasserted Mormon control. In the Cherokee Nation, the submerged tensions of the 1840s resurfaced, as John Ross and Stand Watie once again battled for supremacy, a struggle that revolved around whether to ally with the Confederacy. In the end, Ross reluctantly did so, not as much out of his desire to maintain slavery as to uphold Cherokee unity and maintain Cherokee sovereignty.[20] In southern California, some ex-southerners argued for California's secession and entrance into the Confederacy; other Californians began once again to contemplate an independent Pacific republic, particularly if the North failed to win the war.[21] In ever-moderate Oregon, a minority supported the South's right to secede based on their disdain for federal interference in all state matters. Joseph Lane, the running mate of the southern Democratic presidential nominee, John Breckinridge, in the 1860 election, was an Oregonian.[22] However, once the war came, most of this minority reluctantly supported the Union. Texas, at this point routinely written into the Deep South, made arguments for secession that echoed almost word for word its reasons for declaring independence from Mexico in 1836, which included the federal government's failure to provide frontier protection against Natives.[23]

Yet the West was not the South. Much of the talk of western independence was simply that—talk. In this way, the Texas Moment that reemerged during the Civil War echoed the original Texas Moment: most western Americans continued to be dictated by pragmatism. If the United States won the Civil War, then westerners were willing to remain in the newly strengthened national Union. However, if the Confederacy emerged victorious, then pragmatism dictated other political possibilities: for former southerners living in the West, this may have been joining the Confederacy, but for most Americans in the region, it meant an independent republic or several republics or, for the Mormons, a theocracy. Thus, the Civil War was not just a clash between two sections, North and South, but a clash that also would dictate the political fate of the third section, the West.

The end point of the Texas Moment, therefore, is the same as the end point of the entire early American republic: Union victory in the Civil War. As many scholars have demonstrated, the combination of the Republican Party's ideological project and its various responses to the military crises that arose during the war created a federal government that was significantly more powerful and more activist than its antebellum incarnation. While compared to the post–Progressive Era bureaucratic state, the federal government itself remained small, it was now willing to pay money to private individuals and corporations to build the state on the United States' behalf.[24] In the West, the federal government pursued multiple strategies. It ramped up the policy of incentivizing settlement via legislation such as the 1862 Homestead Act. It also incentivized corporations that would facilitate settlement through measures like the 1862 Pacific Railway Act. In this way, the government helped populate the West with loyal Anglo-Americans at the expense of the region's Native and Hispanic peoples. By the 1880s, part of this strategy included facilitating the dissolution of Indian Territory by declaring it open to white settlement.[25] Even for the most Americanized tribes, like the Cherokees, political autonomy was no longer an option.

While incentivizing settlers was an old federal strategy now employed with greater gusto, another US strategy was relatively new: conquering the remainder of the West with the US Army, which now boasted much greater numbers and military experience thanks to its transformation during the Civil War. The Utah War of 1857 had anticipated this strategy when President James Buchanan sent thousands of soldiers into the Mormons' territory to bring them to heel, but it was not until the late 1860s that the army patrolled the Great Plains on a consistent and permanent basis. Within less than two decades, the army first circumscribed and eventually conquered powerful nomadic peoples, like the Lakotas and the Comanches, whose strength had seemed unassailable as recently as the early 1860s.

Breakaway Americanism made its final appearances overseas between 1860 and 1890, when the United States consolidated its continental empire while proclaiming its lack of interest in an oceanic one. Across the Pacific,

Anglo-American merchants and missionaries in Hawaii had long made their influence felt on the Native Hawaiian population, but in 1887 they fully asserted their power when they forced King Kalākaua to accept the "Bayonet constitution." The new constitution granted voting powers to only those possessing a significant amount of property, most of whom were American sugar planters, thus creating an effective American oligarchy. In 1893, the planters overthrew Queen Liliuokalani, the last Hawaiian monarch, implemented a republic, and hoped for annexation to the United States. Although this strategy echoed the Texas game, the Republic of Hawaii was much more of a farce than Texas had ever been. Yet when President William McKinley agreed to annexation in 1898, he and allies like Theodore Roosevelt argued that they were simply following the wishes of the Hawaiian people.[26] Polk's methods had proven useful once again.

Meanwhile, across the Atlantic, Liberia remained a political anomaly on multiple levels. It was one of only two African countries (alongside Ethiopia) to retain its independence during the European scramble for Africa, and it was governed by a small clique of African Americans who had been persecuted in the United States but had since become persecutors themselves as they asserted their political and military dominance—and their supposed cultural superiority—over the local African population. While Hawaii, with its substantial Anglo-American population, was folded into the US empire in the late 1890s, Liberia was left to its own devices. White breakaway Americans were welcomed back into the union as equals, but nonwhite breakaway Americans were conquered like the Cherokees or abandoned like the Americo-Liberians.

By the turn of the twentieth century, conquest, by and large, had become the dominant strategy of US foreign policy for reasons that would not have been unfamiliar to the breakaway Americans of the 1830s and 1840s. During the 1890s a devastating depression combined with rapid industrialization to curb the economic independence of American men, who, like prior generations, sought ways to validate their masculinity outside their local towns and cities. Unlike the 1830s, however, there was no longer "open" land beyond the frontier, as Frederick Jackson Turner famously proclaimed in 1893, the same year the depression began.[27] And compared to the 1830s, the United States was far more powerful on the world stage and seemingly no longer beset with sectionalism. The resulting solution was far clearer than the Texas Moment had ever been, and white American men responded by supporting— and joining in droves—an explicit war of conquest against Spain and then another against a Philippine insurgency.[28] During the Texas Moment, conquest could be rhetorically submerged beneath migration, expatriation, settlement, and economic opportunity, as white Americans built an American empire—but one with an ambiguous relationship to the United States. By the Spanish-American War, the United States itself was an empire.

Sam Houston first articulated how the era of the Texas Moment would be transformed into the era of Manifest Destiny. But Houston's speech was not the only demonstration of this transformation; so too was Sam Houston himself. For almost his entire life, Houston was the consummate believer in the United States. A Tennessee delegate to the House of Representatives and then its state governor in the 1820s, Houston made poor personal and political choices that forced him to flee to Texas in the early 1830s. As the two-time president of the Texas republic, Houston worked tirelessly to annex it to the United States. He then became a US senator for two terms and served as governor of Texas for two terms. In 1860, Houston again showed his commitment to the Union. While in the 1830s he had worked tirelessly to join Texas to the United States, in 1860 he worked tirelessly to keep Texas in the United States. Vociferously opposed to secession, Houston refused to call a secession convention, but other Texans called it anyway, thereby negating his authority. He died in Texas in 1863, having not seen the coming destruction of the South that he had predicted two years before.

Sam Houston's life epitomizes how Americans viewed—and still view—US expansion. Wherever he went, Houston was not just an American, but an American committed to the United States. His decision to leave US borders in the 1830s was wholly personal, and it was not meant as an expatriation. Most historians and much of the general public remember the migrants of the 1830s and 1840s as, in effect, Sam Houstons. In this view, American Patriots wanted to attach Canada to the United States; the Mormons wanted isolation, but only within US borders; the Cherokees and other removed Natives were defeated peoples relegated to US wards; Americans in California fought to attach the territory to the United States; and Americans in Oregon never even questioned that Oregon would soon be connected to the United States. Like Houston, the majority of the Americans of the era, wherever they traveled and whatever they did, were US nationalists foremost and forever, or at the very least clear-eyed about the future US dominance of the continent.

Yet, as I have demonstrated in this book, Houston was atypical. Indeed, his unionist actions while president of Texas in the 1830s and 1840s should be viewed as just as anomalous as his unionist actions as Texas governor in 1860. In both cases, separation—*breakawayism*—was the dominant trend, not union. While Texas independence in the late 1830s was not as popular as Texas secession in 1860, it was still a part of normal discourse. Indeed, on a broader scale, separation and independence were part of the normal discourse for most of the Americans who left or contemplated leaving US borders during the Texas Moment. Brigham Young had independence in mind when he looked to the Salt Lake Valley in 1845, and John Ross hoped for permanent Cherokee sovereignty when he convened more than a dozen removed Native tribes in Indian Territory in 1843. Rensselaer Van Rensselaer did not hope to expand the United States when he volunteered to fight for the Republic of Canada in 1838, and John Gantt did not plan for the US conquest of California when he signed up for Micheltorena's Mexican army in 1845. Even those who may have longed for US conquest prepared for other contingencies: the Bear Flaggers would not have rebelled if they believed that US conquest was imminent, and Peter Burnett and his "independent party" would not have laid the groundwork for a vigorous Oregon government if they thought Oregon would soon be a US territory. These men were not alone. The thousands of Americans who hoped to create their own idealized versions of an American polity in Texas and Canada, in the Salt Lake Valley and Indian Territory, and in California and Oregon felt the same way. They left a republic that was fragile and fractured, and when they returned it was still fragile and fractured. Almost two centuries later, in ways both similar and different, it remains so.

Introduction

1. Gilbert Belnap, "Autobiography of Gilbert Belnap," 6, MSS FAC 581, Huntington Library, San Marino, CA. All of the following quotations and information about Belnap come from this source. See also Brent J. Belnap, "Life Story of Gilbert Belnap" (1996), *Belnap Family Organization*, http://www.belnapfamily.org/Gilbert_Belnap_SUP_Biog raphy_(1996).htm (accessed Feb. 18, 2019).

2. "Dana (Denna), Lewis," Joseph Smith Papers, https://www.josephsmithpapers .org/person/lewis-dana-denna (accessed Feb. 18, 2019); Lori Taylor, "Telling Stories about Mormons and Indians" (PhD diss., University of Buffalo, 2000), 188–192.

3. Matthew J. Grow et al., *The Joseph Smith Papers: Administrative Records: Council of Fifty, Minutes, March 1844–January 1846* (Salt Lake City, UT: Church Historian's Press, 2016), 255–257, 461–462.

4. Lewis Dana to John Brown, July 5, 1845, Lewis Dana Correspondence, MSS 15551, LDS Church History Library, Salt Lake City, UT (hereafter, CHL).

5. John Brown to Lewis Dana, July 5, 1845, Lewis Dana Correspondence, MSS 15551, CHL.

6. Lansford W. Hastings, *The Emigrants' Guide to Oregon and California* (Cincinnati, 1845).

7. On Hastings, see Will Bagley, "Lansford Warren Hastings: Scoundrel or Visionary?," *Overland Journal* 12, no. 1 (1994): 12–26; Thomas F. Andrews, "The Ambitions of Lansford W. Hastings: A Study in Western Myth-Making," *Pacific Historical Review* 39, no. 4 (Nov. 1970): 473–491; Thomas Richards, Jr., "The Lansford Hastings Imaginary: Visions of Democratic Patriarchy in the Americas," in *Inventing Destiny: Cultural Explorations of US Expansion*, ed. Jimmy L. Bryan (Lawrence: University Press of Kansas, 2019).

8. Americans first used this phrase to describe France in the 1790s and then the Latin American republics in the 1820s. See Caitlin Fitz, *Our Sister Republics: The United States in an Age of American Revolutions* (New York: Norton, 2016).

9. On Manifest Destiny and US expansionism, see, among many works, Albert K. Weinberg, *Manifest Destiny: A Study of Nationalist Expansionism in American History* (Baltimore, MD: Johns Hopkins Press, 1935); Walter Nugent, *Habits of Empire: A History of American Expansion* (New York: Knopf, 2008); Richard Kluger, *Seizing*

Destiny: How America Grew from Sea to Shining Sea (New York: Knopf, 2007); Anne Hyde, *Empires, Nations, and Families: A History of the North American West, 1800–1860* (Lincoln: University of Nebraska Press, 2011), 348–407; Steven E. Woodworth, *Manifest Destinies: America's Westward Expansion and the Civil War* (New York: Knopf, 2010), 57–150; Norman Graebner, *Empire on the Pacific: A Study in American Continental Expansion* (New York: Ronald Press, 1955); Lloyd Garner, Walter LaFeber, and Thomas McCormick, *Creation of the American Empire: U.S. Diplomatic History* (Chicago, IL: Rand McNally, 1973), 120–156; D. W. Meinig, *The Shaping of America*, vol. 2: *Continental America* (New Haven, CT: Yale University Press, 1995), 169–217; R. W. Van Alstyne, *The Rising American Empire* (New York: Oxford University Press, 1960), 100–123; Frederick Merk, *Manifest Destiny and Mission in American History: A Reinterpretation* (Cambridge, MA: Harvard University Press, 1963); Thomas R. Hietala, *Manifest Design: Anxious Aggrandizement in Late Jacksonian America* (Ithaca, NY: Cornell University Press, 1990).

10. John L. O'Sullivan, "Annexation," *United States Magazine and Democratic Review* 17, no. 1 (1845): 5–10. For the compelling argument that Cazneau actually wrote the famous article, see Linda S. Hudson, *Mistress of Manifest Destiny: A Biography of Jane McManus Storm Cazneau, 1807–1878* (Austin: Texas State Historical Association, 2001). On the historiography of the concept, see Andrew C. Isenberg and Thomas Richards, Jr., "Alternative Wests: Rethinking Manifest Destiny," *Pacific Historical Review* 86, no. 1 (Feb. 2017): 4–17.

11. Alan Taylor, *American Colonies: The Settling of North America* (New York: Penguin, 2001), 117–274; Daniel K. Richter, *Before the Revolution: America's Ancient Pasts* (Cambridge, MA: Harvard University Press, 2011), 171–326.

12. By the mid-sixteenth century, a "colony" was defined as being subject to the mother country. See "colony," *Online Etymology Dictionary*, https://www.etymonline .com/word/colony (accessed Feb. 20, 2018). For expatriation from the United States during the Jacksonian era, see Eric Schlereth, "Privileges of Locomotion: Expatriation and the Politics of Southwestern Border Crossing," *Journal of American History* 100, no. 4 (Mar. 2014): 995–1020.

13. "Usonian," *Oxford Living Dictionaries*, https://en.oxforddictionaries.com /definition/usonian (accessed Feb. 18, 2019).

14. John Mack Faragher, *Women and Men on the Overland Trail* (New Haven, CT: Yale University Press, 1979); Hendrik Hartog, *Man and Wife in America: A History* (Cambridge, MA: Harvard University Press, 2002), 93–135.

15. On various filibuster movements and expatriation, see Alan Taylor, *The Civil War of 1812: American Citizens, British Subjects, Irish Rebels, and Indian Allies* (New York: Knopf, 2010), 15–74; Andrés Reséndez, *Changing National Identities at the Frontier: Texas and New Mexico, 1800–1850* (New York: Cambridge University Press, 2005); Andrew Cayton, "Continental Politics: Liberalism, Nationalism, and the Appeal of Texas in the 1820s," in *Beyond the Founders*, ed. Jeffrey L. Pasley, Andrew W. Robertson, and David Waldstreicher (Chapel Hill: University of North Carolina Press, 2005); Sarah Rodríguez, " 'Children of the Great Mexican Family': American Immigration to Northern Mexico, 1810–1861" (PhD diss., University of Pennsylvania, 2015); Gregg Cantrell, *Stephen F. Austin: Empresario of Texas* (New Haven, CT: Yale University Press,

1999); Andrew McMichael, *Atlantic Loyalties: Americans in Spanish West Florida, 1785–1810* (Athens: University of Georgia Press, 2008); David Narrett, *Adventurism and Empire: The Struggle for Mastery in the Louisiana-Florida Borderlands, 1762–1803* (Chapel Hill: University of North Carolina Press, 2017), 129–187; James E. Lewis, Jr., *The Burr Conspiracy: Uncovering the Story of an Early American Crisis* (Princeton, NJ: Princeton University Press, 2017); Kevin T. Barksdale, *The Lost State of Franklin: America's First Secession* (Lexington: University Press of Kentucky, 2009); Jessica Choppin Roney, "1776: Viewed from the West," *Journal of the Early Republic* 37, no. 4 (Winter 2017): 655–700; Michael Bellesiles, *Revolutionary Outlaws: Ethan Allen and the Struggle for Independence on the Early American Frontier* (Charlottesville: University of Virginia Press, 1993).

16. David Armitage, *The Declaration of Independence: A Global History* (Cambridge, MA: Harvard University Press, 2008); Eliga Gould, "Independence and Interdependence: The American Revolution and the Problem of Postcolonial Nationhood," *William and Mary Quarterly* 74, no. 4 (Oct. 2017): 729–752; Seth Cotlar, *Tom Paine's America: The Rise and Fall of Transatlantic Radicalism in the Early Republic* (Charlottesville: University of Virginia Press, 2011), 54–55; Fitz, *Our Sister Republics*, 6–11, 105, 113–115, 209–211.

17. David Waldstreicher, *In the Midst of Perpetual Fetes: The Making of American Nationalism, 1776–1820* (Chapel Hill: University of North Carolina Press, 1987); Benjamin E. Park, *American Nationalisms: Imagining Union in the Age of Revolutions, 1783–1833* (New York: Cambridge University Press, 2018); Anne Norton, *Alternative Americas: A Reading of Antebellum American Culture* (Chicago: University of Chicago Press, 1986); Robert Bonner, *Mastering America: Southern Slaveholders and the Crisis of American Nationhood* (New York: Cambridge University Press, 2009); Lewis, *Burr Conspiracy*, 133–147.

18. Jason Opal, *Avenging the People: Andrew Jackson, the Rule of Law, and the American Nation* (New York: Oxford University Press, 2017).

19. On the Mexican federalist rebellions, see Reséndez, *Changing National Identities at the Frontier*. On the expansion of Native power, see Pekka Hämäläinen, *The Comanche Empire* (New Haven, CT: Yale University Press, 2008); Andrew C. Isenberg, *The Destruction of the Bison: An Environmental History, 1750–1920* (New York: Cambridge University Press, 2000), 63–92; Brian DeLay, *War of a Thousand Deserts: Indian Raids and the U.S.-Mexican War* (New Haven, CT: Yale University Press, 2009); Ned Blackhawk, *Violence over the Land: Indians and Empires in the Early American West* (Cambridge, MA: Harvard University Press, 2006), chap. 4.

20. Amy Greenberg, *Manifest Manhood and the Antebellum American Empire* (New York: Cambridge University Press, 2005); Laurel Clark Shirer, *The Threshold of Manifest Destiny: Gender and National Expansion in Florida* (Philadelphia: University of Pennsylvania Press, 2016); Amy Kaplan, "Manifest Domesticity," *American Literature* 70, no. 3 (Sept. 1998): 581–606; Woodworth, *Manifest Destinies*; Kluger, *Seizing Destiny*; Hietala, *Manifest Design*.

21. For an interpretation that stresses the resilient Loyalism and British nationalism of most Americans, see Brendan McConville, *The King's Three Faces: The Rise and Fall of Royal America, 1688–1776* (Chapel Hill: University of North Carolina Press, 2007).

22. John Ferling, *Almost a Miracle: The American Victory in the War of Independence* (New York: Oxford University Press, 2009); Benson Bobrick, *Angel in the Whirlwind: The Triumph of the American Revolution* (New York: Simon and Schuster, 2011).

23. William W. Freehling, *The Road to Disunion*, vol. 2: *Secessionists Triumphant, 1854–1861* (New York: Oxford University Press, 2007); Michael F. Holt, *The Political Crisis of the 1850s* (New York: Norton, 1983).

24. James M. McPherson, "Why Did the Confederacy Lose?," in McPherson, *Drawn with a Sword: Reflections on the American Civil War* (New York: Oxford University Press, 1997), 113–136.

25. Peter Guardino, *The Dead March: A History of the Mexican-American War* (Cambridge, MA: Harvard University Press, 2017); Amy Greenberg, *A Wicked War: Polk, Clay, Lincoln, and the 1846 U.S. Invasion of Mexico* (New York: Knopf, 2012), 200–213.

Chapter 1 • The Texas Moment

1. Henry Clay to John J. Crittenden, Dec. 5, 1843, in *The Papers of Henry Clay, 1797–1852*, 11 vols., ed. Robert Seager II et al. (Lexington: University of Kentucky Press, 1958–1992), 9:897–899.

2. Stephen L. Hardin, *Texian Iliad: A Military History of the Texas Revolution* (Austin: University of Texas Press, 1996), 195–218.

3. David S. Weber, *The Mexican Frontier, 1821–1846: The American Southwest under Mexico* (Albuquerque: University of New Mexico Press, 1982), 163.

4. Sarah Rodríguez, " 'Children of the Great Mexican Family': American Immigration to Northern Mexico, 1810–1861" (PhD diss., University of Pennsylvania, 2015), 37.

5. Saul Cornell, *The Other Founders: Anti-Federalism and the Dissenting Tradition in America, 1788–1828* (Chapel Hill: University of North Carolina Press, 1999), 107; Tom Slaughter, *The Whiskey Rebellion: Frontier Epilogue to the American Revolution* (New York: Oxford University Press, 1986), 23–60; Jason Opal, *Avenging the People: Andrew Jackson, the Rule of Law, and the American Nation* (New York: Oxford University Press, 2017), 174–181; John R. Van Atta, *Securing the West: Politics, Public Lands, and the Fate of the Old Republic, 1785–1850* (Baltimore, MD: Johns Hopkins University Press, 2014), 45–46; Terry Bouton, *Taming Democracy: "The People," the Founders, and the Troubled Ending of the American Revolution* (New York: Oxford University Press, 2007), 171–256.

6. Opal, *Avenging the People*, 172–225.

7. Opal, *Avenging the People*, 172–205.

8. Eric Schlereth, "Privileges of Locomotion: Expatriation and the Politics of Southwestern Border Crossing," *Journal of American History* 100, no. 4 (Mar. 2014): 995–1020; Eric Schlereth, "Voluntary Mexicans: Allegiance and the Origins of the Texas Revolution," in *Contested Empire: Rethinking the Texas Revolution*, ed. Sam W. Haynes and Gerald D. Saxon (College Station: Texas A&M University Press, 2015), 11–42; Andrés Reséndez, *Changing National Identities at the Frontier: Texas and New Mexico, 1800–1850* (New York: Cambridge University Press, 2005), 148–161; Andrew Cayton, "Continental Politics: Liberalism, Nationalism, and the Appeal of Texas in the 1820s," in *Beyond the Founders*, ed. Jeffrey L. Pasley, Andrew W. Robertson, and David Waldstreicher (Chapel Hill: University of North Carolina Press, 2005); Rodríguez, "Children of the Great Mexican Family"; Gregg Cantrell, *Stephen F. Austin: Empresario*

of Texas (New Haven, CT: Yale University Press, 1999), 132–201; Weber, *Mexican Frontier*, 163–164.

9. Reséndez, *Changing National Identities at the Frontier*, 87–88.

10. Sam W. Haynes, "Imitating the Example of Our Forefathers: The Texan Revolution as Historical Reenactment," in Haynes and Saxon, *Contested Empire*, 43–49.

11. Timothy E. Anna, *Forging Mexico, 1821–1835* (Lincoln: University of Nebraska Press, 2001).

12. For an account of the Texas Revolution that emphasizes the irreconcilable differences between Anglos and Mexicans, see Weber, *Mexican Frontier*, 158–178, 242–266.

13. For historiography that emphasizes the centralist-federalist split as the cause of the Texas Revolution, see Reséndez, *Changing National Identities at the Frontier*; and Rodríguez, "Children of the Great Mexican Family."

14. Weber, *Mexican Frontier*, 248–249.

15. Reginald Horsman, *Race and Manifest Destiny: The Origins of American Racial Anglo-Saxonism* (Cambridge, MA: Harvard University Press, 1981), 209–213.

16. Paul Lack, *The Texas Revolutionary Experience: A Political and Social History, 1835–1836* (College Station: Texas A&M University Press), 78, 110–136; Reséndez, *Changing National Identities at the Frontier*, 164–170; Weber, *Mexican Frontier*, 243–255; Cantrell, *Stephen F. Austin*, 329–347.

17. James Curtis, *The Fox at Bay: Martin Van Buren and the Presidency, 1837–1841* (Lexington: University of Kentucky Press, 1970), 152–169; Major Wilson, *The Presidency of Martin Van Buren* (Lawrence: University Press of Kansas, 1984), 147–153.

18. R. A. Irion to Memucan Hunt, Dec. 31, 1837, in *Diplomatic Correspondence of the Republic of Texas*, vol. 1, ed. George Garrison (Washington, DC: Government Printing Office, 1908), 279.

19. On the lack of attention to the Texas republic, see Kenneth W. Howell and Charles Swanlund, "Introduction," in *Single Star of the West: The Republic of Texas, 1836–1845*, ed. Kenneth W. Howell and Charles Swanlund (Denton: University of North Texas Press, 2017), 4.

20. See 1840 Census, US Census Bureau, https://www.census.gov/history/www /through_the_decades/fast_facts/1840_fast_facts.html; "Census and Census Records," Texas State Historical Association, https://tshaonline.org/handbook/online/articles /ulc01 (accessed Aug. 8, 2017); Robert McCaa, "The Peopling of Mexico from Origins to Revolution," in *A Population History of North America*, ed. Michael R. Haines and Richard H. Steckel (New York: Cambridge University Press, 2000), 279–280.

21. For Texans' understanding of their own exceptionalism, see Joseph G. Dawson III, "Army of the Texas Republic, 1836–1845," in Howell and Swanlund, *Single Star of the West*, 114.

22. See, for example, John Charles Chasteen, *Americanos: Latin America's Struggle for Independence* (New York: Oxford University Press, 2009); Jeremy Adelman, *Sovereignty and Revolution in the Iberian Atlantic* (Princeton, NJ: Princeton University Press, 2007).

23. Haynes, "Imitating the Example of Our Forefathers."

24. Mirabeau Lamar, "The Inaugural Address of Mirabeau Lamar," in *The Papers of Mirabeau Lamar*, vol. 2, ed. Charles Adam Gulick, Jr. (Austin: Texas State Library, 1922), 316–327.

25. Winfield Scott to Joel Poinsett, Jan. 12, 1839, Joel Poinsett Papers, 11-150, Historical Society of Pennsylvania, Philadelphia (hereafter, HSP).

26. Alexis de Tocqueville, *Democracy in America*, ed. Bruce Frohnen, trans. Henry Reeve (1835; repr., Washington, DC: Regnery, 2002), 343.

27. Jessica Lepler, *The Many Panics of 1837: People, Politics, and the Creation of a Transatlantic Financial Crisis* (New York: Cambridge University Press, 2013); Alasdair Roberts, *America's First Great Depression: Economic Crisis and Political Disorder after the Panic of 1837* (Ithaca, NY: Cornell University Press, 2012); Scott Sandage, *Born Losers: A History of Failure in America* (Cambridge, MA: Harvard University Press, 2005), 40–55; Edward Balleisen, *Navigating Failure: Bankruptcy and Commercial Society in Antebellum America* (Chapel Hill: University of North Carolina Press, 2001), 32–41; Scott Reynolds Nelson, *A Nation of Deadbeats: An Uncommon History of America's Financial Disasters* (New York: Knopf, 2012), 117–136; Larry Schweikart, *Banking in the American South, from the Age of Jackson to Reconstruction* (Baton Rouge: Louisiana State University Press, 1987), 48–90.

28. Roberts, *America's First Great Depression*, 21–22; Howard Bodenhorn, *State Banking in Early America: A New Economic History* (New York: Oxford University Press, 2003), 291.

29. Lepler, *Many Panics*, 231–232.

30. Sandage, *Born Losers*, 46.

31. Reeve Huston, *Land and Freedom: Rural Society, Popular Protest, and Party Politics in Antebellum New York* (New York: Oxford University Press, 2000), 88.

32. Roberts, *America's First Great Depression*, 160–170.

33. David Waldo to John Rowland, Aug. 10, 1840, California Historical Documents Collection, MSS HM 40401–40555, Huntington Library, San Marino, CA (hereafter, HL).

34. George Richards to Phineas and Dewey Richards, Mar. 1, 1838, Richards Family Correspondence, MSS HM 65631–65642, HL.

35. Thomas J. Love to James S. Shedden, Jan. 17, 1838, Thomas Love Letters, A00-279, Buffalo and Erie County Historical Society, Buffalo, NY.

36. James Ronaldson to Joel Poinsett, Mar. 2, 1838, Poinsett Papers, HSP.

37. *New York Mercury*, Aug. 6, 1840.

38. Lewis Ray to Charles Ray, Aug. 1, 1843, Charles Henry Ray Papers, MSS RY 1-294, HL.

39. Paul Johnson, *A Shopkeeper's Millennium: Society and Revivals in Rochester, New York, 1815–1837* (New York: Hill and Wang, 1978); Sean Wilentz, *Chants Democratic: New York City and the Rise of the American Working Class, 1788–1850* (New York: Oxford University Press, 1984); David Roediger, *The Wages of Whiteness: Race and the Making of the American Working Class* (New York: Verso, 1991); Jonathan Prude, *The Coming of the Industrial Order: Town and Factory Life in Rural Massachusetts, 1810–1860* (New York: Cambridge University Press, 1983); Charles Sellers, *The Market Revolution: Jacksonian America, 1815–1846* (New York: Oxford University Press, 1991); Walter Johnson, *River of Dark Dreams: Slavery and Empire in the Cotton Kingdom* (Cambridge, MA: Belknap, 2013); Edward Baptist, *The Other Half Has Never Been Told: Slavery and the Making of American Capitalism* (New York: Basic, 2014).

40. Allan Kulikoff, *The Agrarian Origins of American Capitalism* (Charlottesville: University of Virginia Press, 1992).

41. Much of the following two paragraphs is drawn from Paul Wallace Gates, "Land Policy and Tenancy in the Prairie States," *Journal of Economic History* 1, no. 1 (May 1941): 60–82; Paul Wallace Gates, *The Farmer's Age: Agriculture, 1815–1860* (New York: Routledge, 1977), 67–77; John Mack Faragher, *Sugar Creek: Life on the Illinois Prairie* (New Haven, CT: Yale University Press, 1986), 181–186; Clarence H. Danhof, *Change in Agriculture: The Northern United States, 1820–1870* (Cambridge, MA: Harvard University Press, 1969), 16–21, 107–114, 126–130.

42. Van Atta, *Securing the West*, 216.

43. On preemption, see Reeve Huston, "Land Conflict and Land Policy in the United States, 1785–1841," in *The World of the Revolutionary American Republic: Land, Labor, and the Conflict for a Continent*, ed. Andrew Shankman (New York: Routledge, 2014), 324–345; Van Atta, *Securing the West*; Roy Robbins, *Our Landed Heritage: The Public Domain, 1776–1936* (Princeton, NJ: Princeton University Press, 1942), 3–118.

44. Joshua R. Greenberg, *Advocating the Man: Masculinity, Organized Labor, and the Household in New York, 1800–1840* (New York: Columbia University Press, 2008), 49–118; David Pugh, *Sons of Liberty: The Masculine Mind in Nineteenth-Century America* (Westport, CT: Praeger, 1984), 3–44; E. Anthony Rotundo, *American Manhood: Transformations in Masculinity from the Revolution to the Modern Era* (New York: Basic, 1993), 167–221.

45. Michael Kammen, *Mystic Chords of Memory: The Transformation of Tradition in American Culture* (New York: Knopf, 1991), 65–69; Fred Somkin, *Unquiet Eagle: Memory and Desire in the Idea of American Freedom, 1815–1860* (Ithaca, NY: Cornell University Press, 1967), 91–130; Haynes, "Imitating the Example of Our Forefathers," 46–48.

46. Roberts, *America's First Great Depression*, 114.

47. Robert May, "Young American Males and Filibustering in the Age of Manifest Destiny: The United States Army as Cultural Mirror," *Journal of American History* 78, no. 3 (Dec. 1991): 874–875.

48. Mark Voss-Hubbard, "The 'Third Party Tradition' Reconsidered: Third Parties and American Public Life, 1830–1900," *Journal of American History* 86, no. 1 (June 1999): 121–150.

49. David Grimsted, *American Mobbing, 1828–1861: Toward Civil War* (New York: Oxford University Press, 1998); Michael Feldberg, *The Turbulent Era: Riot and Disorder in Jacksonian America* (New York: Oxford University Press, 1980).

50. Steven Mintz, *Moralists and Modernizers: America's Pre–Civil War Reformers* (Baltimore, MD: Johns Hopkins University Press, 1995), 7.

51. Trish Loughran, *The Republic in Print: Print Culture in the Age of U.S. Nation Building* (New York: Columbia University Press, 2007), 1–5.

52. Mintz, *Moralists and Modernizers*, 3–16.

53. Max M. Edling, *A Hercules in the Cradle: War, Money, and the American State, 1783–1867* (Chicago, IL: University of Chicago Press, 2014), 145–177; Peter Guardino, *The Dead March: A History of the Mexican-American War* (Cambridge, MA: Harvard University Press, 2017), 7–18.

54. William J. Novak, "The Myth of the 'Weak' U.S. State," *American Historical Review* 113, no. 3 (June 2008): 752–777; Brian Balogh, *A Government Out of Sight: The Mystery of National Authority in Nineteenth-Century America* (New York: Cambridge

University Press, 2009), chaps. 5 and 6; Laura Smietanka Jensen, *Patriots, Settlers, and the Origins of American Social Policy* (New York: Cambridge University Press, 2003); Paul Frymer, *Building an American Empire: The Era of Territorial and Political Expansion* (Princeton, NJ: Princeton University Press, 2017); Richard R. John, *Spreading the News: The American Postal System from Franklin to Morse* (Cambridge, MA: Harvard University Press, 1995), 64–111; Edling, *Hercules in the Cradle*; Gautham Rao, *National Duties: Custom Houses and the Making of the American State* (Chicago, IL: University of Chicago Press, 2016).

55. Balogh, *Government Out of Sight.*

56. Lamar, "Inaugural Address," in Gulick, *Papers of Mirabeau Lamar*, 2:317.

57. Lamar, "Inaugural Address," 2:321.

58. Lamar, "Inaugural Address," 2:321.

59. Lamar, "Inaugural Address," 2:323.

60. Lamar, "Inaugural Address," 2:322.

61. Mirabeau Lamar, "Notes on the Annexation of Texas," in Gulick, *Papers of Mirabeau Lamar*, 2:324; Andrew J. Torget, *Seeds of Empire: Cotton, Slavery, and the Transformation of the Texas Borderlands, 1800–1850* (Chapel Hill: University of North Carolina Press, 2015), 206–208.

62. Lamar, "Notes on the Annexation of Texas," 2:324–327.

63. Lamar, "Inaugural Address," 2:320.

64. Kenneth W. Howell, "Mirabeau B. Lamar: Blinded by Delusions of Grandeur," in *Single Star of the West: The Republic of Texas, 1836–1845*, ed. Kenneth W. Howell and Charles Swanlund (Denton: University of North Texas Press, 2017), 209–211.

65. Lamar, "Inaugural Address," 2:318, 320.

66. Sylvester Van Horn to William Samson, Mar. 24, 1839, Vaux Family Papers, MSS coll. no. 73, American Philosophical Society, Philadelphia, PA.

67. Torget, *Seeds of Empire*, 310n18.

68. Lamar, "Inaugural Address," 2:317.

69. "Census and Census Records," Texas State Historical Association, https://www.tshaonline.org/handbook/online/articles/ulc01 (accessed Aug. 8, 2017).

70. Mark E. Nackman, "Anglo-American Migrants to the West: Men of Broken Fortunes? The Case of Texas, 1821–1846," *Western Historical Quarterly* 5, no. 4 (Oct. 1974): 449–455.

71. *Charleston (SC) Courier*, July 19, 1839.

72. Randolph Campbell, *Gone to Texas: A History of the Lone Star State* (New York: Oxford University Press, 2003), 159.

73. Pekka Hämäläinen, *The Comanche Empire* (New Haven, CT: Yale University Press, 2008), 215–217; Gary Clayton, *The Conquest of Texas: Ethnic Cleansing in the Promised Land, 1825–1875* (Norman: University of Oklahoma Press, 2005), chap. 11.

74. James E. Crisp, "Who Were the Texians? The Creation of Texas Identity in the Era of the Republic," 81–112; and Francis X. Galán, "A Tainted Friendship: The Betrayal of Tejanos in the Republic of Texas," 437–482, both in Howell and Swanlund, *Single Star of the West*.

75. Roberts, *America's First Great Depression*, 21.

76. Steven Hahn, *A Nation without Borders: The United States and Its World in an Age of Civil Wars, 1830–1910* (New York: Viking, 2016), 85–87.

77. James Oakes, *Slavery and Freedom: An Interpretation of the Old South* (New York: Knopf, 1990), 80–136, esp. 94–96; Baptist, *The Other Half*, 292–297.

78. *The Times; or, The Pressure and Its Causes Examined: An Address to the People by a Citizen of Massachusetts* (Boston, 1837), 9.

79. Nackman, "Anglo-American Migrants," 453–454.

80. B. Waugh to Nathan Bangs, Nov. 17, 1840, Oregon Methodist Missionary Papers, MSS 017, Collins Memorial Library Archives, University of Puget Sound, Tacoma, WA.

81. Sylvester Van Horn to his parents, Nov. 26, 1838, Vaux Family Papers, American Philosophical Society, Philadelphia, PA.

82. Randolph B. Campbell, *An Empire of Slavery: The Peculiar Institution in Texas, 1821–1865* (Baton Rouge: Louisiana State University Press, 1981), 110.

83. Lewis Ross to John Ross, Jan. 5, 1838, in *The Papers of Chief John Ross*, vols. 1–2, ed. Gary Moulton (Norman: University of Oklahoma Press, 1985), 1:577 (hereafter, *Ross Papers*); John Ross to Friedrich Ludwig Von Roenne, in *Ross Papers*, 1:330; Gary Moulton, *John Ross: Cherokee Chief* (Athens: University of Georgia Press, 1978), 61–62.

84. *Niles' Register*, July 2, 1836, in *Ross Papers*, 1:447; John P. Bowes, *Land Too Good for Indians: Northern Indian Removal* (Norman: University of Oklahoma Press, 2016), 214–215.

85. Linda S. Hudson, *Mistress of Manifest Destiny: A Biography of Jane McManus Storm Cazneau* (Austin: Texas State Historical Association, 2001).

86. John L. O'Sullivan, "The Great Nation of Futurity," *United States Magazine and Democratic Review* 6, no. 23 (Nov. 1839): 426–430. See also Robert Sampson, *John L. O'Sullivan and His Times* (Kent, OH: Kent State University Press, 2003), chap. 7; Robert Scholnick, "Extermination and Democracy: O'Sullivan, the *Democratic Review*, and Empire, 1837–1840," *American Periodicals* 15, no. 2 (2005): 123–141.

87. O'Sullivan, "Great Nation of Futurity," 427.

88. John Higham, "From Boundlessness to Consolidation: The Transformation of American Culture, 1848–1860," in Higham, *Hanging Together: Unity and Diversity in American Culture* (New Haven, CT: Yale University Press, 2001), 149–166.

89. Rodríguez, "Children of the Great Mexican Family," 20; James Belich, *Replenishing the Earth: The Settler Revolution and the Rise of the Anglo-American World, 1783–1939* (New York: Oxford University Press, 2009), 85.

90. Horsman, *Race and Manifest Destiny*; Nicole Eustace, *1812: War and the Passions of Patriotism* (Philadelphia: University of Pennsylvania Press, 2012), 1–35.

91. Henry Clay to William Lambert, Jan. 22, 1840, in Seager et al., *Papers of Henry Clay*, 9:322.

92. Daniel Webster to Abijah Bigelow et al., Jan. 23, 1844, in *The Papers of Daniel Webster: Correspondence*, vol. 6: *1844–1849*, ed. Charles M. Wiltse (Hanover, NH: University Press of New England, 1984), 13.

93. Ralph Waldo Emerson, "Lectures," in *The Collected Works of Ralph Waldo Emerson*, vol. 1: *Nature, Addresses, and Lectures*, ed. Robert E. Spiller (Cambridge, MA: Belknap, 1971), 220.

94. David Shields, "The Power to Be Reborn," in *The American Revolution Reborn*, ed. Patrick Spero and Michael Zuckerman (Philadelphia: University of Pennsylvania Press, 2016), 289–299.

95. Major Wilson, *Space, Time, and Freedom: The Quest for Nationality and the Irrepressible Conflict, 1815–1861* (Westport, CT: Greenwood, 1974), 73–119.

96. Webster to Bigelow et al., Jan. 23, 1844, in Wiltse, *Papers of Daniel Webster,* 6:20.

97. *Portsmouth Journal of Literature and Politics,* Nov. 15, 1845.

98. Thomas Jefferson to John Jacob Astor, May 12, 1812, in *The Works of Thomas Jefferson,* vol. 11: *Correspondence and Papers, 1808–1816,* ed. Paul Leicester Ford (New York: Cosimo Classics, 2009).

99. John Calhoun, Speech on the Treaty of Washington, Aug. 19, 1842, in *The Papers of John C. Calhoun,* vol. 16: *1841–1843,* ed. Clyde N. Wilson (Camden: University of South Carolina Press, 1984), 400.

100. Robert J. Miller, "The Doctrine of Discovery, Manifest Destiny, and American Indians," in *Why You Can't Teach United States History without American Indians,* ed. Susan Sleeper-Smith et al. (Chapel Hill: University of North Carolina Press, 2015), 87–98.

101. *New Orleans Bulletin,* reprinted in *Macon Georgia Telegraph,* Aug. 6, 1839.

102. *Daily National Intelligencer,* July 22, 1839.

103. *Portsmouth Journal of Literature and Politics,* Nov. 15, 1845 (emphasis in original). Webster's speech was widely reprinted in many papers.

104. *New Orleans Bulletin,* quoted in *North American and Daily Advertiser* (Philadelphia), Mar. 26, 1840.

105. *Louisville (KY) Journal,* as quoted in the *Daily National Intelligencer,* Feb. 6, 1844.

106. *St. Louis New Era,* as quoted in the *Evansville (IN) Journal,* Sept. 11, 1845.

107. *Southern Patriot* (Charleston, SC), Nov. 22, 1845.

108. John L. O'Sullivan, "Annexation," *United States Magazine and Democratic Review* 17, no. 1 (1845): 9.

109. Reginald Stuart, *United States Expansionism and British North America, 1775–1871* (Chapel Hill: University of North Carolina Press, 1988), 164–165.

110. Henry Clay to *Daily National Intelligencer,* Apr. 17, 1844, in Seager et al., *Papers of Henry Clay,* 10:42–44.

111. Clay to Crittenden, Dec. 5, 1843, in Seager et al., *Papers of Henry Clay,* 9:897.

112. *Albany Evening Journal,* Mar. 28, 1844.

113. *Daily Madisonian* (Washington, DC), Mar. 28, 1844.

114. William E. Unrau, *The Rise and Fall of Indian Country, 1825–1855* (Lawrence: University of Kansas Press, 2007), 1–80; Robert Trennert, Jr., *Alternative to Extinction: Federal Indian Policy and the Beginnings of the Reservation System, 1846–51* (Philadelphia: Temple University Press, 1975), 1–9.

115. Unrau, *Rise and Fall of Indian Country;* Annie Abel, "Proposals for an Indian State, 1778–1878," in *Annual Report of the American Historical Association, 1907* (Washington, DC: Government Printing Office, 1909), 1:93–99.

116. *Richmond Enquirer,* Oct. 22, 1845.

117. *New York Sun,* as quoted in *Ohio Statesman* (Columbus), Nov. 26, 1845.

118. *Baltimore Sun,* Jan. 15, 1840.

119. *Daily National Intelligencer,* June 15, 1838.

120. See, for example, *Southern* (Jackson, MI), reprinted in *Daily National Intelligencer*, Feb. 6, 1844.

121. Sam W. Haynes, *Unfinished Revolution: The Early American Republic in a British World* (Charlottesville: University of Virginia Press, 2010), 204–229.

122. Richard Rush to Joel Poinsett, Jan. 13, 1838, Joel Poinsett Papers, 9-168, HSP.

123. *St. Louis Republican*, as quoted in *Arkansas Gazette*, Oct. 24, 1838.

124. Matt Karp, *This Vast Southern Empire* (Cambridge, MA: Harvard University Press, 2016), 20; Haynes, *Unfinished Revolution*, 217–221.

125. Alan Taylor, *The Internal Enemy: Slavery and War in Virginia, 1772–1832* (New York: Norton, 2013).

126. John C. Calhoun, Speech on the Bill to Distribute the Proceeds of the Sales of Public Lands to the States, Aug. 24, 1841, in *The Papers of John C. Calhoun*, vol. 15, ed. Clyde N. Wilson (Columbia: University of South Carolina Press, 1983), 728; Rebecca Berens Matzke, "Britain Gets Its Way: Power and Peace in Anglo-American Relations, 1838–1846," *War in History* 8, no. 1 (Jan. 2001): 19–46.

127. *Pennsylvania Inquirer* (Philadelphia), Mar. 11, 1840.

128. James Gadsen to Poinsett, Jan. 16, 1838, Poinsett Papers, HSP.

129. A. Mill to Poinsett, June 30, 1838, Poinsett Papers, HSP.

130. Felix Hutson to Poinsett, Apr. 6, 1838, Poinsett Papers, HSP.

131. William Worth to Poinsett, Jan. 30, 1838; Winfield Scott to Poinsett, Feb. 22, 1838; Worth to Poinsett, Dec. 25, 1838, all in Poinsett Papers, HSP.

132. Edward Everett to Poinsett, Apr. 19, 1839, Poinsett Papers, HSP.

133. Ronaldson to Poinsett, Feb. 14, 1838, Poinsett Papers, HSP.

Chapter 2 • Perfecting America in Canada

1. On this neglect, see Maxime Dagenais, "Introduction," in *Revolutions across Borders: Jacksonian America and the Canadian Rebellion*, ed. Maxime Dagenais and Julien Mauduit (Montreal, QC: McGill-Queen's University Press, 2019), 3–18.

2. Richard White, *The Middle Ground: Indians, Empires, and Republics in the Great Lakes Region, 1650–1815* (New York: Cambridge University Press, 1993); Alan Taylor, *The Civil War of 1812: American Citizens, British Subjects, Irish Rebels, and Indian Allies* (New York: Knopf, 2010); Gregory Evans Dowd, *A Spirited Resistance: The North American Indian Struggle for Unity, 1745–1815* (Baltimore, MD: Johns Hopkins University Press, 1993); Jeremy Adelman and Stephen Aron, "From Borderlands to Borders: Empires, Nation-States, and the Peoples in Between in North American History," *American Historical Review* 104, no. 3 (June 1999): 814–841.

3. Marcus Lee Hansen, *The Mingling of the Canadian and American Peoples* (New Haven, CT: Yale University Press, 1940), 105–112; Reginald Stuart, *United States Expansionism and British North America, 1775–1871* (Chapel Hill: University of North Carolina Press, 1988), 109–110.

4. Colin Read, *The Rising in Western Upper Canada, 1837–1388: The Duncombe Revolt and After* (Toronto, ON: University of Toronto Press, 1982).

5. Adam Fergusson, *Practical Notes Made during a Tour in Canada and a Portion of the United States in MDCCCXXXI* (Edinburgh, 1833), 148–149; Jane Errington, *The Lion, the Eagle, and Upper Canada: A Developing Colonial Ideology* (Kingston, ON:

McGill-Queen's University Press, 1987), 121–125; Stuart, *United States Expansionism*, 106–124.

6. Jane Dorothy Baglier, "The Niagara Frontier: Society and Economy in Western New York and Upper Canada, 1794–1854" (PhD diss., State University of New York, Buffalo, 1993), 178–252.

7. John J. Duffy and H. Nicholas Muller, *An Anxious Democracy: Aspects of the 1830s* (Westport, CT: Greenwood, 1982), 21; Jean-Paul Bernard, "Vermonters and the Lower Canadian Rebellions," *Vermont History* 58, no. 4 (Fall 1990): 251–252; J. I. Little, *Loyalties in Conflict: A Canadian Borderland in War and Rebellion, 1812–1840* (Toronto, ON: University of Toronto Press, 2008), 57–77.

8. Colin Read and Ronald J. Stagg, "Introduction," in *The Rebellion of 1837 in Upper Canada*, ed. Read and Stagg (Toronto, ON: McGill-Queen's University Press, 1985), lvi; Read, *Rising in Western Upper Canada*, 78–184.

9. *Buffalo Commercial Advertiser*, Dec. 12, 1837; *Buffalo Daily Star*, Dec.12, 1837; Mary D. Taber to Mrs. Richard Williams, Dec. 17, 1837, Hawes-Taber Family Letters, William L. Clements Library, University of Michigan (hereafter, CL-UM); C. H. McCollom to William Mackenzie, Dec. 22, 1837, Mackenzie-Lindsey Family Fonds (hereafter, MLFF); John Henderston to William Mackenzie, Dec. 28, 1837, MLFF.

10. Nathaniel Wilson Brooks to Caroline Brooks, Dec. 29, 1837, Nathaniel Wilson Brooks Papers, Burton Historical Collection, Detroit Public Library, Detroit, MI (hereafter, BHC-DPL).

11. Duffy and Muller, *Anxious Democracy*, 59–72; Elinor Kyte Senior, *Redcoats and Patriotes: The Rebellions in Lower Canada, 1837–1838* (Stittsville, ON: Canada's Wings, 1985), 152–162; Allan Greer, *The Patriots and the People: The Rebellion of 1837 in Rural Lower Canada* (Toronto, ON: University of Toronto Press, 1993), 345; Bernard, "Vermonters and the Lower Canadian Rebellions," 261; Orrin Edward Tiffany, *The Relations of the United States to the Canadian Rebellion of 1837–38* (Toronto, ON: Coles, 1972), 85–86.

12. Ernest A. Cruikshank, "The Invasion of Navy Island," in *Papers and Records: Ontario Historical Society* (Toronto: Ontario Historical Society, 1937), 7–84.

13. *Buffalo Daily Star*, Dec. 16, 1837; Augustus Porter to Peter Porter, Jan. 10, 1838, reel 10, Peter Porter Papers, Buffalo and Erie County Historical Society, Buffalo, NY (hereafter, BECHS).

14. Catharina V. R. Bonney, *A Legacy of Historical Gleanings*, 2nd ed. (Albany, NY, 1875), 63–80; Lillian F. Gates, *After the Rebellion: The Later Years of William Lyon Mackenzie* (Toronto, ON: Dundurn, 1988), 18–19.

15. *Detroit Free Press*, quoting the *Buffalo Daily Commercial Advertiser*, Dec. 27, 1837; Winfield Scott to Joel Poinsett, Feb. 2, 1838, Joel Poinsett Papers, 10-23, Historical Society of Pennsylvania, Philadelphia (hereafter, HSP).

16. John Anderson to Alexander Anderson, Jan. 15, 1838, John Anderson Papers, Bentley Historical Library, University of Michigan, Ann Arbor.

17. Donald McLeod to William Mackenzie, Nov. 1, 1838, MLFF; Donald E. Graves, *Guns across the River: The Battle of the Windmill, 1838* (Prescott, ON: Friends of Windmill Point, 2013), 227.

18. J. Woolsey Burchard to Rensselaer Van Rensselaer, Dec. 22, 1837, MLFF.

19. Lemuel Cook, Jr., to William Mackenzie, Dec. 28, 1837, MLFF.

20. Bonney, *Legacy of Historical Gleanings*, 79.

21. Thomas Jefferson Sutherland to editor of the *New York Daily Express*, Apr. 26, 1838, MLFF.

22. Thomas Jefferson Sutherland, *The Sword and the Pen: A Journal of Literature, Politics, and Military Science* (New York, 1840), 1–2.

23. Oliver Brodier to William Mackenzie, Nov. 26, 1838, MLFF; Edwin Stacy to Nathaniel Stacy and Susan Clark Stacy, Dec. 9, 1838, Nathaniel Stacy Papers, CL-UM; L. S. Martin to William Mackenzie, Dec. 26, 1837, MLFF; Lemuel Cook, Jr., to William Mackenzie, Dec. 29, 1837, MLFF; John Henderston to William Mackenzie, Dec. 28, 1837, MLFF; John Gates to Rensselaer Van Rensselaer, Dec. 29, 1837, MLFF.

24. Sam W. Haynes, *Unfinished Revolution: The Early American Republic in a British World* (Charlottesville: University of Virginia Press, 2010), esp. 118–126, 209–210.

25. *Buffalo Daily Star*, Dec. 29, 1837; *Albany Evening Journal*, Jan. 2, 1838; *Niles' National Register*, Jan. 6, 1838.

26. B. A. Hill to William Mackenzie, June 3, 1838, MLFF; *Detroit Morning Post*, quoting the *Rochester Democrat*, Dec. 29, 1838; Winfield Scott to Joel Poinsett, Jan. 12, 1839, Poinsett Papers, 11-150, HSP; Edwin Stacy to Nathaniel Stacy and Susan Clark Stacy, Dec. 9, 1838, Nathaniel Stacy Papers, CL-UM; William Upjohn diary, Jan. 8, 1838, BHC-DPL; Lucy Williams Hawes to Lawrence Grinnell, Dec. 30, 1837, Hawes-Taber Family Letters, CL-UM; C. Hudson, "Poem: For the Volunteer," Sept. 1838, MLFF; *Daily Commercial and Advertiser* (Buffalo, NY), Jan. 2, 1838; *Baltimore Sun*, quoting the *Argus* (Albany, NY), June 6, 1838.

27. Out of dozens of letters to Mackenzie and Van Rensselaer during the Navy Island campaign, only one mentions the *Caroline*: Account of a Patriot Meeting, Jan. 4, 1838, MLFF.

28. See, for example, "The Canada Question," *United States Magazine and Democratic Review* 1, no. 2 (Jan. 1838): 217–218; Stuart, *United States Expansionism*, 97–99.

29. John Smyles to Mackenzie, Sept. 4, 1838, MLFF.

30. A. Chappell to Rensselaer Van Rensselaer, Dec. 1837 or Jan. 1838; Stephen Nateson to William Mackenzie, Dec. 26, 1837; George Clinton Westcott and Beakes Rossell to William Mackenzie and Rensselaer Van Rensselaer, Dec. 28, 1837; John Gates to Rensselaer Van Rensselaer, Dec. 29, 1837; George Washington Morgan to Rensselaer Van Rensselaer, Dec. 30, 1837; Eleaser Lewis to Van Rensselaer or Mackenzie, Jan. 5, 1838, all in MLFF.

31. George Russell to William Mackenzie, Jan. 3, 1838, MLFF.

32. Bushnell Strong to Rensselaer Van Rensselaer, Dec. 26, 1837; Stephen Nateson to William Mackenzie, Dec. 26, 1837, both in MLFF.

33. Bonney, *Legacy of Historical Gleanings*, 74–79; Gates, *After the Rebellion*, 18–19; C. H. Graham to "Daniel Brooks" (aka Mackenzie), Feb. 10, 1838; Graham to Mackenzie, Mar. 8, 1838; Van Rensselaer to Mackenzie, Dec. 18, 1838, all in MLFF.

34. Gates, *After the Rebellion*, 22; "Regulations and Pay of the Northwestern Army: On Patriot Service in Upper Canada," Sept. 24, 1839, Broadsides, CL-UM.

35. S. C. Frey to Mackenzie, Oct. 9, 1838, MLFF; "Regulations and Pay of the Northwestern Army"; Patrick Shirreff, *A Tour through North America . . .* (Edinburgh, 1838), 16.

36. James Brewer to Rensselaer Van Rensselaer, Dec. 27, MLFF.

37. E. B. Ward to Eben Ward, Jan. 18, 1838, Ward Family Papers, BHC-DPL; Edmund Kirby to Jacob Brown Kirby, Mar. 3, 1838, Edmund Kirby Papers, MSS EK-1-148, Huntington Library, San Marino, CA (hereafter, HL).

38. H. Perry Smith, *History of Buffalo and Erie Co., New York* (Syracuse, NY: D. Mason, 1884), 1:213.

39. Matilda Anderson to John Anderson, Jan. 24, 1838; John Anderson to Alexander Anderson, Feb. 4, 1838; Eliza Wing to Alexander Anderson, Feb. 25, 1838; John Anderson to Alexander Anderson, June 9, 1838, all in John Anderson Papers, BHC-DPL; J. S. Neysmith to Mackenzie, Nov. 12, 1838, MLFF; W. W. Dodge to J. R. Field, July 20, 1839, Hugh Brady Papers, BHC-DPL; *Detroit Morning Post*, Nov. 26, 1838.

40. Eleaser Lewis to Mackenzie, Jan. 5, 1838; J. S. Neysmith to Mackenzie, Nov. 9, 1838; Thomas Storrow Brown to Mackenzie, [Summer?] 1838, all in MLFF.

41. Tiffany, *Relations of the United States*, 70; Winfield Scott, *Memoirs of Lieutenant-General Scott* (New York, 1864), 308.

42. Kenneth Stevens, *Border Diplomacy: The Caroline and McLeod Affairs in Anglo-American-Canadian Relations, 1837–1842* (Tuscaloosa: University of Alabama Press, 1989), 16–20; James C. Curtis, *The Fox at Bay: Martin Van Buren and the Presidency, 1837–1841* (Lexington: University Press of Kentucky, 1970), 170–181; Major L. Wilson, *The Presidency of Martin Van Buren* (Lawrence: University Press of Kansas, 1984), 157–163.

43. Scott, *Memoirs of Lieutenant-General Scott*, 308.

44. Anonymous to Mackenzie, Jan. 21, 1838, MLFF.

45. Winfield Scott to Joel Poinsett, Feb. 3, 1838, Poinsett Papers, 10-23, HSP.

46. Gates, *After the Rebellion*, 24.

47. Oscar Kinchen, *The Rise and Fall of the Patriot Hunters* (New York: Bookman Associates, 1956), 31–45.

48. Edwin C. Guillet, *The Lives and Times of the Patriots: An Account of the Rebellion of Upper Canada, 1837–1838, and of the Patriot Agitation in the United States, 1837–1842* (Toronto, ON: University of Toronto Press, 1968), 179–180; Kinchen, *Rise and Fall of the Patriot Hunters*, 35–45.

49. Elisabeth S. Smith, "Historic Attempts to Annex Canada to the United States," *Journal of American History* 5 (1911): 224; Marc L. Harris, "The Meaning of Patriot: The Canadian Rebellion and American Republicanism, 1837–1839," *Michigan Historical Review* 23 (Apr. 1997): 53.

50. Thomas Fitnam to Mackenzie, Feb. 13, 1838; Mackenzie to E. B. O'Callaghan, Nov. 22, 1838, both in MLFF.

51. These are extremely rough estimates based on tallies from Kinchen, *Rise and Fall of the Patriot Hunters*; Guillet, *Lives and Times of the Patriots*; and Graves, *Guns across the River*.

52. For this outlook, see Samuel Watson, "U.S. Army Officers Fight the 'Patriot War': Responses to Filibustering on the Canadian Border, 1837–1839," *Journal of the Early Republic* 18, no. 3 (1998): 485–519.

53. Henry Hill to Joel Poinsett, Dec. 23, 1837, 9-143; and V. H. Swayne to Poinsett, Nov. 23, 1838, 11-86, both in Poinsett Papers, HSP; George H. McWhorter to Secretary of the Treasury, Sept. 14, 1838, reprinted in Kinchen, *Rise and Fall of the Patriot*

Hunters, 125–126; E. Brooks to John Allen, Jan. 15, 1838, William Woodbridge Papers, BHC-DPL; *Detroit Daily Advertiser*, Dec. 23, 1837.

54. Don Faber, *The Boy Governor: Stevens T. Mason and the Birth of Michigan Politics* (Ann Arbor: University of Michigan Press, 2012), 102–110; Ivor D. Spencer, *The Victor and the Spoils: The Life of William L. Marcy* (Providence, RI: Brown University Press, 1959), 105–107.

55. B. Bagley to Mackenzie, June 14, 1838, MLFF; William Worth to Joel Poinsett, Dec. 25, 1838, 11-114, Joel Poinsett Papers, HSP; Stevens, *Border Diplomacy*, 42–43.

56. Thomas Storrow Brown to Mackenzie, May 23, 1838, MLFF.

57. Lucy Williams Hawes to Richard Williams, Sr. and Jr., Dec. 29, 1837, Hawes-Taber Family Letters, CL-UM; *Buffalo Daily Commercial Advertiser*, Jan. 22, 1838.

58. Scott, *Memoirs of Lieutenant-General Scott*, 308.

59. Worth to Poinsett, Jan. 30, 1838, Poinsett Papers, HSP.

60. *Washington Daily National Intelligencer*, June 11, 1838.

61. Webster to John Tyler, July 1841, in *Letters of Daniel Webster*, ed. C. H. Van Tyne (New York, 1902), 232–233.

62. *Cleveland Liberalist*, Jan. 13, 1838, as quoted in Andrew Bonthius, "Bald Eagle over Canada: Dr. Samuel Underhill and the Patriot Rebellion of 1837–1838," in Dagenais and Mauduit, *Revolutions across Borders*, 153.

63. Kinchen, *Rise and Fall of the Patriot Hunters*, 85.

64. Robert W. Coakley, *The Role of Federal Military Forces in Domestic Disorders, 1798–1878* (Washington, DC: Center of Military History, 1988), 50–53, 98, 110–119.

65. *Detroit Morning Post*, Dec. 6, 1838.

66. E. A. Theller to Mackenzie, Jan. 5, 1839, MLFF.

67. George Herron to Mackenzie, Dec. 5, 1838, Mackenzie Papers, BHC-DPL.

68. E. A. Theller, *Canada in 1837–38: Showing, by Historical Facts, the Causes of the Late Attempted Revolution, and of Its Failure . . .* (New York, 1841), 2:304, 308–310.

69. Maxime Dagenais, "Parti canadien," http://www.thecanadianencyclopedia.com /en/article/parti-canadien; Fernande Roy, "Patriotes," http://thecanadianencyclopedia .ca/en/article/patriotes, both *Canadian Encyclopedia* (accessed Oct. 25, 2017).

70. Edmund Kirby to Jacob Kirby, Mar. 11, 1838, Edmund Kirby Papers, HL.

71. Jason Opal, *Avenging the People: Andrew Jackson, the Rule of Law, and the American Nation* (New York: Oxford University Press, 2017).

72. Theller, *Canada in 1837–38*, 2:311.

73. Ronald Formisano, *The Birth of Mass Political Parties: Michigan, 1827–1861* (Princeton, NJ: Princeton University Press, 1971), 189–190; *Albany Argus*, quoted in *Detroit Daily Commercial Advertiser*, Dec. 25, 1837; *New York Spectator*, Dec. 7, 1837; *Daily National Intelligencer*, Dec. 21, 1837; *Detroit Daily Advertiser*, Jan. 31, 1838; *Detroit Free Press*, Dec. 10, 1838.

74. *Canadian*, Jan. 1, 1838. Although printed as 1838, the publication date was actually 1839, since the Patriot War events of 1838 are mentioned explicitly in the text.

75. J. Doty to Poinsett, Apr. 30, 1839, Poinsett Papers, 12-97, HSP.

76. *Mackenzie's Gazette* (New York), Aug. 4, Aug. 12, Aug. 18, Aug. 25, and Sept. 1, 1838; Gates, *After the Rebellion*, 44–45; Duncan Koerber, "Political Operatives and Administrative Workers," *Journalism History* 36 (Fall 2010): 164–165.

77. James Mackenzie to William Mackenzie, Oct. 2, 1838, MLFF.

78. D. Hungerford to Mackenzie, Aug. 9, 1838, MLFF.

79. James Mackenzie to William Mackenzie, Aug. 6, 1838, MLFF.

80. Mark Voss-Hubbard, "The 'Third Party Tradition' Reconsidered: Third Parties and American Public Life, 1830–1900," *Journal of American History* 86, no. 1 (June 1999): 121–150; Glenn Altschuler and Stuart Blumin, *Rude Republic: Americans and Their Politics in the Nineteenth Century* (Princeton, NJ: Princeton University Press, 2000), 14–46; Ronald P. Formisano, *For the People: American Populist Movements from the Revolution to the 1850s* (Chapel Hill: University of North Carolina Press, 2008), 91–158, esp. 91–115 for New York; Jonathan H. Earle, *Jacksonian Antislavery: The Politics of Free Soil, 1824–1854* (Chapel Hill: University of North Carolina Press, 2004), 49–77 (New York), 144–162 (Ohio); Eric Foner, *Free Soil, Free Labor, Free Men: The Ideology of the Republican Party before the Civil War* (New York: Oxford University Press, 1970), 149–185.

81. "Mackenzie's Constitution," in Read and Stagg, *The Rebellion of 1837*, 97.

82. William Deverell, "Redemption Falls Short: Soldier and Surgeon in the Post–Civil War Far West," in *Civil War Wests*, ed. Adam Arenson and Andrew R. Graybill (Berkeley: University of California Press, 2015), 139–140.

83. Ruth Dunley, *The Lost President: A. D. Smith and the Hidden History of Radical Democracy in Civil War America* (Athens: University of Georgia Press, 2019).

84. William Gates, *Recollections of Life in Van Diemen's Land* (Lockport, NY: D. S. Crandall, 1850), 14–15; Sutherland, *Sword and the Pen*; *Detroit Morning Post*, Dec. 3, 1838.

85. Margaret Failey, ed., *The Selected Writings of William Lyon Mackenzie, 1827–1837* (New York: Oxford University Press, 1960), 156, 173.

86. "Fourth Annual Report of the American Anti-Slavery Society," ed. Elizur Wright, *Quarterly Anti-Slavery Magazine* 2 (1837): 350.

87. Read and Stagg, "Introduction," xl, lvi; Gerald Horne, *Negro Comrades of the Crown: African Americans and the British Empire Fight the U.S. before Emancipation* (New York: New York University Press, 2012), 116. See also *Detroit Daily Advertiser*, Jan. 1, 1838; *Mackenzie's Gazette*, June 9 and Nov. 3, 1838; Read, *Rising in Western Upper Canada*, 62, 71, 73; Ernest Muller, "Preston King: A Political Life" (PhD diss., Columbia University, 1957), 265–266, 335–336, 378–379.

88. Horne, *Negro Comrades of the Crown*, 114–119; Van Gosse, "'As a Nation, the English Are Our Friends': The Emergence of African American Politics in the British Atlantic World, 1772–1861," *American Historical Review* 113 (Oct. 2008): 1012–1013; Fred Landon, "Canadian Negroes and the Rebellion of 1837," *Journal of Negro History* 7 (Oct. 1922): 377–379.

89. Sutherland to Van Rensselaer, Dec. 1837 or Jan. 1838, MLFF; see also Lucy Hawes to Richard Williams, Jan. 1, 1838, Hawes-Taber Family Letters, CL-UM.

90. Eliza A. Wing to Alexander Anderson, Jan. 5, 1838, John Anderson Papers, BHC-DPL. See also Wilson Brooks to Caroline Brooks, Dec. 29, 1837, Brooks Papers, BHC-DPL; A. Barber to Rensselaer Van Rensselaer, Dec. 28, 1837, MLFF.

91. Anonymous to Mackenzie, Sept. 8, 1838, Mackenzie Papers, BHC-DPL; J. A. Vail to Mackenzie, Dec. 7, 1838, MLFF.

92. Chippewa Chiefs to S. P. Jarvis, Dec. 21, 1837, in Read and Stagg, *Rebellion of 1837*, 328; Adam Hope to his father, Dec. 11, 1846, in *Letters of Adam Hope 1834–1845*,

ed. Adam Crerar (Toronto, ON: Champlain Society, 2007), 241; Graves, *Guns across the River*, 46.

93. Samuel C. Frey to Mackenzie, Jan. 4, 1838, MLFF.

94. *Pennsylvania Inquirer*, Dec. 15, 1837.

95. *Plattsburgh Republican*, Dec. 1, 1838. See also *Connecticut Herald*, Dec. 5, 1837; *Pennsylvania Inquirer*, Dec. 4, 1837; *Baltimore Gazette and Daily Advertiser*, Dec. 16, 1837; Duffy and Muller, *Anxious Democracy*, 43–86, 113; Greer, *Patriots and the People*, 345; Little, *Loyalties in Conflict*, 101; Senior, *Redcoats and Patriotes*, 152.

96. Nelson's declaration (which was written in French) was translated in the *New-Hampshire Gazette*, Nov. 20, 1838, and reprinted in many other American newspapers.

97. Ian Steele, *Betrayals: Fort William Henry and the "Massacre"* (New York: Oxford University Press, 1990), 149–176. See Cooper's *Leatherstocking Tales: The Pioneers* (New York, 1823), *The Last of the Mohicans* (Philadelphia, PA, 1826), *The Prairie* (Philadelphia, PA, 1827).

98. Kinchen, *Rise and Fall of the Patriot Hunters*, app. 2, 127–131; Thomas Fitnam to Mackenzie, Feb. 13, 1839, MLFF; T. R. Preston, *Three Years Residence in Upper Canada, from 1837 to 1839* . . . (London, 1840), 1:159–166.

99. Steven Bullock, *Revolutionary Brotherhood: Freemasonry and the Transformation of the American Social Order, 1730–1840* (Chapel Hill: University of North Carolina Press, 1996), 316.

100. Mary Ann Clawson, *Constructing Brotherhood: Class, Gender, and Fraternalism* (Princeton, NJ: Princeton University Press, 1996), 109.

101. "Mrs. Lount's Letter," *Canadian*, Jan. 1, 1838.

102. Hobart Berrian to Mackenzie, Nov. 21, 1838, MLFF.

103. John Tracey to Mackenzie, Aug. 29, 1838, MLFF.

104. John Griffon to Mackenzie, Jan. 28, 1839, MLFF. See also Haynes, *Unfinished Revolution*, 122–123.

105. Robert May, "Young American Males and Filibustering in the Age of Manifest Destiny: The United States Army as Cultural Mirror," *Journal of American History* 78, no. 3 (Dec. 1991): 874–875.

106. Kathleen Neils Conzen, "A Saga of Families," in *The Oxford History of the American West*, ed. Clyde A. Milner, Carol A. O'Connor, and Martha A. Sandweiss (New York: Oxford University Press, 1994), 315–358.

107. Dunley, *The Lost President*, 29–30.

108. Sir George Arthur to John Colbourne, Mar. 20, 1839, Charles Burow Papers, BHC-DPL.

109. Joshua R. Greenberg, *Advocating the Man: Masculinity, Organized Labor, and the Household in New York, 1800–1840* (New York: Columbia University Press, 2008), 49–118; Amy Greenberg, *Manifest Manhood and the Antebellum American Empire* (New York: Cambridge University Press, 2005), 5–13; David Pugh, *Sons of Liberty: The Masculine Mind in Nineteenth-Century America* (Westport, CT: Praeger, 1984), 3–44; E. Anthony Rotundo, *American Manhood: Transformations in Masculinity from the Revolution to the Modern Era* (New York: Basic, 1993), 167–221.

110. See the essays by Ruth Dunley, Andrew Bonthius, and Albert Schrauwers in Dagenais and Mauduit, *Revolutions across Borders*, xii–xv, 137–160, 174–197.

111. Duncombe, "An Address to the Different Lodges on the Subject of a Joint-Stock Company Bank," as printed in Kinchen, *Rise and Fall of the Patriot Hunters*, 133–135.

112. Graves, *Guns across the River*; Guillet, *Lives and Times of the Patriots*, 132–142; Tiffany, *Relations of the United States*, 66–68; Kinchen, *Rise and Fall of the Patriot Hunters*, 70–78.

113. Stephen Wright, *Narrative and Recollections of Van Dieman's Land . . .* (1844), 7.

114. Theller to Mackenzie, Nov. 27 and Dec. 10, 1838, both in MLFF; Lillian F. Gates, "*Mackenzie's Gazette*: An Aspect of W. L. Mackenzie's Later Years," *Papers of the Bibliographical Society of Canada* 25 (1986), 127.

115. Earl of Durham, *Report on the Affairs of British North America, from the Earl of Durham, Her Majesty's High Commissioner* (Ottawa, 1839), http://eco.canadiana.ca /view/oocihm.32374/2?r=0&s=1; "The Webster-Ashburton Treaty" (1842), https:// avalon.law.yale.edu/19th_century/br-1842.asp.

116. Bonney, *Legacy of Historical Gleanings*, 79.

117. Daniel D. Heustis, *A Narrative of the Adventures and Sufferings of Captain Daniel D. Heustis and His Companions in Canada and Van Dieman's Land during a Long Captivity: With Travels in California and Voyages at Sea* (Boston, 1848), 55–56.

118. Gates, *Recollections of Life*, 14–15; Sutherland, *Sword and the Pen*, 25; *Mackenzie's Gazette*, July 21, 1838.

119. For the numbers of Texas volunteers, see Paul D. Lack, *The Texas Revolutionary Experience: A Political and Social History, 1835–1836* (College Station: Texas A&M University Press, 1995), 129.

120. *Buffalo Daily Commercial Advertiser*, Dec. 21, 1837.

121. John Brooks to Wilson Brooks, Jan. 23, 1838, Brooks Letters, BHC-DPL.

122. Clay to Porter, Dec. 25, 1837, roll 12, Clay-Porter Correspondence, BECHS.

123. Thomas Russell to his father, Nov. 18, 1838, Canada Rebellion Papers, St. Lawrence University, Canton, NY.

124. Stevens, *Border Diplomacy*, 27–28; Albert B. Corey, *The Crisis of 1830–1842 in Canadian-American Relation* (New Haven, CT: Yale University Press, 1941), 49–57.

125. *Daily National Intelligencer*, Jan. 22, 1838.

126. *Congressional Globe*, 25th Cong., 2nd sess., 103–104.

127. *Congressional Globe*, 25th Cong., 2nd sess., 103–104.

128. *U.S. Statutes at Large*, vol. 5, ed. Richard Brown (Boston: Little, Brown, 1856), 209–210.

129. G. H. McCotton to Mackenzie, Feb. 21, 1838, and Anonymous to Mackenzie, May 29, 1838, both in BHC-DPL; A. K. McKenzie to Mackenzie, Feb. 1, 1839, MLFF.

130. Scott to Captain Monroe, July 8, 1841, Winfield Scott Collection, CL-UM.

131. Thomas Love to James Shedden, Jan. 17, 1838, Thomas Love Letters, BECHS.

132. Eben Ward to Emily Ward, Feb. 18, 1838, Ward Family Papers; William Upjohn diary, Dec. 31, 1838, both in BHC-DPL.

133. James Ronaldson to Poinsett, Mar. 2, 1838, Poinsett Papers, 10-61, HSP.

134. *Congressional Globe*, 25th Cong., 2nd sess., 83.

135. *Detroit Free Press*, Nov. 21, 1838.

136. John Mitchell to Rensselaer Van Rensselaer, Jan. 10, 1838, MLFF; Webster to Tyler, July 1841, in Van Tyne, *Letters of Daniel Webster*, 232–233.

137. See the letters to editors in Robert Ross, "The Patriot War," *Michigan Historical Collections* (Lansing, MI, 1894), 21:601–609.

138. Muller, "Preston King," 200–238.

139. Preston King to Mackenzie, Oct. 2, 1838; King to Mackenzie, Oct. 5, 1838, both in MLFF.

140. *New York Times*, Nov. 26, 1865.

141. *New York Herald*, Nov. 15, 1865; *New York Times*, Nov. 26, 1865. See also Robert B. Ross, "The Patriot War," *Michigan Historical Collections* 21 (1894): 606–607.

142. *Daily Albany Argus*, Nov. 20, 1865.

Chapter 3 • *Mormon Zion and the Quest for an American Theocracy*

1. Sidney Rigdon, Council of Fifty Minutes, Apr. 11, 1844, in *The Joseph Smith Papers: Administrative Records: Council of Fifty, Minutes, March 1844–January 1846*, ed. Matthew J. Grow et al. (Salt Lake City, UT: Church Historian's Press, 2016), 88 (hereafter, *CFM*).

2. This is what Jan Shipps termed the historiographic "hole in the doughnut" in "Gentiles, Mormons, and the History of the American West," in Shipps, *Sojourner in the Promised Land: Forty Years among the Mormons* (Urbana: University of Illinois Press, 2006), 17–44.

3. W. W. Phelps, Mar. 1, 1845, *CFM*, 273.

4. Patrick Q. Mason, "'The Wars and Perplexities of Nations': Reflections on Early Mormonism, Violence, and the State," *Journal of Mormon History* 38 (Summer 2012): 87; D. Michael Quinn, *The Mormon Hierarchy: Origins of Power* (Salt Lake City, UT: Signature Books, 1994), 18; Laurel Thatcher Ulrich; *A House Full of Females: Plural Marriage and Women's Rights in Early Mormonism* (New York: Knopf, 2017), xxiv.

5. Phelps, Mar. 1, 1845, *CFM*, 271.

6. Book of Mormon, 2 Nephi 10:11. See also Terryl L. Givens, *By the Hand of Mormon: The American Scripture That Launched a New World Religion* (New York: Oxford University Press, 2002), 46; David Charles Gore, "Mormonism and America as Promised Land in Joseph Smith's Letter from Liberty Jail," in *The Rhetoric of American Exceptionalism: Critical Essays*, ed. Jason A. Edwards and David Weiss (Jefferson, NC: McFarland, 2011), 102–106.

7. Leonard J. Arrington and Davis Bitton, *The Mormon Experience: A History of the Latter-day Saints* (Urbana: University of Illinois Press, 1992), 20–43.

8. Lilburn Boggs, military order, Oct. 27, 1838, reprinted in John P. Greene, *Facts relative to the Expulsion of the Mormons from the State of Missouri* (Cincinnati, OH: R. P. Brooks, 1839), 26.

9. Robert Bruce Flanders, *Nauvoo: Kingdom on the Mississippi* (Urbana: University of Illinois Press, 1965), 16; Robert S. Wicks and Fred R. Foister, *Junius and Joseph: Presidential Politics and the Assassination of the First Mormon Prophet* (Logan: Utah State University Press, 2005), 46–47.

10. Flanders, *Nauvoo*, 92–106.

11. Richard E. Bennett, Susan Easton Black, and Donald Q. Cannon, *The Nauvoo Legion in Illinois: A History of the Mormon Militia, 1841–1846* (Norman, OK: Arthur H. Clark, 2010); Hamilton Gardner, "The Nauvoo Legion, 1840–1845: A Unique Military Organization," in *Kingdom on the Mississippi Revisited: Nauvoo in Mormon History*, ed.

Roger D. Launius and John E. Hallwas (Champaign: University of Illinois Press, 1996), 48–61; Flanders, *Nauvoo*, 109–114.

12. Quinn, *Mormon Hierarchy*, 106.

13. Jan Shipps, *Mormonism: The Story of a New Religious Tradition* (Urbana: University of Illinois Press, 1985).

14. Daniel Walker Howe, *What Hath God Wrought? The Transformation of America, 1815–1848* (New York: Oxford University Press, 2007), 164–202, 285–327; Daniel Walker Howe, "Religion and Politics in the Antebellum North," in *Religion and American Politics: From the Colonial Period to the 1980s*, ed. Mark A. Noll (New York: Oxford University Press, 1990), 121–145; Mark Noll, *America's God: From Jonathan Edwards to Abraham Lincoln* (New York: Oxford University Press, 2002), 161–226.

15. Quinn, *Mormon Hierarchy*, 18–21.

16. Klaus Hansen, *Quest for Empire: The Political Kingdom of God and the Council of Fifty in Mormon History* (Lansing: Michigan State University Press, 1967), 45–71; Richard L. Bushman, *Joseph Smith: Rough Stone Rolling* (New York: Knopf, 2005), 175–176, 404, 519.

17. Patrick Q. Mason, "God and the People: Theodemocracy in Nineteenth-Century Mormonism," *Journal of Church and State* 53, no. 3 (Sept. 2011): 353–356; Andrew Ehat, " 'It Seems like Heaven Began on Earth': Joseph Smith and the Constitution of the Kingdom of God," *Brigham Young University Studies* 20, no. 3 (1980): 253–280.

18. Terryl Givens, *The Viper on the Hearth: Mormons, Myths, and the Construction of Heresy* (New York: Oxford University Press, 1997), 40–59; J. Spencer Fluhman, *"A Peculiar People": Anti-Mormonism and the Making of Religion in Nineteenth-Century America* (Chapel Hill: University of North Carolina Press, 2012), 25–89; W. Paul Reeve, *Religion of a Different Color: Race and the Mormon Struggle for Whiteness* (New York: Oxford University Press, 2015), 14–51; John E. Hallwas, "Mormon Nauvoo from a Non-Mormon Perspective," in Launius and Hallwas, *Kingdom on the Mississippi Revisited*, 160–180; David Brion Davis, "Some Themes of Counter-Subversion: An Analysis of Anti-Catholic, Anti-Masonic, and Anti-Mormon Literature," *Mississippi Valley Historical Review* 47, no. 2 (Sept. 1960): 205–224.

19. Hallwas, "Mormon Nauvoo from a Non-Mormon Perspective," 59–60.

20. Van Buren to Smith, as quoted in *History of the Church*, 7 vols., ed. B. H. Roberts (Salt Lake City, UT: Deseret Book, 1948–1950), 4:80.

21. *Detroit Free Press*, Nov. 21, 1838. The term was ubiquitous among the Mormons. For an earlier reference, see Joseph Smith, diary entry, July 2, 1843, in *An American Prophet's Record: The Diaries and Journals of Joseph Smith*, ed. Scott Faulring (Salt Lake City, UT: Signature Books, 1989), 392.

22. Brent M. Rogers, "To the 'Honest and Patriotic Sons of Liberty': Mormon Appeals for Redress and Social Justice, 1843–44," *Journal of Mormon History* 39, no. 1 (Winter 2013): 36–67.

23. Rogers, "To the 'Honest and Patriotic Sons of Liberty,' " 39.

24. Joseph Smith, *Views of the Powers and Policy of the Government of the United States* (1844; repr., Salt Lake City, UT, 1886).

25. Smith, *Views of the Powers and Policy*, 13, emphasis in original.

26. Smith, *Views of the Powers and Policy*, 8.

27. Smith, *Views of the Powers and Policy*, 15.

28. Smith, *Views of the Powers and Policy*, 19.

29. "The Prophet's Memorial to Congress," in Roberts, *History of the Church*, 6:275–277.

30. Paul Frymer, *Building an American Empire: The Era of Territorial and Political Expansion* (Princeton, NJ: Princeton University Press, 2017), 136; Julius Wilm, *Settlers as Conquerors: Free Land Policy in Antebellum America* (Stuttgart, Germany: Franz Steiner, 2018), 66–114.

31. When I refer to the "Quorum of the Twelve," I do so inexactly, that is, if a majority of the twelve were present during an important meeting, I use the term, instead of specifying who was present and who was not. Additionally, when I use the term "Mormon leaders," I am referring inexactly to those Mormons who were influential during the time described in that particular section of the chapter. For example, "Mormon leaders" in the spring of 1844 refers to the first presidency (Smith and his counselors), the Quorum of the Twelve, and influential members of the Council of Fifty. By 1846, "Mormon leaders" refers to essentially the Quorum of the Twelve alone, the first presidency having been temporarily dissolved and the Council of Fifty having been marginalized.

32. Lyman Wight to Joseph Smith, Feb. 15, 1844, in Roberts, *History of the Church*, 7:257–261.

33. Wight to Smith, Feb. 15, 1844, 7:259.

34. "Volume Introduction: The Council of Fifty in Nauvoo, Illinois," in *CFM*, xiii–xlv.

35. *CFM*, xxxvii; Quinn, *Mormon Hierarchy*, 127–128.

36. Quinn, *Mormon Hierarchy*, 132; Faulring, *American Prophet's Record*, 459, 463, 477.

37. *CFM*, 43–44.

38. Cheryl L. Bruno, "Freemasonry, Polygamy, and the Nauvoo Relief Society, 1842–1844," *Journal of Mormon History* 39, no. 4 (Fall 2013): 170.

39. Thank you to Benjamin Park for this crucial insight, which is found in chapter 5, "Fruit," of his book *Kingdom of Nauvoo: A Story of Mormon Politics, Plural Marriage, and Power in Nineteenth-Century America* (New York: Norton/Liveright, 2020).

40. Gary James Bergera, "Identifying the Earliest Mormon Polygamists, 1841–1844," *Dialogue: A Journal of Mormon Thought* 38, no. 3 (2005): 1–74, esp. 49, which has a table of early polygamists.

41. For differing accounts of Smith's presidential ambitions, see B. H. Roberts, *The Rise and Fall of Nauvoo* (Provo, UT: Maasai Publishing, 2001), 250; Flanders, *Nauvoo*, 334–340; Marvin S. Hill, *Quest for Refuge: The Mormon Flight from American Pluralism* (Salt Lake City, UT: Signature Books, 1989), 137–140; Kenneth H. Winn, *Exiles in a Land of Liberty: Mormons in America, 1830–1846* (Chapel Hill: University of North Carolina Press, 1990), 195–207; Quinn, *Mormon Hierarchy*, 119–124.

42. Quinn, *Mormon Hierarchy*, 117–118.

43. Roberts, *History of the Church*, 6:188; Orson Hyde to Joseph Smith, Apr. 26, 1844, in Roberts, *History of the Church*, 6:373–376.

44. Faulring, *American Prophet's Record*, 446–447; Ronald K. Esplin, "Joseph, Brigham, and the Quest for Promised Refuge in the West," *Journal of Mormon History* 9 (1982): 93–94.

45. Hyde to Smith, Apr. 25, 1844, 6:369–373; Hyde to Smith, Apr. 26, 1844, 6:373–376, both in Roberts, *History of the Church.*

46. Hyde to the Council of Fifty, Apr. 26, 1844, *CFM*, 181.

47. "Hyde's Report of Labors in Washington," Apr. 25, 1844, in Roberts, *History of the Church*, 6:372.

48. Hyde to Sidney Rigdon, June 9, 1844; Hyde to Rigdon, June 11, 1844, both in Journal History of the Church, LDS Church History Library, Salt Lake City, UT (hereafter, Journal History).

49. Wight to Rigdon, June 9, 1844, in Journal History.

50. Woodworth to Houston, July 14, 1844, in Journal History; James Arlington Bennet to Willard Richards, June 4, 1845, Willard Richards Papers, LDS Church History Library, Salt Lake City, UT (hereafter, CHL); George Miller, *Correspondence of Bishop George Miller to the Northern Islander from His Acquaintance with Mormonism Up to Near the Close of His Life* . . . (Burlington, WI, 1855). See also Michael Scott Van Wagenen, *The Texas Republic and the Mormon Kingdom of God* (College Station: Texas A&M University Press, 2002).

51. Woodworth, Mar. 3, 1844, *CFM*, 142.

52. Bennet to Richards, June 4, 1845 (emphasis in original).

53. Miller, *Correspondence*, 20. See also Lucian Woodworth to Reuben Hedlock, May 3, 1844, in Journal History.

54. Faulring, *American Prophet's Record*, 458.

55. Smith, Apr. 8, 1844, in Journal History; *Wilford Woodruff's Journal, 1833–1898*, vol. 2, ed. Scott Kenney (Midvale, UT: Signature Books, 1984), 388–389.

56. For a list of all Texas articles in Nauvoo newspapers between 1842 and 1844, see appendix B in Van Wagenen, *Texas Republic and the Mormon Kingdom*, 77–86.

57. Woodworth to Hedlock, May 3, 1844.

58. John Walton to Joseph Smith, June 3, 1844, in Journal History; Van Wagenen, *Texas Republic and the Mormon Kingdom*, 47–48.

59. See especially the minutes from April 11, 1844, in which the council debated Smith's political platform, settling on "Jefferson" democracy: *CFM*, 90–91.

60. Kimball and Young, Apr. 5, 1844, *CFM*, 82.

61. Apr. 11, 1844, *CFM*, 110–114.

62. March 11 resolution, *CFM*, 54.

63. Joseph Smith, Apr. 11, 1844, *CFM*, 101.

64. John Taylor statement, Apr. 18, 1844, *CFM*, 114.

65. Taylor statement, *CFM*, 114.

66. Smith statement, *CFM*, 137.

67. A few members of the council did voice disdain for the United States, but this was not a prevalent theme of the council meetings held under Smith. For statements of anti-US hostility, see *CFM*, 95–96, 116.

68. Arrington and Bitton, *Mormon Experience*, 79–80; Hallwas, "Mormon Nauvoo from a Non-Mormon Perspective," in Launius and Hallwas, *Kingdom on the Mississippi Revisited*, 171; Quinn, *Mormon Hierarchy*, 138–140.

69. "Prospectus of the *Nauvoo Expositor*," May 10, 1844, in Journal History.

70. For detailed accounts of the events that led to Smith's death, see Bushman, *Joseph Smith*, 526–550; Wicks and Foister, *Junius and Joseph*, 132–179.

71. Woodworth to Houston, July 14, 1844, in Journal History.

72. Quinn, *Mormon Hierarchy*, 143–244; *CFM*, 205–215.

73. "President Young's Discourse," Aug. 18, 1844, in Roberts, *History of the Church*, 7:254–255.

74. Melvin C. Johnson, *Polygamy on the Pedernales: Lyman Wight's Mormon Village in Antebellum Texas* (Logan: Utah State University Press, 2006); Van Wagenen, *Texas Republic and the Mormon Kingdom*, 52–63; David Bitton, "Mormons in Texas: The Ill-Fated Lyman Wight Colony, 1844–1858," *Arizona and the West* 11, no. 1 (Spring 1969): 5–26.

75. Apr. 2, 1847, in Journal History.

76. Wight to the Quorum of the Twelve, Feb. 15, 1844, 6:255–257; Wight to Smith, Feb. 15, 1844, 6:257–260, both in Roberts, *History of the Church*.

77. Wight to Smith, Feb. 15, 1844, 6:258.

78. Wight to the Quorum of the Twelve, Feb. 15, 1844, 6:256.

79. Wight to Smith, Feb. 15, 1844, 6:258.

80. Wight to Smith, Feb. 15, 1844, 6:259.

81. Ronald W. Walker, "Seeking the Remnant: The Native American during the Joseph Smith Period," *Journal of Mormon History* 19, no. 1 (1993): 12–20; Bushman, *Joseph Smith*, 122; Arrington and Bitton, *Mormon Experience*, 146.

82. Walker, "Seeking the Remnant," 22–23. See also Reeve, *Religion of a Different Color*, 52–74; Lori Taylor, "Telling Stories about Mormons and Indians" (PhD diss., University of Buffalo, 2000).

83. Oliver Olney, diary entry, July 20, 1842, MSS 8288, item 8, CHL. See also William Clayton's journal entry, Mar. 1, 1845, in *An Intimate Chronicle: The Journals of William Clayton*, ed. George D. Smith (Salt Lake City, UT: Signature Books, 1995), 158; Ronald K. Esplin, "'A Place Prepared': Joseph, Brigham, and the Quest for Promised Refuge in the West," in *Window of Faith: Latter-day Saint Perspectives on World History*, ed. Roy A. Prete (Provo, UT: Religious Studies Center, Brigham Young University, 2005), 90–91.

84. Taylor, "Telling Stories about Mormons and Indians," 187–210.

85. William Bryan Pace, "Autobiography of William Bryan Pace," typescript, Harold B. Lee Library, Brigham Young University, Provo, UT, http://www.boap.org/LDS/Early-Saints/WPace.html.

86. Richard E. Bennett, "Mormon Renegade: James Emmett at the Vermillion, 1846," *South Dakota History* 15, no. 3 (1986): 217–233; Danny L. Jorgensen, "Building the Kingdom of God: Alpheus Cutler and the Second Mormon Mission to the Indians, 1846–1853," *Kansas History* 15, no. 3 (Autumn 1992): 192–209.

87. Smith, *Intimate Chronicle*, 157; Quinn, *Mormon Hierarchy*, 176.

88. *CFM*, 232–244.

89. Smith, *Intimate Chronicle*, 158; Taylor, "Telling Stories about Mormons and Indians," 242.

90. *CFM*, 336, 341.

91. *CFM*, 299–300.

92. *CFM*, 252–275.

93. Smith, *Intimate Chronicle*, 158.

94. Taylor, "Telling Stories about Mormons and Indians," 245–246.

95. *CFM*, 260.

96. *CFM*, 271.

97. *CFM*, 271.

98. *CFM*, 284.

99. Pekka Hämäläinen, *The Comanche Empire* (New Haven, CT: Yale University Press, 2008), 141–180; Brian DeLay, *War of a Thousand Deserts: Indian Raids and the U.S.-Mexican War* (New Haven, CT: Yale University Press, 2009).

100. *CFM*, 299.

101. *CFM*, 303.

102. Parley Pratt to Brigham Young, June 5, 1845, Brigham Young Office Files, LDS Church History Library, Salt Lake City, UT (hereafter, BYOF).

103. Dana to Young, Dec. 15, 1845, BYOF.

104. Wight to Smith, Feb. 15, 1844, in Roberts, *History of the Church*, 6:258. "Orson Hyde's Second Letter from Washington," Apr. 26, 1844, in Roberts, *History of the Church*, 6:375; Orson Hyde to Joseph Smith, Apr. 30, 1844, in Journal History.

105. *CFM*, 342, 349.

106. *CFM*, 350.

107. *CFM*, 396.

108. *CFM*, 406–408.

109. *CFM*, 342n493.

110. For the Stockbridge Mohicans, see May entries in the Phineas Young Journal, MSS 2799, CHL; and Brigham Young to Thomas Hendrick, Stockbridge chief, Aug. 4, 1845, BYOF; for the Senecas: Smith, *Intimate Chronicle*, 181; for the Cherokees: Jonathan Dunham to Brigham Young, May 31, 1845, BYOF; and Lewis Dana to John Brown, July 5, 1845, Lewis Dana Correspondence, MSS 15551, CHL; for the twenty-one nations: "Letter of Recommendation for Lewis Dana," in Thomas Hendrick to B. Fields, May 18, 1845, Lewis Dana Correspondence, CHL. For more specific discussion of Mormons' relations with each of these tribes, see Taylor, "Telling Stories about Mormons and Indians," 240–252.

111. *CFM*, 469–470.

112. *CFM*, 470.

113. *CFM*, 462.

114. *CFM*, 477–479; Arrington and Bitton, *Mormon Experience*, 94–95; James B. Allen and Glen M. Leonard, *The Story of the Latter-day Saints* (Salt Lake City, UT: Deseret Book, 1976), 208; Leonard Arrington, *Brigham Young: American Moses* (New York: Knopf, 1985), 125–126.

115. Taylor, "Telling Stories about Mormons and Indians," 254–255.

116. Dana to Young, Dec. 16, 1845, BYOF.

117. Hosea Stout, *On the Mormon Frontier: The Diary of Hosea Stout, 1844–1861*, 2 vols., ed. Juanita Brooks (Salt Lake City: University of Utah Press, 1964), 1:152, 1:205.

118. Lewis Clark Christian, "Mormon Foreknowledge of the West," *Brigham Young University Studies* 21 (Fall 1981): 403–415; Esplin, "A Place Prepared," 89–93.

119. *CFM*, 40, also see 40n71; Esplin, "A Place Prepared," 93–94.

120. Thomas Drew to Brigham Young, May 27, 1845, BYOF; Roberts, *History of the Church*, 6:188; Orson Hyde to Joseph Smith, Apr. 26, 1844, in Roberts, *History of the Church*, 6:373–376.

121. The *Quincy Whig*'s story was repeated in a number of papers, for example, *Boston Courier*, Oct. 27, 1845; *Baltimore Sun*, Oct. 28, 1845; *Daily National Intelligencer*, Oct. 28, 1845; *Milwaukee Daily Sentinel*, Nov. 8, 1845.

122. *Barre (MA) Patriot*, quoting the *Sangamo Journal*, Jan. 2, 1846; Governor Ford to Sheriff Backenstos, Dec. 29, 1845, in *Readings in L.D.S. Church History: From Original Manuscripts*, ed. William E. Berrett and Alma P. Burton (Salt Lake City, UT: Deseret Book, 1953), 2:109.

123. Elisha Davis to Wilford Woodruff, Jan.(?), 1846, Wilford Woodruff Journals and Papers, MSS 1352, CHL.

124. *CFM*, 406.

125. *CFM*, 410–411. Taylor lived in Upper Canada during the rebellion in 1837, and he may have been angry at British repression. For more on the Mormons and Upper Canada, see Darren Ferry, "The Politicization of Religious Dissent: Mormonism in Canada, 1833–1843," *Ontario History* 89, no. 4 (Dec. 1997): 285–301.

126. Faulring, *American Prophet's Record*, 340.

127. Dean L. May, "A Demographic Portrait of the Mormons," in *After 150 Years: The Latter-day Saints in Sesquicentennial Perspective*, ed. Thomas Alexander and Jessie Embry (Provo, UT: Charles Redd Center for Western Studies, 1983), 39–66.

128. Brigham Young, Sept. 13, 1857, in *Journal of Discourses*, 26 vols., http://jod.mrm .org/1 (hereafter, *Journal of Discourses*), 5:230–231; George Smith, July 24, 1854, *Journal of Discourses*, 2:22–24; Esplin, "A Place Prepared," 102–103.

129. Young to Stephen Douglas, Dec. 17, 1845, BYOF; *CFM*, 464, 484–485.

130. Charles Lovell to Young, Oct. 20, 1845; E. [Elden?] Warren to Young, Oct. 22, 1845; Samuel Hastings to Young, Dec. 29, 1845; Eli Whitney, Jr., to Young, Jan. 6, 1846, all in BYOF. The Journal History entry for Oct. 31, 1845, also mentions several letters Orson Hyde received from Americans urging the Mormons to move to California.

131. Thomas Ford to Young, Apr. 8, 1845, BYOF.

132. Thomas F. Andrews, "The Ambitions of Lansford W. Hastings: A Study in Western Myth-Making," *Pacific Historical Review* 39 (Nov. 1970): 473–491; Will Bagley, "Lansford Warren Hastings: Scoundrel or Visionary?," *Overland Journal* 12 (Spring 1994): 12–26; Thomas Richards, Jr., "The Lansford Hastings Imaginary: Visions of Democratic Patriarchy in the Americas," in *Inventing Destiny: Cultural Explorations of US Expansion*, ed. Jimmy L. Bryan (Lawrence: University Press of Kansas, 2019).

133. For this scheme, see the letters in Will Bagley, ed., *Scoundrel's Tale: The Samuel Brannan Papers* (Logan: Utah State University Press), 75–85; Gerrit John Dirkmaat, "Enemies Foreign and Domestic: U.S. Relations with Mormons in the U.S. Empire in North America" (PhD diss., University of Colorado, Boulder, 2010), 88–95. On the Mormons' connections with Farnham specifically, see Hyde to Young, Oct. 21, 1845, BYOF; and Oct. 31, 1845, in Journal History.

134. Bagley, *Scoundrel's Tale*, 127–129.

135. *CFM*, 328–329.

136. *CFM*, 353–354.

137. *CFM*, 330.

138. *CFM*, 476; July 13, 1846, in Journal History.

139. See, for example, John Bernhisel to Young, Nov. 26, 1846, and Jan. 18, 1847, both in BYOF.

140. John G. Turner, *Brigham Young: Pioneer Prophet* (Cambridge, MA: Belknap, 2012), 158–159; Jill Mulvay Derr, "Woman's Place in Brigham Young's World," *Brigham Young University Studies* 18, no. 3 (Spring 1978): 388.

141. Turner, *Brigham Young*, 158–159.

142. Dec. 20 and 27, 1845, in Journal History; Christian, "Mormon Foreknowledge of the West," 412–414.

143. Roberts, *History of the Church*, 7:515.

144. *CFM*, 355.

145. Stout, *On the Mormon Frontier*, diary entry, May 27, 1846, 1:163.

146. "A Circular of the High Council," *Times and Seasons* (Nauvoo, IL), Jan. 15, 1846; *New York Daily Tribune*, Feb. 5, 1846.

Chapter 4 • *The Cherokee Nation and the Quest for a Native Republic*

1. William H. Goode, *Outposts of Zion, with Limnings of Mission Life* (Cincinnati, OH, 1864), 69.

2. "Compact between the Several Tribes of Indians," in *The Constitution and Laws of the Cherokee Nation, Passed at Tahlequah, Cherokee Nation, 1839–1851* (Tahlequah, Cherokee Nation, 1852), 87.

3. Winfield Scott, *Memoirs of Lieutenant-General Scott* (New York, 1864), 301–354.

4. *Worcester v. Georgia*, 31 US 515 (1832).

5. James P. Ronda, " 'We Have a Country': Race, Geography, and the Invention of Indian Territory," *Journal of the Early Republic* 19, no. 4 (Winter 1999): 739–755; D. W. Meinig, *The Shaping of America: A Geographical Perspective on 500 Years of History*, vol. 2: *Continental America, 1800–1867* (New Haven, CT: Yale University Press, 1995), 96–103; see 97 for the statistic of 100,000 Natives.

6. Report on the Committee of Indian Affairs, Mar. 15, 1836, as quoted in Ronda, "We Have a Country," 746.

7. "Treaty of New Echota," Cherokee Nation, http://www.cherokee.org/About-The -Nation/History/Trail-of-Tears/Treaty-of-New-Echota (accessed Nov. 9, 2017).

8. Samuel Watson, *Peacekeepers and Conquerors: The Army Officer Corps on the American Frontier, 1821–1846* (Lawrence: University Press of Kansas, 2013), 353.

9. Thank you to Juliana Barr for this helpful framing during her remarks at the panel "Reconsidering Race, Gender, and Power in the Mid-Nineteenth-Century Great Plains," Western History Association Conference, Oct. 18, 2018, San Antonio, TX.

10. Charles S. Maier, *Once within Borders: Territories of Wealth, Power, and Belonging since 1500* (Cambridge, MA: Harvard University Press, 2016).

11. Nicholas Guyatt, " 'The Outskirts of Our Happiness': Race and the Lure of Colonization in the Early Republic," *Journal of American History* 95, no. 4 (Mar. 2009): 986–1011.

12. Brandon Mills, "Situating African Colonization within the History of U.S. Expansion," in *New Directions in the Study of African American Recolonization*, ed. Beverly Tomek and Matthew J. Hetrick (Gainesville: University Press of Florida, 2017), 175.

13. Bronwen Everill, " 'Destiny Seems to Point Me to That Country': Early Nineteenth-Century African American Migration, Emigration, and Expansion," *Journal of Global History* 7, no. 1 (2012): 53–77; Eugene S. Van Sickle, "Reluctant Imperialists:

The U.S. Navy and Liberia, 1819–1845," *Journal of the Early Republic* 31, no. 1 (Spring 2011): 107–134; Mills, "Situating African Colonization."

14. For these numbers, see Pierce Butler to Zachary Taylor, n.d., received June 6, 1842, in Letters Received by the Office of Indian Affairs, M234: Cherokee Agency, National Archives, Washington, DC (hereafter, OIA). There were also two more groups of Cherokees: approximately 1,000 Cherokees remained in North Carolina (their descendants remain to this day as the Eastern Band of the Cherokee Nation), and close to 1,000 Cherokees lived in northern Texas (see page 137).

15. William McLoughlin, *After the Trail of Tears: The Cherokees' Struggle for Sovereignty, 1839–1880* (Chapel Hill: University of North Carolina Press, 1993), 5–6.

16. William McLoughlin, *Cherokee Renascence in the New Republic* (Princeton, NJ: Princeton University Press, 1986), 12–13, 139–140, 161; Circe Sturm, *Blood Politics: Race, Culture, and Identity in the Cherokee Nation of Oklahoma* (Berkeley: University of California Press, 2002), 32, 40–42, 55; Duane Champagne, *Social Order and Political Change: Constitutional Governments among the Cherokee, the Choctaw, the Chickasaw, and the Creek* (Stanford, CA: Stanford University Press, 1992), 101–103.

17. Thurman Wilkins, *Cherokee Tragedy: The Story of the Ridge Family and the Decimation of a People* (New York: Macmillan, 1971), 321–324; John Demos, *The Heathen School: A Story of Hope and Betrayal in the Age of the Early Republic* (New York: Knopf, 2014), 256–265.

18. "The Cherokee Blood Law," *Cherokee Observer*, http://www.cherokeeobserver .org/Issues/bloodlaw.html (accessed Feb. 15, 2018).

19. Champagne, *Social Order and Political Change*, 179.

20. *Cherokee Nation v. Georgia*, 30 US 1 (1931); McLoughlin, *After the Trail of Tears*, 1–58; Andrew Denson, *Demanding the Cherokee Nation: Indian Autonomy and American Culture, 1830–1900* (Lincoln: University of Nebraska Press, 2004), 41–49; Stanley W. Hoig, *The Cherokees and Their Chiefs: In the Wake of Empire* (Fayetteville: University of Arkansas Press, 1998), 191–204; Kenny Franks, *Stand Watie and the Agony of the Cherokee Nation* (Memphis, TN: Memphis State University Press, 1979), 54–106; Gary Moulton, *John Ross: Cherokee Chief* (Athens: University of Georgia Press, 1978), 107–153; Morris Wardell, *A Political History of the Cherokee Nation, 1837–1907* (Norman: University of Oklahoma Press, 1977), 3–75.

21. Old Settlers to William Armstrong, Aug. 19, 1839, Records of the Southern Superintendency, Record Group 75, microfilm 640, National Archives, Washington, DC.

22. Treaty Party resolutions to John Tyler, 1844, OIA.

23. George Paschal, "A Report on the Trial of Stand Watie," 1843, in Cherokee Nation Papers, Western History Collections, University of Oklahoma, Norman; John Rogers, John Smith, and Dutch [Tatsi] to Matthew Arbuckle, Dec. 27, 1839, OIA; Treaty Party preamble and resolutions, Aug. 20, 1839, OIA.

24. Ross et al. to the Senate, Mar. 8, 1836, in *The Papers of Chief John Ross*, vols. 1–2, ed. Gary Moulton (Norman: University of Oklahoma Press, 1985), 1:413 (hereafter, *Ross Papers*).

25. Aquohee Camp Declaration, Aug. 1, 1838, in Emmett Starr, *Starr's History of the Cherokee Indians*, ed. Jack Gregory and Rennand Strickland (Fayetteville, AR: Indian Heritage Association, 1922), 105. See also McLoughlin, *After the Trail of Tears*, 2–5.

26. Ross et al. to William Armstrong, Aug. 27, 1839, *Ross Papers*, 1:760. For other

messages like this, see Ross to Arbuckle, July 9, 1839, 1:731, 734; Ross to Arbuckle, July 20, 1839, 1:739; Ross to Pierce Butler, Richard Mason, and Roger Jones, Dec. 23, 1844, 2:258, all in *Ross Papers*.

27. Ross et al. to John Bell and the House Committee on Indian Affairs, Apr. 20, 1840, in *Ross Papers*, 2:38.

28. Ross et al. to the House and Senate, Apr. 30, 1846, in *Ross Papers*, 2:293–294.

29. Thomas Crawford, *Annual Report of the Commissioner of Indian Affairs* [Nov. 25, 1839] (Washington, DC, 1840), 339.

30. Arbuckle to Joel Poinsett, Dec. 26, 1839, OIA.

31. Brad Agnew, *Fort Gibson: Terminal on the Trail of Tears* (Norman: University of Oklahoma Press, 1980), 185–204; Grant Foreman, *Advancing the Frontier, 1830–1860* (Norman: University of Oklahoma Press, 1933), 49–76; Michael Tate, *The Frontier Army in the Settlement of the West* (Norman: University of Oklahoma Press, 1999), 241–242.

32. Daniel Littlefield, Jr., and Lonnie Underhill, "Fort Wayne and the Arkansas Frontier, 1838–1840," *Arkansas Historical Quarterly* 35, no. 4 (Winter 1976): 334–359; Daniel Littlefield, Jr., and Lonnie Underhill, "Fort Wayne and Border Violence, 1840–1847," *Arkansas Historical Quarterly* 36, no. 1 (Spring 1977): 3–30.

33. Harris to William Armstrong, May 4, 1838, Records of the Southern Superintendency.

34. Hitchcock to John Spencer, Jan. 9, 1842, in Hitchcock, *A Traveler in Indian Territory: The Journal of Ethan Allen Hitchcock, Late Major-General in the United States Army*, ed. Grant Foreman (1930; repr., Norman: University of Oklahoma Press, 1996), 246.

35. Poinsett to Arbuckle, Mar. 7, 1840, OIA.

36. Poinsett to Andrew Jackson, Sept. 19, 1837, Poinsett Papers, 9-19, Historical Society of Pennsylvania, Philadelphia; Francis Ford Prucha, *The Sword of the Republic: The United States Army on the Frontier, 1783–1846* (London: Macmillan, 1969), 339–360; Robert Wooster, *The American Military Frontiers: The United States Army in the West, 1783–1900* (Albuquerque: University of New Mexico Press, 2009), 83, 90–95; Robert P. Wetteman, Jr., *Privilege vs. Equality: Civil-Military Relations in the Jacksonian Era, 1815–1845* (Santa Barbara, CA: Praeger Security International, 2009), 124–125; J. Fred Rippy, *Joel Poinsett: Versatile American* (Durham, NC: Duke University Press, 1935), 190–191.

37. Robert Trennert, Jr., *Alternative to Extinction: Federal Indian Policy and the Beginnings of the Reservation System, 1846–51* (Philadelphia, PA: Temple University Press, 1975), 1–9.

38. Alasdair Roberts, *America's First Great Depression: Economic Crisis and Political Disorder after the Panic of 1837* (Ithaca, NY: Cornell University Press, 2012), 112–114; Prucha, *Sword of the Republic*, 355.

39. Butler to Archibald Yell, Feb. 16, 1844, OIA; Montfort Stokes to William Armstrong, Aug. 9, 1839; Butler to Crawford, Sept. 28, 1842, Jan. 8 and Aug. 12, 1843, all in OIA. See also William Omer Foster, "The Career of Montfort Stokes in Oklahoma," *Chronicles of Oklahoma* 18, no. 1 (Mar. 1940): 35–52; Carolyn Thomas Foreman, "Pierce Mason Butler," *Chronicles of Oklahoma* 30, no. 1 (Mar. 1952): 6–29.

40. Butler to Crawford, Mar. 4, 1842, OIA.

41. *Arkansas Gazette* (Little Rock), Dec. 11, 1839.

42. Hitchcock to Spencer, June 3, 1842, OIA.

43. *Arkansas Gazette*, Apr. 18 and May 9, 1838; speech of Senator Lewis Linn, *Arkansas Gazette*, Nov. 10, 1841; speech of Senator William Fulton, *Arkansas Gazette*, Mar. 14, 1838.

44. *Arkansas Gazette*, May 30, 1838, Sept. 8, 1842, and Nov. 8, 1843; William Armstrong to Edward Cross, July 3, 1843, OIA.

45. *Arkansas Gazette*, Dec. 11, 1839, and Dec. 1, 1840.

46. Paul Frymer, *Building an American Empire: The Era of Territorial and Political Expansion* (Princeton, NJ: Princeton University Press, 2017); Laurel Clark Shirer, *The Threshold of Manifest Destiny: Gender and National Expansion in Florida* (Philadelphia: University of Pennsylvania Press, 2016), 163–193; Julius Wilm, *Settlers as Conquerors: Free Land Policy in Antebellum America* (Stuttgart, Germany: Franz Steiner, 2018), 66–114.

47. *Arkansas Intelligencer*, as quoted in *Arkansas Banner* (Little Rock), Nov. 18, 1843.

48. *Arkansas Banner*, Nov. 25, 1843.

49. Butler to Crawford, Mar. 28, 1843, OIA; Wooster, *American Military Frontiers*, 108.

50. Peter Silver, *Our Savage Neighbors: How Indian Warfare Transformed Early America* (New York: Norton, 2008).

51. Kevin Bruyneel, *The Third Space of Sovereignty: The Postcolonial Politics of U.S.-Indigenous Relations* (Minneapolis: University of Minnesota Press, 2007).

52. George Catlin, *Outline Map of Indian Localities in 1833*, as quoted in Jimmy L. Bryan, Jr., "Unquestionable Geographies: The Empirical and the Romantic in U.S. Expansionist Cartography, 1810–1848," *Pacific Historical Review* 87, no. 4 (2018): 693; Wilm, *Settlers as Conquerors*, 80–81.

53. *Niles' Register*, July 2, 1836, in *Ross Papers*, 1:447.

54. David LaVere, *Contrary Neighbors: Southern Plains and Removed Indians in Indian Territory* (Norman: University of Oklahoma Press, 2000), 85.

55. "Constitution of the Cherokee Nation, 1827," Tennessee Virtual Archive, https://teva.contentdm.oclc.org/digital/collection/tfd/id/328.

56. Julie L. Reed, *Serving the Nation: Cherokee Sovereignty and Social Welfare, 1800–1907* (Norman: University of Oklahoma Press, 2016), 23–90.

57. McLoughlin, *Cherokee Renascence*, 280; Reed, *Serving the Nation*, 63; Lisa Ford, *Settler Sovereignty: Jurisdiction and Indigenous People in America and Australia, 1788–1836* (Cambridge, MA: Harvard University Press, 2010), 152–156; Susan Marie Abram, "'Souls in the Treetops': Cherokee War, Masculinity, and Community, 1760–1820" (PhD diss., Auburn University, 2009), 68–71.

58. George Paschal, "A Report on the Trial of Stand Watie, Charged with the Murder of James Foreman," 1843, 10, in Cherokee Nation Papers, Western History Collections, University of Oklahoma, Norman; Butler to Crawford, Oct. 18, 1843, OIA.

59. Ross to Taylor, Oct. 30, 1843, in *Ross Papers*, 2:185.

60. Reed, *Serving the Nation*, 60–90.

61. John Elliott and James Hose to Pierce Butler, Feb. 12, 1844, OIA.

62. Butler et al. to Ross, Dec. 7, 1844, OIA.

63. Deposition of Ross Brown, in Butler to Crawford, June 28, 1845, OIA.

64. W. Jones Howard to Peter Porter, Aug. 12, 1843; William Armstrong to Crawford, May 24, 1842; Butler to Crawford, Aug. 12, 1843, all in OIA.

65. Walter Prescott Webb, *The Texas Rangers: A Century of Frontier Defense* (Austin: University of Texas Press, 1935), 27–53.

66. Theda Perdue, *Cherokee Women: Gender and Culture Change, 1700–1835* (Lincoln: University of Nebraska Press, 1998), 135–158.

67. Carolyn Ross Johnston, *Cherokee Women in Crisis: Trail of Tears, Civil War, and Allotment, 1838–1907* (Tuscaloosa: University of Alabama Press, 2003), 56–80.

68. For a white missionary's account of this Cherokee powerlessness, see the journal excerpts from Daniel Sabine Butrick in *Voices from the Trail of Tears*, ed. Vicki Rozema (Winston-Salem, NC: John F. Blair, 2003), 138–148.

69. Butrick in Rozema, *Voices from the Trail of Tears*, 148.

70. McLoughlin, *After the Trail of Tears*, 15–17.

71. John Phillip Reid, *A Law of Blood: The Primitive Law of the Cherokee Nation* (New York: New York University Press, 1970), 73–85.

72. Champagne, *Social Order and Political Change*, 179.

73. Ross et al. to the House and Senate, Apr. 30, 1846, in *Ross Papers*, 2:293–294.

74. Bertram Wyatt-Brown, *Southern Honor: Ethics and Behavior in the Old South* (New York: Oxford University Press, 1982).

75. Franks, *Stand Watie*, 95–99.

76. Treaty Party resolution, as quoted in Franks, *Stand Watie*, 91.

77. McLoughlin, *After the Trail of Tears*, 125.

78. Butler to Crawford, June 28, 1845, OIA.

79. McLoughlin, *After the Trail of Tears*, 66–79, 125; Theda Perdue, *Slavery and the Evolution of Cherokee Society, 1540–1866* (Knoxville: University of Tennessee Press, 1987), 99–106; R. Halliburton, Jr., *Red over Black: Black Slavery among the Cherokee Indians* (Westport, CT: Greenwood, 1977), 61–92.

80. Perdue, *Slavery and the Evolution of Cherokee Society*, 78–80.

81. Daniel Littlefield and Lonnie Underhill, "Slave 'Revolt' in the Cherokee Nation, 1842," *American Indian Quarterly* 3, no. 2 (Summer 1977): 121–131; Reed, *Serving the Nation*, 79.

82. *The Constitution and Laws of the Cherokee Nation, Passed at Tahlequah, Cherokee Nation, 1839–1851* (Tahlequah, Cherokee Nation, 1852), 53; Littlefield and Underhill, "Slave 'Revolt' in the Cherokee Nation"; Perdue, *Slavery and the Evolution of Cherokee Society*, 87.

83. Butler to Crawford, Dec. 4 and 14, 1842, OIA. See also Tiya Miles, *Ties That Bind: The Story of an Afro-Cherokee Family in Slavery and Freedom* (Berkeley: University of California Press, 2006), 169–173.

84. Dawn Peterson, *Indians in the Family: Adoption and the Politics of Antebellum Expansion* (Cambridge, MA: Harvard University Press, 2017), 296.

85. Perdue, *Slavery and the Evolution of Cherokee Society*, 84–90; Celia E. Naylor, *African Cherokees in Indian Territory: From Chattel to Citizens* (Chapel Hill: University of North Carolina Press, 2008), 27–31.

86. *Constitution and Laws of the Cherokee Nation*, 7, 19, 44.

87. *Constitution and Laws of the Cherokee Nation*, 7.

88. *Cherokee Advocate*, May 22, 1845.

89. *Constitution and Laws of the Cherokee Nation*, 5.

90. Perdue, *Cherokee Women*, 155–157.

91. Reed, *Serving the Nation*, 76–87.

92. Perdue, *Slavery and the Evolution of Cherokee Society*, 71–72.

93. Hitchcock, *Traveler in Indian Territory*, 240.

94. Butler to Yell, Feb. 16, 1844, OIA.

95. William H. Freehling, *The Road to Disunion*, vol. 1: *Secessionists at Bay, 1776–1854* (New York: Oxford University Press, 1991), 39–58; Stephanie McCurry, *Masters of Small Worlds: Yeoman Households, Gender Relations, and the Political Culture of the Antebellum South Carolina Low Country* (New York: Oxford University Press, 1995), 60–61, 85–91.

96. Robert Armstrong to Stand Watie, May 29, 1846, in *Cherokee Cavaliers: Forty Years of Cherokee History as Told in the Correspondence of the Ridge-Watie-Boudinot Family*, ed. Edward Dale and Gaston Litton (Norman: University of Oklahoma Press, 1969), 42–44.

97. H. L. Smith to Watie, Apr. 21, 1846, Stand and Sarah C. Watie Papers, Cherokee Nation Papers, Western History Collections, University of Oklahoma, Norman.

98. Ross to Roger Jones, Richard Mason, and Pierce Butler, Dec. 9, 1844, OIA.

99. George Hicks et al. to Ross, David Vann, and John Benge, July 8, 1841, in *Ross Papers*, 2:91; Ross et al. to John Bell, Aug. 11, 1841, in *Ross Papers*, 2:96; Montfort Stokes to William Armstrong, Aug. 9, 1839, Records of the Southern Superintendency; *Cherokee Advocate*, July 31, 1845.

100. *Cherokee Advocate*, May 13 and May 20, 1845. See also Izumi Ishii, *Bad Fruits of the Civilized Tree: Alcohol and the Sovereignty of the Cherokee Nation* (Lincoln: University of Nebraska Press, 2008), 99–101.

101. Gregory D. Smithers, *The Cherokee Diaspora: An Indigenous History of Migration, Resettlement, and Identity* (New Haven, CT: Yale University Press, 2015).

102. Dianna Everett, *The Texas Cherokees: A People between Two Fires, 1819–1840* (Norman: University Press of Oklahoma, 1990), 24, 51, 67; Smithers, *Cherokee Diaspora*, 100–105; Jeffrey M. Schulze, *Are We Not Foreigners Here? Indigenous Nationalism in the U.S.-Mexico Borderlands* (Chapel Hill: University of North Carolina Press, 2018), 38–39.

103. John Ross to Friedrich Ludwig Von Roenne, in *Ross Papers*, 1:330; Moulton, *John Ross*, 61–62.

104. Lewis Ross to John Ross, Jan. 4, 1838, in *Ross Papers*, 1:577.

105. John G. Ross to John Ross, June 3, 1841, in *Ross Papers*, 2:90.

106. LaVere, *Contrary Neighbors*, 106–107; Wilm, *Settlers as Conquerors*, 80.

107. See, for example, John Rogers to James Porter, May 18, 1843, OIA.

108. See, for example, W. M. Thompson to Elias Boudinot, Nov. 5, 1838, in Dale and Litton, *Cherokee Cavaliers*, 16.

109. W. Byrd Powell to the *Arkansas Gazette*, Feb. 9, 1842.

110. The first instance I have found using the term "the line" is Butler to Crawford, May 17, 1842, OIA. By 1846 the term had become prevalent enough that the *Cherokee Advocate* could issue reports simply titled "From the Line" (e.g., June 25, 1846).

111. Littlefield and Underhill, "Fort Wayne and Border Violence," 3–30.

112. Littlefield and Underhill, "Fort Wayne and Border Violence," 17–18; William

McLoughlin, *Champions of the Cherokee: Evan and John B. Jones* (Princeton, NJ: Princeton University Press, 1990), 187.

113. Ishii, *Bad Fruits of the Civilized Tree*, 93–109.

114. Bethany R. Berger, " 'Power over This Unfortunate Race': Race, Politics and Indian Law in *United States v. Rogers*," *William and Mary Law Review* 45, no. 5 (2004): 1960–2052; Sidney L. Harring, *Crow Dog's Case: American Indian Sovereignty, Tribal Law, and United States Law in the Nineteenth Century* (New York: Cambridge University Press, 1994), 60–61; John Rockwell Snowden, Wayne Tyndall, and David Smith, "American Indian Sovereignty and Naturalization: It's a Race Thing," *Nebraska Law Review* 80 (2001): 171–238.

115. *Arkansas Gazette*, Apr. 21, 1845; Berger, "Power over This Unfortunate Race," 1991–1992.

116. Per the 1793 Judiciary Act. See Berger, "Power over This Unfortunate Race," 1991.

117. *Cherokee Advocate*, May 22, 1845.

118. *Cherokee Advocate*, June 5, 1845.

119. *Arkansas Gazette*, Apr. 21, 1845.

120. *Cherokee Advocate*, June 5, 1845.

121. *United States v. Rogers*, 45 US 567 (1846).

122. Berger, "Power over This Unfortunate Race," 1997.

123. *Cherokee Advocate*, Jan. 15, 1846; Sarah Watie to John Bell, Apr. 16, 1846, in Dale and Litton, *Cherokee Cavaliers*, 37; J. M. Lynch to Watie, Aug. 1, 1846, Stand and Sarah C. Watie Papers; Rogers to Porter, May 18, 1843, OIA; McLoughlin, *After the Trail of Tears*, 49–50; Wardell, *Political History of the Cherokee Nation*, 62–66.

124. LaVere, *Contrary Neighbors*, 26–30.

125. On councils, see LaVere, *Contrary Neighbors*, 92–108; John Bowes, *Exiles and Pioneers: Eastern Indians in the Trans-Mississippi West* (New York: Cambridge University Press, 2007), 137–151; Foreman, *Advancing the Frontier*, 195–216. On Cherokee exceptionalism, see Butler to Crawford, Feb. 26, 1842, OIA; *Cherokee Advocate*, Apr. 3, 1845; Ethan Allen Hitchcock, Dec. 21, 1843, in Hitchcock, *Traveler in Indian Territory*, 243; Denson, *Demanding the Cherokee Nation*, 47.

126. Robert A. Williams, Jr., *Linking Arms Together: American Indian Treaty Visions of Law and Peace, 1600–1800* (New York: Oxford University Press, 1997).

127. Goode, *Outposts of Zion*, 74.

128. McLoughlin, *After the Trail of Tears*, 43.

129. Butler to Crawford, Jan. 16, 1843, OIA; Petition of Arkansas Citizens, July 3, 1843, OIA.

130. Goode, *Outposts of Zion*, 69–84; Moulton, *John Ross*, 134–135; Bowes, *Exiles and Pioneers*, 141–147; McLoughlin, *After the Trail of Tears*, 43.

131. Goode, *Outposts of Zion*, 71.

132. Goode, *Outposts of Zion*, 76.

133. "Compact between the Several Tribes of Indians," in *The Constitution and Laws of the Cherokee Nation, Passed at Tahlequah, Cherokee Nation, 1839–1851* (Tahlequah, Cherokee Nation, 1852), 87.

134. "Compact between the Several Tribes of Indians," 88.

135. Reed, *Serving the Nation*, 69–70.

136. Goode, *Outposts of Zion*, 75.

137. Gregory Evans Dowd, *A Spirited Resistance: The North American Indian Struggle for Unity, 1745–1815* (Baltimore, MD: Johns Hopkins University Press, 1993), 139–143.

138. Dowd, *Spirited Resistance*, 180.

139. Goode, *Outposts of Zion*, 84.

140. Goode, *Outposts of Zion*, 80.

141. Goode, *Outposts of Zion*, 80.

142. Bowes, *Exiles and Pioneers*, 146.

143. Bowes, *Exiles and Pioneers*, 146.

Chapter 5 • *The Seigneurial Republic of California*

1. See the interviews conducted by H. H. Bancroft and Louisa Thompson that are held in the Bancroft Library, Berkeley, CA (hereafter, BL), including Henry Ford, "On the Bear Flag Revolt," MSS C-E 75; William Baldridge, "Days of 1846," MSS C-D 36; and Thomas Knight interview, MSS C-D 110.

2. Linda Heidenreich, *"This Land Was Mexican Once": Histories of Resistance from Northern California* (Austin: University of Texas Press, 2007), 75–92.

3. Alan Rosenus, *General M. G. Vallejo and the Advent of the Americans: A Biography* (Albuquerque: University of New Mexico Press, 1995), 35.

4. Rosenus, *General M. G. Vallejo*, 184.

5. Steven W. Hackel, "Land, Labor, and Production: The Colonial Economy of Spanish and Mexican Florida," in *Contested Eden: California before the Gold Rush*, ed. Ramón Gutiérres and Richard J. Orsi (Berkeley: University of California Press, 1998), 132.

6. Louise Pubols, *The Father of All: De La Guerra Family, Power and Patriarchy in Mexican California* (San Marino: University of California Press and the Huntington Library, 2009), 30–31.

7. Rosaura Sánchez, *Telling Identities: The Californio Testimonios* (Minneapolis: University of Minnesota Press, 1995), 96–141; Pubols, *Father of All*, 150–151.

8. Sheburne F. Cook, *The Conflict between the California Indian and White Civilization* (Berkeley: University of California Press, 1976), 4.

9. George Harwood Phillips, *Indians and Intruders in Central California, 1769–1849* (Norman: University of Oklahoma Press, 1993), 160–161; Benjamin Madley, *An American Genocide: The United States and the California Indian Catastrophe, 1846–1873* (New Haven, CT: Yale University Press, 2016), 16–41.

10. Michael Gonzalez, "War and the Making of History: The Case of Mexican California, 1821–1846," *California History* 86, no. 2 (2009): 14–20.

11. Doyce B. Nunis, Jr., "Alta California's Trojan Horse: Foreign Immigration," in Gutiérres and Orsi, *Contested Eden*, 306–310; Douglas Monroy, *Thrown among Strangers: The Making of Mexican Culture in Frontier California* (Berkeley: University of California Press, 1990), 154–162.

12. Thomas Larkin to William Hooper, Mar. 22, 1845, in *The Larkin Papers*, 10 vols., ed. George P. Hammond (Berkeley: University of California Press, 1952), 3:84.

13. Thomas Larkin, "Description of California," in Hammond, *Larkin Papers*, 4:332–344.

14. Hubert Howe Bancroft, *History of California*, 7 vols. (San Francisco, CA: History

Company, 1884–1890), 3:385–413. Bancroft's book was largely ghostwritten by Frances Fuller Victor.

15. Doyce B. Nunis, Jr., *The Trials of Isaac Graham* (Los Angeles, CA: Dawson's Book Shop, 1967), 14–18.

16. See the statements of Isaac Graham, Joseph Whitehouse, Thomas Lewis, and Nathan Daily in "Affidavits of Americans in Mexico, 1840," MSS FAC 1652, Huntington Library, San Marino, CA (hereafter, HL).

17. David Weber, *The Mexican Frontier, 1821–1846: The American Southwest under Mexico* (Albuquerque: University of New Mexico Press, 1982), 16–31, 156–157.

18. Weber, *Mexican Frontier*, 255–260; Robert Ryal Miller, *Juan Alvarado: Governor of California, 1836–1842* (Norman: University of Oklahoma Press, 1998), 45–50; Bancroft, *History of California*, 3:455–477.

19. Weber, *Mexican Frontier*, 243.

20. Nunis, *Trials of Isaac Graham*, 22.

21. Miller, *Juan Alvarado*, 42–43.

22. Miller, *Juan Alvarado*, 50.

23. Miller, *Juan Alvarado*, 50; Bancroft, *History of California*, 3:471.

24. The entire declaration is translated in Bancroft, *History of California*, 3:470–471n28.

25. Antonio María Osio, *The History of Alta California: A Memoir of Mexican California*, trans. Rose Marie Beebe and Robert M. Senkewicz (Madison: University of Wisconsin Press, 1996), 158.

26. Bancroft, *History of California*, 3:478–481; Monroy, *Thrown among Strangers*, 123; Weber, *Mexican Frontier*, 257–258; Sánchez, *Telling Identities*, 233; Pubols, *Father of All*, 207.

27. Miller, *Juan Alvarado*, 50–56; Woodrow James Hansen, *The Search for Authority in California* (Oakland, CA: BioBooks, 1960), 26–28; Bancroft, *History of California*, 3:515–533.

28. Sánchez, *Telling Identities*, 96–141, 228–267; Benedict Anderson, *Imagined Communities: Reflections on the Origin and Spread of Nationalism* (New York: Verso, 1983).

29. Henry Jubilee Bee, "Recollections of the History of California," 17–18, 1877, transcribed by Thomas Savage, MSS C-D 41, BL.

30. Thomas Larkin to Abel Stearns, Nov. 9, 1836, in *First and Last Consul: Thomas Oliver Larkin and the Americanization of California*, ed. John A. Hawgood (San Marino, CA: Huntington Library, 1962), 12; Alfred Robinson, *Life in California . . .* (San Francisco, CA, 1846), 176; Bancroft, *History of California*, 3:468–469.

31. Robinson, *Life in California*, 184; Miller, *Juan Alvarado*, 80.

32. Harland Hague and David J. Langum, *Thomas O. Larkin: A Life of Patriotism and Profit in Old California* (Norman: University of Oklahoma Press, 1990), 80–81; Bancroft, *History of California*, 4:8–9n8; John Chamberlain, "Memoirs of California since 1840," transcribed by Thomas Savage, MSS C-D 57, BL; Charles Brown, "Early Events in California," 15, MSS C-D 53, BL.

33. Miller, *Juan Alvarado*, 80–83; Nunis, *Trials of Isaac Graham*, 21–30; Bancroft, *History of California*, 4:1–41.

34. Thomas Jefferson Farnham, *Travels in California, and Scenes in the Pacific Ocean* (New York, 1844), 55–59; Charles B. Churchill, "Thomas Jefferson Farnham:

An Exponent of American Empire in Mexican California," *Pacific Historical Review* 60, no. 4 (Nov. 1991): 517–537; Chamberlain, "Memoirs," 9; Thomas Larkin to John Calhoun, Jan. 25, 1845, in Hammond, *Larkin Papers*, 3:22–24; Thomas Marsh to Thomas Catesby Jones, 1842 draft, Marsh Family Papers, MSS C-B 878, BL.

35. Farnham, *Travels in California*, 61–63.

36. Nunis, "Alta California's Trojan Horse," 313.

37. Norman A. Graebner, *Empire on the Pacific: A Study in American Continental Expansion* (New York: Ronald Press, 1955), 51–64.

38. Albert L. Hurtado, *John Sutter: A Life on the North American Frontier* (Norman: University of Oklahoma Press, 2006), 55.

39. John Sutter to Jacob Leese, Nov. 8, 1841, Vallejo Papers, BL.

40. Rosenus, *General M. G. Vallejo*, 35.

41. Mariano Vallejo, "Historical and Personal Memoirs Relating to Alta California," 5 vols., trans. Earl Hewitt, 1875, MSS C-D 17–19, 3:307–308, BL; Platón Mariano Guadalupe Vallejo, *New Light on the History, before and after the "Gringos" Came, Based on Original Documents and Recollections of Dr. Platón M. G. Vallejo* (Fairfield, CA: James D. Stevenson, 1994), 59; Rosenus, *General M. G. Vallejo*, 40–43.

42. Vallejo to Juan Almonte, 1841 draft, 147-1, Vallejo Papers, BL.

43. John D. Unruh, *The Plains Across: The Overland Emigrants and the Trans-Mississippi West, 1840–1860* (Urbana: University of Illinois Press, 1979), 119.

44. John Bidwell, "California 1841: An Immigrant's Recollections of a Trip across the Plains," in *The Bidwell-Bartleson Party, 1841 California Emigrant Adventure: The Documents and Memoirs of the Overland Pioneers*, ed. Doyce B. Nunis, Jr. (Santa Cruz, CA: Western Tanager Press, 1991), 77.

45. Will Bagley, *So Rugged and Mountainous: Blazing the Trails to Oregon and California, 1812–1848* (Norman: University of Oklahoma Press, 2010), 84–110; John Bidwell, *Echoes of the Past* (New York: Citadel, 1962), 5–76.

46. John Marsh, letter, July 3, 1840, printed in the *Daily Argus*, 1841, in Marsh Family Papers, MSS C-B 878, BL.

47. Bidwell, "California 1841," 77, BL.

48. Marsh, letter, July 3, 1840.

49. Michael J. Gillis and Michael F. Magliari, "Prologue," in *John Bidwell and California*, ed. Gillis and Magliari (Spokane, WA: Arthur H. Clark, 2003), 29.

50. Michael J. Gillis and Michael F. Magliari, "Introduction," in Gillis and Magliari, *John Bidwell and California*, 16.

51. John Bidwell, "A Journey to California, 1841," in Gillis and Magliari, *John Bidwell and California*, 62.

52. Lansford Hastings, *The Emigrants' Guide to Oregon and California* (Cincinnati, 1845), 123; Overton Johnson and William Winter, *Route across the Rocky Mountains, with a Description of Oregon and California, etc., 1843* (Lafayette, IN, 1846), 307.

53. Neil Howison to George Abernethy, Feb. 9, 1847, George Abernethy Papers, MSS 929, Oregon Historical Society, Portland.

54. Bidwell, "Journey to California," 61.

55. Johnson and Winter, *Route across the Rocky Mountains*, 306.

56. Hastings, *Emigrants' Guide*, 110.

57. Bidwell, "Journey to California," 61.

58. Hastings, *Emigrants' Guide*, 132.

59. "Letter of Dr. John Marsh to Hon. Lewis Cass," *California Historical Society Quarterly* 22, no. 4 (Dec. 1943): 321.

60. Hastings, *Emigrants' Guide*, 132.

61. Johnson and Winter, *Route across the Rocky Mountains*, 306.

62. John Sutter to unknown recipient, May 4, 1845, printed in *California Farmer and Journal of Useful Sciences* (San Francisco), Mar. 13, 1857.

63. Hurtado, *John Sutter*, 68–80.

64. Stacey Smith, *Freedom's Frontier: California and the Struggle over Unfree Labor, Emancipation, and Reconstruction* (Chapel Hill: University of North Carolina Press, 2014), 15–24; Andrés Reséndez, *The Other Slavery: The Uncovered Story of Indian Slavery in America* (Boston: Houghton Mifflin Harcourt, 2016), 250–265; Michael F. Magliari, "Free Soil, Unfree Labor: Cave Johnson Couts and the Binding of Indian Workers in California, 1850–1867," *Pacific Historical Review* 73 (2004): 349–389; Michael F. Magliari, "Free State Slavery: Bound Indian Labor and Slave Trafficking in California's Sacramento Valley, 1850–1864," *Pacific Historical Review* 81 (2012): 155–192.

65. As quoted in George R. Stewart, *The California Trail: An Epic with Many Heroes* (New York: McGraw-Hill, 1962), 95.

66. Gillis and Magliari, *John Bidwell and California*, 248–310; Reséndez, *The Other Slavery*, 250–263, esp. 259–262.

67. Robert Semple, "A Sketch of the Country," in Lansford Hastings, *A New History of Oregon and California* (Cincinnati, 1847), 154. This was a reprinted edition of Hastings's 1845 *Emigrants' Guide to Oregon and California*, but with Semple's description and the text of the Oregon Treaty tacked on to the end.

68. Robert Evans, Jr., "The Economics of American Negro Slavery," in *Aspects of Labor Economics* (Princeton, NJ: Princeton University Press, 1962), 199.

69. Nunis, *Bidwell-Bartleson Party*, 74n39.

70. Bidwell to John Townshend, Nov. 26, 1845, John Bidwell Letters, MSS HM 31549, HL.

71. Bidwell to Townshend, Jan. 26, 1846, Bidwell Letters, MSS HM 31549. See also William Barnett and William Hague to John Marsh and John Sutter, May 18, 1841, Marsh Family Papers, BL.

72. Nunis, *Bidwell-Bartleson Party*, 257–258.

73. Nunis, *Bidwell-Bartleson Party*; Gillis and Magliari, *John Bidwell and California*, 73–80, 129–150.

74. See especially Sarah Rodríguez, " 'Children of the Great Mexican Family': American Immigration to Northern Mexico, 1810–1861" (PhD diss., University of Pennsylvania, 2015).

75. Charles Weber, "Proclamation," July 4, 1845, Weber Family Papers, MSS C-B 829, BL.

76. Hastings, *Emigrants' Guide*, 94.

77. Semple, "Sketch of the Country," 156.

78. Edward Brinley, Jr., to Francis Brinley, Jan. 25, 1847, Papers of Edward Brinley Jr., MSS HM 74000–74090, HL.

79. Vallejo to Thomas Marsh, Nov. 11, 1841; San Jose Alvarado pronouncement, Nov. 11, 1841; Vallejo pronouncement, Nov. 13, 1841, all in C-B 10, Vallejo Papers, BL.

80. Faxon Dean Atherton to Larkin, Jan. 13, 1841, in Hammond, *Larkin Papers*, 1:71–72; Henry Edward Vernon to Vallejo, Apr. 16, 1842, Vallejo Papers, BL. See also William Binckley, *The Expansionist Movement in Texas, 1836–1850* (New York: Da Capo, 1970), 16–122.

81. See the discussion of "el lenguaje de la colonia de Austin" in Almonte to Vallejo, May 18, 1841; Anastasio Bustamente to Vallejo, Mar. 10, 1841, both in Vallejo Papers, BL.

82. William L. Lewis to Larkin, Sept. 18, 1841, in Hammond, *Larkin Papers*, 1:120–121.

83. Fredrick Hudson (*New York Herald* office) to Larkin, Oct. 14, 1845, 4:24; George P. Hammond, "Preface," 4:x–xi, both in in Hammond, *Larkin Papers*; Hague and Langum, *Thomas O. Larkin*, 108–110.

84. Charles Wilkes, *Narrative of the United States Exploring Expedition* (Philadelphia, 1845), 5:171–172.

85. Gene Smith, "The War That Wasn't: Thomas ap Catesby Jones's Seizure of Monterey," *California History* 66, no. 2 (June 1987): 104–113.

86. Edward P. Crapol, *John Tyler: The Accidental President* (Chapel Hill: University of North Carolina Press, 2012), 119.

87. Frank A. Knapp, Jr., "Mexican Fear of Manifest Destiny in California," in *Essays in Mexican History*, ed. Thomas Cotner and Carlos Castañeda (Austin: University of Texas Press, 1958), 195; Smith, "War That Wasn't," 113; Larkin to James Gordon Bennett, Feb. 10, 1843, in Hammond, *Larkin Papers*, 2:6; David Pletcher, *The Diplomacy of Annexation: Texas, Oregon, and the Mexican War* (Columbia: University of Missouri Press, 1973), 100–101.

88. Smith, "War That Wasn't," 111; Rosenus, *General M. G. Vallejo*, 54.

89. Gene A. Smith, "Thomas ap Catesby Jones and the First Implementation of the Monroe Doctrine," *Southern California Quarterly* 76, no. 2 (Summer 1994): 139–152.

90. Thomas Richards, Jr., "The Lansford Hastings Imaginary: Visions of Democratic Patriarchy in the Americas," in *Inventing Destiny: Cultural Explorations of US Expansion*, ed. Jimmy L. Bryan (Lawrence: University Press of Kansas, 2019).

91. Lansford Hastings to Thomas Marsh, Mar. 26, 1846, Marsh Family Papers, BL; Bidwell, *Echoes of the Past*, 92–94; Charles Putnam to Joseph Putnam, July 11, 1846, in *Overland in 1846: Diaries and Letters of the California-Oregon Trail*, vol. 2, ed. Dale Morgan (Georgetown, CA: Talisman Press, 1963), 603; Ben E. Green to John C. Calhoun, Apr. 11, 1844, in *The Papers of John Calhoun*, vol. 18: *1844*, ed. Clyde N. Wilson (Columbia: University of South Carolina Press, 1989), 203–204.

92. Bagley, *So Rugged and Mountainous*, 87.

93. Farnham to Marsh, July 6, 1845, Marsh Family Papers, BL.

94. Larkin to Marsh, July 8, 1845, as printed in Hawgood, *First and Last Consul*, 24.

95. George D. Lyman, *John Marsh, Pioneer: The Life Story of a Trail-Blazer on Six Frontiers* (New York: Chautauqua Press, 1931), 262–267.

96. Weber to Marsh, Nov. 25, 1845, and Mar. 8, 1846, both in Marsh Family Papers, BL.

97. On Hastings's connections to Brannan and both of their connections with Farnham, see the letters in Will Bagley, ed., *Scoundrel's Tale: The Samuel Brannan Papers* (Logan: Utah State University Press), 75–85. On the Mormons' connections with Farnham, see Orson Hyde to Brigham Young, Oct. 21, 1845, Brigham Young Office Files, LDS

Church History Library, Salt Lake City, UT; Hyde to Young, Oct. 31, 1845, in Journal History of the Church, LDS Church History Library, Salt Lake City, UT. On the possible McLoughlin connection, see Will Bagley, "Lansford Warren Hastings: Scoundrel or Visionary?," *Overland Journal* 12, no. 1 (1994): 17.

98. Hurtado, *John Sutter*; Bagley, *Scoundrel's Tale*; Bagley, "Lansford Warren Hastings"; Churchill, "Thomas Jefferson Farnham"; Bidwell, *Echoes of the Past*, 68. Hastings's "scoundrel" status also stems from his promotion of the Hastings Cutoff— the mythical shortcut that led to the Donner Party disaster.

99. Robert G. Cowan, *Ranchos of California: A List of Spanish Concessions, 1775–1822; and Mexican Grants, 1822–1846* (Fresno, CA: Academy Library Guild, 1956), 106.

100. Miller, *Juan Alvarado*, 97–101; Carlos Manuel Salomon, *Pío Pico: The Last Governor of Mexican California* (Norman: University of Oklahoma Press, 2010), 71–73; Bancroft, *History of California*, 4:281–297.

101. Bancroft, *History of California*, 4:293–294.

102. For the Mexican use of convict soldiers, see Peter Guardino, *The Dead March: A History of the Mexican-American War* (Cambridge, MA: Harvard University Press, 2017), 52–64.

103. John Coffin Jones to Larkin, Oct. 22, 1842, 1:300–301; Henry Fitch to James McKinlay, June 9, 1842, 1:236, both in Hammond, *Larkin Papers*; Vallejo to Sutter, Dec. 13, 1844, Vallejo Papers, BL; Osio, *History of Alta California*, 212–217; Bancroft, *History of California*, 4:363–367.

104. Hurtado, *John Sutter*, 136–151; Bancroft, *History of California*, 4:455–517.

105. Hurtado, *John Sutter*, 140–141.

106. Sutter to Pierson Reading, Oct. 30, 1844; Sutter to Reading, Jan. 15, 1845, both in John Augustus Sutter Papers, C-B 631, BL.

107. William A. Streeter, "Recollections of Historical Events in California," ed. William Henry Ellison, *California Historical Society* 18, no. 2 (June 1939): 160; Larkin to Calhoun, Jan. 25, 1845, in Hammond, *Larkin Papers*, 3:22–24.

108. Hurtado, *John Sutter*, 142–144.

109. Sutter to Reading, Jan. 16, 1845, Sutter Papers, BL.

110. Sutter to Reading, Jan. 16, 1845; John Bidwell, "California, 1841–1848," 122–126, C-D 8, Bear Flag Memoirs, BL; Lyman, *John Marsh*, 254–257.

111. Streeter, "Recollections," 157–159.

112. Streeter, "Recollections," 157–159; Bancroft, *History of California*, 4:500–501.

113. Alvarado and Castro to Micheltorena, Jan. 6, 1845, as quoted in Bancroft, *History of California*, 4:489–490; Miller, *Juan Alvarado*, 107.

114. Stearns to Larkin, Mar. 11, 1845, in Hammond, *Larkin Papers*, 3:61–62; see also John Coffin Jones to Larkin, Feb. 16, 1845, in Hammond, *Larkin Papers*, 3:45–46.

115. This is also known as the Second Battle of Cahuenga Pass.

116. Streeter, "Recollections," 157–159; Bidwell, "California, 1841–1848," 122–128; Chamberlain, "Memoirs," 15–19; Osio, *History of Alta California*, 219–221; John Gantt to John Marsh, Mar. 11, 1845, Marsh Family Papers; Larkin to Calhoun, Mar. 24, 1845, in Hammond, *Larkin Papers*, 3:95–96; Frank J. Polley, "Americans at the Battle of Cahuenga," *Annual Publication of the Historical Society of Southern California, Los Angeles* 3, no. 2 (1894): 47–54; Bancroft, *History of California*, 4:506–507.

117. Bancroft, *History of California*, 4:507n34.

118. Weber estimated 680 Americans were in California in 1845. Weber, *Mexican Frontier*, 209.

119. Gonzalez, "War and the Making of History." Gonzalez estimated that between 1829 and 1845 there were twelve rebellions, in which a maximum of fifteen people died.

120. Bancroft, *History of California*, 4:543.

121. John Gantt to John Marsh, Mar. 11, 1845, Marsh Family Papers, BL.

122. José Castro to Charles Weber, Apr. 12, 1845, Weber Family Papers, MSS C-B 829, BL.

123. David J. Langum, *Law and Community on the Mexican California Frontier: Anglo-American Expatriates and the Clash of Legal Traditions, 1821–1846* (Norman: University of Oklahoma Press, 1987), 131–278.

124. Weber proclamation, Mar. 27, 1845; Weber to Marsh, Mar. 24, 1845, both in Weber Family Papers, BL.

125. Bancroft, *History of California*, 4:599.

126. Larkin to Micheltorena, Mar. 21, 1845, in Hammond, *Larkin Papers*, 3:74–75.

127. John Coffin Jones to Larkin, Feb. 25, 1845, in Hammond, *Larkin Papers*, 3:49 (emphasis in original).

128. *Daily National Intelligencer*, May 7, 1845. This particular article cited the *Nashville Union* and *New Orleans Courier* as calling for a replay of the "Texas game," which the *National Intelligencer* argued against. The phrase had become ubiquitous enough that a correspondent from New York City used the phrase in a letter to Larkin: Alfred Robinson to Larkin, May 29, 1845, in Hammond, *Larkin Papers*, 3:204–206.

129. The phrase "Defensores de la Patria" is in Micheltorena proclamation, May 11, 1844, Vallejo Papers, BL. See also Miller, *Juan Alvarado*, 100–101; Bancroft, *History of California*, 4:406–408.

130. See, for example, Larkin to James Jackson Jarves, Nov. 4, 1844, 2:271; Larkin to Calhoun, Aug. 18, 1844, 3:204–207; John Parrott to Larkin, June 29, 1844, 2:155; Larkin to Buchanan, Sept. 29, 1845, 3:367; Faxon Dean Atherton to Larkin, Sept. 8, 1845, 3:340–343, all in Hammond, *Larkin Papers*.

131. Bancroft, *History of California*, 4:605.

132. Salomon, *Pío Pico*, 82–85.

133. Salomon, *Pío Pico*, 82–85.

134. Rosenus, *General M. G. Vallejo*, 78.

135. Marsh to Lewis Cass, Jan. 20, 1846, Marsh Family Papers, BL.

136. Stephen Reynolds to Larkin, Apr. 19, 1845, in Hammond, *Larkin Papers*, 3:139–141.

137. John Coffin Jones to Larkin, May 23, 1845, in Hammond, *Larkin Papers*, 3:192–194.

138. Marsh to Larkin, Aug. 12, 1845, in Hammond, *Larkin Papers*, 3:308–310.

139. Larkin to Faxon Dean Atherton, June 6, 1845, Faxon Dean Atherton Papers, MSS 69 A5, BL.

140. Larkin to Marsh, July 8, 1845, Marsh Family Papers.

141. John Bidwell, "Frémont in the Conquest of California" (Feb. 1891), 522, as quoted in Gillis and Magliari, *John Bidwell and California*, 103.

Chapter 6 • *The White Yeomen's Republic of Oregon*

1. *Oregon Spectator*, Feb. 5, 1846; Warren J. Brier, "Political Censorship in the *Oregon Spectator*," *Pacific Historical Review* 31, no. 3 (Aug. 1962): 235–240.

2. *Oregon Spectator*, Feb. 5, 1846.

3. Walter Nugent, *Habits of Empire: A History of American Expansion* (New York: Vintage, 2008), 157.

4. See, for example, the Sons and Daughters of Oregon Pioneers, http://oregonsdop .org; Oregon Territory and Its Pioneers, http://www.oregonpioneers.com/ortrail.htm.

5. Melinda Marie Jetté, *At the Hearth of the Crossed Races: A French-Indian Community in Nineteenth-Century Oregon, 1812–1859* (Corvallis: Oregon State University Press, 2015), 12–69; Anne Hyde, *Empires, Nations, and Families: A History of the North American West, 1800–1860* (Lincoln: University of Nebraska Press, 2011), 89–133.

6. Jetté, *At the Hearth*, 67; Robert Boyd, "Lower Chinookan Disease and Demography," in *Chinookan Peoples of the Lower Columbia*, ed. Robert Boyd, Kenneth Ames, and Tony Johnson (Seattle: University of Washington Press, 2013), 239–241.

7. Jetté, *At the Hearth*, 69; William L. Lang, "The Chinookan Encounter with Euro-Americans in the Lower Columbia River Valley," in Boyd, Ames, and Johnson, *Chinookan Peoples*, 268.

8. Robert Loewenberg, "Saving Oregon Again: A Western Perennial?," *Oregon Historical Quarterly* 78, no. 4 (Dec. 1977): 346; Robert Loewenberg, *Equality on the Oregon Frontier: Jason Lee and the Methodist Mission, 1834–1843* (Seattle: University of Washington Press, 1976); Malcolm Clark, *Eden Seekers: The Settlement of Oregon, 1818–1862* (Boston: Houghton Mifflin, 1981), 92–164; Clifford Drury, *Marcus and Narcissa Whitman and the Opening of Old Oregon*, 2 vols. (Glendale, CA: Arthur H. Clark, 1973), chaps. 10–15.

9. John Unruh, *The Plains Across: The Overland Emigrants and the Trans-Mississippi West, 1840–1860* (Urbana: University of Illinois Press, 1979), 90–92.

10. Unruh, *Plains Across*; Will Bagley, *So Rugged and Mountainous: Blazing the Trails to Oregon and California, 1812–1848* (Norman: University of Oklahoma Press, 2010), 66–67.

11. Jetté, *At the Hearth*, 92–121.

12. Jason Lee to Methodist Missionary Board, Mar. 15, 1841, Oregon Methodist Missionary Papers, MSS 017, Collins Memorial Library Archives, University of Puget Sound, Tacoma, WA (hereafter, UPS).

13. Alvan Waller to Amos Cooke, Nov. 30, 1841, Amos Cooke Letters, MSS 1223, Oregon Historical Society, Portland (hereafter, OHS); Marcus Whitman to David Greene, Nov. 1, 1843, in Letters and Papers of the American Board of Commissioners for Foreign Missions, vol. 138: Oregon Indians, 1838–1844, 723, MSS 1200, OHS (hereafter, LPABC).

14. Unruh, *Plains Across*, 119.

15. Jason Lee and J. H. Frost to Charles Pitman, Mar. 30, 1843, UPS.

16. Unruh, *Plains Across*, 93–94; Dorothy Johansen, "A Working Hypothesis for the Study of Migrations," *Pacific Historical Review* 36 (Feb. 1967): 1–12.

17. Dean May, *Three Frontiers: Family, Land, and Society in the American West, 1850–1900* (New York: Cambridge University Press, 1994), 41–42; Bagley, *So Rugged and Mountainous*, 129.

18. James Christy Bell, Jr., *Opening a Highway to the Pacific, 1838–1846* (New York: AMS Press, 1968), 124–125; William A. Bowen, *The Willamette Valley: Migration and Settlement on the Oregon Frontier* (Seattle: University of Washington Press, 1978), 17–18.

19. Melvin C. Jacobs, *Winning Oregon: A Study of an Expansionist Movement* (Caldwell, ID: Caxton Printers, 1938), 56–58.

20. John McCoy, "Memoirs," MSS 1166, OHS.

21. John Mack Faragher, *Women and Men on the Overland Trail* (New Haven, CT: Yale University Press, 1979), 20–24.

22. John Couch to John Cushing, Mar. 24, 1845, Elkanah Walker Papers, MSS WA 1-86, Huntington Library, San Marino, CA (hereafter, HL).

23. Michael Husband, "Senator Lewis Linn and the Oregon Question," *Missouri Historical Review* 66, no. 1 (Oct. 1971): 1–20.

24. Law of Land Claims, July 5, 1843, in Joseph Brown, *Brown's Political History of the Oregon Government . . .* (Portland, OR, 1892), 104.

25. Julius Wilm, *Settlers as Conquerors: Free Land Policy in Antebellum America* (Stuttgart, Germany: Franz Steiner, 2018), 13–65.

26. Roy M. Robbins, *Our Landed Heritage: The Public Domain, 1776–1936* (Princeton, NJ: Princeton University Press, 1942), 72–91; Reeve Huston, "Land Conflict and Land Policy in the United States, 1785–1841," in *The World of the Revolutionary American Republic: Land, Labor, and the Conflict for a Continent*, ed. Andrew Shankman (New York: Routledge, 2014), 324–345; John R. Van Atta, *Securing the West: Politics, Public Lands, and the Fate of the Old Republic, 1785–1850* (Baltimore, MD: Johns Hopkins University Press, 2014), 228–231.

27. Jeremy Atack, "Tenants and Yeomen in the Nineteenth Century," *Agricultural History* 62, no. 3 (Summer 1988): 31.

28. Peter Burnett, *Recollections of an Old Pioneer* (New York, 1880), 98.

29. Kathleen Neils Conzen, "A Saga of Families," in *The Oxford History of the American West*, ed. Clyde A. Milner, Carol A. O'Connor, and Martha A. Sandweiss (New York: Oxford University Press, 1994), 315–358.

30. Medorem Crawford, *A Letter from Medorem Crawford, 1845* (Eugene: Friends of the Library, University of Oregon), 2.

31. Joseph Williams, *Narrative of a Tour from the State of Indiana to the Oregon Territory in the Years 1841–2* (Cincinnati, OH, 1843), 22–23.

32. Alva Shaw, letter, 1844, MSS 941, OHS.

33. Abraham H. Garrison, "Reminiscences, 1903–1906," Abraham Garrison Recollections and Correspondence, MSS 874, OHS.

34. Bell, *Opening a Highway*, 126; May, *Three Frontiers*, 43; James Oakes, *Slavery and Freedom: An Interpretation of the Old South* (New York: Knopf, 1990), 80–136, esp. 94–96; Edward Baptist, *The Other Half Has Never Been Told: Slavery and the Making of American Capitalism* (New York: Basic, 2014), 292–297.

35. Bell, *Opening a Highway*, 126; Robert Johannsen, *Frontier Politics and the Sectional Conflict: The Pacific Northwest on the Eve of the Civil War* (Seattle: University of Washington Press, 1955), 18–21.

36. Richard Rowland to unknown recipient (likely his sister), Nov. 1840, MSS 1180, OHS.

37. Peter Burnett, letter to *Jefferson Inquirer*, 1845, as quoted in Kenneth R. Cole-

man, *Dangerous Subjects: James D. Saules and the Rise of Black Exclusion in Oregon* (Corvallis: Oregon State University Press, 2017), 111.

38. Dana Elizabeth Weiner, *Race and Rights: Fighting Slavery and Prejudice in the Old Northwest, 1830–1870* (DeKalb: Northern Illinois University Press, 2013), 42–45.

39. Burnett, *Recollections of an Old Pioneer*, 221.

40. Coleman, *Dangerous Subjects*, 89–118; Thomas C. McClintock, "James Saules, Peter Burnett, and the Oregon Black Exclusion Law of June 1844," *Pacific Northwest Quarterly* 86, no. 3 (Summer 1995): 121–130, 126–127; Quintard Taylor, "Slaves and Free Men: Blacks in the Oregon Country, 1840–1860," *Oregon Historical Quarterly* 83, no. 2 (Summer 1982): 156.

41. Gordon Wood, *The Creation of the American Republic, 1776–1787* (Chapel Hill: University of North Carolina Press, 1969); Daniel T. Rodgers, "Republicanism: The Career of a Concept," *Journal of American History* 79, no. 1 (June 1992): 11–38.

42. Charlotte Mathery Kirkwood, "Reminiscence of Journey to Oregon in 1843 and Life in Oregon," Robert Lockley Collection, HL.

43. *St. Louis Gazette*, Nov. 10, 1845.

44. Nancy M. Bogart, "Reminiscences of Journey across the Plains in 1843 with Dr. Marcus Whitman's Caravan and Early Life in Oregon," Fred Lockley Papers and Addenda, 1849–1958, HL.

45. "A Bill to Authorize the Adoption of Measures for the Occupation and Settlement of the Territory of Oregon," Jan. 3, 1843, Oregon Methodist Missionary Papers, UPS; "The Donation Land Claim Act (1850)," University of Oregon, http://pages .uoregon.edu/mjdennis/courses/hst469_donation.htm (accessed Apr. 6, 2018).

46. See, for example, John McLoughlin to Henry Spalding and Marcus Whitman, Apr. 1837, in LPABC, 50.

47. Overton Johnson and William Winter, *Route across the Rocky Mountains* (Lafayette, IN, 1846), 64.

48. "Oregon Provisional Government Enacting Prohibition, 1844," Oregon State Archives, http://sos.oregon.gov/archives/exhibits/highlights/Documents/prohibition -law-document-1209.pdf (accessed Apr. 6, 2018).

49. Bowen, *Willamette Valley*, 18–21; Jacobs, *Winning Oregon*, 62–65; Conevery Bolton Valencius, *The Health of the Country: How American Settlers Understand Themselves and Their Land* (New York: Basic, 2002), 24–25, 79–84.

50. Bagley, *So Rugged and Mountainous*, 121–125.

51. John Minto, "Reminiscences of Experiences on the Oregon Trail in 1844," ed. H. S. Lyman, *Quarterly of the Oregon Historical Society* 2, no. 2 (June 1901): 130.

52. Abner Sylvester Baker, "The Oregon Pioneer Tradition in the Nineteenth Century" (PhD diss., University of Oregon, 1968), 56–84; Frederick Merk, *The Oregon Question: Essays in Anglo-American Diplomacy and Politics* (Cambridge, MA: Harvard University Press, 1967), 235–236, esp. 236n6 for an older literature taking this attitude.

53. William Gray diary, William Gray Papers, MSS 1201, OHS; Robert Newell, "Account of 1843 Champoeg Meeting," Robert Newell Papers, MSS 1197, OHS; *Oregon Spectator*, July 4, 1846.

54. Walter C. Woodward, *Political Parties in Oregon, 1843–1868* (Portland, OR: J. K. Gill, 1913), 28–30.

55. John Hussey, *Champoeg, Place of Transition: A Disputed History* (Portland: Oregon Historical Society, 1967), 136.

56. Gustavus Hines, *Life on the Plains of the Pacific: Oregon: Its History, Conditions, and Prospects . . .* (Buffalo, NY, 1852), 420.

57. Hines, *Life on the Plains*, 421.

58. Robert Carlton Clark, *History of the Willamette Valley, Oregon* (Chicago, IL: Clarke, 1927), 231–235; Clark, *Eden Seekers*, 143–145.

59. Henry Viola, "The Wilkes Expedition on the Pacific Coast," *Pacific Northwest Quarterly* 80, no. 1 (Jan. 1989): 21–31.

60. Viola, "Wilkes Expedition," 25.

61. According to Wilkes's 1845 published account, he told several Methodist missionaries that the United States would soon "extend their jurisdiction" over them, but in his original diary he made no mention of such a claim, and the diary aligns much more closely to other accounts of his trip to Oregon. In all likelihood, Wilkes added the line about US annexation when he was reworking his account for publication, for by that time expansionism was once again popular (and Wilkes, for various reasons, was not), and Wilkes could portray himself as an agent of US empire. Edmund S. Meany, ed., "Diary of Wilkes in the Northwest," *Washington Historical Quarterly* 16, no. 1 (Jan. 1926): 48–49; Charles Wilkes, *Narrative of the United States Exploring Expedition*, 5 vols. (Philadelphia, PA, 1845), 4:352–353.

62. Wilkes, *Narrative*, 5:171–172.

63. "Petition of Citizens of Oregon in 1843," as quoted in William Gray, *A History of Oregon, 1792–1849* (Portland, OR, 1870), 293; Clark, *History of the Willamette Valley*, 145; Clark, *Eden Seekers*, 143–145.

64. Jonathan Richmond to G. P. Disoway, Aug. 18, 1841, Oregon Methodist Missionary Papers, UPS.

65. "Petition of 1840," as quoted in Gray, *History of Oregon*, 194 (emphasis in original).

66. Whitman to David Greene, May 30, 1843, LPABC, 714–716.

67. Whitman to Greene, Nov. 1, 1843, LPABC, 723–724; Jason Lee to Missionary Board, Mar. 15, 1841, Oregon Methodist Missionary Papers, UPS; David Leslie to Charles Pitman, Nov. 20, 1842, Oregon Methodist Missionary Papers, UPS; Alvan Waller to Amos Cooke, Aug. 25, 1842, Amos Cooke Letters, MSS 1223, OHS; Walker to Greene, Oct. 10, 1843, LPABC, 556–559.

68. Jason Lee to the Mission Board, Sept. 23, 1841, Oregon Methodist Missionary Papers, UPS.

69. Loewenberg, *Equality on the Oregon Frontier*, 188–194; Dorothy Nafus Morrison, *Outpost: John McLoughlin and the Far Northwest* (Portland: Oregon Historical Society, 1999), 390–396. See also *The Letters of John McLoughlin*, 7 vols., ed. E. E. Rich (Toronto, ON: Champlain Society, 1944), 7:195–210 (hereafter, *LJM*).

70. Petition of Alvan Waller to Roger Taney, Feb. 8, 1844, Alvan Waller Papers, MSS 1210, OHS.

71. Hyde, *Empires, Nations, and Families*, 141.

72. McLoughlin to the HBC, Oct. 31, 1842, *LJM*, 4:76–77. White was a former Methodist missionary who had left the mission over conflicts with Jason Lee.

73. Husband, "Senator Lewis Linn"; William A. Hansen, "Thomas Hart Benton and the Oregon Question," *Missouri Historical Review* 63, no. 4 (July 1969): 489–497.

74. Hussey, *Champoeg*, 119–172; Morrison, *Outpost*, 365–372; Dorothy Johansen and Charles Gates, *Empire of the Columbia: A History of the Pacific Northwest*, 2nd ed. (New York: Harper and Row, 1967), 188–190; Hubert Howe Bancroft, *History of Oregon* (San Francisco, CA, 1886), 1:166–178, 203–221.

75. Robert Newell to *Oregon Herald*, Jan. 22, 1867, Newell-Gray Letters, Robert Newell Papers, MSS 1197, OHS.

76. Robert Loewenberg, "Creating a Provisional Government in Oregon: A Revision," *Pacific Northwest Quarterly* 68, no. 1 (Jan. 1977): 13–24; Loewenberg, *Equality on the Oregon Frontier*, 140–168, 195–228; Hines, *Life on the Plains*, 422.

77. Minutes of Champoeg Meeting, June 25, 1843, in Brown, *Brown's Political History*, 97.

78. Oregon Organic Laws, May 1844, in "The Oregon Archives, 1841–1843," ed. David C. Duniway and Neil. R. Riggs, *Oregon Historical Quarterly* 60, no. 2 (June 1959): 273.

79. Loewenberg, "Creating a Provisional Government," 22–24.

80. P. L. Edwards, "Instructions to Immigrants," letter to *St. Louis New Era*, May 25, 1843, MSS 235, OHS.

81. "State," in *American Dictionary of the English Language* (1828), http://websters dictionary1828.com/Dictionary/state.

82. Leslie to Pitman, Nov. 20, 1842.

83. Frederick Merk, "The Oregon Pioneers and the Boundary," in Merk, *Oregon Question*, 233–254.

84. Husband, "Senator Lewis Linn," 15–16.

85. Johansen and Gates, *Empire of the Columbia*, 191–194; Hussey, *Champoeg*, 168–170; Jetté, *At the Hearth*, 172–179; Woodward, *Political Parties in Oregon*, 20–23.

86. Hussey, *Champoeg*, 168–170. See also Bancroft, *History of Oregon*, 1:471.

87. Executive Committee to Legislative Committee, June 18, 1844, in Brown, *Brown's Political History*, 131–132.

88. Executive Committee to Legislative Committee, Dec. 16, 1844, in Brown, *Brown's Political History*, 135–136.

89. Executive Committee to Legislative Committee, Dec. 16, 1844.

90. John McLoughlin to the Governor, Deputy, Commissioner, and Committee of the HBC, Nov. 20, 1844, 7:32; McLoughlin to HBC, July 4, 1844, 6:199; McLoughlin to HBC, Mar. 28, 1845, 7:73; McLoughlin to HBC, Dec. 12, 1845, 7:153; McLoughlin to John Pelly, July 12, 1846, 7:162, all in *LJM*; Peter Burnett, "Letter from Peter Burnett, Esq.," *Quarterly of the Oregon Historical Society* 24, no. 1 (Mar. 1923): 108; Elijah White to the Bureau of Indian Affairs, Apr. 4, 1845, in White, *A Concise View of Oregon Territory, Compiled from Letters and Official Reports, Together with the Organic Laws of the Colony* (Washington, DC, 1846), 54; J. Quinn Thornton, *Oregon and California in 1848* (New York, 1849), 2:34.

91. White, *Concise View of Oregon Territory*, 54.

92. John McLoughlin, "Remarks," as quoted in P. S. Ogen and J. Douglas to Sir George Simpson, Mar. 16, 1847, in *LJM*, 7:296.

93. Burnett, "Letter," 107–108.

94. McLoughlin to the HBC, Dec. 12, 1845, in *LJM*, 7:153. For a similar statement, see Benjamin Stark, Jr., to Benjamin Stark, Nov. 15, 1845, Benjamin Stark Papers, MSS 115, OHS.

95. Thornton, *Oregon and California in 1848*, 2:40.

96. Andrew J. Torget, *Seeds of Empire: Cotton, Slavery, and the Transformation of the Texas Borderlands, 1800–1850* (Chapel Hill: University of North Carolina Press, 2015), 252.

97. James Nesmith to Samuel Wilson, June 27, 1845, James Nesmith Papers, MSS 577, OHS; Jason Lee to Gustavus Hines, Apr. 24 and July 1, 1844, Gustavus Hines Papers, MSS 1215, OHS; Joseph Showalter Smith, biography, MSS 2105, OHS; *Oregon Spectator*, Mar. 19, June 25, July 4, Aug. 6, Aug. 20, and Sept. 3, 1846.

98. Thornton, *Oregon and California in 1848*, 2:37.

99. Unruh, *Plains Across*, 156–200.

100. McLoughlin to HBC, Nov. 20, 1844, in *LJM*, 7:32.

101. This argument is inferred from the *Oregon Spectator*, Apr. 2, 1846, detailed below.

102. James R. Gibson, *Farming the Frontier: The Agricultural Opening of the Oregon Country, 1786–1846* (Seattle: University of Washington Press, 1985), 144; Bowen, *Willamette Valley*, 65–94.

103. Benjamin Stark to William Stark, Nov. 15, 1845, Benjamin Stark Papers, MSS 1155, OHS.

104. McLoughlin to Pelly, July 12, 1846.

105. Three overland parties traveled from Oregon to California: the Hastings Party in 1843, the Kelsey Party in 1844, and the McMahon-Clyman Party in 1845. Other evidence for Oregon-California connections can be found in Samuel McMahan [*sic*] to John Marsh, June 16, 1844, Marsh Family Papers, MSS C-B 878, Bancroft Library, Berkeley, CA (hereafter, BL); McLoughlin to HBC, Nov. 15, 1843, in *LJM*, 6:136; John Sutter to William Leidesdorff, Aug. 5, 1846, John Augustus Sutter Papers, MSS C-B 631, BL; Ewing Young to Juan Alvarado, Mar. 10, 1837, MSS WA 1-86, Elkanah Walker Papers, HL.

106. White to Office of Indian Affairs, Apr. 4, 1845, as reprinted in Elijah White, *A Concise View of Oregon Country, Its Colonial and Indian Relations, Compiled from Official Letters and Reports, Together with the Organic Laws of the Colony* (Washington, DC: T. Barnard, 1846), 54.

107. Thornton, *Oregon and California in 1848*, 2:34.

108. McLoughlin to Pelly, July 12, 1846; Burnett, "Letter," 108.

109. McLoughlin to HBC, Nov. 20, 1845, in *LJM*, 7:109

110. James Douglas to McLoughlin, Mar. 5, 1845, in *LJM*, 7:179.

111. Philip Foster to Francis Ermatinger, June 18, 1845, Philip Foster Letters, MSS 996, OHS.

112. Hussey, *Champoeg*, 169; Woodward, *Political Parties in Oregon*, 25–26; Clark, *Eden Seekers*, 194; Clark, *History of the Willamette Valley*, 308.

113. Unfortunately, no records exist that detail anything beyond the number of votes that rejected the constitutional convention. Therefore, in order to analyze the various constituencies, I place this vote alongside the vote for governor from the same election. In this election, the moderate George Abernethy won with 283 votes, defeating another moderate (75 votes), an independent of British background (130 votes),

and an Ultra-American (71 votes). Extrapolating from these numbers, I tentatively assume that the 71 Ultras from the vote for governor also rejected the constitutional convention, while the 130 independents approved it. Thus, the remaining moderates rejected the constitutional convention by a vote of 212–60. There remains a significant discrepancy in the two vote tallies: 86 more men voted in the election for governor. There are several possible explanations: perhaps the elections took place on different days, perhaps some men abstained from the question about a constitution, or perhaps the archival data are flawed. Nevertheless, the broad trend—a three-to-one ratio— seems safe to assume.

114. Oregon Provisional Government, Memorial to Congress, June 28, 1845, in Brown, *Brown's Political History*, 160–162.

115. Hussey, *Champoeg*, 169.

116. David M. Pletcher, *The Diplomacy of Annexation: Texas, Oregon, and the Mexican War* (Columbia: University of Missouri Press, 1973), 273–351.

117. White to *Daily Union*, Feb. 10, 1846, Elijah White Papers, MSS 1217, OHS.

118. Morrison, *Outpost*, 413–419; Clark, *Eden Seekers*, 176; McLoughlin to HBC, Nov. 20, 1845, in *LJM*, 7:98–102.

119. "Organic Law of the Provisional Government of Oregon," in Brown, *Brown's Political History*, 166.

120. McLoughlin to HBC, Aug. 30, 1845, in *LJM*, 7:109.

121. *Oregon Spectator*, Sept. 3, 1846.

122. Oregon Provisional Government, Memorial to Congress, June 28, 1845, in Brown, *Brown's Political History*, 161 (emphasis added).

123. James Madison, "The Federalist Papers: No. 10" (1787), *Avalon Project: Documents in Law, History, and Diplomacy*, https://avalon.law.yale.edu/18th_century/fed10 .asp.

124. *Oregon Spectator*, Apr. 2, 1846.

125. "Petition of 1840," as quoted in Gray, *History of Oregon*, 194.

Chapter 7 • *The End of the Texas Moment*

1. Alasdair Roberts, *America's First Great Depression: Economic Crisis and Political Disorder after the Panic of 1837* (Ithaca, NY: Cornell University Press, 2012), 114.

2. Ephraim Douglass Adams, *British Interests and Activities in Texas, 1838–1846* (Baltimore, MD: Johns Hopkins Press, 1910), 155–218.

3. Sam W. Haynes, *Unfinished Revolution: The Early American Republic in a British World* (Charlottesville: University of Virginia Press, 2010), 204–273; Thomas Hietala, *Manifest Design: American Exceptionalism and Empire* (Ithaca, NY: Cornell University Press, 1985), 10–54; William W. Freehling, *The Road to Disunion*, vol. 2: *Secessionists Triumphant* (New York: Oxford University Press, 2007), 372–425; Frederick Merk, *Slavery and the Annexation of Texas* (New York: Knopf, 1972), 12–31; Frederick Merk, *The Monroe Doctrine and American Expansionism, 1843–1848* (New York: Random House, 1966), 9–39.

4. *Times-Picayune* (New Orleans), June 18, 1845.

5. Letter from Andrew Jackson, Jan. 1, 1845, quoted in *Ohio Statesman* (Columbus), Jan. 21, 1845.

6. *Richmond Enquirer*, Nov. 13, 1845.

7. *New York Herald*, Feb. 22, 1845 (emphasis added).

8. *Southern Patriot* (Charleston, SC), Dec. 15, 1843.

9. *Milwaukee Weekly Sentinel*, May 27, 1843.

10. *St. Louis New Era*, quoted in *Evansville Journal*, Sept. 11, 1845.

11. *Jeffersonian Republican* (Stroudsburg, PA), quoting the *Sangamo (IL) Journal*, Feb. 5, 1846.

12. *Boon's Lick Times* (Fayette, MO), quoting the *Platte Argus*, Nov. 15, 1845.

13. *Public Ledger* (Philadelphia, PA), July 25, 1843.

14. *Congressional Globe*, Jan. 8, 1846, 29th Cong., 2nd sess., app., 278. Note that this came after Texas annexation, demonstrating that Texas was not the only concern for anglophobic Democrats.

15. John L. O'Sullivan, "Annexation," *United States Magazine and Democratic Review* 17, no. 1 (1845): 5.

16. On the importance of contingency, see William W. Freehling, *Road to Disunion*, vol. 1: *Secessionists at Bay, 1776–1854* (New York: Oxford University Press, 1991); William W. Freehling, *The Road to Disunion*, vol. 2: *Secessionists Triumphant, 1854–1861* (New York: Oxford University Press, 2007); Gary Kornblith, "Rethinking the Coming of the Civil War: A Counterfactual Exercise," *Journal of American History* 90, no. 1 (June 2003): 76–105.

17. Kenneth Anderson to Polk, Mar. 25, 1837, in *Correspondence of James K. Polk*, 12 vols., ed. Hubert Weaver (Knoxville: University of Tennessee Press, 1969–2013), 4:81–82 (hereafter, *CJP*); C. B. Raines to Polk, Sept. 10, 1842, in *CJP*, 6:647; Charles Sellers, *James K. Polk: Jacksonian, 1793–1843* (Princeton, NJ: Princeton University Press, 1957), 336–337.

18. John H. Schroeder, "Annexation or Independence: The Texas Issue in American Politics, 1836–1845," *Southwestern Historical Quarterly* 89, no. 2 (Oct. 1985): 138.

19. *Old School Democrat* (St. Louis, MO), reprinted in the *Madisonian* (Washington, DC), Jan. 19, 1844.

20. Michael Holt, *The Rise and Fall of the American Whig Party: Jacksonian Politics and the Onset of the Civil War* (New York: Oxford University Press, 2003), 105–113; Michael Holt, "The Election of 1840, Voter Mobilization, and the Emergence of the Second American Party System," in *A Master's Due: Essays in Honor of David Herbert Donald*, ed. William Cooper, Jr., Michael Holt, and John McCardell (Baton Rouge: Louisiana State University Press, 1985), 16–58. For contrasting accounts, see Ronald Formisano, "The New Political History and the Election of 1840," *Journal of Interdisciplinary History* 23, no. 4 (Spring 1993): 661–682; Robert Gray Gunderson, *The Log-Cabin Campaign* (Lexington: University of Kentucky Press, 1957).

21. Holt, "Election of 1840," 54.

22. Michael Morrison, "Westward the Curse of Empire: Texas Annexation and the American Whig Party," *Journal of the Early Republic* 10, no. 2 (Summer 1990): 221–249; Nolan Fowler, "Territorial Expansion—A Threat to the Republic?," *Pacific Northwest Quarterly* 53, no. 1 (Jan. 1962): 34–42.

23. John Tyler to Daniel Webster, Oct. 11, 1841, in *Letters and Times of the Tylers*, vol. 2, ed. Lyon G. Tyler (New York: Da Capo, 1970), 126.

24. Matt Karp, *A Vast Southern Empire: Southerners at the Helm of American Foreign Policy* (Cambridge, MA: Harvard University Press, 2016), 103.

25. Freehling, *Road to Disunion*, 2:364–407; Upshur to Tyler, Mar. 13, 1843, reprinted in William Freehling, "Unlimited Paternalism's Problems: The Transforming Moment on My Road toward Understanding Disunion," in Freehling, *The Reintegration of American History: Slavery and the Civil War* (New York: Oxford University Press, 1994), 125–129.

26. Edward P. Crapol, *John Tyler: The Accidental President* (Chapel Hill: University of North Carolina Press, 2012), 218; Freehling, *Road to Disunion*, 2:388–401; Michael Morrison, "Martin Van Buren, the Democracy, and the Partisan Politics of Texas Annexation," *Journal of Southern History* 61, no. 4 (Nov. 1995): 699.

27. Thomas Hart Benton, *Thirty Years' View* (New York, 1856), 2:581.

28. Clay to Leverett Saltonstall, Dec. 4, 1843, in *The Papers of Henry Clay, 1797–1852*, 11 vols., ed. Robert Seager II et al. (Lexington: University of Kentucky Press, 1958–1992), 9:896.

29. Aaron Brown to James Polk, Dec. 9, 1843, in *CJP*, 6:370.

30. Polk's first mention of Texas annexation occurred in early 1844: Polk to Salmon Chase, Mar. 30, 1844, in *CJP*, 7:106.

31. Walker's letters are reprinted in Frederick Merk, *Fruits of Propaganda in the Tyler Administration* (Cambridge, MA: Harvard University Press, 1971), 221–252. See also Freehling, *Road to Disunion*, 1:418–424; Merk, *Fruits of Propaganda*, 95–120; Hietala, *Manifest Design*, 27–32; Charles Sellers, *James K. Polk: Continentalist, 1843–1846* (Princeton, NJ: Princeton University Press, 1966), 50–63; Schroeder, "Annexation or Independence," 159–160.

32. Calhoun to Richard Pakenham, Apr. 18, 1844, in *The Papers of John Calhoun*, vol. 18: *1844*, ed. Clyde N. Wilson (Columbia: University of South Carolina Press, 1989), 273–281.

33. *Daily National Intelligencer*, Apr. 27, 1844; *Daily Globe* (Washington, DC), Apr. 27, 1844; Clay to Thomas Peters and John Jackson, July 27, 1844, in Seager et al., *Papers of Henry Clay*, 10:89–91.

34. Robert Remini, *Henry Clay: Statesman for the Union* (New York: Norton, 1991), 644–645.

35. Edwin A. Miles, " 'Fifty-Four Forty or Fight': An American Political Legend," *Mississippi Valley Historical Review* 44, no. 2 (Sept. 1957): 291–309.

36. Major Wilson, *Space, Time, and Freedom: The Quest for Nationality and the Irrepressible Conflict, 1815–1861* (Westport, CT: Greenwood, 1974), esp. 108–112.

37. Cave Johnson to Polk, Mar. 10, 1844, in *CJP*, 7:87; Miles, "Fifty-Four Forty or Fight," 293–294.

38. Sellers, *Polk: Continentalist*, 76–107; Morrison, "Martin Van Buren."

39. Morrison, "Martin Van Buren."

40. Sellers, *Polk: Continentalist*, 159; David Pletcher, *The Diplomacy of Annexation: Texas, Oregon, and the Mexican War* (Columbia: University of Missouri Press, 1973), 179.

41. *The Texas Question, Reviewed by an Adopted Citizen* (New York, 1844).

42. *Daily Globe* (Washington, DC), June 1, 1844, as quoted in Miles, "Fifty-Four Forty or Fight," 295 (emphasis added).

43. *Illinois State Register* (Springfield), July 12, 1844.

44. This interpretation is frequently repeated in syntheses. See Steven Hahn, *A Nation without Borders: The United States and Its World in an Age of Civil Wars, 1830–*

1910 (New York: Viking, 2016), 169; Daniel Walker Howe, *What Hath God Wrought? The Transformation of America, 1815–1848* (New York: Oxford University Press, 2007), 688; Sean Wilentz, *The Rise of American Democracy: Jefferson to Lincoln* (New York: Norton, 2005), 574.

45. Holt, *Rise and Fall*, 194–206.

46. Joel Sutherland to Polk, Nov. 9, 1844, 8:297; John Mumford to Polk, June 6, 1844, 7:230; Edwin Croswell to Polk, Nov. 30, 1844, 8:382; Gansevoort Melville to Polk, Oct. 26, 1844, 8:224, all in *CJP*. See also Julien Mauduit, "Canadian Interference in American Politics: The 1840 Presidential Election," in *Revolutions across Borders: Jacksonian America and the Canadian Rebellion*, ed. Maxime Dagenais and Julien Mauduit (Montreal, QC: McGill-Queen's University Press, 2019), 239–263.

47. John Quincy Adams, May 25, 1843, in *Memoirs of John Quincy Adams*, vol. 11, ed. Charles Francis Adams (New York: AMS Press, 1970), 346.

48. Charles McCoy, *Polk and the Presidency* (New York: Haskelly House, 1973); Leonard D. White, *The Jacksonians: A Study of Administrative History, 1829–1861* (New York: Macmillan, 1954), 50–66; John Pinheiro, *Manifest Ambition: James K. Polk and Civil-Military Relations during the Mexican War* (Westport, CT: Praeger Security International, 2007), 131–154; Robert Merry, *A Country of Vast Designs: James K. Polk, the Mexican War, and the Conquest of the American Continent* (New York: Simon and Schuster, 2010), 1–12; Amy S. Greenberg, *A Wicked War: Polk, Clay, Lincoln, and the 1846 U.S. Invasion of Mexico* (New York: Knopf, 2012), 67–110. Amy S. Greenberg has also argued that Polk's wife, Sarah, was a crucial influence on Polk and indeed may have been the hidden driver of many of his crucial decisions. Greenberg, *Lady First: The World of First Lady Sarah Polk* (New York: Knopf, 2019), chaps. 4 and 5.

49. Crapol, *John Tyler*, 127.

50. Andrew Kennedy, as quoted in Crapol, *John Tyler*, 121.

51. Tyler to Caleb Cushing, Oct. 14, 1845, in Tyler, *Letters and Times of the Tylers*, 2:445–446.

52. Alexander Anderson to James Polk, July 11, 1844, 7:339; Polk to Andrew Jackson, July 22, 1844, 7:380, both in *CJP*.

53. Freehling, *Road to Disunion*, 1:446–449; Ken S. Mueller, *Senator Benton and the People: Master Race Democracy on the Early American Frontiers* (DeKalb: Northern Illinois University Press, 2014), 195–221.

54. Polk to William Haywood, Jr., Aug. 9, 1845, in *CJP*, 10:140.

55. J. George Harris to Polk, June 5, 1844, 7:199; Alexander Anderson to Polk, July 11, 1844, 7:339–341; Andrew J. Donelson to Polk, Dec. 24, 1844, 8:461; Jacob Martin to Polk, Jan. 25, 1845, 9:72–73; Donelson to Polk, 9:80; Thomas Ritchie to Polk, Feb. 17, 1845, 9:113–114; James Hamilton to Polk, Feb. 23, 1845, 9:129–130; Leonard Cheatham to Polk, Mar. 7, 1845, 9:179; Donelson to Polk, Mar. 18, 1845, 9:205–207; Donelson to Polk, Mar. 19, 1845, 9:207–208; Archibald Yell to Polk, Mar. 28, 1845, 9:227–228, all in *CJP*.

56. Peter Daniel to Polk, Mar. 22, 1845, in *CJP*, 9:223.

57. Stanley Siegel, *A Political History of the Texas Republic, 1836–1845* (Austin: University of Texas Press, 1956), 246–254.

58. "Ordinance of Annexation: Approved by the Texas Convention on July 4, 1845," Texas State Library and Archives Commission, https://www.tsl.texas.gov/ref/abouttx /annexation/4july1845.html (accessed Sept. 14, 2017).

59. Paul Frymer, *Building an American Empire: The Era of Territorial and Political Expansion* (Princeton, NJ: Princeton University Press, 2017); Laura Smietanka Jensen, *Patriots, Settlers, and the Origins of American Social Policy* (New York: Cambridge University Press, 2003), 123–186.

60. "Polk's First Annual Message," Dec. 2, 1845, in *A Compilation of the Messages and Papers of the Presidents*, comp. James D. Richardson (1902), http://www.gutenberg.org/files/12463/12463.txt.

61. James K. Polk, *The Diary of James K. Polk, 1845–1849*, 4 vols., ed. Milo Milton Quaife (Chicago, IL: A. C. McClurg, 1910), 1:70; Merk, *Monroe Doctrine and American Expansionism*, 6, 66, 181–182, 208.

62. "Polk's Third Annual Message," Dec. 7, 1847, in Richardson, *Compilation*, http://www.gutenberg.org/files/12463/12463.txt.

63. Polk, *Diary of James K. Polk*, 1:205–206; Gerrit John Dirkmaat, "Enemies Foreign and Domestic: U.S. Relations with Mormons in the U.S. Empire in North America" (PhD diss., University of Colorado, Boulder, 2010), 109.

64. July 6, 1846, in Journal History of the Church, LDS Church History Library, Salt Lake City, UT (hereafter, Journal History).

65. Little to Polk, June 1, 1846, in *Army of Israel: Mormon Battalion Narratives*, ed. David L. Bigler and Will Bagley (Logan: Utah State University Press, 2000), 34, also 31–32; Matthew J. Grow, *"Liberty to the Downtrodden": Thomas L. Kane, Romantic Reformer* (New Haven, CT: Yale University Press, 2009), 49–50; Dirkmaat, "Enemies Foreign and Domestic," 115–116.

66. Polk, *Diary of James K. Polk*, 1:443–450.

67. Bigler and Bagley, *Army of Israel*, 23.

68. Wilford Woodruff, June 26, 1846, in *Wilford Woodruff's Journal, 1833–1898*, ed. Scott Kenney (Midvale, UT: Signature Books, 1983–1985), 3:54–55.

69. Hyde to Young, Apr. 22, 1846, Brigham Young Office Files, LDS Church History Library, Salt Lake City, UT (hereafter, BYOF).

70. June 6, July 6, and Aug. 7, 1846, all in Journal History. Pickett would also assume a leadership role during the journey west and in Utah, printing money for the Mormons while in Iowa (June 11, 1848), counting votes for elections (Oct. 5, 1848), and becoming a territorial delegate for Utah (Sept. 6, 1849) (all in Journal History).

71. "A Concise View of the Policy of the Latter Day Saints in Reference to Their Emigration to California," 1846, BYOF; July 16, 1846, in Journal History.

72. John L. O'Sullivan, "Annexation," *United States Magazine and Democratic Review* 17 (1845): 10.

73. Sellers, *Polk: Continentalist*, 421–423.

74. James Buchanan to Thomas Larkin, Oct. 17, 1845, in *The Larkin Papers*, 10 vols., ed. George P. Hammond (Berkeley: University of California Press, 1952), 4:44; Harland Hague and David J. Langum, *Thomas O. Larkin: A Life of Patriotism and Profit in Old California* (Norman: University of Oklahoma Press, 1990), 116.

75. Larkin to Jacob Leese, Abel Stearns, and Jonathan Trumbull Warner, Apr. 17, 1846, in Hammond, *Larkin Papers*, 4:295–297.

76. Larkin, "Opinion of State of Affairs in California," Apr. 1846, in Hammond, *Larkin Papers*, 4:297–300.

77. Larkin to Leese, Stearns, and Warner, Apr. 17, 1846, in Hammond, *Larkin Papers*, 4:296.

78. Oct. 30, 1845, in Polk, *Diary of James K. Polk*, 1:83–84.

79. Larkin to José Castro and Manuel Castro, Mar. 6, 1846, 4:231; Larkin to James Buchanan, Mar. 27, 1846, 4:270–273; José Castro, Proceedings of Military Junta, 4:282–284; Larkin to Buchanan, Apr. 2, 1846, 4:275, all in Hammond, *Larkin Papers*.

80. Frémont to Larkin, Mar. 9, 1846, in Hammond, *Larkin Papers*, 4:235.

81. Tom Chaffin, *Pathfinder: John Charles Frémont and the Course of American Empire* (Norman: University of Oklahoma Press, 2014), 180–208.

82. For the historiography surrounding the secret orders, see Robert Utley, *A Life Wild and Perilous: Mountain Men and the Path to the Pacific* (New York: Henry Holt, 1997), 362n30.

83. Mariano Vallejo, "Historical and Personal Memoirs Relating to Alta California," trans. Earl Hewitt, 5 vols., 1875, C-D 19, 5:58–74, Bancroft Library, Berkeley, CA (hereafter, BL); John Sutter to John Marsh, Apr. 3, 1846, John Augustus Sutter Papers, MSS C-D 631, BL; Larkin to William Leidesdorff, Apr. 13, 1846, in Hammond, *Larkin Papers*, 4:284; Larkin to Abel Stearns, in *First and Last Consul: Thomas Oliver Larkin and the Americanization of California*, ed. John A. Hawgood (San Marino, CA: Huntington Library, 1962), 61–62; Joseph Revere, *A Tour of Duty in California* . . . (New York, 1849), 23–31; William Heath Davis, *Seventy-Five Years in California*, ed. Douglas Watson (San Francisco, CA: J. Howell, 1929), 141–142. For an assessment of the evidence of the meeting, see especially Myrtle M. McKittrick, *Vallejo, Son of California* (Portland, OR: Binsford and Mort, 1944), 248–253; Hague and Langum, *Thomas O. Larkin*, 256nn33 and 34. For the contrarian view, see Hubert Howe Bancroft, *History of California*, 7 vols. (San Francisco, CA: History Company, 1884–1890), 5:59–63; Rosaura Sánchez, *Telling Identities: The Californio Testimonios* (Minneapolis: University of Minnesota Press, 1995), 246–254.

84. Vallejo, "Historical and Personal Memoirs," 5:64.

85. Revere, *Tour of Duty in California*, 28–30.

86. Chaffin, *Pathfinder*, 290–291.

87. Francisco Guerrero y Palomares to William Alexander Leidesdorff, Apr. 30, 1846, in Hammond, *Larkin Papers*, 4:354.

88. William B. Ide, *Who Conquered California?* (Claremont, NH, 1880), 29–30.

89. For various interpretations of the Bear Flag Revolt, see Neal Harlow, *California Conquered: The Annexation of a Mexican Province, 1846–1850* (Berkeley: University of California Press, 1989), 74–114; Chaffin, *Pathfinder*, 289–335; Alan Rosenus, *General M. G. Vallejo and the Advent of the Americans: A Biography* (Albuquerque: University of New Mexico Press, 1995), 81–134; Bancroft, *History of California*, 5:77–190; Linda Heidenreich, *"This Land Was Mexican Once": Histories of Resistance from Northern California* (Austin: University of Texas Press, 2007), 75–92; Barbara Warner, *The Men of the California Bear Flag Revolt and Their Heritage* (Sonoma, CA: Clark Publishing for the Sonoma Valley Historical Society, 1996), 13–74.

90. William Hargrave, "California in 1846," transcribed by Ivan Petroff, C-D 97, BL.

91. Bidwell, "Statement of Mr. John Bidwell of Chico, California, Concerning the Conquest of California, in Letters to the Rev. Mr. Willey, 1876," 19, C-B 468, BL.

92. John A. Hawgood, "The Pattern of Yankee Infiltration in Mexican Alta California, 1821–1846," *Pacific Historical Review* 27, no. 1 (Feb. 1958): 33.

93. John Bidwell, "California, 1841–1848," 159–161, C-D 8, BL.

94. For biographies of individual Bears, see Warner, *Men of the California Bear Flag Revolt*.

95. These percentages are approximate, based on overland immigrant totals in John D. Unruh, *The Plains Across: The Overland Emigrants and the Trans-Mississippi West, 1840–1860* (Urbana: University of Illinois Press, 1979), 119.

96. William B. Ide, proclamation, June 18, 1846, Documents for the History of California, BL.

97. Fred Rogers, *William Brown Ide, Bear Flagger* (San Francisco, CA: J. Howell, 1962).

98. John Sutter to Andrew Sutter, Feb. 10, 1847, Sutter Papers, BL.

99. Henry Ford, "On the Bear Flag Revolt," MSS C-E 75, BL. See also Benjamin Kelsey and Mary E. Foy, "The Bear Flag Revolution," *Quarterly of the Historical Society of Southern California* 28, no. 2 (June 1946): 67; Joseph Owen William Russell, Jan. 28, 1886, Bear Flag Memoirs, MSS C-D 270, BL.

100. Fred Blackburn Rogers, *William Brown Ide: Bear Flagger* (San Francisco, CA: J. Howell Books, 1962), 56; Simeon Ide, *A Biographical Sketch of the Life of William Ide* (Claremont, NH, 1880), 100–103, 193–208; Harlow, *California Conquered*, 113; Bancroft, *History of California*, 5:243; Vallejo, "Historical and Personal Memoirs," 5:108.

101. Pío Pico, proclamation, June 23, 1846, 22–24, Bear Flag Papers, C-B 70, BL; Larkin to Anthony Ten Eych and Joel Turill, June 21, 1846, in Hammond, *Larkin Papers*, 5:62.

102. Bidwell, "Statement," 3. See also Baldridge, "Days of 1846," 56; Ford, "On the Bear Flag Revolt."

103. Kelsey and Foy, "Bear Flag Revolution," 65.

104. Leonard Pitt, *The Decline of the Californios: A Social History of the Spanish-Speaking Californians* (Berkeley: University of California Press, 1968), 83–103, 195–213.

105. "Polk's First Annual Message," Dec. 2, 1845.

106. *Daily Union* (Washington, DC), Oct. 9, 1845.

107. James W. Nesmith to Samuel Wilson, June 27, 1845, MSS 577, Oregon Historical Society, Portland (hereafter, OHS).

108. *Oregon Spectator*, Mar. 19, 1846. See also June 25, July 4, Aug. 6, Aug. 20, and Sept. 3, 1846.

109. *Oregon Spectator*, Nov. 26, 1846.

110. Entries from Oct. 24, 1845, and May 16, May 21, May 22, and May 25, 1846, in Polk, *Diary of James K. Polk*, 70, 404, 414, 416, 424.

111. *Oregon Spectator*, Nov. 12, 1846.

112. George Abernethy to Neil Howison, Dec. 21, 1846, George Abernethy Papers, MSS 929, OHS.

113. Polk to Martin Van Buren, Aug. 8, 1838, in *CJP*, 4:526.

114. William McLoughlin, *After the Trail of Tears: The Cherokees' Struggle for Sovereignty, 1839–1880* (Chapel Hill: University of North Carolina Press, 1993), 52–56.

115. *Arkansas Gazette*, Apr. 18, 1838, and Nov. 11, 1840; Yell to Polk, Sept. 5, 1845, in *CJP*, 10:487.

116. Wilson Lumpkin to James Polk, July 8, 1845, in *CJP*, 10:33.

117. Aug. 13, 1846, in Polk, *Diary of James K. Polk*, 2:81–82.

118. Gary Moulton, *John Ross: Cherokee Chief* (Athens: University of Georgia Press, 1978), 149.

119. William S. Coodey to Polk, July 8, 1845, 10:36; John Howard Payne to Polk, Feb. 5, 1846, 11:70–72, both in *CJP*.

120. Shelly Streeby, *American Sensations: Class, Empire, and the Production of Popular Culture* (Berkeley: University of California Press, 2002); Robert Johannsen, *To the Halls of the Montezumas: The Mexican War in the American Imagination* (New York: Oxford University Press, 1985); Peter Guardino, *The Dead March: A History of the Mexican-American War* (Cambridge, MA: Harvard University Press, 2017), 32, 110, 127, 218.

121. *True American* (Lexington, KY), June 17, 1846.

122. Payne to Polk, Feb. 5, 1846.

123. *Rogers v. United States*, 45 US 567 (1846).

124. Sidney L. Harring, *Crow Dog's Case: American Indian Sovereignty, Tribal Law, and United States Law in the Nineteenth Century* (New York: Cambridge University Press, 1994), 60–61.

125. John Rockwell Snowden, Wayne Tyndall, and David Smith, "American Indian Sovereignty and Naturalization: It's a Race Thing," *Nebraska Law Review* 80, rev. 171 (2001): 171–238.

126. Bethany R. Berger, " 'Power over This Unfortunate Race': Race, Politics and Indian Law in *United States v. Rogers*," *William and Mary Law Review* 45, no. 5 (2004): 1965–1966.

127. Berger, "Power over This Unfortunate Race," 2008–2018; R. Kent Newmyer, *The Supreme Court under Marshall and Taney* (Arlington Heights, IL: Harlan Davidson, 1969), 113.

128. "Polk to the Senate and House of Representatives," Apr. 13, 1846, in Richardson, *Compilation*, https://www.gutenberg.org/dirs/1/2/4/6/12463/12463.txt.

129. Ross et al. to the Senate and House of Representatives, Apr. 30, 1846, in *The Papers of Chief John Ross*, vols. 1–2, ed. Gary Moulton (Norman: University of Oklahoma Press, 1985), 2:296–299 (hereafter, *Ross Papers*).

130. Emmett Starr, *Starr's History of the Cherokee Indians*, ed. Jack Gregory and Rennard Strickland (Fayetteville, AR: Indian Heritage Association, 1922), 137–142.

131. John Ross, Annual Message, Nov. 12, 1846, *Ross Papers*, 2:320.

132. *Cherokee Advocate*, Sept. 3 and Oct. 8, 1846.

133. The last mention I found of such an alliance was in the *Arkansas Gazette*, July 7, 1845.

134. Richard Trotter, "For the Defense of the Western Frontier: Arkansas Volunteers on the Indian Frontier, 1846–1847," *Arkansas Historical Quarterly* 60, no. 4 (Winter 2001): 394–400.

135. *Arkansas Gazette*, June 1, 1846.

136. *Cherokee Advocate*, June 4, 1846.

137. *Cherokee Advocate*, June 18, 1846.

138. Committee of Commerce, as quoted in Brandon Mills, "Situating African Colonization within the History of U.S. Expansion," in *New Directions in the Study of*

African American Recolonization, ed. Beverly Tomek and Matthew J. Hetrick (Gainesville: University Press of Florida, 2017), 176.

139. Mills, "Situating African Colonization"; Bronwen Everill, " 'Destiny Seems to Point Me to That Country': Early Nineteenth-Century African American Migration, Emigration, and Expansion," *Journal of Global History* 7, no. 1 (2012): 53–77; James Ciment, *Another America: The Story of Liberia and the Former Slaves Who Ruled It* (New York: Hill and Wang, 2013), chap. 4.

Epilogue

1. Sam Houston, *Speech of Mr. Houston, of Texas, on the Oregon Question: Delivered in the Senate of the United States, April, 1846* ([Washington, DC?], 1846).

2. Houston, *Speech of Mr. Houston*, 7.

3. Brent M. Rogers, *Unpopular Sovereignty: Mormons and the Federal Management of Early Utah Territory* (Lincoln: University of Nebraska Press, 2017), 197–198, discusses the Mormons' attempt at a Native alliance during the Utah War.

4. *Rogers v. United States*, 45 US 567 (1846).

5. William McLoughlin, *After the Trail of Tears: The Cherokees' Struggle for Sovereignty, 1839–1880* (Chapel Hill: University of North Carolina Press, 1993), 86–121; Julie Reed, *Serving the Nation: Cherokee Sovereignty and Social Welfare, 1800–1907* (Norman: University of Oklahoma Press, 2016), 60–90.

6. John P. Bowes, *Exiles and Pioneers: Eastern Indians in the Trans-Mississippi West* (New York: Cambridge University Press, 2007), 145–151.

7. McLoughlin, *After the Trail of Tears*, 158–159.

8. Robert W. Johannsen, *To the Halls of the Montezumas: The Mexican War in the American Imagination* (New York: Oxford University Press, 1985), 21–44; Peter Guardino, *The Dead March: A History of the Mexican-American War* (Cambridge, MA: Harvard University Press, 2017), 94–95.

9. Amy Greenberg, *Manifest Manhood and the Antebellum American Empire* (New York: Cambridge University Press, 2005), 12–13.

10. Robert E. May, *Manifest Destiny's Underworld: Filibustering in Antebellum America* (Chapel Hill: University of North Carolina Press, 2002).

11. William H. Freehling, *The Road to Disunion*, vol. 2: *Secessionists Triumphant, 1854–1861* (New York: Oxford University Press, 2007); David M. Potter, *The Impending Crisis: America before the Civil War, 1848–1861* (New York: HarperCollins, 1976).

12. Larkin to Stearns, Apr. 24, 1856, in *First and Last Consul: Thomas Oliver Larkin and the Americanization of California*, ed. John A. Hawgood (San Marino, CA: Huntington Library, 1962), 104.

13. Samuel Thurston to J. Butterfield, May 5, 1851, Thurston Family Papers, MSS 379, Oregon Historical Society, Portland (hereafter, OHS).

14. Elam Young to Samuel Thurston, July 24, 1850, Thurston Family Papers, MSS 379, OHS.

15. Abner Sylvester Baker, "The Oregon Pioneer Tradition in the Nineteenth Century" (PhD diss., University of Oregon, 1968); Frederick Merk, *The Oregon Question: Essays in Anglo-American Diplomacy and Politics* (Cambridge, MA: Harvard University Press, 1967), 234–254.

16. Anne Hyde, *Empires, Nations, and Families: A History of the North American West, 1800–1860* (Lincoln: University of Nebraska Press, 2011), 409–450.

17. Hyde, *Empires, Nations, and Families*, 429–431.

18. Benjamin Madley, *American Genocide: The United States and the California Indian Catastrophe, 1846–1873* (New Haven, CT: Yale University Press, 2016); Gary Clayton Anderson, *The Conquest of Texas: Ethnic Cleansing in the Promised Land, 1820–1875* (Norman: University of Oklahoma Press, 2005), 212–326.

19. James K. Polk, *The Diary of James K. Polk during His Presidency, 1845–1849,* 4 vols., ed. Milo Milton Quaife (Chicago, IL: A. C. McClurg, 1910), 4:375–376.

20. McLoughlin, *After the Trail of Tears*, 176–200.

21. Glenna Matthews, *The Golden State in the Civil War: Thomas Starr King, the Republican Party, and the Birth of Modern California* (New York: Cambridge University Press, 2012), 66, 84–91; Joseph Waldo Ellison, "Sentiments in California for a Pacific Republic, 1843–1861" (master's thesis, University of California, 1919), 66–104.

22. Jeff LaLande, "'Dixie' of the Pacific Northwest: Southern Oregon's Civil War," *Oregon Historical Quarterly* 100, no. 1 (Spring 1999): 32–81.

23. Sarah Rodríguez, "'Children of the Great Mexican Family': American Immigration to Northern Mexico, 1810–1861" (PhD diss., University of Pennsylvania, 2015), 399–430.

24. Rogers, *Unpopular Sovereignty*, 270–291; Heather Cox Richardson, *West from Appomattox: The Reconstruction of America after the Civil War* (New Haven, CT: Yale University Press, 2007); Richard White, *The Republic for Which It Stands: The United States during Reconstruction and the Gilded Age, 1865–1896* (New York: Oxford University Press, 2017), 103–135.

25. Paul Frymer, *Building an American Empire: The Era of Territorial and Political Expansion* (Princeton, NJ: Princeton University Press, 2017), 155–167.

26. Tom Coffman, *Nation Within: The History of the American Occupation of Hawaii* (Durham, NC: Duke University Press, 1998), 109–262.

27. Frederick Jackson Turner, "The Significance of the Frontier in American History," *Annual Report of the American Historical Association* (1893): 199–227.

28. Kristin L. Hoganson, *Fighting for American Manhood: How Gender Politics Provoked the Spanish-American and Philippine-American Wars* (New Haven, CT: Yale University Press, 2010).